HUMANITY

*A Moral History of
the Twentieth Century*

HUMANITY

*A Moral History of
the Twentieth Century*

Jonathan Glover

JONATHAN CAPE
LONDON

Published by Jonathan Cape 1999

2 4 6 8 10 9 7 5 3 1

Copyright © Jonathan Glover 1999

Jonathan Glover has asserted his right under the
Copyright, Designs and Patents Act 1988 to be identified
as the author of this work

First published in Great Britain in 1999 by
Jonathan Cape
Random House, 20 Vauxhall Bridge Road,
London SW1V 2SA

Random House Australia (Pty) Limited
20 Alfred Street, Milsons Point, Sydney,
New South Wales 2061, Australia

Random House New Zealand Limited
18 Poland Road, Glenfield,
Auckland 10, New Zealand

Random House South Africa (Pty) Limited
Endulini, 5A Jubilee Road, Parktown 2193, South Africa

Random House UK Limited Reg. No. 954009

A CIP catalogue record for this book
is available from the British Library

ISBN 0–224–05240–3

Papers used by Random House UK Limited are natural,
recyclable products made from wood grown in sustainable forests.
The manufacturing processes conform to the environmental
regulations of the country of origin.

Typeset by Deltatype Ltd, Birkenhead, Merseyside
Printed and bound in Great Britain by
Biddles Ltd, Guildford and King's Lynn

To Ruth

Contents

The chief business of twentieth-century philosophy is to reckon with twentieth-century history.

R.G. Collingwood, *An Autobiography*

Preface

I have been writing this book for over ten years. One stimulus came from a first visit to Poland, where Tony Quinton had generously invited me to hear his Tanner Lecture on Human Values in Warsaw and to take part in the associated conference on ethics. Poland then had a Communist government. At lunch on the first day, I sat next to a Polish philosopher, Klemens Szaniawski. During our conversation he told me about his life. He was a teenager when the Nazis invaded in 1939. His father, a journalist, was shot for refusing to write for a Nazi newspaper. Klemens studied philosophy at the Underground University and took part in the Warsaw uprising, in which many of his friends were killed. He was arrested and sent to Auschwitz. Later he was moved to Mauthausen, where he worked as a slave labourer in the quarries. At the end of the war he was liberated by the Americans. He went back to Poland and taught philosophy through the Stalinist period and after. He was one of the founders of a discussion group which later played a part in the Solidarity movement. When we met, he had recently been elected Rector of the University of Warsaw, but the government had rejected him on political grounds and had removed his passport.

As his history emerged, I was struck by the range of experience that he and other Polish philosophers could bring to thinking about ethics, and also by the way much English-language writing on ethics is limited by relative insulation from some of the twentieth century's man-made disasters. There must be lessons for ethics in the events of this violent century. English people of my generation and the subsequent one have been lucky in being largely spared both war and other atrocities. Only a fool would regret this; but thinking about ethics is likely to be enriched by learning what we can about the causes of the events we have been lucky to avoid. This book was written partly in response to this thought.

But, in another way, I have been thinking about this book for most of my adult life. Since I first heard about the Nazi genocide, I have wondered how people could bring themselves to commit such acts. The question has kept recurring and has been present in most of what I have written in philosophy. I have written books on ethical issues about taking life and about the applications of genetic knowledge. The relevance of those topics to the project of building more secure defences against any revival of Nazi policies is obvious. But, even when writing about apparently more neutral topics such as personal identity, I found my obsession with recent human barbarism bursting out almost against my will. So it seemed sensible to say what I had to say directly rather than in the margins of another subject.

This book is an attempt to give ethics an empirical dimension. It uses ethics to pose questions to history and it uses history to give a picture of the parts of human potentiality which are relevant to ethics. To do this I have had to discuss many issues which other people know and understand better than I do. Where they think I have got the story wrong, I would be delighted to provoke them to carry out the project better.

Ten years is a long time to spend writing a book. In that time much has happened to Vivette and me and to our three – now grown-up – children, Daniel, David and Ruth. I hope the book reflects some of the ways I have been shaped by sharing life with Vivette. I hope it also reflects some of the many things I have learnt from each of our children over these years.

I dedicate this book to Ruth. With some hesitation, as she may have reservations about being linked with a book about the horrors of the century. But in places it is about people with humanity and courage. With those parts of the book in mind, I dedicate it to Ruth with admiration and love.

Acknowledgements

Parts of this book have been used elsewhere. An early version of part of the section on the Nazis was used in a lecture to the Program in Ethics and the Professions at the Kennedy School of Government at Harvard, and in lectures at the University of Colorado at Boulder. A later version was used in my Gilbert Ryle Lectures at Trent University, Ontario, and in some lectures at the University of Copenhagen. Some of the chapter on bombing was used in a talk at the Free University in Berlin. Parts of the discussion of moral identity and of nationalism were used in talks at the Maison des Sciences de l'Homme and at the Centre National de la Recherche Scientifique in Paris. Many parts of the book have also been used in talks, both in New York and in Oxford at the Consortium in Medical Ethics, which links Mount Sinai Hospital, the University of Oxford and King's College London. I am grateful to all those whose invitations to give those talks encouraged me to make progress with the book and whose comments on those occasions have stimulated my thinking.

Inevitably, on this subject, most of the time I am trespassing on territory which others have far more knowledge of than I have. It will be obvious how much I have drawn on the work of historians and journalists. I cannot possibly thank them all here, but I hope the References will give some idea of what I owe them. The book also uses people's accounts of their own experiences. I do not wish to thank tyrants, torturers and those who have supported them, but, with those exceptions, I am grateful to all whose experiences and reflections I have drawn on. I hope they will approve of the uses to which their accounts are put here.

Far more people have given me help or encouragement than it is possible to mention, but among those who helped, either by answering specific queries, by directing me to what I should read, by turning me towards a particular topic, by telling me their own experiences, or by making comments on drafts of chapters, are: Tom and Bobbie Farsides, Christoph Fehige, Patrick Gardiner, Michael Hechter, Polly Markandya, Alexei Medvedev, Igor Novović, Steve Paulsson, Hilary Putnam, Scott

Rhind, Thomas Schramme, Gerry Smith, David Spurrett, Dan Stone, Laurence Thomas, Barry Trachtenberg, Geoffrey Warnock, Jeff Wilson and David Worswick.

Other people have given me a great deal of encouragement and support while I have been writing this book. They include: Catherine Atherton, Avi Barbasch, Stefan Baumrin, Karin Boxer, Michael Burleigh, John Campbell, Ann Davis, Julia Driver, Jim Griffin, Dick Hare, John Harris, Tony Hope, Dolores Iorizzo, Dale Jamieson, Nathan Kase, Jeff McMahan, Dan Moros, Martha Nussbaum, Gunilla Öberg, Onora O'Neill, Anthony Price, Frankie Raben, Rosamond Rhodes, Alan Ryan, David Shapiro, Jim Strain, David Wiggins, Bernard Williams and Dan Wikler.

Felicity Bryan has acted as my agent, but her encouragement and patience have gone far beyond what that suggests. I have been lucky with my publishers too. The mixture of critical comments and helpful suggestions provided by Will Sulkin and Jörg Hensgen at Jonathan Cape have greatly improved the book.

Most of all I have been helped by Richard Keshen. Many years ago I supervised his graduate work. I wish I could believe I gave him then anything like the encouragement and constructive criticism he has generously given me with this book.

CHAPTER I

Never Such Innocence Again

In Europe at the start of the twentieth century most people accepted the authority of morality. They thought there was a moral law, which was self-evidently to be obeyed. Immanuel Kant had written of the two things which fill the mind with admiration and awe, 'the starry heavens above me and the moral law within me'. In Cambridge in 1895, a century after Kant, Lord Acton still had no doubts: 'Opinions alter, manners change, creeds rise and fall, but the moral law is written on the tablets of eternity.'[1] At the start of the twentieth century, reflective Europeans were also able to believe in moral progress, and to see human viciousness and barbarism as in retreat. At the end of the century, it is hard to be confident either about the moral law or about moral progress.

Some, however, are still unwavering about the moral law. In a letter to a newspaper about the Gulf War, Father Denis Geraghty wrote, 'The use of weapons of mass destruction is a crime against God and man and remains a crime even if they are used in retaliation or for what is regarded as a morally justified end. It is forbidden to do evil that good may come of it.'[2] Many other people, including some who are sympathetic to his opinions, will view Father Geraghty's tone with a mixture of envy and scepticism. Confidence such as his was easier a century ago. Since Acton, the writing on the tablets of eternity has faded a little.

The challenge to the moral law is intellectual: to find good reasons for thinking that it exists and that it has any claim on us. The problem is hardly new; Plato wrote about it. But the collapse of the authority of religion and decline in belief in God are reasons for it now being a problem for many who are not philosophers. There is a further challenge to religious ethics, one which Dostoyevsky put into the mouth of Ivan Karamazov.

Pointing to features of the world which God is said to have created, Karamazov questions God's credentials for the role of a moral authority. He first concedes much of the religious picture. He believes in a wise God with a purpose unknown to us, and in an ultimate harmony: 'something so precious that it will suffice for all hearts, to allay all indignation, to redeem all human villainy, all bloodshed; it will suffice not only to make forgiveness possible, but also to justify everything that has happened with men'.[3]

This ultimate harmony is not something Ivan Karamazov can accept. It will be the culmination of a universe which includes what the Turks did in Bulgaria, where they burnt, killed and raped women and children. They hanged prisoners after first making them spend their last night nailed by the ear to a fence. ('No animal could ever be so cruel as a man, so artfully, so artistically cruel.') They used daggers to cut babies out of women's wombs. They tossed nursing infants in the air, catching them on bayonets: 'the main delight comes from doing it before their mothers' eyes'. What claim can the creator of a harmony, of which all this is a part, have to be a moral authority?

The other belief, in moral progress, has also been undermined. The problems have come from events. The twentieth-century history of large-scale cruelty and killing is only too familiar: the mutual slaughter of the First World War, the terror-famine of the Ukraine, the Gulag, Auschwitz, Dresden, the Burma Railway, Hiroshima, Vietnam, the Chinese Cultural Revolution, Cambodia, Rwanda, the collapse of Yugoslavia. These names will conjure up others. Because of this history, it is (or should be) hard for thinking about ethics to carry on just as before.

This book is an attempt to bring ethics and this history together. The title, *Humanity: a Moral History of the Twentieth Century*, needs some explanation. The topic is the twentieth-century moral history of the human race. But 'humanity' is also being used in a different sense, in which it is contrasted with inhumanity. One of the book's aims is to fill out this idea of humanity.

The project of discussing the recent moral history of the human race may strike the reader (as it strikes me) as rather grandiose. It is worth indicating at once some limitations of scope. The history is highly selective in the episodes discussed. Some places (India, and many others) are either hardly mentioned or quite unmentioned. This does not reflect a view that the history of some parts of humanity is unimportant, but rather the limitations of what is well or availably documented. It also reflects the much more severe limitations of my own knowledge.

There is more to our recent moral history than the ethical debates and the man-made horrors discussed here. A more generous conception would also include changes in the family, in the way children are treated, and in the relations between men and women. Among much else, it would also include attitudes to poverty, religious changes, the impact of science on our thinking about how to live, attitudes to sex and to death, the relations between different cultures, and attitudes towards animals, to the natural world and to the environment. No single discussion could hope to cover all this without superficiality – any serious discussion has to be selective. These other aspects repay study; but perhaps no apology is needed for giving the twentieth-century atrocities a central place in our recent moral history.

To bring out the links between ethics and twentieth-century history it is worth saying something about the approach first to history and then to ethics.

First, history.

To talk of the twentieth-century atrocities is in one way misleading. It is a myth that barbarism is unique to the twentieth century: the whole of human history includes wars, massacres, and every kind of torture and cruelty: there are grounds for thinking that over much of the world the changes of the last hundred years or so have been towards a psychological climate more humane than at any previous time.

But it is still right that much of twentieth-century history has been a very unpleasant surprise. Technology has made a difference. The decisions of a few people can mean horror and death for hundreds of thousands, even millions, of other people.

These events shock us not only by their scale. They also contrast with the expectations, at least in Europe, with which the twentieth century began. One hundred years of largely unbroken European peace between the defeat of Napoleon and the First World War made it plausible to think that the human race was growing out of its warlike past. In 1915 the poet Charles Sorley, writing home a few months before being killed in battle, found it natural to say, 'After all, war in this century is inexcusable: and all parties engaged in it must take an equal share in the blame of its occurrence.'[4] More recently, some of those going to fight in the Gulf may also have felt war to be inexcusable, but they are less likely to have found it particularly so in the twentieth century. In 'MCMXIV' Philip Larkin describes the queues to enlist at the start of the First World War:

> The crowns of hats, the sun
> On moustached archaic faces
> Grinning as if it were all
> An August Bank Holiday lark.

His late-century comment was 'Never such innocence again'.

The thoughts developed here on twentieth-century history are an attempt to see some of the century's events in an appropriate human perspective. We have an incessant flow of information about the unfolding story of our times, so many facts that it is hard to stand back and think about their meaning and their relative importance. Milan Kundera described one of the effects of the flow of news:

The bloody massacre in Bangladesh quickly covered the memory of the Russian invasion of Czechoslovakia, the assassination of Allende drowned out the groans of Bangladesh, the war in the Sinai desert made people forget Allende, the Cambodian massacre made people forget Sinai, and so on and so forth until ultimately everyone lets everything be forgotten.[5]

In retrieving some of these events, there are many ways in which they could be grouped and interpreted. This is not a narrative history, but a discussion, an attempt at analysis. Immanuel Kant, talking of how the mind does not passively receive knowledge, but actively interprets the world in terms of its concepts and categories, said that we should interrogate nature, not like a pupil, but like a judge. This applies to history too. Here I use ethics to pose questions in the interrogation of history.

There has been much philosophical discussion about what factors restrain people from ruthlessly selfish treatment of others, and what reasons there are for accepting moral restraints on conduct. These 'moral resources' will be central. There are questions about what happened to them when the First World War started, when the atomic bomb was dropped, in Stalin's Russia, in Nazi Germany, or, more recently, in Bosnia and in Kosovo. The aim in using ethics to interrogate history is to help understand a side of human nature often left in darkness.

It will also be argued that, in understanding the history, philosophical questions about ethics cannot be ignored. Poor answers to these questions have contributed to a climate in which some of the disasters were made possible.

One problem about trying to see these events in perspective comes from not having experienced them. I am acutely aware that, being lucky in where and when I have lived, I lack first-hand knowledge of the events that I am discussing. I write about war having not fought in one. I write about Nazism and Stalinism, about dictatorships in Latin America and elsewhere, having not lived under any of them. Readers who have experienced these things will at times notice my limitations. In a different field, medical ethics, philosophers sometimes write with an over-confidence which betrays that they have not experienced the human reality of the dilemmas. The same must be true many times over of someone who, without having experienced them, writes of Vietnam or Auschwitz.

All the same, while it would be better to write from experience, there are reasons for an attempt even by an inexperienced person.

No one can have experienced more than a small number of these episodes. To be daunted by inexperience might result in no one trying to see as a whole events from which so much can be learnt. Towards the end of the Second World War, the philosopher Glenn Gray was in an American division in Germany which overran a concentration camp, and he spent a day with the survivors: 'The whole range of human character seemed to be exhibited there by these few hundred survivors during the first day of their liberation, and I was conscious of having stumbled onto an hour of truth that would hardly be repeated, even by them, in later days.'[6] Glenn Gray published his reflections on this and other experiences, but those who record what seem to be important war experiences are at the time often too preoccupied to reflect on them. Sometimes they express the hope that others, in time of peace, will extract from their experiences some help towards saving future people from having to repeat them.

Some atrocities are not past but present. Those of us who are lucky in living elsewhere should not be inhibited from thinking about them. Journalists risk their lives to let us know the terrible things that are being done while we live in relative security. Victims painfully narrate their experiences so that we may understand. Often they do this in the belief that, if the world hears, there will be an outcry and something will be done.

Journalists can be disappointed by the response. Ed Vulliamy, who reported the war in Bosnia, wrote:

> Most of us thought we could make a difference, at first. It seemed incredible that the world could watch, read and hear about what was happening to the victim people of this war, and yet do nothing – and worse. As it turned out, we went unheeded by the diplomats and on occasions were even cursed by the political leaders.[7]

The victims and those close to them also note the response. Selma Hecimović looked after Bosnian women who had been raped:

> At the end, I get a bit tired of constantly having to *prove*. We had to prove genocide, we had to prove that our women are being raped, that our children have been killed. Every time I take a statement from these women, and you journalists want to interview them, I imagine those people, disinterested, sitting in a nice house with a hamburger and beer, switching channels on TV. I really don't know what else has to happen here, what further suffering the Muslims have to undergo . . . to make the so-called civilised world react.[8]

Those of us who think about these episodes at a distance will sometimes get things wrong. And, of course, understanding is not enough to stop the horrors. But the alternative, the passive response, helps keep them going.

Next, ethics, which could be more empirical than it is.

There has been a shift of emphasis in philosophical discussion of ethics, away from purely abstract questions to more practical ones. Discussions of the right and the good, or of the analysis of moral judgements, have given some ground. Now there are discussions of the just war, moral dilemmas in medicine, social justice, human rights, feminism, nuclear deterrence, genetic engineering, animal rights and environmental issues. This shift of concern towards 'applied ethics' has been beneficial. What is humanly most important has been moved from the margins to the centre.

Even in applied ethics awareness is often missing. The tone of much writing suggests that John Stuart Mill is still alive and that none of the twentieth century has happened. ('Never such innocence again' has not been applied to ethics.) I hope to help change this by encouraging an idea of ethics as a more empirical subject.

It is possible to assume too readily that a set of moral principles simply needs to be 'applied'. The result can be the mechanical application of some form of utilitarianism, or list of precepts about justice, autonomy, benevolence and so on. When this happens, the direction of thought is all one way. The principles are taken for granted, or 'derived' in a perfunctory way, and practical conclusions are deduced from them. What is missing is the sense of two-way interaction. The principles themselves may need modifying if their practical conclusions are too Procrustean, if they require us to ignore or deny things we find we care about when faced with the practical dilemmas.

Many philosophers are sympathetic to a more pragmatic form of ethics, where principles are put forward tentatively, in the expectation that they will be shaped and modified by our responses to practical problems. The mutual adjustment between principles and our intuitive responses is the process leading to what John Rawls has called, perhaps optimistically, 'reflective equilibrium'.

But the pragmatism could be taken further, to encompass the idea that our ethical beliefs should also be revisable in the light of an empirical understanding of people and what they do. If, for instance, the great atrocities teach lessons about our psychology, this should affect our picture of what kinds of actions and character traits are good or bad.

Some intellectual disciplines are highly abstract, and perhaps understanding people is unimportant in those fields, but ethics is not one of them. I hope this book will help to bring closer to the centre of ethics some questions about people and what they are like. This project of bringing ethics and psychology closer to each other involves thinking about the implications of some of the things we now know civilized people are capable of doing to each other.

At the start of the century there was optimism, coming from the Enlightenment, that the spread of a humane and scientific outlook would lead to the fading away, not only of war, but also of other forms of cruelty and barbarism. They would fill the chamber of horrors in the museum of our primitive past. In the light of these expectations, the century of Hitler, Stalin, Pol Pot and Saddam Hussein was likely to be a surprise. Volcanoes thought extinct turned out not to be.

Now we tend to see the Enlightenment view of human psychology as thin and mechanical, and Enlightenment hopes of social progress through the spread of humanitarianism and the scientific outlook as naïve. John Maynard Keynes said of Bertrand Russell, a follower of the Enlightenment, that his comments about life and affairs were 'brittle' because there was 'no solid diagnosis of human nature underlying them'.[9]

Opponents of the Enlightenment can seem to grasp truths which elude its followers, and repudiation of the Enlightenment is now fashionable among philosophers.

One of this book's aims is to replace the thin, mechanical psychology of the Enlightenment with something more complex, something closer to reality. A consequence of this is to produce a darker account. But another aim of the book is to defend the Enlightenment hope of a world that is more peaceful and more humane, the hope that by understanding more about ourselves we can do something to create a world with less misery. I have qualified optimism that this hope is well founded. There are more things, darker things, to understand about ourselves than those who share this hope have generally allowed. Yet, although this book contains much that is exceptionally dark, the message is not one of simple pessimism. We need to look hard and clearly at some monsters inside us. But this is part of the project of caging and taming them.

PART ONE

ETHICS WITHOUT THE MORAL LAW

That girls are raped, that two boys knife a third,
Were axioms to him, who'd never heard
Of any world where promises were kept,
Or one could weep because another wept.

W.H. Auden, *The Shield of Achilles*

CHAPTER 2

Nietzsche's Challenge

> As the will to truth thus gains self-consciousness – there can be no doubt of that – morality will gradually *perish* now: this is the great spectacle in a hundred acts reserved for the next two centuries in Europe – the most terrible, most questionable, and perhaps also the most hopeful of all spectacles.
>
> Friedrich Nietzsche, *The Genealogy of Morals*

Nietzsche's words put it dramatically. He rightly saw a crisis for the authority of morality, but he drew conclusions which, after the experience of the first of his 'next two centuries in Europe', should dismay us.

The books Nietzsche wrote were published between 1872 and 1895 and he died in 1900. Some of his ideas became background assumptions to much of twentieth-century life and thought.

Nietzsche saw that the idea of a moral law external to us is in deep trouble. He wrote of the death of God, and took for granted that religious belief was no longer a serious intellectual option. He thought the implications of this, particularly for morality, had not yet been understood. Like rays of light from a distant star, its implications had not yet reached us.[1]

A century later, many people share Nietzsche's scepticism about a religious basis for morality, but Nietzsche's own outlook, the basis for his 'revaluation of values', contains much that is terrible. It includes intermittent racism, contempt for women, and a belief in the ruthless struggle for power. He rejected sympathy for the weak in favour of a willingness to trample on them.

Unsurprisingly, some of his ideas were congenial to the Nazis, who admired a highly selected and distorted version of his work. His many modern defenders rightly point out the distortions, but perhaps they explain away too much. A sense that Nietzsche is harmless may be created. I want to remove this impression. In our time, the problem is how to accept his scepticism about a religious authority for morality while escaping from his appalling conclusions.

The Attack on Judaeo-Christian Morality

Nietzsche attacked the dominant morality in the modern Western world, which derived from Judaism and Christianity. His attack was based partly on some historical claims about that morality.

He thought that every higher culture had begun with conquest by barbarians, 'men of prey still in possession of an unbroken strength of will and lust for power'. The nobles came from these barbarians: 'their superiority lay, not in their physical strength, but primarily in their psychical – they were *more complete* human beings (which, on every level, also means as much as "more complete beasts")'. The values of the barbarian noble caste, these more complete human beings, were subverted and replaced by the 'moral' values of people inferior to them.

Nietzsche saw a shift in the concept of goodness, away from aristocratic nobility towards compassion and love of one's neighbour, as the catastrophic triumph of the Judaeo-Christian tradition. This was the long-term triumph of the enslaved Jewish people over their more warlike conquerors. They had preached the virtues of the poor and weak: 'With the Jews there begins *the slave revolt in morality*: that revolt which has a history of two thousand years behind it and which we no longer see because it has been victorious.'[2]

Nietzsche saw the victory of the Jewish slave morality as a kind of poisoning: 'Everything is visibly becoming Judaized, Christianized, mobized (what do the words matter!). The progress of this poison through the entire body of mankind seems irresistible.'[3]

He detested the idea of morality being validated by any kind of religion. He came across a passage in which Ernest Renan wrote that man is nearest to the truth when he is most religious, and that when man is good he wants virtue to correspond to an eternal order. Nietzsche's response to 'these words with their upside-down truth' was that in Renan he had found his antipodes: 'It is so pleasant, so distinguishing, to possess one's own antipodes!'[4]

Without correspondence to an eternal order, Nietzsche thought that judgements of good and evil are exposed to a new question. What value do they themselves have? We should ask whether they indicate 'the plenitude, force, and will of life, its courage, certainty, future', or whether they reveal distress, impoverishment and degeneration.

Self-creation

The denial that religious morality has the authority it claims, together with the debunking historical account of its origins and allegedly poisonous effects, are the destructive part of Nietzsche's 'revaluation of values'. He believed that the destruction of Judaeo-Christian morality would make room for something better. In his new values, a central place is given to deciding what sort of person you want to be and then going on to create yourself. His belief that self-creation is possible comes from his scepticism about objective truth (his 'perspectivism').

Religion is one way in which people derive the values they live by from a picture of the world: other pictures are scientific or metaphysical. These pictures often suggest some point or meaning in life, but Nietzsche is severely critical of any idea that a meaning can be discovered in the world. The death of God can be interpreted in a wider sense, to include the death of scientific or metaphysical 'religions' as well:

> It is still a *metaphysical faith* that underlies our faith in science – and we seekers after knowledge of today, we godless ones and anti-metaphysicians, we, too, derive *our* flame from the fire ignited by a faith millennia old, the Christian faith, which was also Plato's, that God is truth, that truth is divine.[5]

Nietzsche wanted to preside at the funeral of *any* faith in a set of beliefs as the objective truth about things, or in external validation of anyone's way of life.

He believed the world has no intrinsic meaning. We can either live with meaninglessness or we can try to create our own meaning and impose it on the world. Or, more realistically, we can try to impose our own meaning on a small part of the world, in particular on our own lives. The collapse of the idea of an objective meaning leaves us free to create our own lives and ourselves.

Self-creation is how the 'will to power' expresses itself in human life and Nietzsche sees the will to power throughout nature. He uses the idea in an all-embracing way; he applies it to people, races, animals and species, even to physics. The concept is too vague to have much explanatory use, but the image of a constant struggle at all levels of existence colours his picture of human self-creation.

The collapse of the external authority of morality removes one of the main obstacles to conscious projects of self-creation. Nietzsche says that moral judgement should be left to the majority of people, who live in the past: 'We, however, *want to become those we are* – human beings who are new, unique, incomparable, who give themselves laws, who create themselves.'[6]

We tend to think of a person as having a particular character, which is displayed in the pattern of his or her actions. But perspectivism (which perhaps is at its most plausible here) stresses that there are alternative patterns into which a set of actions can be fitted – which of the things I did were expressions of central aspects of myself and which were marginal? Because our self picture has this fluidity we have scope to shape ourselves. We can use our future actions to highlight chosen aspects of our past, and so to create ourselves across a lifetime.

Because Nietzsche wants people to create themselves, he cannot lay down exactly what they should be like. But there are some qualities which (perhaps because he thinks they are necessary for self-creation) he indicates will be possessed by the kind of man he wants to see. He thought women were not suited to his ideal:

> One half of mankind is weak, typically sick, changeable, inconstant . . . she needs a religion of weakness that glorifies being weak, loving, and being humble as divine . . . Woman has always conspired with the types of decadence, the priests, against the 'powerful', the 'strong', the men.[7]

To create oneself is to impose coherence on what would otherwise be a collection of disunited personal characteristics. So long as unity can be imposed on them, the greater the variety of characteristics the better. Nietzsche did not want men without passions, whose self-creation might produce something insipid. Greatness of soul includes having intense passions, but ensuring by asceticism and self-discipline that they are mastered by a strong will: '*In summa: domination* of the passions, *not* their weakening or extirpation!'[8]

Nietzsche said of Goethe, 'What he aspired to was *totality*; he strove against the separation of reason, sensuality, feeling, will (preached in the most horrible scholasticism by Kant, the antipodes of Goethe); he disciplined himself to a whole, he *created* himself.'[9] Self-creation requires self-discipline. Cultivating some characteristics and curbing others requires 'hardness', as Nietzsche called it, towards oneself. As advocated by the Stoic philosophers, desires and impulses have to be strictly under control.

The reward of hardness towards yourself is to become what you have the potential to be: the artist and creator of your own life.

The Constraints of Morality and Life as a Struggle

The Judaeo-Christian tradition places a high value on altruism. Self-sacrifice for the sake of others is admired, and feelings of guilt are an appropriate reaction to the fact that you have trampled on others in pursuit of your own goals. For Nietzsche, this is all misguided. Moral restraints on self-creation are the result of self-deception. The idea of loving your neighbour is a disguise for mediocrity. People too weak to override others disguise their weakness as moral virtue, though this may be a necessary stage on the way to something higher: he says that 'the bad conscience is an illness, there is no doubt about that', but goes on to say that it is an illness as pregnancy is an illness.

The man Nietzsche admires will overcome bad conscience, which is the mark of slave morality, and will want to dominate others. He believed that egoism is essential to the noble soul, and he defines 'egoism' as the faith that 'other beings have to be subordinate by nature, and sacrifice themselves to us'.[10] This attitude is the sign of a healthy aristocracy, which 'accepts with a good conscience the sacrifice of innumerable men who *for its sake* have to be suppressed and reduced to imperfect men, to slaves and instruments'.[11]

He believed in opportunity for the creative minority. To provide a basis for great art and for highly developed forms of human perfection, the minority had to subordinate the majority ruthlessly: 'Accordingly, we must agree to the cruel sounding truth that slavery belongs to the essence of culture; . . . the wretchedness of struggling men must grow still greater in order to make possible the production of a world of art for a small number of Olympian men.'[12]

Nietzsche despised the majority, including most Europeans of his own time. He refers to 'the surfeit of ill-constituted, sickly, weary and exhausted people of which Europe is beginning to stink today'.[13] He even says, 'the great majority of men have no right to existence, but are a misfortune to higher men. I do not yet grant the failures the right. There are also peoples that are failures.'[14]

The impact of Social Darwinism was at its height in Nietzsche's lifetime. Many believed that societies and groups were engaged in a constant struggle for survival, in which the strong would win and the weak would go under. Nietzsche was contemptuous of Darwin and yet was influenced by Social Darwinism. His writings contain dismissive references to English biologists and to Darwin: 'I incline to the prejudice that the school of Darwin has been deluded everywhere.'[15]

Despite this, Nietzsche's ideas are close to Social Darwinism in that he sees life as a struggle. For him, any regret about this rests on a sentimental lack of realism: 'That lambs dislike great birds of prey does not seem strange: only it gives no ground for reproaching these birds of prey for bearing off little lambs.'[16]

Struggle was not merely to be accepted, but was also noble. Zarathustra says, 'You should love peace as a means to new wars. And the short peace more than the long . . . You say it is the good cause that hallows even war? I tell you: it is the good war that hallows every cause.'[17] Nietzsche admired the products of the struggle for survival. Before the struggle was mitigated by modern society, it produced a noble version of man, a beast of prey who might inspire fear but who also deserved to inspire respect. Modern

European man, after centuries of Christianity, is a 'measly, tame, domestic animal'.[18]

Christian morality's rejection of the law of the jungle had almost ruined the human species: for Nietzsche, it was more than time for that morality to be overturned.

Not Sympathy but Hardness

Nietzsche looks forward to 'philosophers of the future' who will be hard. Self-creation requires hardness: 'in man there is matter, fragment, excess, clay, mud, madness, chaos; but in man there is also creator, sculptor, the hardness of the hammer'. This hardness is part of greatness: 'strength of will, the hardness and capacity for protracted decisions, must constitute part of the concept "greatness" '.[19]

The hardness Nietzsche advocates sometimes takes a Stoic form, in being directed against your own impulses, but at other times it spills over into hardness towards others. The philosophers of the future will have 'a certain self-possessed cruelty which knows how to wield the knife with certainty and deftness even when the heart bleeds. They will be *harder* (and perhaps not always only against themselves) than humane men might wish.'[20]

He believes that all creators have to be hard in order to make an impact on history. He expresses this in vague but disturbing metaphors about 'cutting to pieces' and writing on metal:

> And if your hardness will not flash and cut and cut to pieces: how can you one day create with me? For creators are hard. And it must seem bliss to you to press your hand upon millennia as upon wax, bliss to write upon the will of millennia as upon metal – harder than metal, nobler than metal. Only the noblest is perfectly hard. This new law-table do I put over you, O my brothers: *Become hard!*[21]

Nietzsche advocates more than the hardness needed for self-mastery. His hardness requires the rejection of pity as something unmanly. He refers to modern Europeans with a morbid sensitivity to pain, who suffer from 'tenderization', and talks of 'the *unmanliness* of that which is in such fanatic circles baptized "pity" '.[22] His version of hardness, with its rejection of unmanly compassion, supports the domination, even the cruel domination, of others:

> To see others suffer does one good, to make others suffer even more: this is a hard saying but an ancient, mighty, human, all-too-human principle to which even the apes might subscribe; for it has been said that in devising bizarre

cruelties they anticipate man and are, as it were, his 'prelude'. Without cruelty there is no festival . . .²³

Nietzsche moves beyond this praise of making others suffer. The rejection of sympathy for the weak is taken to encompass even participating in their destruction: 'The weak and ill-constituted shall perish: first principle of *our* philanthropy. And one shall help them to do so. What is more harmful than any vice? Active sympathy for the ill-constituted and weak — Christianity.²⁴

The Limits of Self-creation

The austere universe left when religious metaphysics is stripped away still allows us to lead rich and satisfying lives. This satisfaction is often linked to the Nietzschean idea of creating ourselves according to our own values.

But some of us drawn to these ideas may feel aghast at where they took Nietzsche. Struggle, egoism, dominance, slavery, the majority having no right to existence, peoples that are failures, hardness, the festival of cruelty, the replacement of compassion for the weak by their destruction. If such a world is really the result of Nietzsche's thought, it seems a nightmare.

These chilling Nietzschean conclusions do not follow from his premises about the value of self-creation and the absence of an external moral law. People's projects of self-creation may be guided by quite different values from his. Some of us do not want to be all dominance and assertion. We are free to reject any predetermined pattern, whether laid down by God or by Nietzsche. To value self-creation is not necessarily to think that it is the only object of life, which has to override everything else.

Nietzsche's self-creation pushes aside people who get in the way, but self-creation can be seen as one value among others. Some who create themselves may also care about other people, and dislike the egoism and ruthlessness admired by Nietzsche. He believed in *unrestrained* self-creation, perhaps thinking that only an external authority could provide a basis for restraint, but this assumption is false. My caring about the sort of person I am motivates the project of self-creation. Why should not my caring about other people set limits to it?

The Nietzschean nightmare does not follow from Nietzschean premises, but a troubling question remains. Perhaps there are people, either individuals or whole groups, whose projects of self-creation are close to that of Nietzsche's 'noble soul'. And perhaps they do not have countervailing values which restrain their ruthless projects. Does the fading of the moral law mean that we have nothing to say to a Nietzschean amoralist?

CHAPTER 3

Self-interest as a Restraint

Amoralists are sceptics about the claims of morality. They do not have to be ruthlessly selfish – they may have generous impulses and care about other people – but they are sceptical about claims that they *ought* to do things for others. An amoralist says about 'ought' what Oscar Wilde said about 'patriotism': it is not one of my words. The generous, caring amoralist is in practice not much of a problem. It is the ruthlessly selfish amoralist who arouses the hope that amoralism can be refuted.

Some speakers in Plato's dialogues advance powerful, sceptical arguments against morality. In *The Republic*, Thrasymachus argues for the 'Marxist' account: that ideas of what is just or right reflect the interests of the strong, who impose them on the weak. Callicles, in the *Gorgias*, argues the 'Nietzschean' case: the strong are naturally dominant like lions, but the rest of us try to tame them with the charms and spells of moral dogma. Nietzsche predicted that morality will gradually perish.

How serious are the consequences of amoralism? Any picture of universal savagery and social collapse is exaggerated. The first correction to this must be that it is often in our own interest to behave well to other people. Society usually works to reinforce this.

Self-interest and Co-operation

Rational self-interest will lead to a good deal of 'reciprocal altruism'. Not all generous acts are repaid, but a generous approach to the needs of others makes it more likely that friends will be there when you need them.

Narrow selfishness can be self-defeating. This is shown by the prisoners' dilemma. Two people who conspired to commit a crime are captured and kept out of communication with each other. To obtain a confession, the police interrogate them separately. Each of them is told, 'If neither of you confesses, you will each get one year in jail. If you confess and your accomplice does not, you will go free and he will get twelve years. If your accomplice confesses and you do not, those sentences will be reversed. If you both confess, you will each get five years.'

A narrowly self-interested prisoner will work out that, whichever decision the other takes, it is better to confess. If both are narrowly self-interested, both will then confess. They will both go to jail for five years. If they had been more altruistic, each considering both of their interests rather than sticking to self-interest, and each knowing the other would do this, they would both have stayed silent rather than confessed. Paradoxically, greater altruism here serves each of them better than selfishness.

This holds if the prisoners' dilemma is an isolated case, but things become different in a series of repeated dilemmas. Then co-operation can build up trust which may pay off next time and not co-operating may be followed by retaliation. The future impact of present decisions may tilt the self-interested balance towards co-operation.

Robert Axelrod ran a 'repeated prisoners' dilemma' tournament on computers.[1] Mathematicians, computer scientists, physicists, biologists, psychologists, economists, political scientists and sociologists submitted strategies aimed at doing best in a series of repeated two-person prisoners' dilemmas. Some complex strategies were submitted, but the winning one was very simple. It was TIT FOR TAT: I will co-operate with you unless you defect. If you defect, I will defect next time. If you co-operate, I will co-operate next time.

The success of TIT FOR TAT gives support to co-operation. To the extent that social life is like a series of repeated prisoners' dilemmas, self-interested people will be wise to consider this conditional form of co-operation.

However, there are limits to the case made for co-operation by the success of TIT FOR TAT. Axelrod's is only one version of the tournament. Later versions incorporate more features of the world and of human psychology. One version includes the fact that players may make mistakes. Another includes the human tendency to repeat winning strategies and to change losing ones. Other versions have more than two players. In some of these modified tournaments, TIT FOR TAT is not the winner.[2]

In a one-off prisoners' dilemma, purely self-interested people find themselves mutually trapped. And, even if TIT FOR TAT co-operation evolves, it will break down in the last game, where building trust no longer leads to future rewards. The last game would be won by a solitary defector, but because both 'prisoners' can see this, mutual trust collapses and they are back in the trap. They could only be saved by a trust based on more than self-interested calculation.

Prisoners' dilemma also requires a particular structure of rewards and penalties. If the prison sentences for confession or silence had been set differently, selfishness might not have been self-defeating. A lot depends on how many real-world conflicts of interest have the structure of the prisoners' dilemma, and how many have pay-offs which give a different result. A lot also depends on how likely you are to have a repeat session with the same people.

The lesson of prisoners' dilemma is not that co-operation is always to a person's advantage. It is that *under some conditions* co-operation is more successful than selfishness. Those of us who want to see co-operation rather than conflict have a reason to rig the social rewards and penalties so that co-operation becomes a winning strategy. One attempt at this is to have rules backed by social sanctions.

Social Pressures and Conventional Moral Rules

Thomas Hobbes thought that humans' natural state was to be at war with each other, and that it was worth doing almost anything necessary to escape from the life this mutual war caused: 'continualle feare, and danger of violent death; And the life of man, solitary, poore, nasty, brutish, and short.'[3] His solution was that everyone should submit to an absolute ruler, who would have the power to set penalties sufficiently severe to enforce social rules. The history of how absolute rulers have used their power suggests that Hobbes's solution is a desperate one, to be used at best as a very last resort. Fortunately there are degrees of social pressure which fall short of political dictatorship.

Conventional moral rules can be useful in shifting the balance away from selfishness. It is better to be accepted as a member of society in good standing than to be excluded or disapproved of. But a sophisticated calculation of self-interest may suggest that what matters is reputation and image, rather than what you are really like. Glaucon, in Plato's *Republic*, supports this with a thought experiment. He cites the story of Gyges, a shepherd who found a ring which made its wearer invisible at will. Glaucon argues that the advantages of morality over immorality are all bound up with being detected, so they disappear for anyone who has the ring of Gyges. People benefit from seeming, rather than from being, moral. This need to seem moral may still make people co-operative, but it is possible that this is only a surface conformity. Many will feel that amoralism remains a threat unless there is a deeper convergence of outlook.

R.M. Hare has suggested that self-interest can lead to this deeper convergence.[4] He says that the concealment strategy is very difficult. In the real world there are no rings of Gyges, so the easiest way to seem upright is to be upright. And the best way for parents to promote the interests of their children is to encourage the development of moral feelings which will motivate obedience to society's moral rules.

There is some plausibility in this. Being moral may sometimes give better results than concealed amoralism, but there may also be times when a mixed strategy (of genuine commitment to some parts of the moral code and concealed lack of commitment to other parts) gives better results. Perhaps it will benefit our children if we can cultivate a moral outlook in them, but, for ourselves, it seems paradoxical to aim at genuine moral commitment for this kind of reason.

Even if Hare's claim goes too far, social pressures seem likely either to create some moral commitment or at least to provide reasons for a fairly substantial show of conformity. Those who remain amoralists are unlikely to be outwardly Nietzschean unless they are very powerful.

However, these restraining effects are limited to where the social pressures are felt, but there are contexts in which the social pressures against harm to others may be weak or non-existent.

Sometimes the social pressures which normally operate against harming others are actually reversed. To protect Jews in Hitler's Germany, or to help a 'reactionary' in the Chinese Cultural Revolution, was to risk stigma and sometimes punishment. Those motivated by sympathy, or by revulsion at subjecting people to humiliation and cruelty, found themselves trapped. To act on these decent impulses could bring heavy penalties. These are cases of people wanting to help others who may be deterred by the costs of doing so.

And one whole sphere hardly affected by these pressures is that of relations between groups, for instance nations. The bank robber may be imprisoned and stigmatized, but the political leader who sends an army to capture a weaker neighbour's territory may be a national hero.

CHAPTER 4

The Moral Resources: Humanity

Sometimes self-interest restrains ruthlessness and mutual harm. This is usually when co-operation brings benefits, or when there are relevant social rewards and penalties. However, we have seen that rational self-interest does not always support co-operation, and sometimes the social pressures are weak or even reversed. We may hope that decent behaviour has other roots as well as calculating self-interest.

Fortunately, there are also the 'moral resources', certain human needs and psychological tendencies which work against narrowly selfish behaviour. These tendencies make it natural for people to display self-restraint, and to respect and care for others. They make it unlikely that 'morality' in a broad sense will perish, despite the fading of belief in a moral law.

What are the moral resources?

We have distinctive psychological responses to different things people do: acts of cruelty may arouse our revulsion; we may respond to some mean swindle with contempt; courage or generosity may win our respect or admiration. These responses to others are linked to our sense of our own 'moral identity'. Many people have their own, often very un-Nietzschean, projects of self-creation. We have a conception of what we are like, and of the kind of person we want to be, which may limit what we are prepared to do to others.

Other moral resources, to be looked at first, are the 'human responses'. Two of these human responses, in particular, are important restraints. One is the tendency to respond to people with certain kinds of respect. This may be bound up with ideas about their dignity or about their having a certain status, either as members of our community or just as fellow human beings. The other human response is sympathy: caring about the miseries and the happiness of others, and perhaps feeling a degree of identification with them.

Respect and Moral Standing

There is a widespread disposition to show respect to people, or at least to some people. Sometimes the respect is for status: in a hierarchy, such as an army or a structured church, the respect is mainly shown by subordinates to superiors. There is a more egalitarian kind of respect, which is shown to all members of a community, and which is sometimes thought of as respect for people's dignity, expressed through social conventions of politeness.

Behaviour showing respect for someone's dignity symbolizes that person's moral standing. Those who are weak are protected by social conventions about the respect they should be shown. These conventions are backed up by social pressures, but they also have psychological backing. The idea of humiliating a blind beggar appals us. Narrow self-interest might lead someone to take the blind beggar's money away: retaliation would be unlikely, and there will be no social sanctions if no one else is around to see. But the idea disgusts most of us.

Immanuel Kant saw respect for dignity as owed not just to those with standing in a community, but simply to human beings:

> Humanity itself is a dignity; for a man cannot be used merely as a means by any man . . . but must always be used at the same time as an end. It is just in this that his dignity (personality) consists . . . so neither can he act contrary to the equally necessary self-esteem of others . . . he is under obligation to acknowledge, in a practical way, the dignity of humanity in every other man.[1]

Our inclination to show this respect, and our disgust at someone's humiliation, is a powerful restraint on barbarism. The weakening of this restraint may have contributed to the Amritsar massacre. In 1919, in India, troops under General Dyer fired for ten minutes into a peaceful Indian political meeting. They killed between 500 and 1,000 people and wounded a similar number. How could General Dyer have ordered this atrocity?

The explanation may be linked to the way the British authorities in that part of India humiliated Indians. If a European approached, Indians had to 'salaam'. They had to dismount, lower their umbrellas and step into the road. One Indian who failed to salaam was made to kiss the boots of the officer he ignored. For the same offence, others were made to lie down, rub their noses in the dust and grovel.

Some British officers devised 'fancy punishments' for Indians. A group of men who visited a brothel during a curfew were ordered to be flogged in front of the prostitutes by Captain Doveton, who punished people for other offences by making them skip and touch the ground with their foreheads. Some Indians said an officer had punished them by covering them with whitewash. General Dyer himself had a triangle put up for publicly whipping offenders. He also issued a 'crawling order': all Indians going along a particular lane had to squirm along on their stomachs. If they lifted their legs or arms, soldiers would prod them with rifles.[2] To order the massacre might have been harder if the Indians' protective dignity had not already been violated.

Sympathy

Our entanglements with people close to us erode simple self-interest. Husbands, wives, lovers, parents, children and friends all blur the boundaries of selfish concern. Francis Bacon rightly said that people with children have given hostages to fortune. Inescapably, other forms of friendship and love hold us hostage too. The deeper levels of relationships are denied to people who hold large parts of themselves back. And to give yourself means that part of you belongs to the person you care for. There is a constant pull towards new kinds of sympathy and commitment. Narrow self-interest is destabilized.

We can also feel sympathy for people we do not know. We may be moved to help by the television reports from refugee camps in Ethiopia. We feel compassion when we hear of a mother visiting her son before his execution.

And sympathy may grow with our own experience of what it is to suffer. In Lebanon Brian Keenan was held hostage for five years under grim conditions and was sometimes beaten by his captors. He remembered the experience of hearing another prisoner being beaten:

> With each tortured cry I felt my own fear claw at and crawl over my flesh. There is a capacity in each of us and sometimes I think even a need to reach out to others in pain. Why that is I didn't know at the time but have since learnt a lot about it. The more we discover the different degrees and different aspects of our own unhappiness the greater our capacity to sympathize instinctively or to reach out to someone in distress.[3]

People vary in how they respond to their own unhappiness. Some grow more shut in and self-absorbed, and some hardly respond to anyone else's unhappiness. But the alternative, reaching out to others, is widespread, and is a strong constraint on ruthlessness and cruelty.

Humanity as Fact and Aspiration

Respect and sympathy are 'human responses' which human beings do not always have. Our frequent inhumanity is the theme of this book, but it contrasts with these widespread and deep-rooted responses, which are part of our humanity.

Someone decent to other people merely out of self-interested calculation, with no independent inclination towards respect or sympathy, could be said to lack humanity.

Human responses are the core of the humanity which contrasts with inhumanity. They are widely distributed, but to identify them with humanity is only partly an empirical claim. It remains also partly an aspiration.

CHAPTER 5

The Moral Resources: Moral Identity

Narrow self-interest is also limited by the way we care about being one sort of person rather than another. This can take many forms: I may want to be more confident; I am not the sort of person who takes bribes; I am someone people can talk to; I would not have a haircut like that; I am quite a good parent some of the time; I am glad I am not a television evangelist.

Character, Commitments and Moral Identity

This sense of identity has a moral charge when it is not a matter of style or personality but is of deeper character. A person's character, as Aristotle saw, comes partly from individual decisions and actions. Repeated, these become the habits which set into character. The ways we respond to things that happen and to things people do also play a part. These responses may have no reference to ourselves. We may respect loyalty or detest cruelty when we see them in others. They leave a residue of personal commitment, perhaps to being a loyal friend, being a good Catholic, being someone who would not work for a tobacco company, or being someone willing to speak out in an unpopular cause. Few people could easily give a list of what their own commitments are. We may only recognize them when they are challenged. But these commitments, even if hardly conscious, are the core of moral identity.

Under extreme duress, a sense of moral identity can give courage and strength. Brian Keenan describes how, after being beaten by one of his captors, his first thoughts of revenge were replaced by something else:

As my anger diminished I felt a new and tremendous kind of strength flooding me. The more I was beaten the stronger I seemed to become. It was not strength of arm, nor of body but a huge determination never to give in to these men, never to show fear, never to cower in front of them. To take what violence they meted out to me and stand and resist and not allow myself to be humiliated. In that resistance I would humiliate them. There was a part of me they could never bind nor abuse nor take from me. There was a sense of self greater than me alone which came and filled me in the darkest hours.[1]

To Live at Peace with Oneself: the Argument of Socrates

The question of the sort of person you want to be is central to the argument given by Socrates against the view that it is in our interest to seem moral but not to *be* moral.

Socrates believed that the method of using questions to elicit people's beliefs and values, and then the method of arguing by presenting counter-examples, can lead us to a clearer understanding of our deepest desires and values. (This Socratic method is, even today, the best thing in philosophy.) Socrates accepted that people may get much of what they want through immorality, but he claimed that the self-knowledge gained by questioning and criticism shows that immorality does not lead to true happiness.

Those who gain this self-knowledge see that their happiness depends on psychological integration, or wholeness. We need to be at peace with ourselves. Inner conflict is a threat to happiness. Disharmony involves slavery to madness, and allows the beast in man to gain control. 'It would be better for me to have a musical instrument or a chorus which I was directing in discord and out of tune, better that the mass of mankind should disagree with me and contradict me than that I, a single individual, should be out of harmony with myself and contradict myself.'[2] And to be at peace with yourself depends on your anarchic and conflicting desires being subjected to the discipline of morality.

This argument has various steps which can be questioned. Why does Socrates think that only people with psychological unity can be happy? And is morality the only way of imposing discipline on anarchic desires? Why should the amoralist be torn apart by conflict?

On its own, the Socratic argument seems weak. But it makes more sense if we presuppose the moral resources. Most of us have to some degree the human responses of respect and sympathy. Most of us do care, at least a little, about what sort of person we are. These dispositions all conflict with ruthless selfishness, greatly raising its psychological cost. This is, of course, 'only' an empirical point. People look to philosophy for the knockdown argument and the decisive refutation, but ethics, being bound up with people, cannot escape soft-edged psychology, all dispositions and tendencies rather than hard universal laws.

The Socratic argument would have no force for a 'natural', ruthless amoralist, in whom moral resources were non-existent, but for the rest of us it contains an important truth. The psychological conflict generated by trampling on others will be often (though not always) unacceptably great.

Limitations: the Melian Dialogue

Different ethical theories base morality either on self-interest or else on one of the moral resources. They tend to urge the claims of one of these factors to be *the* basis of morality. Deals based on self-interested calculation are at the heart of the contractarian theory. Sympathy for others is at the heart of utilitarianism. Respect for other people, as a form of recognition of their moral standing, is the centre of Kantian ethics and of moralities based on rights. Concern with one's own moral identity is one source of ethics centred on virtues.

Despite the popularity of theories proposing a single basis for morality, self-interest and the different moral resources all have a role to play. Together they help to explain why, in most societies, scepticism about the moral law has not resulted in unlimited conflict and social breakdown.

But, outside the boundaries of a single community, both self-interest and the moral resources have severe limitations.

Self-interested calculation finds the structure of rewards and penalties very different in dealings with members of a different community. There are far weaker social pressures against hostile treatment of members of other groups. And in war the pressures often support group hostility.

The moral resources also have less power. Claims to be treated with respect are often linked to standing within a group. The claim of an outsider may be minimal. Sympathy has similar limitations. The sympathies which really engage us are often stubbornly limited and local. I may move mountains for my child, but perhaps I will not cross the street to be a good Samaritan to a stranger. Sympathy may hardly extend to those outside a particular community.

These limitations help to explain a moral gap which is increasingly evident. Many moralities are 'internal', giving weight to the interests of those inside a community, but doing little against the common indifference or even hostility towards those outside. It is increasingly obvious that this moral gap is a human disaster.

The limitations of an internal morality are strikingly illustrated by the 'Melian dialogue' recounted by Thucydides. In the Peloponnesian War, the inhabitants of the island of Melos tried to be neutral between Athens and Sparta. But Athenian attacks turned them into enemies. Athens sent negotiators, who offered peace if the Melians would pay them tribute. In the discussions, as recounted by Thucydides, the Athenians explicitly rejected appeals to morality. They would not use 'fine phrases' about having a right to their empire, nor appeal to injuries done by the Melians. And they asked the Melians

> not to imagine that you will influence us by saying . . . that you have never done us any harm . . . since you know as well as we do that, when these matters

are discussed by practical people, the standard of justice depends on the equality of power to compel and that in fact the strong do what they have the power to do and the weak accept what they have to accept.[3]

The Melians claimed that it would be in the interests of the Athenians to preserve the principle of fair play and just dealing, since they themselves might one day be defeated. The Athenians replied that such a risk weighed less with them than that of seeming weak if they let a small island remain neutral.

The Melians then made a direct appeal to morality ('Is that your subjects' idea of fair play?'), which the Athenians brushed aside: 'So far as right and wrong are concerned they think that there is no difference between the two.' The Athenians held a grim view, which they took to be realism:

> It is a general and necessary law of nature to rule wherever one can. This is not a law we made ourselves, nor were we the first to act upon it when it was made. We found it already in existence, and we shall leave it to exist for ever among those who come after us. We are merely acting in accordance with it, and we know that you or anybody else with the same power as ours would be acting in precisely the same way.

The Melians refused to subordinate themselves to Athens, offering a treaty by which they would remain neutral. The Athenians then besieged the city of Melos and the next winter the Melians surrendered. The Athenians killed all the men of military age and sold the women and children into slavery.

The Athenians presented hard amoralism as mere realism. Echoes of this have been heard many times since, for example in a comment by Stalin on the policies of countries at war: 'Whoever occupies a territory also imposes on it his own social system. Everyone imposes his own system as far as his army has power to do so. It cannot be otherwise.'[4]

Nietzsche, in his thoughts on the Melian dialogue, made no criticism of the Athenians. Predictably, his contempt was reserved for those with sympathy for the Melians' moral appeals:

> Do you suppose perchance that these little Greek free cities, which from rage and envy would have liked to devour each other, were guided by philanthropic and righteous principles? Does one reproach Thucydides for the words he put into the mouths of the Athenian ambassadors when they negotiated with the Melians on the question of destruction or submission? Only complete Tartuffes could possibly have talked of virtue in the midst of this terrible tension – or men living apart, hermits, refugees, and emigrants from reality – people who negated in order to be able to live themselves.[5]

The brutal 'realism' of Nietzsche's comments is not answered by what has been said so far. Sophisticated self-interest and our deeper psychological needs may generate an internal morality, but this was not enough to restrain the Athenians on Melos. More than two thousand years later, events not so different took place in Bosnia and then in Kosovo, both a few hundred miles north of Melos. We still need an answer to the hardness of the Athenians and of Nietzsche.

CHAPTER 6

The Festival of Cruelty

Barbed wire enclosed an arbitrary spot
Where bored officials lounged (one cracked a joke)
And sentries sweated for the day was hot:
A crowd of ordinary decent folk
Watched from without and neither moved nor spoke
As three pale figures were led forth and bound
To three posts driven upright in the ground.

The mass and majesty of this world, all
That carries weight and always weighs the same
Lay in the hands of others; they were small
And could not hope for help and no help came:
What their foes liked to do was done, their shame
Was all the worst could wish; they lost their pride
And died as men before their bodies died.

W.H. Auden, *The Shield of Achilles*

Ivan Karamazov could not accept the moral authority of a God who created a world containing the Bulgarian atrocities. There are questions to ask about any God who made a world in which people are hanged after spending their last night nailed by the ear to a fence, or in which babies are cut out of their mothers' wombs with daggers. There are also questions to ask about human beings: 'no animal could be so artfully, so artistically, cruel'.

More than a century after the atrocities in Bulgaria, journalists covering the Gulf War described what Saddam Hussein's Iraqi forces had done to the Kuwaitis. Among the many cruel acts reported, a few individual cases stand out. Hisham al-Abadan, the gynaecologist at Mubarak al-Kabeer hospital, who gave medical treatment to people the Iraqis did not approve of, was found dead with his nails and eyes gouged out.[1] A twenty-year-old woman who was arrested by the Iraqis had all her hair cut off, was repeatedly raped over a period of two months, and, pregnant, was electrocuted. Before she died she had 'her breasts cut off and her belly sliced open'.[2]

Ahmad Qabazard was a nineteen-year-old Kuwaiti held by the Iraqis. An Iraqi officer told his parents he was about to be released.

> They were overjoyed, cooked wonderful things, and when they heard cars approaching went to the door. When Ahmad was taken out of the car, they saw that his ears, his nose and his genitalia had been cut off. He was coming out of the car with his eyes in his hands. Then the Iraqis shot him, once in the stomach and once in the head, and told his mother to be sure not to move the body for three days.[3]

Journalists from outside were able to visit places in Iraq where prisoners of Saddam Hussein's regime had been held. When the Kurds captured Kirkuk, Gwynne Roberts described a visit:

> The Kurds guided me into the pitch-black vaults of the security building used as a torture centre. In one cell pieces of human flesh – ear lobes – were nailed to the wall, and blood spattered the ceiling. A large metal fan hung from the ceiling and my guide told me prisoners were attached to the fan and beaten with clubs as they twirled. There were hooks in the ceiling used to suspend victims. A torture victim told me that prisoners were also crucified, nails driven through their hands into the wall. A favourite technique was to hang men from the hooks and attach a heavy weight to their testicles.[4]

These reports were rightly front-page news, but that was partly because Saddam Hussein was the enemy in the Gulf War. The appalling nature of his regime was highly visible and the world was ready to listen to such accounts. For years Amnesty International and others had been reporting similar tortures in Iraq, with little resulting publicity.

And from Kuwait, soon after the Iraqis were driven out, came reports that it was the turn of Palestinians to be tortured. Victims of the new wave of torture were interviewed in Farwaniya Hospital. One Palestinian had half his body paralysed and could not talk. He wrote on a pad: 'I was tortured with electrical shocks. I became paralysed . . . I was held by an intelligence unit . . . I do not know what is my destiny. I was captured only because I am a Palestinian. They threw me in this hospital. I want to get out of here . . . out of Kuwait . . . Please help me.'[5]

In its report issued that year, 1991, Amnesty International recorded protests against human rights abuses in over fifty countries, the protests to thirteen countries making specific reference to torture.[6] These are the kinds of thing many of us have a vague background awareness of, without there being much publicity unless the perpetrators are some currently loathed regime, or unless some highly visible Westerner is among the victims. The reality is that in many countries torture of the most revolting cruelty happens routinely, often under the auspices of governments with good relations with Europe and the United States, sometimes using equipment knowingly supplied by Western companies. There is little reason to think torture is in retreat. The festival of cruelty is in full swing.

What is it about human beings that makes such acts possible?

Three factors seem central. There is a love of cruelty. Also, emotionally inadequate people assert themselves by dominance and cruelty. And the moral resources which restrain cruelty can be neutralized.

The Love of Cruelty

Sometimes cruel treatment is a means to an end, such as intimidation. Fear of abduction and torture was used to deter criticism by the military dictatorship in Argentina. Some Argentinians who brought *habeas corpus* cases on behalf of people who had 'disappeared' started to 'disappear' themselves.

Physical or psychological torture can be used to make people say things, but there is doubt about the reliability of the resulting information. People might confess to anything, or denounce anyone, to bring the agony to a halt. The paradox of using torture to obtain information raises the question of whether this is the real motive.

The instrumental uses of torture and other kinds of cruelty are not enough to explain their prevalence or the artistry with which they are carried out. It is impossible to believe that what was done to Ahmad Qabazard resulted from some careful calculation of how to frighten the Kuwaitis. Deep in human psychology, there are urges to humiliate, torment, wound and kill people.

Some of the appeal is that of exercising power over victims. Jacobo Timerman was tortured in Argentina under the military regime. He noticed sometimes a bond developed between torturer and victim, who could come to need each other. The victim could need a human voice. 'For the torturer, it is a sense of omnipotence . . . the torturer needs to be needed by the tortured.' He described one of the men offering him coffee, food and a blanket. Timerman refused the man's offer to go to bed with a woman prisoner. His refusal made the man angry: 'In some way he needs to demonstrate to me and to himself his capacity to grant things, to alter my world, my situation. To demonstrate to me that I need things that are inaccessible to me and which only he can provide.'[7] Those higher up also enjoyed the exercise of power. General Galtieri visited a centre where prisoners were held. To one woman, who had been blindfolded and tortured for months, he said, 'If I say you live, you live, and if I say you die, you die. As it happens, you have the same Christian name as my daughter, and so you live.'[8]

For some, especially when the victims are women, the pleasure of cruelty is sexual. Typical are the cruelties and humiliations inflicted on Brazilian women tortured under the military regime, who describe being paraded naked, having their nipples repeatedly pinched, being genitally violated with bits of wood, and being made to work naked while being subjected to a barrage of obscenities and jokes.[9]

The savage and violent history of punishment can only really be understood in the context of a love of cruelty. People are excited by executions. Louis-Sebastien Mercier described the reaction when the French revolutionaries guillotined Louis XVI:

> His blood flowed and cries of joy from eighty thousand armed men struck my ears . . . I saw the schoolboys of the Quatre-Nations throw their hats in the air; his blood flowed and some dipped their fingers in it; one tasted it . . . An executioner on the boards of the scaffold sold and distributed little packets of hair and the ribbon that bound them . . . I saw people pass by, arm in arm, laughing, chatting familiarly as if they were at a fête.[10]

As Nietzsche saw, the ingenuity of methods of torment and of death does not come from calculation about deterrence. The widespread enthusiasm even now for capital punishment seems to reflect something more than a concern to reduce crime rates. When capital punishment was the law in Britain, there were about five applications a week for the post of executioner.

Some People and not Others

The psychological appeal of acts of cruelty is not their whole explanation. Many people do not torture, maim or kill.

Most torturers are men. Physical cruelty seems to have less appeal to women, although female Red Guards did some fairly terrible things in the Chinese Cultural Revolution. This raises questions about how far this gender difference reflects biological differences, and how far it is the result of differences of upbringing and opportunity. As with other 'nature or nurture' issues, the evidence is opaque and disputed.

It is less disputed that there are relevant individual differences between people. Those who practise cruelty are often in one way or another emotionally stunted. Those who abducted and ill-treated Brian Keenan were in their twenties but had the immaturity of thirteen-year-olds. He wrote, 'I could see the man, a man not defined by Islam or by ethnic background, perhaps a man more confused than the man in chains, a man more hurt and anguished than the man he had just beaten.' They were obsessed with sex. They were humourless and felt threatened by the humour of their captives. They were afraid of being by themselves, needing the distraction of endless radio and television. They became dependent on their prisoners, sometimes begging them to talk.

Brian Keenan thought about where the brutality came from:

> Cruelty and fear are man-made, and men who perpetrate them are ruled by them. Such men are only half-made things. They live out their unresolved lives by attempting to destroy anything that challenges the void in themselves. A child holds a blanket over its face in fear. A fear-filled man transposes his inadequacy onto another. He blames them, hates them, and hopes to rid himself of his unloved self by hurting, or worse, destroying them.[11]

The fact that many people are not emotionally stunted is part of the explanation of why acts of brutality are comparatively rare, but it is not the whole story. There are also the restraining effects of self-interest and of the moral resources: the sense of moral identity and the human responses.

The Erosion of Moral Identity

Some of those who carry out acts of cruelty may once have had a conception of themselves as being a very different kind of person. But there are ways in which moral identity can be eroded.

People slide by degrees into doing things they would not do if given a clear choice at the beginning. Each of the early steps may seem too small to count, but later anxiety about the moral boundary may only suggest the uncomfortable thought that it has already been passed. The prisoners abducted in the Argentinian state terror would sometimes be given improved conditions in exchange for co-operation, which would start with small cleaning jobs. A few went by degrees to taking part in interrogation and even torture.

Weakening the Human Responses

Atrocities are easier if the human responses are weakened. Torturers have to suppress sympathy, or 'squeamishness' as they come to think of it. One way is to stress that victims do not belong. They are usually assigned to some other, stigmatized, group. The excluding classification may be ideological. According to where you are, it may be easier to ill-treat someone seen as an imperialist or as a Communist than someone seen just as a person.

Atrocities are easier to commit if respect for the victims can be neutralized. For this reason, humiliation handed out by those with power can be ominous. The link between humiliation and atrocity is often found. The Argentinian torturers made their prisoners run naked shouting such things as 'My mother's a whore . . . The whore who gave birth to me . . . I masturbate . . . I must respect the corporal on guard . . . The police love me.'[12]

People in Argentina who 'disappeared' were made less likely to resist by being blindfolded. This practice, called 'walling up', also eroded their dignity by making them helpless and dependent on their tormentors. As Dr Norberto Liwsky put it, 'The normal attitude of the torturers and guards towards us was to consider us less than slaves. We were objects. And useless, troublesome objects at that. They would say: "You're dirt." '[13]

Sometimes the humiliation is linked to ethnicity or religion. The Argentinian torturers were influenced by a pervasive anti-Semitism, with conscious echoes of Nazism. Jews were humiliated; sometimes they were painted with swastikas or made to shout 'Heil Hitler!' They were singled out for special tortures, such as having a rat inserted in their anus, from where it would eat its way out.[14] Jacobo Timerman described his captors' obsession with Jewish 'conspiracies' against Argentina. He remembered how his Jewishness was used to add humiliation to his torture with electric shocks:

> Now they're really amused, and burst into laughter. Someone tries a variation while still clapping hands: 'Clipped prick . . . clipped prick.' Wherupon they begin alternating while clapping their hands: 'Jew . . . Clipped prick . . . Jew . . . Clipped prick . . .' It seems they're no longer angry, merely having a good time.[15]

A central part of the torturer's craft is to make his job easier by stripping the victim of protective dignity.

The Cold Joke

Among the strongest expressions of lack of respect is the cold joke. During the occupation of Kuwait, some Iraqis who had killed a boy told his family they wanted money to pay for the bullet.[16] They could have simply forced Kuwaitis at random to give them money. The added cruel humour in this demand is what makes it a cold joke.

The language used by people carrying out atrocities is riddled with cold jokes. The Iraqi military security under Saddam Hussein uses Kadhemya prison in Baghdad for torturing political prisoners. The tank of battery acid into which they are thrown to their deaths is known as 'the swimming pool'.[17] Argentinian soldiers under the junta called the machine they used to give people massive electric shocks, 'Susan', and a prisoner's interroga- tion by these means was called 'a chat with Susan'.[18] Under apartheid, South African interrogators had nicknames for kinds of torture: 'telepho- ning', 'playing the radio', 'the submarine', 'the aeroplane ride', and so on.[19] Some of the same terms crop up in Argentinian accounts, showing that there is a revolting international language in which to be amusing about torture.

The cold joke mocks the victims. It is an added cruelty and it is also a display of power: we can put you through hell merely for our mild amusement. It adds emphasis to the difference between 'us' and 'them': we the interrogators are a group who share a joke at the expense of you the victims. It is also a display of hardness: we are so little troubled by feelings of sympathy that we can laugh at your torment; but the display may be a clue that suppression of sympathy is not so easy and needs help.

It is not only the torturers themselves who use the cold joke, but sometimes also those a stage or two further back in the system. A cell has been set up in the Special Branch headquarters in Dubai:

with a terrifyingly loud sound system and a white noise generator designed to pulse sound at a frequency which will ultimately destroy the human body, 11 hertz. Synchronised with the white noise generator was a strobe light, also set at 11 hz. The combined effect would be to reduce anyone inside the cell to a screaming, helpless supplicant within moments.

The British company who installed this torture chamber were reported as calling it the 'House of Fun'.[20]

This use of the cold joke is not an extra cruelty, nor is it a display of power. It seems to be more a device by which businessmen and technicians do not have to face up to precisely what they are doing. It is a defensive flippancy, enabling the torment they are preparing for other people to be referred to without being taken seriously.

Breakthrough of the Human Responses

The techniques for switching off respect and sympathy are powerful, but sometimes the human responses break through the carefully constructed defences.

In 1985, in the old apartheid South Africa, there was a demonstration in Durban. The police attacked the demonstrators with customary violence. One policeman chased a black woman, obviously intending to beat her with his club. As she ran, her shoe slipped off. The brutal policeman was also a well-brought-up young Afrikaner, who knew that when a woman loses her shoe you pick it up for her. Their eyes met as he handed her the shoe. He then left her, since clubbing her was no longer an option. (I am grateful to David Spurrett, an eye-witness, for this account.)

Such episodes are rare and less likely in the more controlled situation of torture. The shoe coming off took the policeman by surprise and this combined with his learned politeness to produce the small act of helping restore a woman's dignity. This act and the eye-meet together triggered the breakthrough of normal human responses and their tendency to inhibit violence. Although such breakthrough is rare, that it can occur at all is important for thinking about resisting the side of our psychology that makes atrocities possible.

The Tradition of Cruelty and the Hope of Its Defeat

Cruelty has deep roots in human psychology, but its details and techniques are a tradition which is passed on. It is not an accident that the language of torture is similar in different countries. Nor was it coincidence that Jacobo Timerman was subjected to Nazi-type anti-Semitism in Argentina. Primo Levi once wrote that 'the silent Nazi diaspora has taught the art of persecution and torture to the military and the political men of a dozen countries, on the shores of the Mediterranean, the Atlantic and Pacific'. And the torturers working for Saddam Hussein were trained by the Stasi of the old East Germany, who in turn had learned from the Gestapo. The tradition, like a virus, is easily carried across national and ideological frontiers.

This may seem to support great pessimism about torture and similar cruelty. To stress the ease of its transmission, and how deeply it penetrates inside us, may suggest its inevitability. Certainly its defeat will not be easy.

But, tentatively, I think its defeat may be possible. There is some hope to be drawn from the fading of the terrible punishments, such as being boiled in oil, or being torn apart by horses while tied to their legs, rightly cited by Nietzsche as an expression of the human love of cruelty.

Immanuel Kant wrote:

So there can be disgraceful punishments that dishonour humanity itself (such as quartering a man, having him torn by dogs, cutting off his nose and ears). Not only are such punishments more painful than loss of possessions and life to one who loves honour (who claims the respect of others, as everyone must); they also make a spectator blush with shame at belonging to a species that can be treated that way.[21]

Even more, to blush with shame at belonging to a species that can do such things. It is true that in some countries people are still punished by being flogged, by having limbs amputated, by being stoned to death, or by being sent to the electric chair. But, in many parts of the world, revulsion against these punishments has been strong enough for them to be abolished. None of this shows that either torture or cruel punishment is certain to fade away as the human race grows up. But at least it gives a reason for thinking that the ending of the festival of cruelty may be possible.

CHAPTER 7

Answering Nietzsche

But why does Nietzsche think the night has no stars, nothing but bats and owls and the insane moon?

W.B. Yeats, marginal note in his copy of *The Genealogy of Morals*

Jean Améry grew up in Vienna. His name then was Hans Maier. He was Jewish, a student of philosophy, and an opponent of Nazism. At the time of the Anschluss he fled to Belgium, joining the Belgian Resistance when the Nazis invaded. He was arrested, tortured by the Gestapo and sent to Auschwitz, which he survived. After the war he returned to Belgium. He abandoned his German name and wrote philosophy under his new one. He wrote of Nietzsche as 'the man who dreamed of the synthesis of the brute with the superman', saying, 'He must be answered by those who witnessed the union of the brute with the sub-human; they were present as victims when a certain humankind joyously celebrated a festival of cruelty, as Nietzsche himself has expressed it.'[1]

Améry wrote of the temptation for an intellectual victim of Nazism to see Auschwitz as giving support to one kind of amoralism:

Were not those who were preparing to destroy him in the right, owing to the undeniable fact that they were the stronger ones? . . . Yes, the SS could carry on just as it did: there are no natural rights, and moral categories come and go like the fashions. A Germany existed that drove Jews and political opponents to their death, since it believed that only in this way could it become a full reality. And what of it? Greek civilization was built on slavery and an Athenian army had run wild on the Island of Melos as had the SS in Ukraine . . . That is the way history was and that is the way it is. One had fallen under its wheel and doffed one's cap when a murderer came along.[2]

Améry did not endorse these thoughts. Instead he thought Nietzsche must be answered by those who witnessed the Nazi festival of cruelty. Some of the rest of us may also feel it is worth trying to answer Nietzsche.

The prospects of reviving belief in a moral law are dim. Looking for an external validation of morality is less effective than building breakwaters. Morality could be abandoned, or it can be re-created. It may survive in a more defensible form when seen to be a human creation. We can shape it consciously to serve people's needs and interests, and to reflect the things we most care about.

In trying to answer Nietzsche, I assume that a central part of morality should be concerned with avoiding repetition of man-made disasters of the kind the Nazis brought about.

Growing Out of Barbarism

For most people, most of the time, the virtues which matter are local and personal. In ordinary life kindness counts for more than belief in human rights. In thinking about how to live, small is beautiful. It is right to emphasize honesty in relationships, generosity to friends, warmth towards children, doing work that is creative, and being disposed to like people.

This close-up focus is adapted to the lives of most of us, but, on its own, it is too limited. We are not only parents, friends, and neighbours. We are also part of the human species as it struggles to escape from its brutal history.

Our species won a dominant position on earth partly by using intelligence to devise methods of killing at a distance. And the packs of hunters who survived were often those who were best at killing other humans who were members of rival packs. Human consciousness has developed in ways which transcend these grim origins. Having emerged through being good at killing, the human species has invented codes of ethics. It also includes pacifists and vegetarians.

But we are still disfigured by our origins. We still live in tribes with apparently unending epidemics of mutual killing. The numbers of late-twentieth-century political dead indicate that our social arrangements for containing violence are still massively failing us. The festival of cruelty continues. But, because this massive social failure is recognized as such, there is the chance of a remedy.

We are a species both brutal and sickened by brutality. This conflict between our cruelty and our aspirations goes as far as we can see back in human history. However, it is not parochial to think of our own time as particularly important. The outbreaks of killing are now especially dangerous because technology makes them a threat to the survival of the whole species.

Modern technology has also made us more aware of distant atrocities as they happen. As I write this, it is virtually certain that people in the Bosnian town of Cerska are being mutilated, raped and killed because their

Islamic religion makes them alien to the soldiers who have captured the town. By the time you read this, it will not be Cerska but somewhere else. We all know that it is always happening somewhere. Unless we are linked to the perpetrators, we are all revolted by it. This should be enough to make the elimination of these horrors a central human project.

Because we live in the first period in history in which there is such full awareness of cruelty and killing as they happen, our response is particularly important. We can start to establish a tradition that, with our knowledge of the atrocities, we find them intolerable and will do what we can to eradicate them. Or we can help to continue a tradition which accepts them fatalistically.

Already we can see early faltering attempts at a political machinery of intervention to prevent atrocities and wars. There are international peace conferences, United Nations peace-keeping forces, and international war crimes tribunals. Gradually recognition is growing that violations of national sovereignty may be justified to prevent genocide and other crimes. These responses have obvious problems and failures, but they are a sign that the world will not always accept brutal group acts with resigned fatalism.

The international machinery needs to be developed much further, but it is only part of what is needed. A change in the climate of opinion is also important. International intervention could be stronger if the attitude that war and persecution are utterly intolerable was more deeply rooted. And the atrocities themselves do not just happen: people commit them. In a different moral climate, it could be harder to take part.

Partly what is needed is to re-create ethics, giving more weight to the public dimension of individual conduct and character. It is easy to think this public dimension is unimportant. Most of the time what matters is the local and personal. But the great public disasters can strike the most unlikely places. A military coup in Argentina or the death of Tito in Yugoslavia can bring atrocities and war to towns and villages which seemed peacefully remote from politics. Developing a climate of opinion which limits the damage is like paying taxes to fund the fire brigade. You hope you will not need it, and probably you won't, but if your house catches fire you will be glad of it.

If we are serious about wanting to grow away from our barbaric past, this extra dimension has to be made central to ethics. Ideas about how to live should be shaped partly by awareness of collective disasters.

Some Human Causes of Human Misery

This public dimension is only one aspect of morality. And the project of reconstruction discussed here, which concerns wars and other forms of barbarism, relates to only one part of the public dimension. It ignores the psychology relevant to environmental damage or to the spread of AIDS.

The first topic to be discussed here is war: the psychology of waging war and of committing atrocities in it, whether in close combat or by technological means at a distance. Then there is the psychology of how wars arise, both 'tribal' wars reflecting local divisions and more complex conflicts like the two world wars. 'The psychology of war' is something I take to be present as much in civilians who support and sustain wars as in soldiers. Then the discussion turns to mass atrocities not directly connected with war: the political killings of Stalin, Hitler and others. I will argue that these issues have a unity which comes partly from having a cluster of psychological weaknesses in common.

The aim is to construct a more empirical form of ethics, which looks at the psychology which has contributed to this set of man-made disasters. What are the limitations of the moral resources? How can we start to overcome these limitations? Which parts of our psychology are dangerous? How far can they be changed or contained? What countervailing tendencies can we develop?

One approach to these questions will be to take a particular form of human destructiveness, such as armed combat. A picture of its psychology will be drawn from descriptions given by participants. There are suggestive similarities between thoughtful accounts of war given by American soldiers who experienced Vietnam and by Soviet soldiers who experienced Afghanistan.

Another approach will be to look at particular historical episodes. Man-made disasters are not the product of the psychology of individuals in isolation. They are rather the product of interaction, of people misunderstanding each other, putting pressure on each other, hating each other, obeying others, fearing each other, and so on. It is only by looking at actual events that these processes can be seen.

These disasters show weak points in the moral resources we rely on to restrain savagery. Our moral resources either turn out not to work in a particular context, or else they are deliberately neutralized or overridden. The psychological causes come in layers, with different layers making different contributions according to how close the participant is to the victims. The close-up psychology of atrocity is very different from the psychology of killing at a distance.

Historical events are not just explained by individual psychology. The First World War and the depression of 1929–31 may have contributed more to Nazism than the motives and beliefs of particular Nazis. But in this discussion the emphasis will be on the role of individual people. The murders did not just happen impersonally: they needed the actions of individual Nazis. One central question will be 'How can people have done these things?' And, if their actions came from deeply rooted features of human psychology, these psychological characteristics continue to matter, despite the disappearance of the depression and the First World War into increasingly distant history.

PART TWO

THE MORAL PSYCHOLOGY OF WAGING WAR

CHAPTER 8

Close Combat

A plain without a feature, bare and brown,
No blade of grass, no sign of neighbourhood,
Nothing to eat and nowhere to sit down,
Yet, congregated on its blankness, stood
An unintelligible multitude.
A million eyes, a million boots in line,
Without expression, waiting for a sign.
> W.H. Auden, *The Shield of Achilles*

Estimates of numbers of people killed in a war are not precise, but they give a rough idea. In the Iran–Iraq war between 1980 and 1988, a million people were killed; 2 million were killed in Vietnam; 3 million were killed in the Korean War. An estimate for the period from 1900 until 1989 is that war killed 86 million people.[1]

Eighty-six million is a small proportion of all those alive during the ninety years, and is a small number compared to those who have died from hunger and preventable diseases. All the same, death in twentieth-century war has been on a scale which is hard to grasp. Any averaging out of the numbers of deaths is artificial, since about two-thirds (58 million) were killed in the two world wars. But, if these deaths had been spread evenly over the period, war would have killed around 2,500 people every day, That is over 100 people an hour, round the clock, for ninety years.

How can people take part in these mass outbreaks of mutual killing? This is a cluster of different questions. Why do people fight in battle? Why do they join the army? Why do governments go to war? Why do populations support them?

First, the people who fight wars. There is a psychology of long-range war, of bombing raids and missile attacks, but the most common event is close-range war, soldiers fighting on the ground. How is close combat possible? How can people, who might have been drinking companions or fellow students, kill each other at close range?

Rational self-interest can be turned upside down. In ordinary life restraining social pressures make killing unthinkable. In war the effect of their removal, or even reversal, is dramatic.

Close combat also requires overcoming the moral resources. Combatants need to escape the inhibitions of human responses: of respect and sympathy for others. They need to escape the restraints of moral identity: of their sense of not being a person who would wound and kill.

Mostly, the moral resources fail to prevent killing in combat because they are neutralized. Armies need to produce something close to a 'robot psychology', in which what would otherwise seem horrifying acts can be carried out coldly, without being inhibited by normal responses.

Sometimes the moral resources are not so much neutralized as overwhelmed. There are the altered emotional states induced by war. Combat can have a deep emotional appeal. People find actions which they would never have thought themselves capable of suddenly appearing, as if they were suddenly released, or as if they were the result of an inner explosion.

'A Plain Without a Feature'

A recruit is removed from everyday life, first to army training and then to battle. A sense of unreality blurs habitual guidelines. The moral landscape fades into Auden's 'plain without a feature'. People who could not possibly kill in their home town, close to neighbours and their children, lose inhibitions in war. One former Soviet soldier said he could never kill anyone at home: 'If we buy a live chicken from the market, it's my wife who has to slaughter it. Those first few days I was there, with the bullets slicing off the mulberry branches, there was a sense of unreality. The psychology of war is so different from anything else.' This loss of moral landmarks can be reinforced by the physical landscape of a foreign battlefield. A Soviet artillery captain talked of the exotic feel of Afghanistan: 'There are places there which remind you of the moon with their fantastic, cosmic landscapes.'[2] An American soldier described the moral effects of the atmosphere of unreality in Vietnam:

> The landscape doesn't change much. For days and days you see just about nothing. It's unfamiliar – always unfamiliar . . . But you feel like it's not all real . . . You're in Vietnam and they're using real bullets . . . Here in Vietnam they're actually shooting people for no reason . . . Any other time you think, it's such an extreme. Here you can go ahead and shoot them for nothing.[3]

Neutralizing the Human Responses

Normal moral restraints emphasize the respect for people's dignity, which protects them from barbaric treatment.

In war this inhibition is selectively removed. A Soviet soldier in Afghanistan described his unit being taught to humiliate the Afghans. The battalion commander told them to call Afghans of any age '*batcha*', which means 'boy'. Then, seeing an old man, the commander pushed his turban off his head and poked his fingers in his beard. The soldier went on to say, 'To kill or not to kill? That's a post-war question . . . The Afghans weren't people to us.'[4]

An American company in Vietnam stopped in a village on a hot day and were helped to have showers by a farmer. He pulled water up from a well and sloshed it over the soldiers. He was old and blind, and he smiled and laughed as he helped them. Tim O'Brien described how one of the soldiers, for no reason, threw a carton of milk in the old man's face:

> The carton burst, milk spraying on the old man's temples and into his cataracts. He hunched forward, rocking precariously and searching for balance. He dropped his bucket, and his hands went to his eyes then dropped loosely to his thighs. His blind gaze fixed straight ahead, at the stupid soldier's feet. His tongue moved a little, trying to get at the cut and tasting the blood and milk. No one moved to help.[5]

Respect for the dignity of people on the other side can be linked with denial of their humanity. They may even be seen as animals. J. Glenn Gray reports a talk to a class of his by a veteran of the Second World War in the Pacific. He described how his unit found a single Japanese soldier hiding when the rest of the Japanese army had left the island. They took their rifles and used him as a target while he dashed frantically round the clearing. They found his movements hilarious and their laughter slowed down their eventual killing of him. They were cheered by the incident and joked about it for days. In telling the story, the veteran said they had seen him as being like an animal:

> None of the American soldiers even considered that he may have had human feelings of fear and the wish to be spared. What puzzled the veteran in retrospect was why his comrades and he found the incident so humorous. Now, a few years later, it appeared to him grisly and cruel enough; at the time, he had had no conscience about it whatever.[6]

Sympathy is also selectively weakened. Training includes a gradual adjustment to the hardness of battle. John Keegan, drawing on his experience of teaching at Sandhurst, writes of an implicit agreement to shield the cadets from the worst horrors. He suggests an analogy with the way medical students are encouraged to develop a detached attitude to the pain and distress of patients.[7] Doctors are more effective if they are not overwhelmed by gusts of sympathetic emotion. Soldiers are more likely to avoid panic in battle if they think in impersonal learned categories. This is plausible, but the clinical training of soldiers is also part of a gradual anaesthetization of the sympathy which would make it hard to kill and wound.

In battle one defence is to distance the people on the other side. The person you maim or kill is not seen as someone as frightened as you, whose mother and father want him to come back from the war. Instead he is typed by his alien beliefs or race, in Vietnam as a Communist or a gook. One former sergeant who opposed this testified to the pressures behind it: 'The colonels called them gooks, the staff all called them gooks. They were dinks, you know, subhuman. They used to deal with them in this way, so they [my troops] took the cue from that and they considered me some kind of weird freak.'[8]

The denial of humanity may again take the form of thinking of opponents as animals. In the Gulf War the killing of thousands of retreating enemy soldiers was described as a 'turkey shoot'. Sometimes comparisons with particularly repulsive kinds of life are resorted to. Again in the Gulf War, a lieutenant-colonel in the US Marines was asked what it was like to see Iraqi troops in Kuwait from his plane. He said, 'It was like turning on the kitchen light late at night and the cockroaches started scurrying . . . We finally got them out where we could kill them.'[9]

Such distancing of opponents is part of a defensive hardness. Jeff Needle noted this in Vietnam:

> A very sad thing happened while we were there – to everyone. It happened slowly and gradually so no one noticed when it happened. We began slowly with each death and every casualty until there were so many deaths and so many wounded, we started to treat deaths and loss of limbs with callousness, and it happens because the human mind can't hold that much suffering and survive.[10]

J. Glenn Gray, in his Second World War diary, noticed his failure to be moved by a dead German soldier: 'Somehow I have grown quite hard in the past months . . . God in Heaven, help me to keep my humanity.'[11]

The Erosion of Moral Identity

Even those who resist the change may find their personality disappears under a crust of hardness. J. Glenn Gray described in his diary how he read the words of a German soldier quoted in a captured newspaper, saying that in the long war he had lost his 'Ich', his personality. Gray agreed: 'I shuddered. He spoke for me . . . Formerly I tried to be mild and kind, now I interrogate the miserable civilians and take pride in sternness and indifferency to their pleas.'[12]

Former soldiers can see their actions in war as coming from a different identity. Vietnam veterans sometimes spoke of 'the person in me that fought the war'.[13] Others come back thinking their original identity has gone. A private in a Soviet Grenadier Regiment said, 'I went to Afghanistan thinking I'd come home with my head held high. Now I realize the person I was before this war has gone forever.'[14]

Military training has to make people do things which they would not do in civilian life. Weakening civilian constraints helps to erode civilian identity and values. Erich Maria Remarque described how German army training in the First World War required 'a renunciation of personality such as one would not ask of the meanest servants', imposed by sergeants who made them learn that 'a bright button is weightier than four volumes of Schopenhauer'.[15] Seventy years later a Soviet soldier in Afghanistan described the same process:

> Before I went into the army it was Dostoyevsky and Tolstoy who taught me how I ought to live my life. In the army it was sergeants. Sergeants have unlimited power. There are three to a platoon. 'Now hear this! Repeat after me! What is a para? Answer: a bloody-minded brute with an iron fist and no conscience! Repeat after me: conscience is a luxury we can't afford!' The message of the twice weekly political seminar given to some of the Soviet army in Afghanistan was: 'The army must keep healthy and we must banish pity from our minds.'[16]

The erosion of identity is helped by psychological remoteness from ordinary life. Peter Bourne, a psychiatrist who studied American recruits' basic training in the Vietnam period, describes the recruit being stripped of his civilian identity, through physical and verbal abuse and humiliation. His head is shaved and every detail of his life is entirely programmed by others. He has to change the way he talks, being reduced to 'a vocabulary of monosyllabic conformity interspersed with obscenities'. Bourne also writes, 'Drill sergeants with Vietnam experience have been noted for boasting to recruits about the way they have tortured prisoners and committed other atrocities.' Many recruits were pressured into accepting, or at least seeming to accept, the values of these sergeants.[17]

The fact that soldiers are often young men who need some recognition of their adulthood also plays a part. Tim Lynch, a veteran of the Falklands War, describes how the period in which identity is broken down (called 'beasting' in the British army) is followed by the passing out ceremony, which marks the transition to being an adult soldier. He writes of the British killing of Argentinian prisoners with bayonets on Mount Longdon:

Take a young man, desperate to establish an identity in the adult world, make him believe military prowess is the epitome of masculinity, teach him to accept absolutely the authority of those in command, give him an exaggerated sense of self-worth by making him part of an elite, teach him to value aggression and to dehumanize those who are not part of his group and give him permission to use any level of violence without the moral restraints which govern him elsewhere.[18]

Although the traditional moral rules of war may be taught formally, a very different informal message can come across. In Vietnam there were 'free fire zones' in which any civilian could be killed, and 'search and destroy' missions, on which anyone could be killed, or 'wasted'. The country was saturated with high-tech destruction, for instance defoliants were used which kill human embryos as well as plants. The informal message was expressed by some Vietnam veterans as, 'It's okay to kill them . . . that's what you're supposed to do.' Things which at first shocked soldiers morally or emotionally later became accepted. There was the first sight of a troop carrier driving by with about twenty human ears tied to the antenna. The first shock ('It was kind of hard to believe. They actually had ears on the antenna') was overcome. Some came back with ears as trophies of their own.[19] This erosion also took place among the Soviet troops in Afghanistan: 'Have you ever seen necklaces of dried ears? Yes, trophies of war, rolled up into little leaves and kept in matchboxes! Impossible? You can't believe such things of our glorious Soviet boys? Well, they could and did happen.'[20]

Battle and the experience of seeing death close up can make a soldier feel that his identity has changed. A private in the Soviet army in Afghanistan described this:

Within two or three weeks there's nothing left of the old you except your name. You've become someone else . . . This new person doesn't have to imagine: he *knows* the smell of a man's guts hanging out; the smell of human excrement mixed with blood. He's *seen* the scorched skulls grinning out of a puddle of molten metal, as though they'd been laughing, not screaming, as they died only a few hours before. He knows the incredible excitement of seeing a dead body and thinking, that's not me! It's a total transformation, it happens very quickly, and to practically everyone.[21]

Breakthrough

Robot psychology, defensive hardness and distancing, and the assault on moral identity, all have their limits. Sometimes the old, more human, psychology breaks through the new hard crust.

Sometimes it is sympathy which breaks through. One Vietnam veteran described how the men in his platoon had felt unease on removing belongings from dead Vietnamese. Pictures of parents, girlfriends, wives and children made them think, 'They're just like us.'[22]

A sense of shared humanity can also break through. George Orwell fought against the fascists in the Spanish Civil War. He later described how a fascist soldier came in sight, half-dressed and running, holding up his trousers with both hands: 'I refrained from shooting at him . . . I did not shoot partly because of that detail about the trousers. I had come here to shoot at "Fascists"; but a man who is holding up his trousers isn't a "Fascist", he is visibly a fellow creature, similar to yourself, and you don't feel like shooting at him.'[23]

At other times moral revulsion breaks through. A Soviet soldier had become hardened to close-up killing in Afghanistan. But he could have other responses:

Only once something snapped inside me and I was struck by the horror of what we were doing. We were combing through a village. You fling open the door and throw in a grenade in case there's a machine-gun waiting for you . . . I threw the grenade, went in and saw women, two little boys and a baby in some kind of box making do for a cot. You have to find some kind of justification to stop yourself going mad.[24]

Sometimes soldiers, ordered to do something terrible, have an intact sense of their moral identity. They see what obedience would mean. In the Gulf War British army helicopters were ordered to attack the retreating Iraqi tanks. They would circle over the tanks as a warning to the crews, who could escape before the tanks were destroyed. Socrates would have understood what one of the pilots said: 'That way we could feel at peace with ourselves. We had total superiority, but we didn't use it.'[25]

Moral identity may seem lost, but something may trigger the half-forgotten moral commitments. A regimental doctor in Vietnam was treating an enemy soldier, and found himself remembering the Hippocratic oath when his commanding officer said, 'Just keep him alive for a few minutes so we can question him. After that he can die. It doesn't matter to me.'[26]

Explosion and Release

Some cases of mass killing in combat give the impression that the killers went berserk. There is a sudden explosion of violence, as if the killing has burst through a dam which held it back.

There are distinctive emotional states linked with outbursts of violence.

It is worth distinguishing two patterns of such outbursts. One, 'explosion', is linked with feelings of humiliation or resentment. The other, 'release', is linked with more pleasurable feelings. These may be a sense of comradeship in a group, or a sense of heightened experience which sometimes reaches a level of ecstasy.

Explosion can be triggered in combat by the experience of seeing friends wounded or killed. Second Lieutenant Mike Ransom described his reaction in Vietnam when one of his men jumped on a mine:

> Both his feet were blown off, both legs were torn to shreds – his entire groin area was completely blown away. It was the most horrible sight I've ever seen . . . I talked to the mechanized platoon leader who is with us and he said that as he left the area to return to his fire base, the people in the village he went through were laughing at him because they knew we had been hit. I felt like turning my machine-guns on the village to kill every man, woman and child in it.[27]

Soviet soldiers in Afghanistan reported the same responses. One was with another soldier who was killed: 'He pushed open a hut door with his leg and was shot point-blank with a machine-gun. Nine rounds. In that situation hatred takes over. We shot everything right down to the domestic animals.' Another Soviet private described the same reaction:

> One time, our column was going through a *kishlak* when the leading vehicle broke down. The driver got out and lifted the bonnet – and a boy, about ten years old, rushed out and stabbed him in the back, just where the heart is. The soldier fell over the motor. We turned that boy into a sieve. If we'd been ordered to, we'd have turned the whole village to dust.[28]

Some of the emotional states in combat are very different from the pent-up humiliation or vengefulness which can explode in violence. These other states are exhilarating, and with the violence comes a sense of liberation from normal restraints. One source of this release is the sense of comradeship in a group.

Even outside war, groups get carried away and do things together they would not do as individuals. To this, military combat adds something extra; battle creates the comradeship of trying to achieve a shared goal. Shared danger breaks down the barriers between people. Glenn Gray saw that, for some people, battle was a high point in their lives: 'Despite the horror, the weariness, the grime, and the hatred, participation with others in the chances of battle had its unforgettable side, which they would not want to have missed.'[29]

The shared and intoxicating liberation can transform attitudes to killing. One Soviet soldier found this in Afghanistan: 'It's frightening and unpleasant to have to kill, you think, but you soon realize that what you really find objectionable is shooting someone point-blank. Killing *en masse*, in a group, is exciting, even – and I've seen this myself – fun.'[30] During the first week of the Gulf War, one fighter pilot was quoted as saying, 'I was gung-ho the whole way. It was kinda neat!' Another was asked 'Are you looking forward to doing it again?' and replied 'Absolutely!' One said, 'I feel like a young athlete after his first football match!'[31]

The exhilaration comes partly from our passion to experience things. The intense experience of battle strikes many people as something not to be missed: 'gentlemen in England now a-bed shall think themselves accursed they were not here'. Glenn Gray uses the biblical phrase 'the lust of the eye', and says this will be recognized by anyone who has seen the faces of people at a fire, or who has watched people crowding round an accident. He talks about how battle can have a sublime beauty for those who experience it, something 'ecstatic in the original meaning of the term, namely, a state of being outside the self'.[32]

A Soviet artillery captain saw how danger and holding the lives of others in your hands heighten experience:

> We'll never walk, or make love, or be loved, the way we walked and loved and were loved over there. Everything was heightened by the closeness of death: death hovered everywhere and all the time. Life was full of adventure: I learnt the smell of danger . . . We're homesick for it, some of us; it's called the 'Afghan syndrome'.[33]

'I Loved It in Strange and Troubling Ways'

It is easy to see the appeal of comradeship and the passion for intense experience, but the appeal of battle has more troubling ingredients. Some Soviet soldiers in Afghanistan took pleasure in killing: 'One junior lieutenant I know went back home and admitted it. "Life's not the same now, I actually want to go on killing," he said. 'They spoke about it quite coolly, some of those boys, proud of how they'd burnt down a village and kicked the inhabitants to death.'[34]

J. Glenn Gray also talks of 'the satisfaction that men experience when they are possessed by the lust to destroy and to kill their kind'. He says this delight in destruction will be known by 'anyone who has watched men on the battlefield at work with artillery, or looked into the eyes of veteran killers fresh from slaughter, or studied the descriptions of bombardiers' feelings while smashing their targets'.[35]

His Second World War account is strikingly echoed in the reflections of William Broyles Jr on his experience as a lieutenant in Vietnam. As well as hating war, men can love it as much as anything in their lives. Broyles says he is not a violent person, has not been in a fight since grade school, and says that, as a father, he is a natural enemy of what war does to children. But he admits that he misses the war, and that this is 'because I loved it, loved it in strange and troubling ways'.[36]

Broyles gives some of the reasons for the emotional pull of war. Like J. Glenn Gray, he mentions the passion for experience, and the intense comradeship of a group entrusting each other with their lives. He gives other reasons. People in ordinary life often prefer being told what to do, and army discipline replaces this with a liberating urge to break the rules. It is an escape from the duties of everyday life, from the bonds of family, community and work. Men love games and 'war is a brutal, deadly game, but a game, the best there is'.

But for Broyles this is not the whole story: 'For all these reasons, men love war. But these are the easy reasons, the first circle, the ones we can talk about without risk of disapproval, without plunging too far into the truth or ourselves. But there are other, more troubling reasons why men love war.' These are seeing death close up, the excitement of killing and destruction, and the heightened sexuality which is linked with all this. War 'is, for men, at some terrible level the closest thing to what childbirth is for women: the initiation into the power of life and death. It is like lifting off a corner of the universe and looking at what's underneath.'

William Broyles gives some illustrations of the delight in war. After one ambush his men brought back the body of a North Vietnamese soldier.

> I later found the dead man propped against some C-ration boxes. He had on sunglasses, and a *Playboy* magazine lay open in his lap; a cigarette dangled jauntily from his mouth, and on his head was perched a large and perfectly formed piece of shit. I pretended to be outraged, since desecrating bodies was frowned on as un-American and counterproductive. But it wasn't outrage I felt. I kept my officer's face on, but inside I was . . . laughing. I laughed – I believe now – in part because of some subconscious appreciation of this obscene linkage of sex and excrement and death; and in part because of the exultant realization that he – whoever he had been – was dead and I – special unique me – was alive.

This was not the only time when war was bliss. After one operation in which a group had killed dozens of enemy troops, they had to load for removal the naked, muddy bodies of those they had killed:

> there was a look of beatific contentment on the colonel's face that I had not seen except in charismatic churches. It was the look of a person transported into ecstasy. And I – what did I do, confronted with this beastly scene? I smiled back, as filled with bliss as he was. That was another of the times I

stood on the edge of my humanity, looked into the pit, and loved what I saw there.

CHAPTER 9

The Case of My Lai

On 16 March 1968 Vietnamese civilians were massacred by American soldiers in the village of My Lai. 'Charlie Company' was 120 infantrymen under the command of Captain Ernest Medina. Four of them had been killed and thirty-eight wounded in seven weeks of guerrilla war. They were to be part of an attack on a Vietcong battalion thought to be in My Lai. Medina received orders that the men were to show aggression in the attack. He briefed them the night before about the 'search and destroy' mission. It was a chance to get their own back: houses were to be burnt down; cattle and crops were to be destroyed; wells were to be wrecked. A second briefing was then given by Lieutenant William Calley. He said the villagers were nearly all enemy supporters: that men had weapons, women carried packs, and the children were future Vietcong. On one account, he said they should kill anything that moved.

Early in the morning the soldiers were landed in the village by helicopter. Many were firing as they spread out, killing both people and animals. There was no sign of the Vietcong battalion and no shot was fired at Charlie Company all day, but they carried on. They burnt down every house. They raped women and girls and then killed them. They stabbed some women in the vagina and disembowelled others, or cut off their hands or scalps. Pregnant women had their stomachs slashed open and were left to die. There were gang rapes and killings by shooting or with bayonets. There were mass executions. Dozens of people at a time, including old men, women and children, were machine-gunned in a ditch. In four hours nearly 500 villagers were killed.

Obedience and Conformity

Much of the massacre was in obedience to orders. There were the earlier orders from senior officers to show aggression. Soldiers obeyed the orders of officers on the spot and fired their machine-guns on the villagers in the ditch.

My Lai shows military discipline in two different lights. One of the causes of the massacre was an absence of discipline. Charlie Company had drifted slightly away from normal obedience to rules and orders. Michael Bernhardt realized this when he saw some of its members starting to commit atrocities: 'Little by little, I began to see that this group of men was getting out of control. Without military discipline they were there alone in the country with no point of reference. The things that they had brought from their families and schools were far away and beginning to disappear.'[1] Military discipline often functions as a substitute for the moral pressures of family and home community. It stops a military unit from becoming a pack of wild men. This restraint was absent at My Lai.

But another aspect of military discipline contributed to the massacre. Effectiveness as a soldier may depend on instant obedience. To question an order may be to risk lives. From this perspective, Sergeant Hodges saw nothing wrong in the conduct of those who obeyed orders in My Lai: 'As one of the sergeants who trained Charlie Company, I was very pleased with the way they turned out. They turned out to be very good soldiers. The fact that they were able to go into My Lai and carry out the orders they had been given, I think this is a direct result of the good training they had.'[2]

Ronald Ridenhour, who knew many of the men of Charlie Company, later described how this training could make soldiers instantly obey orders which went against their own characters:

in a context in which they'd been trained, prepared to follow orders, they do what they're told, and they shouldn't have, and they look back a day later and realize they probably made the biggest mistake of their lives. [There were] only an extraordinary few people who had the presence of mind and the strength of their own character that would see them through. Most people didn't.[3]

Obedience was not the whole story. Pressures to conform pulled the wrong way. Charlie Company was isolated and they depended on each other for their lives. A strong sense of comradeship grew up and later a number of them said the company was like a family. Their isolation and solidarity created a private moral world with its own social pressures. Michael Bernhardt, who refused to join in the massacre, described these effects of isolation:

What people think of you back home don't matter . . . What matters is how the people around you are going to see you. Killing a bunch of civilians in this way – babies, women, old men, people who were unarmed, helpless – was wrong. Every American would know that. And yet this company sitting out here isolated in this one place didn't see it that way. I'm sure they didn't. This group of people was all that mattered. It was the whole world. What they thought was right was right. And what they thought was wrong was wrong. The definitions for things were turned round.[4]

The Erosion of the Moral Resources

Sympathy for the villagers was reduced by seeing them as a threatening enemy, not as victims. Some of the time the soldiers acted out this denial of reality. While shooting, they knelt and crouched as if in battle. One said later, 'If you're actually thinking in terms of a massacre or murder, going in and shooting a bunch of defenceless people, why crouch? . . . Because your judgement is all screwed up . . . they actually look like the enemy, or what you think is the enemy.'[5]

The loss of sympathy was reinforced by the fact that the 'enemy' was also thought of in terms which dehumanized them. Lieutenant Calley expressed this at his trial: 'When my troops were getting massacred and mauled by an enemy I couldn't see, I couldn't feel and I couldn't touch, nobody in the military system ever described them as anything other than Communism. They didn't give it a race, they didn't give it a sex, they didn't give it an age.'[6]

When former members of Charlie Company look back, they sometimes comment on the way moral constraints fell away. It could start with seeing other people doing things normally impermissible. One of those who took part in the massacre, Greg Olsen, moved from the strict Mormon morality of his upbringing to something closer to the outlook of the Athenians in the Melian dialogue. He described the erosion of his morality:

> I remember seeing people butted in the head with rifles. But you start losing your sense of what's normal. You don't give up your morals, but you become a lot more tolerant. We believed this behaviour was pretty commonplace. I didn't think we were doing anything different from any other unit. You really do lose your sense . . . not of right or wrong, but your degree of wrong changes.[7]

Moral restraints were eroded by degrees. The first breaches seem relatively small, but then no clear barrier exists against further erosion. Michael Bernhardt described this in the case of killing: 'It started with just plain prisoners – prisoners you thought were the enemy. Then you'd go on to prisoners who weren't the enemy, and then the civilians because there was no difference between the enemy and civilians. It came to the point where a guy could kill anybody.'[8]

Moral erosion was reinforced by a cult of hardness which stigmatized moral doubts as sentimental weakness. A chaplain, Captain Carl Cresswell, attended when the soldiers were given a briefing before the assault on My Lai. His own expression of moral doubts elicited a display of hardness by a major: 'I remember he said: "We're going in there, and if we get one round out of there, we're gonna level it." And I looked at him and I said: "You know, I didn't really think we made war that way." And he looked at me and he said: "It's a tough war, chaplain." '[9]

Some members of the company later saw that their sense of identity had been eroded. At My Lai, the company's radio operator, Fred Widmer, killed two small children:

Why? Why did I do that? That is not me. Something happened to me. You reach a point where you snap, that is the easiest way to put it, you finally snap. Somebody flicks a switch and you are a completely different person. There is a culture of violence, of brutality, with people all around you doing the same thing.[10]

Explosion: 'My Mind Just Went'

Lieutenant Calley's actions may have been influenced by emotional responses to humiliation. He was not respected by his men, one of whom thought he was like a small guy who had been pushed around a lot by bigger people before he joined the army. A squad leader said that he was nervous and excitable, and that he yelled a lot. He was 'so disliked by members of the unit that they put a bounty on his head'. Captain Medina ridiculed Lieutenant Calley in front of his men, calling him 'Lieutenant Shithead', and often saying to him, 'Listen, sweetheart . . .'[11]

In some, the desire for retaliation played its part. One account of the talk by Captain Medina before the attack reported him as saying, 'We lost a lot of guys. Pinkville caused us a lot of hell. Now we're gonna get our revenge. Everything goes.'[12] And revenge clearly coloured the psychology of the soldiers as they killed the villagers. Some shouted: 'VC bastards, you dirty VC bastards,' 'That's for Bill Weber,' and 'Cry, you dirty gook bastards, cry like you made us cry.'[13]

As one soldier later put it, 'you have a need to explode'.[14] Varnado Simpson described how, from the inside, an explosion of violence seemed drained of emotion. In My Lai, Simpson killed about twenty-five people: 'Personally. Men, women. From shooting them, to cutting their throats, scalping them, to . . . cutting off their hands and cutting out their tongue. I did it.' When asked why he did these things, he said, 'I just went. My mind just went . . . Once I started, the . . . the training, the whole programming part of killing, it just came out.' He was asked whether his training had told him to scalp people or cut their ears off. He replied, 'No. But a lot of people were doing it. So I just followed suit. I just lost all sense of direction, of purpose. I just started killing any kinda way I could kill. It just came. I didn't know I had it in me.'

The psychological explosion came after he killed a woman and child:

> But like I say, after I killed the child, my whole mind just went. And once you start, it's very easy to keep on. Once you start. The hardest – the part that's hard is to kill, but once you kill, that becomes easier, to kill the next person and the next one and the next one. Because I had no feelings or no emotions or no nothing. No direction. I just killed. It can happen to anyone.[15]

Breakthrough

There were soldiers who were appalled by what they were ordered to do. Lieutenant Calley ordered Dennis Conti and Paul Meadlo to kill a group of villagers which included babies, children and very old women. Both tried to evade the order, but Calley lost his temper and repeated it. Conti continued to evade it, making an excuse about saving ammunition, but Meadlo joined Calley in shooting the villagers. After a minute or so he was in tears and could not go on. He left Calley to finish the massacre. In Conti, the breakthrough of conscience or of sympathy protected him against obeying Calley. That the similar breakthrough in Meadlo at first did not stop his obedience is a grim tribute to the military programming.

In some cases breakthrough led to effective resistance to the massacre. Hugh Thompson was a 25-year-old helicopter pilot with a reputation for courage in combat. Flying over My Lai, he saw wounded people and left smoke markers as a signal for help. Later he saw some soldiers near one of the injured people he had marked, a woman of about twenty. He hovered a few feet above her and sent a signal to the troops: 'You have wounded over where the bubble is hovering.' He saw an infantry captain come to the woman, prod her with his foot, and then kill her. Later they saw bodies of people, some still alive, in a ditch, with soldiers sitting smoking nearby. Thompson landed and asked if any help was needed by the people in the ditch. A sergeant said the only way to help them was to put them out of their misery. Lieutenant Calley then said he was in charge of the ground troops and it was none of Thompson's business. Thompson took off again and then one of his crew, Glenn Andreotta, said the sergeant was shooting people in the ditch.

Hugh Thompson thought about how the Nazis had massacred people by making them lie in ditches and shooting them. He saw civilians, including children, running to a bomb shelter pursued by a group of soldiers. He landed between the villagers and the soldiers and sent a radio signal for help. He ordered his crew to use their machine-gun against the American troops if they fired on the villagers. He went to the bomb shelter and persuaded the civilians to come out. He called the two helicopter gunships nearby for help in rescuing the civilians. When his request was queried, he cursed and pleaded, and said that his machine-gunner would fire on the infantry if they fired on the civilians. Hugh Thompson could not talk directly to the infantry, but the helicopter gunships arranged for a signal to be sent to them to stop the killing. The gunships then landed and flew out to safety the people Hugh Thompson and his crew had saved: two men, two women and five or six children.

As Thompson was taking off again, Glenn Andreotta saw something moving in the ditch. They landed again and went back to the ditch, which was filled with about a hundred dead men, women and children. Andreotta went down among the corpses. He eventually found a child about three years old, probably a boy, covered in blood and slime, but not injured. Hugh Thompson, who had a son about that age, was crying as they flew the boy to hospital. Charlie Company started to pick up over the radio the clear order to 'stop killing civilians'.

War crimes like My Lai rightly arouse horror, but the psychology of such episodes is related to the psychology of much 'normal' combat. Of course the deliberate massacre of defenceless civilians is morally different from fighting armed enemy forces. Morally different, but in its psychology disturbingly close.

CHAPTER 10

The Shift to Killing at a Distance

Traditional wars have been fought at close range. This is why soldiers have to be programmed to lose their inhibitions against killing. The emotional explosions and the strange ecstasy of war are evoked by close combat.

The great twentieth-century change in warfare has been the power of mass killing at a distance. Our thinking about the psychology of war is dominated by episodes which shock us, such as the My Lai massacre. But, in modern war, what is most shocking is a poor guide to what is most harmful. Technology has created forms of cold violence which should disturb us far more than the beast of rage in man. The great military atrocities now use bombs or missiles. The decisions are taken coldly, far away.

Civilians are often the victims of this cold and distant killing. Of course this is not new. Whether at My Lai or in Bosnia, civilians have been killed at close range. At the start of the twentieth century, massacres by soldiers were seen as aberrations. Perhaps this was too optimistic. Mass killing of civilians at a distance, having been made easier by technology, is now central to modern war and should be at the centre of the study of the psychology of war.

The bombing of civilians in the Second World War, whether 'conventional' bombing or the use of atomic bombs on Hiroshima and Nagasaki, is an obvious product of technology. These were later stages in the twentieth century's slide towards mass killing of civilians far away.

The British Naval Blockade

The start of the slide needed technology no more sophisticated than warships. It was the economic blockade of Germany in the First World War.

The blockade was hardly noticed when it began, although the military historian and theorist Sir Basil Liddell Hart considered the act of starting it to have been 'perhaps the most decisive of the war'. In July 1914 the British fleet sailed for Scapa Flow, and from then until the German fleet was handed over in 1918, 'Germany's arteries were subjected to an invisible pressure which never relaxed.'[1]

The German naval strategy was defensive, aimed at avoiding battles until the stronger British navy had been weakened by mines and submarines. The response of the British navy was not to seek battle, but to command the North Sea and keep up pressure on German supplies.

At the start of the war, the British government had accepted the 1909 Declaration of London, which severely restricted the use of blockade, but Germany declared the waters round the British Isles a war zone, where German submarines would sink foreign ships. In retaliation Britain abandoned restrictions and started to intercept ships taking goods to Germany. The squeeze was greatly increased in 1917, when the United States entered the war. Liddell Hart judged the blockade to have been 'the decisive agency in the struggle'. He said that no historian would underrate 'the direct effect of the semi-starvation of the German people in causing the final collapse of the "home front" '.[2]

The number of deaths caused by the blockade is hard to calculate. It is also hard to know how the food shortages should be apportioned between the blockade and the economic priority given to the war effort, or how many of the deaths in the influenza epidemic of 1918 should be ascribed in part to severe undernourishment. After the war an official German calculation put the deaths caused by the blockade at 762,000. A British government White Paper put the figure at 800,000. Some later estimates were substantially lower, one putting the figure at 424,000.[3]

After the Armistice, the blockade was extended to the Baltic ports and continued until the Allies were satisfied with German compliance with their demands. The journalist Walter Duranty visited Lübeck in 1919 and found people living on potatoes and black bread. They had no meat, butter, milk or eggs. A doctor told him that 90 per cent of the children were anaemic or below weight, and that more than half of them had rickets or tuberculosis.[4]

The hostility engendered by the war meant that, outside Germany, there was little public pressure to end the blockade. One who did want to end it was Winston Churchill, but, as he put it, 'Public opinion in the Allied countries was callous.'[5] In March 1919 it was agreed to lift the blockade, but people in Germany went on dying until food started to get through in May.

The importance of the blockade as a human disaster goes far beyond the great suffering it caused. It soured the peace, making a poor climate for reconciliation. Churchill described the understandable German response: 'These bitter experiences stripped their conquerors in their eyes of all credentials except those of force.'[6] The blockade was used to impose the 'war guilt' clauses of the Versailles treaty. The senior German delegate at Versailles, Graf Ulrich von Brockdorff-Rantzau, expressed some of the resentment: 'The hundreds of thousands of noncombatants who have perished since November 11 because of the blockade were destroyed coolly and deliberately, after our opponents had won a certain and assured victory. Think of that, when you speak of guilt and atonement.'[7]

The 'war guilt' clauses contributed to the resentful German nationalism of the inter-war period. One of the things which seem strange in Nazi speeches is the frequent harping on the idea of Germans as victims. The explanation of the Nazi horrors, and of the war the Nazis started, has to include the contribution of Versailles to the sense that German pride needed to be reasserted.

The blockade's importance as a human disaster goes further still. It was a stage in the development of a new psychology of war, a psychology adapted to large-scale killing of civilian populations. The blockade is an early and technically primitive instance of this shift. It displays clearly a small number of simple psychological patterns some of which contributed to later, more technological, atrocities.

Moral Identity as the Remaining Restraint

When war is conducted at a distance, the psychology is different. The moral resources are not threatened by the ecstasy which overwhelms them in close combat. But, on the other hand, little has to be done to neutralize the inhibitions linked to respect and sympathy. Those running the policy are far away from those killed. Humiliations are not seen. And sympathy is minimal.

To make long-range war possible, moral identity, above all, must be neutralized. At the start of the twentieth century, many politicians, soldiers and others would have repudiated the idea that they would condone the deliberate killing of civilians, yet during the century, many condoned or even took part in such killing. This neutralization of moral identity was more complex than the neutralizing needed for close combat. Something more subtle was needed than the bullying sergeant.

The conflict with moral identity is reduced if killing civilians seems justifiable. Those who in general oppose killing may make an exception for self-defence against a potential killer. In wartime retaliation in kind has the same appeal. Those supporting the blockade could point to the fact that it was started in response to the German blockade of Britain.

Embarking on such a policy is less morally troubling if at the start no civilian deaths are aimed at, or even thought about. In 1914 those who cheered the war may have been exhilarated by the Royal Navy going to Scapa Flow. They did not have in mind making German children starve or giving them rickets. This gap between what people first intended and what resulted has become a commonplace of twentieth-century war on civilians.

If the policy starts without the intention of killing civilians, the introduction of such killing is easier to accept if it comes by degrees. This was true of the blockade. When the navy went to Scapa Flow, blockade was formally excluded. At first the blockade was only partly effective because of the need to cause minimum affront to powerful neutrals such as the United States. Before the United States entered the war, there was no decision to be made about a devastatingly powerful blockade. When American participation made it much more effective, no new blockade initiative had to be decided on. A phased decision can avoid there being a key moment when the moral issue about killing civilians has to be confronted. Participants and supporters escape the moment of recognition that they have become people who accept such things.

Moral identity is less threatened when the deaths appear to be caused 'negatively': where, as in the blockade, people die from *not* getting food rather than from being shot.

Participants also feel less of a threat to their moral identity when the implementation of the policy is spread over many people, acting indirectly. The sense of individual responsibility is diluted.

The navy did not think they decided policy, and the politicians and officials felt part of a bureaucratic machine operating only indirectly and at a distance on the starvation in Germany. This comes out in the description given by John Maynard Keynes of how the question of the continuing blockade was dealt with at the peace conference. The Americans wanted the blockade lifted. The British at first supported the French view that it should continue.

Keynes, who wanted it lifted, gives two explanations of the early British support for the French view. One was that some negotiators were more concerned with their own position than with the issue itself. Lord Reading, in charge of British policy on the matter, 'was intriguing at that time day and night to be one of the party for Paris and was terrified of identifying himself too decidedly with anything controversial'. Keynes's second explanation was again bureaucratic:

> The Blockade had become by that time a very perfect instrument. It had taken four years to create and was Whitehall's finest achievement; it had evoked the qualities of the English at their subtlest. Its authors had grown to love it for its own sake; it included some recent improvements, which would be wasted if it came to an end; it was very complicated, and a vast organization had established a vested interest.[8]

None of these thoughts seems coloured by much sympathy for the children this inertia would kill. And the bureaucratic interaction of so many people probably left no one with a sense of personal responsibility for the deaths.

These ways of making it psychologically easier to kill civilians were to appear again in the bombing of Germany in the Second World War, and again in the use of the atomic bomb.

CHAPTER II

Bombing

> I thought it would be fine if the ones who order the bombing and the ones who do the bombing would walk on the ground sometime and see what it is like.
>
> Martha Gellhorn, 'Bombs on Helsinki, December 1939',
> in *The Face of War*

> As I write, highly civilized human beings are flying overhead, trying to kill me. They do not feel any enmity against me as an individual, nor I against them. They are 'only doing their duty', as the saying goes. Most of them, I have no doubt, are kind-hearted law-abiding men who would never dream of committing murder in private life. On the other hand, if one of them succeeds in blowing me to pieces with a well-placed bomb, he will never sleep any the worse for it.
>
> George Orwell, *The Lion and the Unicorn*

The use of the blockade against Germany to starve large numbers of people to death broke through the moral barrier against the mass killing of civilians. It was the precedent for the 'conventional' bombing of civilians in the Second World War and then for the use of the atomic bomb. There has been a revulsion against these acts, but later wars make it hard to believe that the moral barrier has been restored.

A key episode in this change of outlook is the British use of bombing in the Second World War.

1 THE BOMBING OFFENSIVE AGAINST GERMANY

The bombing campaign fell into three phases. In the early phase, up to the summer of 1941, the intended policy was selective bombing of military targets only. Because the British did not have command of the air, daylight raids were impossibly costly. The policy shifted rapidly to night bombing. In the middle phase, from the summer of 1941 to the summer of 1944, the

British and then the Allies still did not have command of the air, but by then it was understood that night bombing was not sufficiently precise to hit military targets. There was a switch to indiscriminate 'area bombing', or rather, the switch was from unintentional to intentional area bombing. In the last phase of the campaign, after the summer of 1944, the Allies had command of the air, and daylight precision bombing was possible, but there was also substantial area bombing in this last phase.

The Early Phase: The Ban on Civilian Targets

There was influential backing in world opinion for a ban on civilian targets. At the beginning of the war British bombing policy was not directed at civilians, the targets were to be military. It was recognized that bombing was inaccurate and that civilians often lived or worked near military installations. The inevitable civilian casualties were accepted as a reasonable price to pay for helping to defeat Hitler.

Even at that time, some saw the ban on civilian targets as mainly a matter of propaganda. In 1939, the Chief of the Air Staff wrote of 'a phase when for political reasons we are confined to a course of action which is neither economical nor fully effective'.[1]

Churchill authorized an early departure from the ban. At first, in its raids on Britain, the Luftwaffe had also confined itself to military targets. But on 24 August 1940 bombs intended for an oil-storage depot fell on the City of London and the East End. Churchill, over-ruling the RAF, ordered a raid the next day on Berlin. The Luftwaffe responded by unleashing the Blitz on London. Retaliation in kind started to seem more acceptable. There were a few exceptions to the ban on targeting cities, and raids on Berlin continued. On 16 December 1940 there was a raid on Mannheim in retaliation for raids on Coventry and Southampton. These were cases of area bombing, which blankets part of a city with bombs, and so inevitably targets civilians, but the general policy remained one of sticking to military targets.

Reports by aircrews on precision bombing suggested success,[2] but it was hard to get convincing photographic evidence of the damage done. In 1941 a report by David Butt on the results of bombing, based on analysis of photographs, was sent to the Cabinet. Of bomber crews claiming to have hit their targets, only a third were within five miles of them.[3] What was happening was actually unintended area bombing.

The Middle Phase: Area Bombing and the 'Second Front'

When this was discovered, something had to give. The choice was between abandoning bombing altogether or intentionally continuing to bomb civilians. What gave way was the ban on civilian targets. In the summer of 1941 British options for striking back at Hitler were few. To give up bombing might have made people on both sides think that Britain was prepared to abandon the fight. Bombing could only be indiscriminate attacks on cities, but the case for it was accepted. The middle phase of the campaign included the thousand-bomber raids on Cologne and other cities, and huge attacks on Hamburg, the Ruhr and Berlin.

One of the campaign's aims was to be seen to give support to Russia. After Hitler's attack to the east, the Soviet army was fighting on a long front with massive casualties. Russia was bearing the brunt of the European war, and Stalin was pressing for a second front to be opened in the West. It was important to show the Soviet Union that Britain was still actively in the war. But the British government, afraid of a re-run of the First World War, did not want to launch an allied invasion of occupied Europe before there was a very good chance of success. To carry on bombing was an alternative way of giving support.

Allegations of British cowardice were made in the Soviet press and also in messages from Stalin. Churchill therefore went to Moscow in August 1942 to explain to Stalin why an invasion of France at that stage would not succeed. Churchill later described Stalin's 'very glum' response, and also his comments: 'A man who was not prepared to take risks could not win a war. Why were we so afraid of the Germans? His experience showed that troops must be blooded in battle. If you did not blood your troops you had no idea what their value was.' And in a later session, 'he said a great many disagreeable things, especially about our being too much afraid of fighting the Germans, and if we tried it like the Russians we should find it not so bad'.[4]

Later comments by Molotov suggest that this tone was a pose, and that Stalin understood that a second front in France at that time would fail. According to Molotov, Stalin kept up the pressure to extract other forms of support:

> Churchill flew to Moscow and insisted they couldn't open a second front in Europe in 1942. I saw that Stalin accepted this calmly. He understood it was impossible. But he needed that paper agreement. It was of great importance for the people, for politics, and for future pressure on the Allies . . . We didn't believe in a second front, of course, but we had to try for it. We took them in: You can't? But you promised . . . That was the way.[5]

In the discussions, Churchill moved the relationship onto a better footing. He outlined the projected invasion of North Africa and reminded Stalin of British bombing of Germany. He noted that mention of this 'gave general satisfaction'. Stalin 'emphasised the importance of striking at the morale of the German population. He said that he attached the greatest importance to bombing, and that he knew our raids were having a tremendous effect in Germany.'[6]

Roosevelt's envoy, Averell Harriman, noted how mention of the bombing started to dispel the hostile atmosphere:

> Here came the first agreement between the two men. Stalin took over the argument himself and said that homes as well as factories should be destroyed. The Prime Minister agreed that civil morale was a military objective, but the bombing of working men's houses came as a by-product of near-misses on factories. The tension began to ease and a certain understanding of common purpose began to grow. Between the two of them, they soon had destroyed most of the important industrial cities of Germany.[7]

It was hoped to use air power to help the eastern front against Hitler. Support there had to be visible enough to help keep Russia in the war. Stalin was promised more bombing of Germany, and was sent photographs of the devastation. Dresden was bombed partly in response to Churchill's demand for some highly visible evidence before he met Stalin at Yalta.

The claim that area bombing kept Russia in the war is implausible. (The argument could reasonably have carried weight with Churchill, as he did not have Molotov's knowledge of Stalin's real view.) Stalin accepted the impossibility of an early invasion of Western Europe. The North African operation was a demonstration of British and American seriousness about the war. And it is hard to see Stalin, betrayed once by Hitler, being willing to settle for less than his defeat.

But there was something in the view that the air campaign was a kind of second front. German aircraft, which could have been used against Russia, were diverted for use against the bombers. And some military production had to be diverted. Richard Overy has pointed out that, in 1942, over half the new German combat aircraft were bombers, many for use on the eastern front. The need for fighter defence against allied bombers changed this. In 1944 only 18 per cent of German combat aircraft produced were bombers.[8]

Although he thought that direct damage to German industry by bombing was not very serious, Albert Speer, Hitler's Munitions Minister, gave some support to the 'second front' view:

> The real importance of the air war consisted in the fact that it opened a second front long before the invasion of Europe. That front was the skies over Germany . . . The unpredictability of the attacks made the front gigantic . . . Defence against air attacks required the production of thousands of anti-aircraft guns, the stockpiling of tremendous quantities of ammunition all over

the country, and holding in readiness hundreds of thousands of soldiers . . . this was the greatest lost battle on the German side.[9]

If this is right, there is a case for area bombing in the middle phase of the campaign. The diversion of resources may have helped to defeat the Nazis.

The Last Phase: Command of the Air

The air campaign against Germany was given huge boosts by the build-up of the American Air Force, and, after the Normandy invasion, by the use of bases in France. From August 1944 the Allies had command of the air: they could ignore the Luftwaffe. And aiming techniques had improved. Daylight precision bombing was now possible. Some favoured oil installations as the prime target, while others gave priority to destroying the German transport system. The head of Bomber Command, Sir Arthur Harris, supported continued area bombing.

Late in the war Allied bombing started to create real oil shortages in Germany. The Luftwaffe could not fly its new aircraft. Parts of the army were immobilized or reduced to using horses. Concentrating attacks on oil targets could have wrecked resistance to the Allied advance In May 1944 Albert Speer said to Hitler, 'The enemy has struck us at one of our weakest points. If they persist at it this time, we will no longer have any fuel production worth mentioning. Our one hope is that the other side has an air force General Staff as scatter-brained as ours!'[10] In his memoirs Speer mentions attacks on factories making ball-bearings, needed for aircraft and vehicles, as a special threat.

The importance of attacks on oil and on vehicle production was recognized by the Chief of Air Staff, Sir Charles Portal, and by the American commanders. In September 1944 oil was made the sole 'first priority' target, with transport links and tank and vehicle production as second priority.

Was There a Case for Area Bombing in the Last Phase?

In the last phase of the bombing campaign, from the summer of 1944 onwards, two things were different. There was a second front on the ground and Allied command of the air made precision bombing possible. In this last phase, arguments for area bombing had to show that it was better than attacks on oil or transport. The main arguments used were that area bombing saved Allied lives, that it disrupted German industry, and that it weakened morale.

The first claim was that the bombing campaign might be a way to victory without the kind of war of attrition against which Churchill himself had protested at the time of the Battle of the Somme. Sir Arthur Harris claimed that it was a comparatively humane method: 'For one thing, it saved the flower of the youth of this country and of our Allies from being mown down by the military in the field, as it was in Flanders in the war of 1914–18.'[11]

Harris put the case strongly in 1945: 'The destruction of those cities has fatally weakened the German war effort and is now enabling allied soldiers to advance into the heart of Germany with negligible casualties.' The attacks 'are strategically justified in so far as they tend to shorten the war and so preserve the lives of Allied soldiers. To my mind we have absolutely no right to give them up unless it is certain that they will not have this effect.'[12]

How was area bombing supposed to shorten the war, or to make easier the task of Allied troops? The answers given were that it disrupted industry and undermined morale.

Sir Arthur Harris said that area bombing would disrupt German industry by causing a huge loss of man hours. This has been disputed, both by Albert Speer and by post-war surveys. (These pieces of evidence are part of the advantage of hindsight. In fairness to Sir Arthur Harris, if his belief was mistaken, this was not obvious at the time.)

During Albert Speer's interrogation, he said that sustained attacks on the chemical industry could have rendered Germany defenceless. But, up to the end of the war, area bombing did not diminish output in the industries which fed the war. 'The night attacks did not succeed in breaking the will to work of the civilian population.' Even after the bombing of Dresden, industrial activity recovered quickly. 'Consequently, it can be said in conclusion that a bomb load is more effective if it is dropped upon economic targets than if it is expended upon towns and cities.'[13]

Speer's conclusion is supported by the post-war survey carried out by the British Bombing Survey Unit. The British survey suggested that war production lost because of area bombing ranged from a low of 0.25 per cent in 1942 to a high of 3.8 per cent in the second half of 1943. Broadly similar conclusions were reached by the United States Strategic Bombing Survey.[14] The other claim was that area bombing weakened the morale of the German population. Sir Arthur Harris was sceptical about attacking morale in a police state such as Germany.[15] And Churchill, although he authorized abandonment of the traditional restraints, had always been doubtful about how effectively bombing would undermine morale. In 1917 he had written that German air raids had roused, not quelled, the combative spirit of the people.[16] In 1941 he was still sceptical: 'All that we have learnt since the war began shows that its effects, both physical and moral, are greatly exaggerated . . . The most we can say is that it will be a heavy and I trust a seriously increasing annoyance.'[17]

The great supporter of the morale argument was Lord Cherwell. His calculations were simple. A ton of bombs destroys the homes of 100–200 people. He expected 10,000 bombers to be produced over 15 months. Before being shot down, each bomber should drop about 10 tons of bombs (nearly 14 sorties carrying 3 tons of bombs each time). If half (200,000 tons) of the resulting bombs hit the main German cities, the homes of 20–40 million people should be destroyed.

Cherwell's calculations were flawed. They overestimated the chance of bomber-production targets being met. They ignored the need for bombers to protect Atlantic shipping from U-boats. They assumed it was acceptable for all the bombers to be destroyed in the course of the campaign. They were unrealistic about the accuracy of bombing. And they assumed that more bombs dropped will destroy houses at the same rate as fewer bombs, without allowing for some bombs falling on places which had already been destroyed.

These criticisms were used to challenge Cherwell's estimates at the time. Sir Henry Tizard thought they were five times too high. Cherwell accepted some of the criticisms, but said that his estimates were only intended to indicate the rough magnitude of the likely damage.[18] After the war a study of the actual results suggested that the estimates had been ten times too high.

It is doubtful that even the high levels of destruction of civilian targets which Cherwell expected would have been an important factor in defeating Hitler. The German people were well trained in civil defence. And, as in the Blitz on London, civilians attacked may become more determined to resist.

Military Drift

In the last phase of the campaign the supposed policy-makers were not entirely in control. What took place can be called 'military drift': the tendency for military policies to escape from political control. The policies take on a life of their own in the minds of those carrying them out.

The official historians of the bombing campaign wrote of Sir Arthur Harris that he 'was a man of strong convictions and unshakable determination . . . He had a facility for concentrating on one side of a question, and of regarding the other as a mere obstruction.'[19] Bomber Command under Harris resisted the priority given to oil. In October 1944, 6 per cent of the effort was directed against oil. Between October and

December, 14 per cent was directed against oil and 58 per cent against cities.[20]

In November 1944, Sir Charles Portal wrote to Harris:

> I have, I must confess, at times wondered whether the magnetism of the remaining German cities has not in the past tended as much to deflect our bombers from their primary objectives as the tactical and weather difficulties which you described so fully . . . I would like you to reassure me that this is not so. If I knew you to be as wholehearted in the attack on oil as in the past you have been in the matter of attacking cities, I would have little to worry about.[21]

In December, Harris wrote to Portal that the oil offensive was a 'panacea'. In January he wrote that he had little faith in selective bombing and 'none whatsoever in this present oil policy'. Knowing that at that stage of the war it would be politically difficult to dismiss him, his response to further pressure to carry out the oil policy was to suggest Portal should consider replacing him.[22] Portal never managed to establish proper control over Harris.

This military drift eased the position of the German army in the closing stages of the war. Of the stopping of attacks on ball-bearings factories, Speer wrote, 'Thus, the Allies threw away success when it was already in their hands. Had they continued the attacks of March and April with the same energy, we would quickly have been at our last gasp.'[23]

The Bomber Crews

Many of those who flew the bombers were killed. Sir Arthur Harris estimated that in the whole period of the war about 125,000 air crew entered Bomber Command units, of whom about 50,000 were killed in action. (Many others were wounded or captured, and a further 10,000 were killed handling bombs or in other ways.) Of the crews flying in 1943, 33 per cent could expect to survive their first tour of duty and only 16 per cent could expect to survive their first and second tours of duty. The historian and former bomber navigator Noble Frankland has said that Bomber Command lost more air crews in the Second World War than the British army lost officers in the First.[24] After Passchendaele, General Gough was known among the troops as 'Butcher' Gough. There was an echo of this in Bomber Command, where to his staff Sir Arthur Harris was known as 'Butch'.

Area bombing was obviously very different from the First World War, not least in having primarily civilian targets. But the bomber crews sometimes had a sense of being trapped which echoes the feelings in the trenches. The parallel was enhanced by the harsh treatment of cases of 'lack of moral fibre'. Many of those who turned back had previously shown great courage in completing other raids. Max Hastings estimates that about one in seven among air crews failed to complete a tour for medical or morale reasons. He quotes one commander of a bomber station: 'LMF could go through a squadron like wildfire if it was unchecked. I made certain that every case before me was punished by court martial, and where applicable by an exemplary prison sentence, whatever the psychiatrists were saying.'[25]

Another parallel with the entrapment of both sides in the First World War was the mutual sympathy which sometimes arose between the combatants. Members of Bomber Command or of the Luftwaffe who baled out close to where they had bombed risked being killed by enraged crowds. Luftwaffe men often saved RAF men from such mobs. Stewart Harris was escorted by three Luftwaffe men through Düsseldorf, which had just been heavily bombed. The mother of one of the escort had lost both her home and her place of work, but she provided four packed lunches.[26]

As in the trenches, the psychology was mixed. There was a great deal of commitment to the war and a recognition that Hitler had to be defeated, but the disciplinary pressures and the extremely poor chances of survival left bomber crews in a trap. The power to change the policy lay, not with them, but with those more senior.

On the Ground

One American estimate suggested that the area bombing of Germany may have killed 305,000 non-combatants. The Federal Statistical Office in Wiesbaden after the war put the number of civilians killed at 593,000. It is necessary to look at the reality behind the figures.

In 1943, between 24 July and 3 August, Hamburg was systematically attacked by six huge air raids, four British and two American. Harris, whose plan it was, later wrote that no previous air raid had been so terrible.

On the night of the 27th, there was an hour's highly concentrated bombing. Hermann Bock, a teacher called up into the army, later spoke of the early stages of the raid:

Hamburg's night sky became in minutes, even seconds, a sky so absolutely hellish that it is impossible even to try to describe it in words. There were aeroplanes, held in the probing arms of the searchlights, fires breaking out, billowing smoke everywhere, loud, roaring waves of explosions, all broken up by great cathedrals of light as the blast bombs exploded, cascades of marker bombs slowly drifting down, stick incendiary bombs coming down with a rushing noise. No noise made by humans – no outcry – could be heard. It was like the end of the world.[27]

The incendiary bombs caused a series of fires, which joined up in a firestorm. At its centre the temperature was about 800°C. The fire sucked in air with hurricane force. The storm grew with fires caused by further bombing.

The firestorm sucked air out of bomb shelters, killing people inside. Some escaped through the streets, but the firestorm melted the road surface. Many found their feet were stuck in the molten asphalt. Their hands stuck too when they used them to try to escape. Trapped people were on their hands and knees screaming.

Those trapped in buildings either suffocated or burned to death. Anne-Lies Schmidt found the bodies of her parents, and saw what had happened to others:

> Women and children were so charred as to be unrecognizable; those that had died through lack of oxygen were half charred and recognizable. Their brains tumbled from their burst temples and their insides from the soft parts under their ribs. How terribly must these people have died. The smallest children lay like fried eels on the pavement. Even in death they showed signs of how they must have suffered – their hands and arms stretched out as if to protect themselves from the pitiless heat.[28]

The firestorm killed about 40,000 people.

On 11 September 1944 a raid on Darmstadt created a firestorm a mile high. Terrified by the roaring of the storm, people stayed in their shelters and mainly died of suffocation. Carolin Schaeffer covered her children's eyes as they fled through the corpses, 'because I felt that if the boys were to see this, they could never grow up to lead happy lives'. But the horror was everywhere and she had to give up trying to hide it.[29] Over 12,000 were killed in raids on Darmstadt, the great majority that night.

On 13 February 1945 Dresden was repeatedly bombed and again there was a huge firestorm. Erika Dienel, who was twenty at the time, has described the experience: 'Children began to cry as, minute by minute, the detonations grew more violent. Each time the whistling noise of a heavy bomb came nearer, we expected that it would hit us. Some began to pray; others were numb with fear. It seemed endless. We died a thousand times. Hell could not be worse.'[30]

There was a tremendous bang as a petrol-filled incendiary bomb hit their house and set it on fire. They escaped through wrecked buildings:

> But our nightmare was not over. As soon as we jumped into the street, we saw the inferno outside. Like the flakes in a snowstorm, fire showered down on us.

My mother looked at it all, panicked, and started running towards the city. Thinking of water, I quickly managed to get her to run with me to the end of our road, to the embankment of the Elbe. We were just in time: soon after we passed, the houses on both sides of the street collapsed and blocked the end of the road. And had it not been such a short distance, the heat of the firestorm would have set our hair and our clothes alight, turned us into human candles.

Erika Dienel goes on to describe people who had been turned into living torches jumping into the Elbe.

Margaret Freyer described searching for her fiancé among the dead, who were everywhere, some as black as charcoal:

> what I saw is so horrific I shall hardly be able to describe it . . . Most people looked as if they had been inflated, with large yellow and brown stains on their bodies. People whose clothes were still glowing . . . I think I was incapable of absorbing the meaning of this cruelty any more, for there were also so many little babies, terribly mutilated . . . I was aware that I had constantly to brush hands away from me, hands which belonged to people who wanted me to take them with me, hands which clung to me. But I was much too weak to lift anyone up.[31]

For the survivors, there were to be many weeks of burying the dead amid disease spread by a larger population of bigger rats. One of the lower estimates is that 30,000 people died through the bombing and the firestorm.

What was the psychology which made this bombing possible?

2 THE MORAL RESOURCES AND THE BOMBING

Distance

Where the targets were in occupied countries, those doing the bombing were acutely aware of the potential harm to people on the ground. The Gnome-Rhône aero-engine factory at Limoges was bombed in 1944. Group Captain Leonard Cheshire avoided killing any of the 300 Frenchwomen who worked there. He risked flying low backwards and forwards across the factory to warn them to evacuate.[32]

The air crews bombing Germany did not easily feel the same concern. There was the psychological distancing of those on the other side. Area bombing of Germany began after 30,000 people in Britain had already been killed by German bombing. Among those attacked by the Luftwaffe in the war Hitler had made, satisfaction that 'the Germans' should now be on the receiving end of the Blitz is understandable. But, if the physical distance could have been stripped away, there might have been doubts about this way of thinking. It is not so satisfying to make a firestorm around Carolin Schaeffer's children.

The effects of physical distance were described by one RAF bomber pilot who took part in a raid on Duisburg in 1943: 'The burning horror beneath us meant the "success" of an operation designed to damage the production of an evil dictator. Even though I had known what it was like to be on the receiving end of bombing raids during the London Blitz, I had little difficulty in banishing the human victims from my mind.'[33] The mechanisms of psychological distancing which make close combat possible are hardly needed when physical distance makes killing so much easier.

Hardness

In 1942 Lord Cherwell argued that the main targets should be working-class houses. Middle-class houses, being more spread out, would waste bombs. He claimed that in eighteen months half the houses in the larger German towns could be destroyed.

Afterwards some of those involved recognized the hardness needed for such calculations. Sir Charles Snow later remembered that opponents of Cherwell, himself included, had been worried by the poor calculations rather than by the ruthlessness. But, looking back in 1960, he also reflected on the hardness:

> It is possible, I suppose, that some time in the future people living in a more benevolent age than ours may turn over the official records and notice that men like us, men well educated by the standards of the day, men fairly kindly by the standards of the day, and often possessed of strong human feelings, made the kind of calculation I have just been describing . . . Will they say . . . that we were wolves with the minds of men? Will they think that we resigned our humanity? They will have the right.[34]

Hardness also developed in Sir Arthur Harris. In the letter in which he argued that it would be wrong to give up attacks on German cities because they might save Allied lives, Harris also said, 'I do not personally regard the whole of the remaining cities of Germany as worth the bones of one British Grenadier.' This cold joke played on Bismarck's remark about the Balkans not being worth the bones of a single Pomeranian Grenadier.

The cold joke also made an appearance in one of Harris's references to the bombing of Dresden: 'The feeling, such as there is, over Dresden could easily be explained by any psychiatrist. It is connected with German bands and Dresden shepherdesses. Actually Dresden was a mass of munition works, an intact government centre, and a key transportation point to the East. It is now none of those things.'[35] The code name of the attack on Hamburg was also a cold joke: 'Operation Gomorrah'.

Harris admitted 'the fact that our aircraft occasionally killed women and children'. On the page in his book before this comment, he wrote, 'No air raid ever known before had been so terrible as that which Hamburg had endured; the second largest city in Germany, with a population of nearly 2,000,000, had been wiped out in three nights.'[36]

It must be difficult to command a bomber force in war and remain sensitive to civilian casualties on the other side. But this policy required quite a lot of hardness.

Breakthrough of Sympathy

Thoughts about the victims sometimes broke through. Some of those involved in a raid on Wuppertal in 1943 felt unhappy because they were told that part of its aim was to catch the thousands of refugees from the flooding caused by the earlier 'Dambuster' raid. No doubt sympathy breaks through more easily when refugees are being bombed, but 'normal' area bombing could trigger similar thoughts: 'After our first Hamburg trip, my navigator and I cycled to Huntingdon and took a boat out on the river. We drifted quietly downstream and Nick said, "What about those poor sods under those fires?" I couldn't think of anything to say. We drifted quietly on.'[37]

For a few, awareness was unavoidable. The bomber pilot, whose description of the raid on Duisburg was quoted earlier, revisited the Ruhr the next night in a raid on Bochum. His aircraft was shot down. He parachuted down, was arrested and taken to Düsseldorf:

> We had to change trains at Duisburg and I had an opportunity to see some of the results of my own handiwork. It was not the stench and the stark, still-smouldering ruins of buildings that impressed me so much as the people, the dazed, grimy, hurt, angry people, trying to come to terms with a world gone mad, with losses too deep for tears. They were indistinguishable from some of the people I had seen in London during the Blitz. That night in Düsseldorf, I cowered with my captors and numerous German civilians in an air-raid shelter as the sirens wailed. I shared their terror as the mighty force of bombers droned endlessly overhead. They were bound elsewhere, but it was some time before we were sure of that. When I was repatriated two years later, I found that Bomber Command had become a kind of scapegoat for the nation's guilt. More than a few of us felt that guilt keenly.[38]

Eroding the Restraints of Moral Identity

There was little chance that the policy-makers would be inhibited by sympathy. The people the bombs fell on were always distant and invisible. As with the blockade, the sense of moral identity was the most plausible brake on the policy. Those directing the campaign did not think of themselves as people who killed children in firestorms.

Sometimes qualms about moral identity surfaced. They were felt at least once by Winston Churchill, who was an advocate of area bombing for most of the war. In June 1943, at Chequers with the Australian Minister, Richard Casey, he watched film of the bombing taken from the air. He turned to Casey and asked, 'Are we beasts? Are we taking this too far?'[39] But, as with the blockade, the inhibitions could fade. The raids on Hamburg, Darmstadt and Dresden were still to come.

For some, concern about moral identity may have been quieted by a reluctance to recognize the reality of bombing. In 1942 Cherwell wrote a Cabinet paper supporting area bombing. In it he wrote of a third of the German population 'being turned out of house and home'. He said this would undermine morale: 'There seems little doubt that this would break the spirit of the people.'[40] Bombing houses tends to kill their occupants. Saying they will be turned out of house and home evades the reality.

The bombing was widely thought to be justified. In another echo of the blockade, retaliation seemed to confer legitimacy. The Nazis had bombed civilians first, in Warsaw and in Rotterdam. Bombing civilians was also made more acceptable by German bombing of British towns. In 1941 Churchill was cheeered in London when he said, 'If tonight the people of London were asked to cast their votes whether a convention should be entered into to stop the bombing of all cities, the overwhelming majority would cry, "No, we will mete out to the Germans the measure, and more than the measure, that they have meted out to us." '[41]

The Fragmentation of Responsibility

Moral and emotional inhibitions against the shift to making civilians targets were partly neutralized by diluting personal responsibility. Like the sailors implementing the blockade, the air crews were carrying out a policy decided by others, so a pilot could see himself as just a cog in a machine. The Air Ministry felt Sir Arthur Harris was out of control, and decision-making shifted around. Harris's deputy, Air Vice-Marshal Robert Saundby later wrote about the bombing of Dresden:

> I was not in any way responsible for the decision to make a full-scale air attack on Dresden. Nor was my Commander-in-Chief, Sir Arthur Harris. Our part

was to carry out, to the best of our ability, the instructions we received from the Air Ministry. And, in this case, the Air Ministry was merely passing on instructions received from those responsible for the higher direction of the war.[42]

The Phased Decision and the Blurring of Moral Boundaries

Sometimes moral boundaries became blurred in people's minds because the decision about whether to cross them came, unintentionally, after the event. The move to deliberate bombing of civilians seemed less radical because an unintended form of area bombing had been going on for years. Psychologically, the move to a deliberate version of what is already in place is less of a leap than opting for a policy which is in every respect new.

During the transition period to deliberate area bombing, moral inhibitions were also weakened by a planned blurring of the boundary between military and civilian targets. In the summer of 1941, as Sir Arthur Harris put it, 'the targets chosen were in congested industrial areas and were carefully picked so that bombs which overshot or undershot the actual railway centres under attack should fall on these areas, thereby affecting morale. The programme amounted to a halfway stage between area and precision bombing.'[43] The slide away from the traditional ban on aiming at civilians was made easier by this period, when the civilian deaths were not the primary aim yet were intended.

3 THE MORAL DEBATE

The Lesser Evil and the Just War

Not everyone had their moral inhibitions neutralized or overcome. As area bombing became public knowledge, critics initiated a moral debate which still continues. Area bombing was not intended in the first phase of the campaign. The moral issue is mainly raised by the middle and last phases.

For the last phase, when precision bombing was possible, the case is highly unconvincing. The evidence does not support claims about the disruption of industry and undermining of morale. With alternatives available, and without overwhelming reason for rejecting them, to choose the mass killing of civilians is an indefensible atrocity.

For the middle phase of the campaign, the defence of area bombing is more plausible. The diversion of German energies may have helped defeat Hitler. The moral issue raised by this defence of the middle phase is a deep one, however. The targets were German towns, including the civilians living in them. The bombing of Hamburg came in this phase. If there was a good chance that this intentional killing of civilians would make the defeat of Hitler significantly more likely, was it then justified?

Some people say that no end, however good, can justify the intentional killing of innocent people. (In this context, to be 'innocent' does not require general moral virtue, but only that you are not part of the military threat.) Against this absolute prohibition, others say that Hitler's victory would probably have led to far greater numbers of innocent deaths. Those who take a consequentialist approach to ethics accept that such considerations might justify a policy which includes the intentional killing of the innocent.

The absolute prohibition finds a natural home in the traditional Judaeo-Christian theory of the Just War, which has been developed particularly in Catholic moral theology.[44] Within this theory, there is an absolute prohibition on intentionally killing an innocent person, but it also allows some actions which have the foreseen but unintended consequence that innocent people die. The good has to be sufficient to outweigh the harm. The destruction of a ball-bearings factory is a good act because it contributes to the defeat of Hitler. So long as the numbers are not disproportionately large, some foreseen but unintended civilian deaths can be morally acceptable. Yet it remains wrong intentionally to kill innocent people as a means to bringing about a good end. Even if creating terror in the German population by mass bombing of civilians is the most effective way to defeat Hitler, it is not permissible.

Cases such as bombing the ball-bearings factory are allowed as exceptions on the basis of the 'doctrine of double effect'. Typically, the acts it deals with are ones which have both good and bad effects. According to the doctrine, the morality of the act is tied to whether the bad effect is merely foreseen or actually intended. A merely foreseen bad effect may be permissible, so long as the badness is not out of proportion to the good being pursued.

The doctrine of double effect has difficulties: one is whether what is intended can really be distinguished sharply from a merely foreseen side effect. Yet the doctrine also has intuitive appeal. Intention is important in moral thinking. A doctor whose negligence foreseeably kills a patient is open to severe criticism, but we do not put this in the same category as murder. And to many of us it feels intuitively right that there is an important moral difference between unintentionally killing civilians in a raid on the ball-bearings factory and deliberately bombing a housing estate.

The central question about the Just War approach concerns the absolute prohibition on the intentional killing of innocent people. What if, by intentionally killing a small number of innocent people, you can save a much larger number? Suppose the result of keeping to the rules of the Just War had been a Nazi victory? Apart from all the other vile aspects of a Nazi Europe, such a victory would probably have cost even more innocent lives than the bombing. Is it so clear that restraint then would be morally right?

Part of the appeal of absolute prohibition is that it requires that potential victims are made the focus of attention. It is linked to Kant's idea that people should always be treated as ends in themselves and never merely as means. One worry about the consequentialist approach is that it can lead to simply 'looking through' the potential victims. Carolin Schaeffer, trying to shield her children's eyes from what they might see, or the children fried like eels on the pavement, become mere numbers in Lord Cherwell's multiplication sums. It is often said that only absolute prohibitions provide a firm barrier against the slide to these multiplication sums. Moral absolutes limit what can be done to individual people on the basis of calculation of consequences.

There is obviously some force to this claim, but the argument may not support this particular prohibition. One alternative is absolute pacifism: the view that all intentional killing in war, rather than just that of civilians, is wrong.

Absolute pacifism has considerable appeal, but few are prepared to be as unconcerned with consequences as it requires. To many people, the Second World War was justified because it was necessary to prevent the worse evil of the triumph of Nazism. Those of us who accept this claim cannot be absolute pacifists and Just War theory allows this kind of case.

But if the appeal to consequences is allowed to override the universal prohibition of intentional killing, why does the prohibition on civilian killing turn out to be absolute? One answer is that the moral law has been laid down in this way, by God perhaps. But for those of us who are sceptical about the moral law, this is no answer. It seems paradoxical to justify fighting a bloody war by saying Hitler must be defeated, and then to accept absolute restrictions which may mean the war is followed by Hitler's victory. Some argument other than an appeal to authority is needed.

And the point about not just 'looking through' the victims can be used on both sides of the debate. Lord Cherwell's sums 'look through' the horrors done to the children of Hamburg, but absolute prohibitions can be accused of 'looking through' the people (again particular individuals, and again often children) who would be Hitler's victims if he won the war.

For this reason, it is hard to accept the principle that bombing civilians should be absolutely rejected even where it would ensure Hitler's defeat.

Despite this, there are good grounds for siding with the moral critics of the bombing policy, even in its middle phase. Bombing civilians did not make the difference between defeat and victory. (Allowance, of course, has to be made for the participants' lack of hindsight.) Even for those of us who do not accept the absolute prohibition, it is very hard to justify intentional bombing of civilians. There has to be a substantial case that it is highly likely to prevent worse horrors. It is hard to think this true of the area bombing of Germany. And there is a further reason, seen at the time only by a few, for objecting to the bombing on grounds of its longer-term consequences.

The Wartime Moral Debate

The moral case for area bombing was contested within Bomber Command itself. The chaplain at Bomber Command Headquarters at High Wycombe was John Collins. (In the 1960s, and by then Canon Collins, he was a well-known leader of the Campaign for Nuclear Disarmament. There is something surreal about John Collins and Sir Arthur Harris having to work together.)

John Collins invited the Minister of Aircraft Production, Sir Stafford Cripps, to High Wycombe to give a talk on the subject 'Is God My Co-Pilot?' Cripps argued that officers should only send men on bombing raids which they thought were morally as well as militarily justified.

Sir Arthur Harris replied by arranging a lecture on 'The Ethics of Bombing'. This was given by T.D. ('Harry') Weldon, a Fellow in Philosophy at Magdalen College, Oxford. He later wrote a book on Kant and an austere linguistic work on political philosophy, *The Vocabulary of Politics*. He was Personal Staff Officer to Sir Arthur Harris in Bomber Command and drafted the communications Harris sent to the Cabinet and the Air Ministry. Predictably, his talk was rather different from that given by Cripps. When Weldon had finished, Collins asked whether Weldon had not taken his subject to be 'The Bombing of Ethics'?[45]

(Sir Arthur Harris comes out of this story with some credit. It is hard to imagine the German equivalents of John Collins and Sir Stafford Cripps using Luftwaffe headquarters for an ethical lecture critical of the German bombing policy. And, if they had, Hermann Goering's response might not have taken the form of a rival ethical lecture by a philosopher.)

The most forceful religious opponent of area bombing was George Bell, the Bishop of Chichester, who had early been a vocal opponent of Nazism. His opposition to area bombing annoyed Churchill, and is said to have cost Bell his expected promotion to Archbishop of Canterbury.

Bishop Bell put his case most forcefully in a speech in the House of Lords in 1944. His views were generally both disagreed with and respected. Before he spoke he was told by his friend, the Conservative peer Lord Woolton, 'George, there isn't a soul in this House who doesn't wish you wouldn't make the speech you are going to make. You must know that. But I also want to tell you that there isn't a soul who doesn't know that the only reason why you make it, is because you believe it is your duty to make it as a Christian priest.'[46]

Bishop Bell accepted that the Luftwaffe had started the large-scale bombing of towns. He accepted the legitimacy of heavy attacks on military and industrial targets, and that this made the killing of civilians inevitable: 'But there must be a fair balance between the means employed and the purpose achieved. To obliterate a whole town because certain portions contain military and industrial establishments is to reject the balance.'

He spoke about the 'unutterable destruction and devastation' caused in Hamburg, 'the most democratic town in Germany where the anti-Nazi opposition was strongest'. He spoke of phosphorus bombs used on residential parts of Berlin so that 'men and women have been lost, overwhelmed in the colossal tornado of smoke, blast and flame'.

Most of all, Bishop Bell was concerned with what seemed to him a blindness to the long-term effects of such methods of war:

> Why is there this blindness to the psychological side? Why is there this inability to reckon with the moral and spiritual facts? Why is there this forgetfulness of the ideals by which our cause is inspired? How can the War Cabinet fail to see that this progressive devastation of cities is threatening the roots of civilization? How can they be blind to the harvest of even fiercer warring and desolation, even in this country, to which the present destruction will inevitably lead when the members of the War Cabinet have long passed to their rest? . . . This is an extraordinarily solemn moment. What we do in war – which, after all, lasts a comparatively short time – affects the whole character of peace, which covers a much longer period.[47]

No doubt it would have been an honour to have been made Archbishop of Canterbury. But it is far surpassed by the honour of having made that speech at that time.

The Moral Slide

The debate over whether intentionally choosing civilian targets can ever be part of the 'fair balance' between the means employed and the purpose achieved still continues. With hindsight, one aspect seems particularly important. This was singled out by George Bell, but seems to have been invisible to most of his contemporaries. Terrible methods of war are not adopted in historical isolation. Their defenders appeal to precedents and uses of these new methods are cited in turn as precedents for later horrors.

Defenders of area bombing cited the civilian deaths caused by the blockade of Germany at the end of the First World War. In 1944 J.M. Spaight, recently retired as Principal Assistant Secretary at the Air Ministry, published his book *Bombing Vindicated*. He claimed that the policy was to aim at military targets, with civilians being killed only incidentally, and he quoted figures of deaths caused by the naval blockade.

He then claimed that the civilian toll through bombing was 'almost trivial in comparison with that due to blockade', and said that 'air power could never reap such a terrible harvest'.[48]

Air Marshal Harris cited the same precedent: 'The point is often made that bombing is specially wicked because it causes casualties among civilians. This is true, but then all wars have caused casualties among civilians. For instance, after the last war the British Government issued a White Paper in which it was estimated that our blockade of Germany had caused nearly 800,000 deaths.'[49]

The blockade made it easier to embark on area bombing. In turn, the raids on Hamburg, Darmstadt and Dresden meant there was relatively little outcry when the American Air Force embarked on the fire-bombing of Tokyo. And that in turn eased the way to Hiroshima and Nagasaki.

CHAPTER 12

Hiroshima

Nuclear weapons have changed everything, except our modes of thought.
Albert Einstein

Some of those who first saw the release of nuclear energy did not understand what it could mean. Lord Rutherford spoke to the British Association in September 1933. *The Times* quoted him as saying, 'it was a very poor and inefficient way of producing energy, and anyone who looked for a source of power in the transformation of atoms was talking moonshine'.[1]

There was no single moment when the policy of developing the atomic bomb for use against Japan was adopted. As with the British bombing of German civilians, moral doubts were weakened by the decision being phased.

The decision to develop the bomb was taken to deter a possible atomic threat from Nazi Germany. The decision to use it against Japan was arrived at in a different climate. Policy-makers had become hardened to devastating conventional bombing. And the new climate was partly created by the very fact of the bomb's development.

1 THE FEAR OF A GERMAN ATOMIC BOMB

Warnings

During the Second World War four atomic bomb programmes were started. In addition to the ultimately successful American–British programme, there were Soviet and Japanese programmes, neither of which came near success during the war. But, in Britain and the United States, there was fear of the German atomic programme.

In 1939, when atomic energy began to seem a serious possibility, Leo Szilard was one of the first to think of the danger of a Nazi bomb: 'I thought that if neutrons are in fact emitted in fission, this fact should be kept secret from the Germans.'[2]

In 1940 Otto Frisch did a calculation about the amount of uranium-235 needed for an explosive chain reaction: 'To my amazement it was very much smaller than I had expected; it was not a matter of tons, but something like a pound or two.' Frisch discussed this at once with Rudolf Peierls, and together they calculated that it would take only weeks to produce: 'At that point we stared at each other and realized that an atomic bomb might after all be possible.'[3]

Frisch and Peierls saw the ethical objections to using an atomic bomb. The possibility of a German bomb led them to invent the idea of nuclear deterrence:

> the bomb could probably not be used without killing large numbers of civilians, and this may make it unsuitable as a weapon for use by this country . . . The most effective reply would be a counter-threat with a similar bomb. Therefore it seems to us important to start production as soon and as rapidly as possible, even if it is not intended to use the bomb as a means of attack.[4]

A government committee supported this case. The report was shown to Roosevelt, who gave instructions to start exploratory work on an atomic bomb. Leo Szilard, Edward Teller and other physicists supported an atomic programme.

In Germany, Werner Heisenberg used heavy water from Norway for experiments on the possibility of a chain reaction, which led him to take the idea of a bomb seriously. He went to Copenhagen to consult the strongly anti-Nazi Danish physicist Niels Bohr about the implications of this. Heisenberg felt he had to speak cautiously, as he knew that the German authorities were watching Bohr, whose later remarks might be passed back to Germany. He gave Bohr a drawing of the reactor he was trying to build.

Heisenberg later gave an account of the conversation. He asked whether it was right for physicists to do nuclear research in wartime.

> Bohr understood the meaning of this question immediately, as I realized from his slightly frightened reaction. He replied as far as I can remember with a counter-question: 'Do you really think that uranium fission could be utilized for the construction of weapons?' I may have replied: 'I know that this is in principle possible, but it would require a terrific technical effort, which, one can only hope, cannot be realized in this war.' Bohr was shocked by my reply, obviously assuming that I had intended to convey to him that Germany had made great progress in the direction of manufacturing atomic weapons. Although I tried subsequently to correct this false impression I probably did

not succeed in winning Bohr's complete trust . . . I was very unhappy about the result of this conversation.[5]

Accounts of Heisenberg's visit derived from Bohr were very different. On one account Heisenberg expressed his hope and belief that if the war lasted it would be won by German nuclear weapons.[6] Bohr also had the impression that Heisenberg was trying to find out what he knew. His response combined reticence with indignation that Heisenberg might perhaps hope for his co-operation with Germany.

The conversation was a disaster. If Heisenberg was appealing for co-operation to avert the development of nuclear weapons, he only succeeded in conveying the frightening message that Nazi Germany was working on the bomb.

The Failure of the German Programme

In 1942 Heisenberg and other physicists won funding for the German programme by winning over Bernhard Rust, the Minister for Education. The dangerous physical work was partly done by slave labour: the uranium plates used in the attempt to build an atomic reactor were made by 2,000 women from the camp at Sachsenhausen.

In 1943 Niels Bohr escaped to Scotland, taking with him Heisenberg's drawing of a reactor. It seemed vital to cut off the German supply of heavy water. The Germans had enlarged the Norsk Hydro plant at Rjukan in Norway to produce larger quantities of heavy water.[7] Commandos had wrecked the plant once, but it had been back in production until it was put out of action again by a bombing raid. The Nazis now decided to dismantle the plant and to take it and the heavy water to Germany.

It was vital to stop the heavy water reaching Germany, but there was no time for a full-scale raid on the plant. Only one trained commando, Knut Haukelid, was available locally, who could not destroy the plant. The water would go by train, crossing a lake by rail-ferry. The train would be hard to blow up and would be crowded with passengers. The ferry carried fewer people, but blowing it up would still kill passengers. And killing the guards would lead to reprisals against civilians. Haukelid was told that the results were important enough to justify these losses.

The plant's transport engineer supported the plan, but was concerned to keep loss of life to a minimum. He saw that the water went on the relatively uncrowded Sunday ferry. Haukelid and others blew up the ferry, killing twenty-six of the fifty-three people aboard, but also sending all the heavy water to the bottom of the lake. Kurt Diebner, a physicist in the Ordnance Department of the Wehrmacht, later said, 'right up to the end of the war, in 1945, there was virtually no increase in our heavy water stocks in Germany . . . it was the elimination of German heavy water production in Norway that was the main factor in our failure to achieve a self-sustaining atomic reactor before the war ended'.[8]

This was not the only factor inhibiting the German atomic programme. Because of scientific advice that the 'uranium project' would take three or four years to develop, it was shelved, but the Allies did not know this until nearly the end of the war, when captured documents about the German project showed how far away from success it was. In the meantime, the Manhattan Project, the American and British atomic programme, was continuing to counter the threat of a Nazi bomb.

The Role of the German Scientists

What were the attitudes of the German atomic physicists? In 1939 the German army had set up a nuclear power research programme. Advice that results would take years led to it being shelved. Was this advice given in good faith? Were the scientists influenced by the terrible nature of atomic weapons, and appalled by the idea of a world dominated by a victorious Nazi nuclear state? Did they deliberately frustrate the project?

There is no single answer to this question. Physicists disagreed about the project. After the war the German nuclear physicists were interned at Farm Hall, a country house near Cambridge, where British Intelligence bugged their conversations on hearing the news of Hiroshima.

Otto Hahn, whose work had shown that nuclear fission was possible, was against the project. The commanding officer of Farm Hall described his reaction to Hiroshima:

> Hahn was completely shattered by the news and said he felt personally responsible for the deaths of hundreds of thousands of people, as it was his original discovery which made the bomb possible. He told me that he had originally contemplated suicide when he realized the terrible potentialities of the discovery and he felt that now these had been realized and he was to blame.

He was recorded as saying, 'I thank God on my bended knees that we did not make an uranium bomb.' And, when Heisenberg said that Walther Gerlach had been committed to the project because he was working for Germany, Hahn replied that he too loved his country and that, strange as it might appear, it was for this reason that he had hoped for her defeat.[9]

Carl Friedrich von Weizsäcker was recorded as having a similar view to Hahn. He said, 'if we had all wanted Germany to win the war we would have succeeded . . . We must admit that we didn't want to succeed'.[10]

When the bomb started to look possible, Werner Heisenberg chose Niels Bohr as the person to consult. The choice of Bohr, a man known for his moral integrity and for his open anti-Nazism, is consistent with Heisenberg either being opposed to making the bomb, or at least wanting real discussion of moral doubts about it. Bohr's suspicion that Heisenberg might be trying to find out about the state of Allied atomic progress, or even to enlist his co-operation in a Nazi project, seems engagingly lacking in self-knowledge. Heisenberg would hardly choose Bohr with either of these ends in mind.

Heisenberg seems to have had doubts about the bomb project and may have deliberately dragged his feet. He told Speer that the results would be too far off to help the war. Heisenberg had refused to join the Nazi Party, and had been attacked for his defence of the 'Jewish physics' of Einstein.

The picture of Heisenberg deliberately but subtly killing the German atomic bomb project has plausibility, but there is some evidence on the other side. Heisenberg wanted German victory. He caused offence at Bohr's institute by his pleasure at German military successes, and by saying war was a biological necessity.[11]

The Farm Hall transcripts make it clear that, early on, Heisenberg had helped to persuade the authorities that the bomb could be made, but the transcripts contain other passages which suggest reluctance. He said that 'although we were not 100 per cent anxious to do it, on the other hand we were so little trusted by the state that even if we had wanted to do it, it would not have been easy to get through.' Talking of the diversion of the German programme from a bomb to a nuclear reactor, he said, 'at the bottom of my heart I was really glad that it was to be an engine and not a bomb, I must admit that'. And he said that they might have succeeded with the bomb but for the fact that they did not want Hitler to win.[12]

Heisenberg was in two minds. He wanted and did not want Germany to win the war. He convinced Rust that the bomb was possible and then convinced Speer that it was not. Being in two minds, Heisenberg was representative of many of the German atomic physicists. With a few exceptions like Otto Hahn, they were sleepwalking through the moral decision they had to take. It was not moral heroism. Heisenberg's phrase 'not 100 per cent anxious to do it' seems to get it right. But the missing few per cent may have saved the world from the Nazi bomb.

2 THE USE OF THE BOMB AGAINST JAPAN

The Allied atomic project, started in response to the possible Nazi threat, was continued with a new aim. Its eventual use against Japan was defended by citing the need to end the war quickly. Part of this defence is relatively easy to accept: a prolonged war would have had terrible human costs.

What is more debatable is whether the bomb had to be used to end the war. Critics say that a harmless demonstration in an empty place might have ended the war without the horrors of Hiroshima and Nagasaki. They also say that the Japanese government was seeking peace and would have admitted defeat if the Allies had dropped their demand for unconditional surrender. These alternatives were considered and rejected.

Both these decisions, to reject a harmless demonstration and to insist on unconditional surrender, seem to have been taken by sleepwalkers. They were taken with one eye on other matters, and were not thought about with the necessary energy and clarity.

The Human Cost of a Longer War

When the war was over in Europe, a prolonged struggle in the Pacific seemed likely, the human cost of which would be great. Japanese occupation of Asian countries was bloody and cruel. People were beheaded, or cut in half from top to bottom, and put on display to frighten others. People from China, India and Malaya, as well as Allied prisoners, were used as forced labour for such projects as the Burma–Siam Railway. Deep-rooted bamboo had to be torn out by hand and with ropes, earth had to be cleared by hand, and immensely heavy lengths of steel rail had to be lifted, positioned and nailed onto wooden sleepers. The slave labourers were given little food. At night they were plagued by mosquitoes. In the day they were driven to work themselves literally to death under the hot sun. It was estimated that for every sleeper on the line one man died. Many others suffered from illnesses and injuries which lasted for the rest of their lives.

The cruelty of the Japanese went beyond slave labour. Eric Lomax was one of a group who made a radio to hear news of the war. For this they were made to stand to attention in the blazing sun, with nothing to drink, for twelve hours. Then each in turn was beaten. They were knocked down with a heavy blow on the back from a pickaxe handle. Then they were beaten again and again, all over the body, with pickaxe handles until they were unconscious. Eric Lomax afterwards remembered boots stamping on the back of his head, crunching his face into the gravel, breaking his teeth. He remembered hearing the cracks when his bones broke.

In the period that followed, they were kept in cramped cages, trying to crouch in ways that would do least damage to their broken bones. Lomax was beaten and tortured. His head was held under water repeatedly. A jet of water from a hose was repeatedly forced down his nose and throat. Again and again he nearly drowned as the water filled his windpipe, lungs and stomach. After all this torture, he was sent to prison. The regime there was total silence and extreme hunger. The prisoners developed revolting skin diseases. 'This was a place in which the living were turned into ghosts, starved, diseased, creatures wasted down to their skeletal outlines.'[13] Any slow end to the war would prolong all this.

An invasion of Japan would also mean enormous casualties on both sides.

Early in 1945 General Curtis LeMay took command of the American air assault on Japan. His strategy for speeding up the end of the war against Japan was similar to that of Air Marshal Harris against Germany. He ordered a huge fire-bombing raid on Tokyo, which killed about 100,000 people in one night. (General LeMay later talked of the people of Tokyo being 'scorched and boiled and baked to death'.)[14] This was followed up by the fire-bombing of Nagoya, Osaka and Kobe. After all this, the bloody struggle still seemed set to continue.

A longer war would have cost many more American and Japanese lives. The capture of Saipan in 1944 had been at the cost of 3,000 American and 30,000 Japanese military casualties. In addition, 22,000 Japanese civilians had committed suicide by hurling themselves from cliffs. The capture of Iwo Jima had cost nearly 7,000 American and 20,000 Japanese lives. (Little more than 1,000 Japanese soldiers were taken prisoner.) Okinawa had cost 12,500 American and 100,000 Japanese lives.

The case for shortening the war was overwhelming. But, at the time, some questioned whether this required using the bomb, or whether even this end would justify its use. General Dwight Eisenhower was a sceptic on both grounds: 'First, the Japanese were ready to surrender and it wasn't necessary to hit them with that awful thing. Second, I hated to see our country be the first to use such a weapon.'[15] He failed to persuade President Truman.

Use or Demonstration?

It was suggested that Japan might be induced to surrender by a harmless demonstration of the bomb. The case for this was partly the obvious humanitarian one. Niels Bohr strongly believed that the atomic bomb was so dangerous that it should be brought under international control. Leo Szilard argued that its military use might make it difficult for countries to resist following the precedent. A bomb on Japan might be 'opening the door to an era of devastation on an unimaginable scale'.[16]

The decision to reject the harmless demonstration in favour of destroying Japanese cities was formally taken by President Truman, and was partly delegated to the 'Interim Committee', chaired by the Secretary of War, Henry Stimson.

The Interim Committee considered the idea of a harmless demonstration apparently for about ten minutes over lunch, and rejected it.[17] Stimson later explained that they did not think it would make Japan surrender and there was a danger that the demonstration bomb would not work. There were also too few bombs for one to be diverted to this use. The committee reported, 'We can propose no technical demonstration likely to bring an end to the war; we see no acceptable alternative to direct military use.'[18]

Truman was in a weak position to check military drift. The Manhattan Project, set up to counter the threat of a Nazi bomb, had taken on a life of its own. General Groves, who commanded the project, was described by one scientist close to him as obsessed by the fear that the war would be finished before his bomb was ready. Even after the capitulation of Germany, he urged that 'we must not lose a single day'. And Groves queried Truman's claim that his 'yes' decided the issue of dropping the bomb: 'Truman did not so much say "yes" as not say "no". It would indeed have taken a lot of nerve to say "no" at that time.'[19]

Whether a harmless demonstration of the bomb could end the war was not the only consideration in Truman's thinking. He and his administration had half an eye on the impression different choices would make on the Soviet Union. Despite Churchill's strong pressure for a mid-June meeting with Stalin, Truman postponed it until mid-July when the bomb would have been tested. Truman's influential representative on the Interim Committee, James Byrnes, discussed the bomb with Leo Szilard and other scientists. He did not argue that the bomb was needed to defeat Japan, but that 'our possessing and demonstrating the bomb would make Russia more manageable in Europe'.[20]

Those who played a part in the decision did not always give full attention to the central question: whether a quick end to the war could have been brought about in a less terrible way.

Unconditional Surrender

Might Japan have surrendered without the bomb being dropped? The Japanese government was known to have asked the Soviet Union to act as an intermediary with the Allies.

The Japanese War Cabinet was divided. Even after the second bomb on Nagasaki, half the War Cabinet wanted to continue the war, but the Emperor himself and some senior ministers wanted to end it. The War Cabinet might have accepted a negotiated surrender but not the Allied demand for unconditional surrender. Resistance to unconditional surrender was linked to their fear that their Emperor would be forced to step down.

The Foreign Minister, Shigenori Togo, sent cables to the Japanese ambassador in Moscow (of which some were intercepted by American intelligence) about negotiating a surrender. But one of the cables also said, 'if the enemy insists on unconditional surrender to the very end, then our country and His Majesty would unanimously resolve to fight a war of resistance to the bitter end. Therefore, inviting the Soviet Union to mediate fairly does not include unconditional surrender; please understand this point in particular.'[21]

The demand for unconditional surrender had arisen virtually by accident. Roosevelt and Churchill had discussed unconditional surrender at Casablanca in 1943, but it was not agreed. When Roosevelt spoke at the press conference, the phrase slipped out: he demanded the unconditional surrender of Germany, Italy and Japan. Roosevelt later said that he had been thinking that getting the French Generals Giraud and de Gaulle to see each other was as hard as arranging a meeting between Generals Grant and Lee. 'And then suddenly the press conference was on, and Winston and I had had no time to prepare for it, and the thought popped into my mind that they had called Grant "Old Unconditional Surrender", and the next thing I knew I had said it.' Churchill was taken by surprise, but supported Roosevelt to avoid public disunity.[22]

In July 1945, at the Potsdam Conference, Churchill argued for more flexibility. The Potsdam declaration issued to Japan did not use the phrase, but it still laid down non-negotiable terms, and did not say that Japan could keep the Emperor. It urged Japan to surrender in order to avoid 'prompt and utter destruction'. The Japanese Prime Minister rejected it on 29 July.

On 2 August the Japanese ambassador in Moscow was instructed to approach the Russians again to act as mediators for peace, but the Russians wanted the advantages of joining the war and the ambassador was told that Stalin and Molotov were unavailable.

'What Did They Think Would Happen if They Dropped It?'

Early on the morning of 6 August 1945, the atomic bomb called 'Little Boy' was dropped from an American bomber called the Enola Gay on Hiroshima.

The explosion released light, blast, heat and nuclear radiation.

One doctor described the effects of the light: 'Those who were watching the plane had their eye-grounds burned. The flash of light apparently went through the pupils and left them with a blind area in the central portion of their visual fields. Most of the eye-ground burns are third-degree, so cure is impossible.'[23]

The blast started at a speed of two miles a second. One boy was in a room looking out at the river:

As the house fell apart he was blown from the end room across the road on the river embankment and landed on the street below it. In that distance he passed through a couple of windows inside the house and his body was stuck full of all the glass it could hold. That was why he was completely covered in blood like that.[24]

The temperature at the centre reached 5,400°F. Many people were burnt to a cinder. A group of construction workers were doing gymnastics when they were killed. A survivor who saw them said to Dr Michihiko Hachiya, 'A human being who has been roasted becomes quite small, doesn't he? Those people all looked like little boys after the explosion.'[25]

People had their hair burnt off. Many were blackened and severely blistered by the burn of the flash. Their skin was then torn loose by the blast, so that even on their faces it hung down like rags. One of Dr Hachiya's patients described some soldiers, burned from the hips up:

Where the skin had peeled, their flesh was wet and mushy. They must have been wearing their military caps because the black hair on top of their heads was not burned. It made them look like they were wearing black lacquer bowls. And they had no faces! Their eyes, noses and mouths had been burned away, and it looked like their ears had melted off. It was hard to tell front from back.[26]

The scenes of pain and horror were unending. There were people with their bowels and brains coming out, and many children with dead mothers. There was 'a woman with her jaw missing and her tongue hanging out of her mouth' wandering around in the rain crying for help. One man stood holding his torn-out eye in his hand.[27]

This was only the beginning. These were the victims of light, blast and heat. Radiation sickness was to follow: nausea, vomiting, extreme thirst, loss of appetite, diarrhoea, fever, convulsions, delirium, purple spots on the body, loss of hair from the roots, and bleeding: in the urine, the retina, the mouth, the rectum or the respiratory passages. Death was preceded by the decay of internal organs. The committee set up to study the bomb's effects described what the radiation did:

It destroyed the actively regenerating cells in the body and greatly devastated the vital defensive mechanism. These heavy doses were the main reason for the poor repair, the prevalence of infection, and the extremely high mortality in atomic bomb injury. The atomic bomb not only brought tragic and horrible injuries to the exposed but also hindered the basis for the reparative and regenerative processes of the living body.[28]

This too was only the beginning. The survivors among those exposed to radiation had a greatly increased risk of contracting leukaemia, and showed high rates of other physical illnesses, and of psychiatric disorders. There were high infant mortality rates among foetuses exposed to radiation in the womb, and those who survived often had retarded growth and abnormally small heads. Up to the end of 1945 the Hiroshima bomb caused 140,000 deaths. Five years later the total had reached 200,000. And there was to be a continuing toll of radiation-induced chromosomal and genetic disorders in children conceived years after the bomb.[29]

And the bombing of Hiroshima was itself only the beginning. Just after eleven a.m. on 9 August the atomic bomb called 'Fat Man' was dropped from an American bomber on Nagasaki. There 70,000 died by the end of the year and five years later the total had reached 140,000.

One girl who was five years old at the time of Hiroshima wrote, 'the more you hear the sadder the stories get'. One boy of five wrote later, 'Since just in my family there is so much sadness from it, I wonder how much sadness other people must also be having.'[30]

A woman who was a schoolgirl at Hiroshima asked, 'Those scientists who invented the atomic bomb, what did they think would happen if they dropped it?'[31]

3 ERODING THE RESTRAINTS OF MORAL IDENTITY

For scientists and others involved in the bomb, sympathy was inhibited by distance. They were only faintly aware of the people who were to be burnt, blinded, blistered, shrivelled, irradiated and killed.

What might have held them back was a sense of moral identity. Few would hope to be remembered as people who ruined and destroyed so many. But again, in a developed version of the psychology of the blockade and of area bombing, this restraint was eroded.

The sense of moral identity is shaped by values which are only partly autonomous. Moral identity is often about being a 'good enough' person, in terms of a base line set by others. In the decision to use the bomb the base line had shifted down during the moral slide from the blockade to the area bombing of Germany and to the fire-bombing of Japan. Predictably, one member of Stimson's committee made the point that the 'number of people that would be killed by the bomb would not be greater in general magnitude than the number already killed in fire raids'.[32]

Participation in a massacre is less threatening to the picture of yourself as a kindly and humane person if the horrors seem to have little to do with you. To diminish the sense of personal responsibility is to weaken the restraining effects of moral identity. The sense of personal responsibility for the atomic bomb was weakened by distance and by evasion, but, above all, was weakened by the way contributions to the use of the bomb were shared among so many people.

Distance

Distance does not just reduce sympathy. It also reduces the feeling of responsibility.

This contrasts with close-up participation, as in the My Lai massacre. Immediacy often causes stronger emotional revulsion. The need to overcome this revulsion generates a stronger awareness of personal agency. It strengthens the sense of being responsible, and increases awareness of the kind of person you have to be to do such things. This awareness can restrain someone from acting, or else can lead to guilt afterwards.

Distance has the opposite effect; by weakening the emotional revulsion, it makes the act easier. This reduces the feeling of responsibility and reduces awareness of the kind of person you become in doing it. There is less restraining pressure against the act, and less guilt afterwards. With the atomic bomb, this had paradoxical effects. Some of those who came closest to the victims had strong feelings of responsibility and guilt. While some of those further away, whose responsibility was really much greater, were enabled by the distance to live comfortably with what they did.

Those who actually dropped the bombs were less responsible than people who took the decisions higher up the chain of command. In modern technological war, psychological responses are poorly correlated with degrees of responsibility. In people further back up the chain, this causal distance reduces the psychological resistance they have to overcome.

It is easier to drop a bomb than to kill people by hand on the ground. But bombing can have its own psychological costs.

There were variations between those closely involved in the bombing. The night before 6 August the Enola Gay's navigator, Captain Van Kirk, found it necessary to take two sleeping pills. He then spent the night playing poker. Perhaps these were signs of stress. But some people were relatively untroubled. Before take-off, a Protestant chaplain was able to ask God 'to be with those who brave the heights of Thy heaven and who carry the battle to our enemies'. And Colonel Paul Tibbetts, the pilot of the Enola Gay, was later able to re-enact the bombing at model aircraft shows.

Others felt differently. The Enola Gay was preceded over Hiroshima by a reconnaissance aircraft, commanded by Major Claude Eatherly, who sent the go-ahead signal. Coming back from Hiroshima, he said a prayer in which he resolved to dedicate his life to abolishing war and nuclear weapons. Afterwards he was haunted by nightmares of the bomb. He sent envelopes of money to Hiroshima. In 1950 he attempted suicide. Later he forged a cheque for a very small sum of money, which he paid to a fund for the children of Hiroshima. He staged a hold-up, but took no money. He was eventually compulsorily detained for psychiatric treatment in hospital.

On one view, Major Eatherly was not psychiatrically ill, but was a sane man incarcerated in hospital to discredit his anti-nuclear protests. He later wrote that the dedication of his life to that cause 'has cost me much because of the mental and emotional disturbances, caused by the guilt of such a crime. I have spent nearly eight of those years in hospitals and a short time in jails. I always seemed to be happier in jails because I had a release of guilt by being punished.' He also wrote that 'the fact is that society simply *cannot* accept the fact of my guilt without at the same time recognizing its own far deeper guilt'.[33]

On another view, his method of seeking punishment for his guilt was a symptom of psychiatric disturbance. Either way, he paid a heavy price for involvement in Hiroshima.

Further away from the bombing, the mood was good. General Leslie Groves, the commander of the Manhattan Project, was positively cheerful as he passed the news of Hiroshima to Robert Oppenheimer: 'I am very proud of you and all your people . . . Apparently it went with a tremendous bang.' And President Truman, when told the news at lunch on board ship, said to the sailors at his table, 'This is the greatest thing in history.'[34]

Still further back in the causal chain were the scientists. Some were appalled. Leo Szilard's immediate reaction was that 'using atomic bombs against Japan is one of the greatest blunders of history'. Otto Frisch was sombre, but his description of some of his colleagues shows that others were not:

I still remember the feeling of unease, indeed nausea, when I saw how many of my friends were rushing to the telephone to book tables at the La Fonda Hotel in Santa Fe, in order to celebrate. Of course they were exalted by the success of their work, but it seemed rather ghoulish to celebrate the sudden death of a hundred thousand people, even if they were 'enemies'.[35]

Evasion

The restraining effects of moral identity can be weakened by evading any clear recognition of what you are doing.

In his private diary Truman wrote a passage on the bomb. Given the decision he was making, there is something disappointing about the quality of his thought:

We have discovered the most terrible bomb in the history of the world. It may be the fire destruction prophesied in the Euphrates Valley Era, after Noah and his fabulous Ark. Anyway we 'think' we have found a way to cause a disintegration of the atom. An experiment in the New Mexican desert was startling – to put it mildly . . . This weapon is to be used against Japan between now and August 10th. I have told the Sec. of War, Mr Stimson, to use it so that military objectives and soldiers are the target and not women and children. Even if the Japs are savages, ruthless, merciless and fanatic, we as the leader of the world for the common welfare cannot drop this terrible bomb on the old capital or the new. He & I are in accord. The target will be a purely military one and we will issue a warning statement asking the Japs to surrender and save lives. I'm sure they will not do that, but we will have given them the chance.[36]

The passage gives evidence of the need to escape from any clear, plain statement of what he was about to do. There is the denial of the full human impact of the bomb by seeing the victims as 'Japs' and savages. There is the half-suggestion that the bomb may not work anyway: we only 'think' we have found a way to split the atom. We are exonerated because we are giving them a warning, even though we know they will ignore it.

Above all, there is the evasion of the fact that an atomic bomb dropped on a city cannot possibly be directed at purely military targets. In Hiroshima civilians outnumbered soldiers by more than six to one. President Truman certainly had some idea of the civilian casualties later. After Nagasaki he stopped the atomic bombing, saying that the thought of wiping out another 100,000 people was too horrible, and that he did not like the idea of killing 'all those kids'.[37] Perhaps at some level he knew about this before Hiroshima. If not, his concern for the children was too small to prompt him to find out.

It was not only the President who had to face or evade a moral decision. The scientists who developed the bomb were also faced with a question of conscience. While some confronted it, others took refuge in evasion.

Many of the physicists involved were aware of the moral dilemmas quite early. Some faced them directly and refused to participate. I.I. Rabi turned down Oppenheimer's invitation to be the Associate Director of the Manhattan Project, partly because he did not want to make three centuries of physics lead up to an atomic bomb. Some, like Szilard, Frisch and Peierls, also faced the dilemmas directly and decided that the threat of a Nazi bomb made it right to work on the project. Others found the dilemmas hard to think about and put them out of their minds in order to work on the project.

A way of evading moral questions was to concentrate single-mindedly on the job. One line of thought assumed that responsibility for consequences was limited by people's roles: it was the scientists' role to make discoveries, but what was done with them was up to politicians or 'society'. Some thought that knowledge was intrinsically worth pursuing, whatever the consequences. Others thought that research was something which scientists were virtually unable to give up.

Robert Oppenheimer spoke about the irresistible appeal of scientific and technological projects:

It is my judgement in these things that when you see something that is technically sweet you go ahead and do it and you argue about what to do about it only after you have had your technical success. That is the way it was with the atomic bomb. I do not think anybody opposed making it; there were some debates about what to do with it after it was made.[38]

Perhaps Oppenheimer was projecting onto scientists in general his own total susceptibility to intellectual or technical beauty. Not all scientists would do what is 'technically sweet' regardless of consequences. But some of Oppenheimer's account of the psychology is confirmed by a self-critical physicist, who talked anonymously to Robert Jungk about the Nagasaki bomb:

I dreaded the use of this 'better' bomb. I hoped that it would not be used and trembled at the thought of the devastation it would cause. And yet, to be quite frank, I was desperately anxious to find out whether this type of bomb would also do what was expected of it, in short, whether its intricate mechanism would work. These were dreadful thoughts, I know, and still I could not help having them.[39]

Although there were honourable exceptions like Bohr, Szilard and Peierls, naïve assumptions about moral and political thought were common among the atomic scientists. No doubt this intellectual limitation in the scientific community deserves criticism. Off stage there is another community also open to criticism. Philosophers will not be impressed by the weak and confused quality of Oppenheimer's thinking about making the bomb. It is clear that scientists, including Oppenheimer, had no idea of the existence of a kind of thinking which they lacked. Their ignorance is only part of the general failure of philosophy, at least at that time, to make a serious impact on the thinking of the wider community. By omission, philosophers who only talk to each other bear some responsibility for a climate conducive to the evasive thought which contributed to Hiroshima.

The Fragmentation of Responsibility

Above all, the sense of personal responsibility was reduced by the way agency was fragmented. Among the airmen who obeyed the order to drop the bomb, the many scientists who helped to make it, the President, the many political and military advisers involved in the decision, who killed the people of Hiroshima? No one seems to have felt that the responsibility was fully his.

Truman's thinking about the question of a harmless demonstration was effectively delegated to Stimson's committee. He saw the decision as mainly technical, and himself as constrained by expert advice.

In Truman's memoirs, 561 pages are devoted to 1945. The decision to use the atomic bomb is explained briefly on page 491. He said that he knew that the bomb would inflict casualties beyond imagination:

> On the other hand the scientific adviser of the committee reported, 'We can propose no technical demonstration likely to bring an end to the war; we see no acceptable alternative to direct military use.' It was their conclusion that no technical demonstration they might propose, such as over a deserted island, would be likely to bring the war to an end. It had to be used against an enemy target. The final decision about where and when to use the bomb was up to me. Let there be no mistake about it. I regarded the bomb as a military weapon and never had any doubt that it should be used. The top military advisers to the President recommended its use, and when I talked to Churchill he unhesitatingly told me that he favoured the use of the atomic bomb if it might aid to end the war.[40]

It is striking that Truman's claim that the decision was up to him took the form of saying that 'the final decision *about where and when to use the bomb* was up to me'. This comes just after saying the committee had concluded that it had to be used against an enemy target. This central decision seems to have been delegated by Truman to the committee.

Stimson's committee considered a harmless demonstration, but rejected it on several grounds. The Japanese might suspect it was a trick. Or they might attack the aircraft used in the demonstration, or take Allied prisoners to the target area. The bomb might not work, or it might not be impressive enough to stop the war. If the demonstration did not result in surrender, the bomb's shock value would be lost. The committee reported that they could propose no technical demonstration likely to end the war: 'we see no acceptable alternative to direct military use'.[41]

Although Truman handed over discussion of this question to Stimson's committee, they do not seem to have seen themselves as considering all aspects of the decision, but only the 'technical' issues involved in it. One member of the committee, Robert Oppenheimer, was later asked about influences on their decision. He said:

> What was expected of this committee of experts was primarily a technical opinion on new questions . . . President Roosevelt and Sir Winston Churchill showed their complete accord with the fact that the atomic bomb had to be used if it proved necessary to end the war. This opinion weighed heavily in the scale. Unfortunately, time was lacking. It seems possible that a more thorough study of the problem, more prolonged, would have led those responsible to a

more precise or even different conception of what was necessary to do with these new weapons.[42]

An interview thirteen years later may not fully reflect the original deliberations, but Oppenheimer's answer gives the impression that he, and perhaps others, did not bring clear thinking to the issue. His point about Roosevelt and Churchill is confused. He refers to their view that the bomb should be used if this was necessary to end the war. But this view is irrelevant to the 'technical' question the committee saw itself answering: *was* the use of the bomb necessary to end the war? If this opinion really 'weighed heavily in the scale', the thinking of the committee was confused.

Oppenheimer gives the impression that the committee was not seriously or fully engaged with whether there were other ways of ending the war. They seem to have felt the decision had already been taken, at least partly, by Roosevelt and Churchill. The decision imposed a huge weight of responsibility. Understandably, the committee wanted to think it was not just theirs. President Truman had the same reason for wanting to think it was not just his decision, but a technical one to delegate to them.

To look closely at this, one of the central decisions of the twentieth century, is to become aware of a moral vacuum. No one seems to have felt sufficiently responsible for the decision to look with energy and imagination for alternatives.

4 THE MORAL DEBATE

These two bombs killed over a third of a million people, both adults and children, in a hell we cannot adequately imagine.

The moral debate about the use of the bombs is about two central issues. Could the war have been stopped by other means? And, if there were no alternative ways of stopping the war, would this justify dropping these bombs?

Were There Other Ways of Ending the War?

Perhaps there was no certain way of ending the war without the use of the bomb, but it is not hard to see the outlines of an approach worth trying.

The Japanese government could have been told of the bomb. They could have been given photographs and other evidence from the test already carried out in New Mexico. They could have been invited, quietly through diplomatic channels, to send representatives, including physicists, to another demonstration of the bomb in the United States. A guarantee of safe conduct could have been given. Japanese physicists could have had discussions with American physicists and been told enough to show that the bomb was genuine. This could have been combined with an invitation, again given quietly through diplomatic channels, to negotiate peace. It could have been said that surrender need not be unconditional, and that the Allies would not depose the Emperor.

A bomb demonstration in the United States would have met the main worries of the Stimson committee. The Japanese would have been less likely to reject the bomb as a fake. They could not sabotage the demonstration by moving Allied prisoners to the site or by shooting down an aircraft carrying the bomb.

For the Japanese to have accepted the public ultimatum issued at Potsdam would have involved a loss of face. They were not prepared to accept unconditional surrender or the loss of the Emperor. A quiet invitation to negotiate, coupled with abandonment of the demand for unconditional surrender and an assurance about the Emperor, might have ended the war without dropping the bomb.

In fairness to Truman, it should be remembered that he did not have the advantages of hindsight. He was taking decisions under all the pressures of a wartime presidency. And there is obviously no certainty that the kind of approach suggested would have ended the war. But, in the light of what happened to the people of Hiroshima and Nagasaki, the thought is unavoidable that such an approach should have been tried.

Ends and Means

Suppose using the bomb had been the only way of shortening the war. Would it then have been justified?

One contribution to this debate was made in 1956, when it was proposed that Oxford University should award an honorary degree to President Truman. Proposals for honorary degrees were always accepted and few University members bothered to vote on them. But on the day Truman was proposed, Congregation was full because there was a controversial proposal to include less of the Greek New Testament in the Theology degree.

One witness described the occasion:

The House was preparing to snooze through the routine business before coming to what was the real reason for their presence, but suddenly and startlingly, Miss Anscombe rose and (after duly seeking the VC's [Vice Chancellor's] permission to speak English) delivered an impassioned speech against the award of an Oxford degree to the 'man who pressed the button' of the Bomb. The VC called for a vote: she was in a minority of one.

This speech elicited only 'the complete silence and impassivity of those present ... not the slightest sign of approval or disapproval, not a murmur, not a rustle, not a change of countenance, but only utter imperturbability'.[43] Memories of the occasion vary. In a different account, four people voted against the degree, including another philosopher, Philippa Foot.

The content of Elizabeth Anscombe's speech is reproduced in a paper she published at the time on 'Mr Truman's Degree'. She correctly saw how area bombing had prepared the way for the atomic bomb. She accepted that, in the circumstances, dropping the bomb probably saved many lives, but pointed out that the circumstances included the Allies' demand for unconditional surrender and their disregard of Japan's known desire for a negotiated peace.

Elizabeth Anscombe's central moral claim was that to kill innocent people as means to an end is always murder. The state has a right to order killing in a war fought either to protect its own people or to protect others who are treated unjustly. There is no right intentionally to kill innocent people, those who are neither waging the war nor supplying its means. Attacking military targets as carefully as possible may involve unintended but foreseen civilian deaths, and this is not murder. But it is not acceptable to attack where the military objective can only be hit by taking as your target something which includes large numbers of innocent people: 'Then you cannot very well say they died by accident. Here your action is murder.'[44]

Elizabeth Anscombe finished on a rhetorical flourish. She said that she would fear to go to the degree ceremony 'in case God's patience suddenly ends'. Afterwards, Harry Weldon, Air Marshal Harris's former colleague, offered to arrange comprehensive air cover.

It is hard to warm to the response of those who heard Miss Anscombe and then voted in a way that left her in such a small minority. Just possibly, each person who voted against her may have had good reasons. But their silence and utter imperturbability now seem extraordinary. Was there too little time for discussion, because of the pressing issue of Greek New Testament in the Theology degree? Did no one think that this courageous and powerful speech deserved the compliment of rational opposition? Apart from Philippa Foot, where were the philosophers?

The moral framework assumed in this criticism of Truman's decision is the Just War doctrine of the Judaeo–Christian tradition. On this view, the intentional killing of innocent people ('murder') is absolutely forbidden. Although it is recognized that modern warfare inevitably results in the deaths of innocent people, the absolute ban on murder does not entail pacifism. The doctrine of double effect is invoked to permit some acts which will foreseeably kill innocent people. Where these deaths are foreseen but not intended consequences, and where they are not out of proportion to the good aimed at, the act is permissible.

There are questions to raise, both about the appeal to the doctrine of double effect and about the absolute prohibition on killing innocent people.

One question about the doctrine of double effect is about how to decide which consequences of an act are intended and which are merely foreseen. One possible test is whether the consequences in question are wanted. This test would allow the bombing of Dresden or of Hiroshima, if those who took the decisions could say sincerely, 'We only wanted to destroy the city, and regret that there was no way of doing this without also killing the people there.' This test seems not nearly demanding enough, and is certainly not the one relied on by Miss Anscombe.

A more demanding test says that you still intend even unwanted consequences if they are so close to the act as to be inextricable from it. Some test of this sort seems to be what Miss Anscombe relied on. She excluded taking a target which included large numbers of innocent people: 'then you cannot very well say they died by accident. Here your action is murder.' There is a problem of how close or how inextricable actions and consequences have to be for the consequences to count as intended. What reasons can be given for drawing the boundary in one place rather than another, and what is the moral case for regarding the boundary as so important?

Apart from these boundary problems, there is a deeper issue. If the weaker test ('Were these consequences wanted?') allows too much, some of us find the stronger version ('Were the deaths so bound up with the act that we cannot say they died by accident?') allows too little. It can be argued that this test is so restrictive that it undermines the view that the intentional killing of the innocent is in all circumstances wrong.

Take the case of the ferry carrying the heavy water from Norway, which was blown up. If the heavy water had reached Germany, a Nazi atomic bomb would not have been certain, but would have been more likely. Letting Hitler have an atomic bomb would risk huge numbers of deaths and perhaps a Nazi victory. With so much at stake, it seems worth paying a substantial price to keep the chance of such a bomb as low as possible. No one wanted the deaths of the twenty-six people who were killed when the ferry was blown up. But it would be hard to argue that it would have been better to have risked the heavy water reaching Germany.

The absolute prohibition on intentional killing of innocent people seems a good deal less plausible if it tells us that Knut Haukelid and his colleagues were wrong to sink the ferry. But it may have this consequence.

The absolute prohibition is usually defended against such objections by the doctrine of double effect. If the deaths of the ferry passengers were not intended, the sinking is permitted and the objection fails.

If the weaker test of intention ('Were the deaths wanted?') is used, the deaths were unintended. Trouble was taken to reduce loss of life by having the water sent on the Sunday morning ferry. And if there had been no passengers, those who blew it up would have been relieved.

But the weaker test allows too much, perhaps even the bombing of Hiroshima. It is natural to follow Miss Anscombe in opting for the stronger test: 'Were the deaths so bound up with the act that we cannot say they died by accident?' But then it is hard to avoid the implausible view that Haukelid acted wrongly. The justification for what Haukelid did was that it reduced the risk of a far greater evil. Haukelid does not need the strange defence that, when the ferry was blown up killing half the passengers, they died by accident.

What does need this strange defence is the absolute prohibition on intentionally killing innocent people even where this averts a much greater evil. The absolute prohibition is central to Miss Anscombe's argument that, no matter how terrible the alternative, the use of the bomb on Hiroshima could not possibly have been justified. The strength of the absolute prohibition is that it insists that we do not treat the people of Hiroshima as transparent, just looking through them to the lives saved through ending the war. In the ferry case the absolute prohibition is in deep trouble. Unless rescued by an absurd stretching of the idea of accidental death, it tells us not to blow up the ferry. We have to risk Hitler getting the atomic bomb. In this case we have to look away from the people Hitler's bomb might kill. It is hard to rely on a moral doctrine which has, in human terms, so poor a sense of proportion.

This unfavourable view of the absolute prohibition is hard to escape when it is judged in terms of its human impact. It is usually defended by those who assume a moral law whose authority is independent of its consequences for people. Elizabeth Anscombe's references to acts being 'forbidden' and to God's patience were not mere rhetoric. She relied on the doctrine of the Just War, taught by the Catholic Church as part of God's law. In that context, criticisms about it being disastrous in human terms miss the point. But, equally, to those of us who judge these things in terms of their human impact, such appeals to authority miss the point.

Some of Miss Anscombe's reasons for her view are implausible outside her religious framework of belief. But we have seen that there are other reasons for agreeing that those who used the bomb did not have enough justification for doing so. Miss Anscombe's vote was right, and those who silently voted her down were wrong.

Niels Bohr and the Open World

The lack of proper exploration of other ways of ending the war is the obvious reason why Truman's decision is hard to defend. But there is also the issue of whether using the bomb would weaken the chance of putting atomic weapons under international control.

With hindsight, it is hard to be sure whether the use of the bomb by one country led to the post-war nuclear arms race. There is an alternative view, that using the bomb demonstrated its horror in a way no harmless experiment could have done, and so helped to sober up the world. Perhaps an arms race was inevitable and this one was restrained by memory of Hiroshima and Nagasaki. Or perhaps, as the Franck Report suggested in June 1945, restraint could have led to international control instead of the arms race.

Two things are clear. The question of international control, raised by Niels Bohr and even now unresolved, was not given the attention it deserved. And, as Bohr saw, it is the fundamental issue of the nuclear age.

Niels Bohr was the most distinguished theoretical physicist to play a role in the development of the bomb. His contribution to the debate on the use of atomic weapons reflected both his moral seriousness and his habit of fundamental thinking. These qualities turned out to be not enough for his ideas to make the necessary impact on decision-makers.

Bohr escaped from occupied Denmark. Because of the threat of a Nazi bomb, he was willing to work on the Manhattan Project. He started to think about the deeper problems of atomic weapons and realized that, since the United States had made the bomb, the Soviet Union would soon follow. The choice was simple: international control or a nuclear arms race. He saw international control as the only safe option.

In 1944 Bohr's ideas persuaded Felix Frankfurter, who passed them on to Roosevelt. The President asked Frankfurter to tell Bohr that he wanted to discuss safeguards with Churchill. Bohr returned to England, and persuaded the President of the Royal Society, Sir Henry Dale, of the importance of the issue. Dale was among those who persuaded Churchill to see Bohr. Thinking of voluntary abstention from using the bomb, in the interests of future international control, Dale wrote to Churchill: 'It is my serious belief that it may be in your power even in the next six months to take decisions which will determine the future course of human history. It is in that belief that I dare to ask you, even now, to give Professor Bohr the opportunity of brief access to you.'

Privately, Dale expressed the fear that Bohr's 'mild, philosophical vagueness of expression and his inarticulate whisper' might mean he would not get through to 'a desperately preoccupied Prime Minister'.[45]

The meeting was not a success. Lord Cherwell was present and much of the time was taken up with argument between him and Churchill on points irrelevant to Bohr's purpose. According to Bohr's own 'very vivid memories' of the interview, recounted to Margaret Gowing, the main point was never reached. 'Professor Bohr was unable to bring the Prime Minister's mind to bear on the implications of the bomb or to tell him of his belief that the President himself was giving the subject such serious thought.' Churchill disliked the meeting. Bohr asked if he could send a memorandum on the subject to Churchill:

> The Prime Minister replied that he would always be honoured to receive a letter from Professor Bohr but hoped that it would not be about politics. Bohr came away greatly disappointed at the way the world was apparently governed, with small points exercising a quite irrational influence. 'We did not speak the same language,' said Bohr afterwards.[46]

Bohr sent a memorandum to Roosevelt, saying that 'the terrifying prospect of a future competition between nations about a weapon of such formidable character can only be avoided by a universal agreement in true confidence'. Prevention of a secret arms race would call for 'such concessions regarding exchange of information and openness about industrial efforts including military preparations as would hardly be conceivable unless at the same time all partners were assured of a compensating guarantee of common security against dangers of unprecedented acuteness'.

In August 1944 the two men met. Roosevelt told Bohr he shared the hopes expressed in the memorandum, and asked Bohr to enlarge on it. But when Roosevelt met Churchill at Hyde Park a few weeks later, it was Churchill's view of Bohr which prevailed. The *aide-mémoire* of their conversation, probably drawn up by Churchill, included the point that 'Enquiries should be made regarding the activities of Professor Bohr and steps taken to ensure he is responsible for no leakage of information particularly to the Russians.'[47]

Bohr's idea was not seen at all by Churchill. It was glimpsed and then forgotten by Roosevelt. His failure to persuade was not surprising. Neither his clogged written prose nor his mumbling conversational style were best suited to engaging political leaders. And the idea was so radical. The time and thought it needed would not have been readily forthcoming, either from a desperately busy wartime Prime Minister or from an equally busy and fatally ill wartime President.

After the war, Bohr tried again. In 1950 he wrote an *Open Letter to the United Nations*, urging 'the ideal of an open world, with common knowledge about social conditions and technical enterprises, including military preparations, in every country'.[48] But this time the attention of the United Nations, and of the world, was diverted by the outbreak of the Korean War. The open world was again put aside.

Bohr's account of his idea left a number of loose ends. It was not a proposal for replacing nation-states by a world government. Nations were to agree on openness. But the possibility of cheating on the agreement suggests the need for policing, and so for some kind of supra-national authority in nuclear matters. And there is the question of what to do if some countries refuse to join the open world. How much pressure on them would be justified? The nature of the compromise between national independence and a world nuclear authority was left vague.

Despite the sketchy nature of the proposal, Bohr's central idea is right. Nuclear weapons (and comparable biological and chemical weapons) are so dangerous that international monitoring and control are essential. And this does mean giving up some degree of national sovereignty. The dangers of not having international control of nuclear weapons were frighteningly apparent during the nuclear arms race of the Cold War. When that arms race ended, many people relaxed about the issue. But, since the end of the Cold War, the proliferation of nuclear-armed nation-states keeps the danger alive in a different form. The open world is something we may be unwise to put aside for too long.

CHAPTER 13

War and the Moral Resources

In close combat the moral resources of those fighting may be eroded and at times overwhelmed. The human responses may be eroded by a culture of combat in which opponents are humiliated or dehumanized, or by soldiers developing a defensive hardness. Moral identity may be neutralized by training or by the remote and alien context of the battlefield. Additional weakening may come from the contempt for scruples expressed within the culture of combat: 'It's a tough war, Chaplain.'

The restraints of the human responses or of moral identity may simply be overwhelmed by an emotional explosion in which 'my mind just went', whether caused by vengeance or by a reaction to humiliation. Or the moral resources may be disconnected by the emotional release combat can bring – by the exhilaration, heightened responses and the strange ecstasy of war.

Sometimes, despite all this, the human responses break through, as happened to George Orwell when he saw the enemy soldier holding up his trousers. Sometimes moral identity breaks through, as when the doctor in Vietnam remembered the Hippocratic oath, or when Hugh Thompson saw that soldiers on his own side were shooting people in ditches as the Nazis had done.

The moral psychology of close combat is bound up with this conflict between the weakening or overwhelming of the moral resources and the tendency for the soldiers' humanity to break through. The moral psychology of long-range, high-technology war is both simpler and more complex.

The Centrality of Moral Identity in Long-range War

In long-range war, distance virtually excludes human responses of any strength. It is possible for someone firing a missile to imagine the impact on people at the receiving end, but nothing has the immediacy of actually seeing a man holding up his trousers.

Moral identity becomes the key moral resource. Distance does not so easily erode intellectual awareness that you are someone who is killing people.

Moral identity can still be neutralized as a restraint in long-range war. But because it has a greater intellectual component than the human responses, it is neutralized in more complex and interesting ways. The main ones have to do with passivity, the fragmentation of responsibility, and the moral slide from one precedent to another.

Institutional Momentum and Moral Inertia

A policy can be started because there are circumstances which seem to justify it and then it can take on a life of its own. The circumstances change to remove the justification. If the policy were not already in existence, it would not be embarked on. But, because it has been institutionalized, it carries on with its own momentum. And people do not feel guilty about participating in it, as they would about proposing it in the new circumstances.

Keynes described the officials who had perfected the instrument of the blockade of Germany and so were reluctant to give it up when the war was over. It is inconceivable that those officials would have had a clear conscience if, after the war, they had proposed to start starving German civilians by a blockade.

In the Second World War area bombing was drifted into partly because accurate night bombing of military targets was impossible and partly as a substitute in Stalin's eyes for a second front. In the last stage of the campaign, which included the bombing of Dresden, the second front was successfully established and command of the skies made possible accurate daytime bombing of military targets, but the policy had a momentum of its own and carried on in conditions in which it would not have been started.

The atomic bomb was developed as a deterrent against a possible Nazi bomb and probably would not have been developed simply as a weapon against Japan, but removal of the Nazi threat did not stop the programme.

In all these cases, many people were relatively untroubled by thoughts about their own participation in killing civilians. Although the difference in response is dubiously rational, going with the momentum of the established policy is far less troubling to the sense of moral identity than actively starting a new policy. Conscience is protected by a kind of moral inertia.

The Fragmentation of Responsibility

So many people had a role in the blockade that no one in particular felt responsible. With the possible exception of Sir Arthur Harris, the same could be said of area bombing.

The extreme case was the atomic bomb. The pilots and air crew were obeying orders. The officers who gave the orders were part of a chain of command stretching back to the President. Some of the scientists thought they were just doing their job, turning over atomic power to mankind at large, to deal with according to its lights and values. Stimson's committee apparently felt constrained by what they thought were the opinions of Roosevelt and Churchill. And the President himself apparently thought the committee had decided the bomb's use was necessary and that his role was to decide only the time and place. No one had to feel any qualms about being the person who rained down horrors on the people of Hiroshima and Nagasaki.

The Moral Slide

The blockade slid by degrees from having a slight effect to having a devastating impact. The blockade made area bombing seem acceptable. Area bombing was reached by a gentle slide from military bombing. The bombing of German cities made acceptable the bombing of Japanese ones, which in turn allowed the slide to the atomic bomb. The slide went on from the Hiroshima bomb to Nagasaki. Bishop Bell's worries about precedent effects were more completely vindicated even than, at his most pessimistic, he can have expected.

If worries about moral identity were avoided by this gradual slide, this suggests a widespread concern with what can be called relative moral identity. On this approach, what matters is not just what sort of person you are. The main concern is how you compare with other people. The question is not whether you are prepared to be someone who destroys a town, killing by horrible means most of the people in it. It is how you compare with previous commanders who did things like that.

Moral Debate and Moral Identity

The human responses are usually quick and fairly unreflective. You see the man holding up his trousers and you feel he is a fellow human being whom you cannot shoot. The sense of moral identity has an intellectual content which contrasts with this. How you feel about being a person who takes part in a bombing raid depends in quite large part on what you think about the justification given for it.

The debates about the Just War, about the intentional killing of civilians and about the doctrine of double effect are all relevant to people's moral identity. There is plausibility in the view that, if an act is morally the best one open to you, then you are not morally a worse person for carrying it out. (Some challenge this view, but they would accept that it is still relevant that the act was morally the best – or least bad – of those possible.)

This part of our moral resources is open-ended: it can be strengthened or weakened by thought and discussion. This is of some importance, particularly in view of the assumptions behind some popular ways of weakening the restraints of moral identity in war. When explicitly spelled out, appeals to institutional momentum and moral inertia, to the fragmentation of responsibility, and to relative moral identity all invite criticism. This part of our psychology does not have to be taken as given.

PART THREE

TRIBALISM

We had fed the heart on fantasies,
The heart's grown brutal from the fare;
More substance in our enmities
Than in our love . . .
> W.B. Yeats, 'The Stare's Nest by My Window',
> in *Meditations in Time of Civil War*

CHAPTER 14

Rwanda

This was not death as I had seen it in South Africa, or Eritrea, or Northern Ireland. Nothing could have prepared me for the scale of what I witnessed. It is this immensity of evil that prompts me to speak of the 'soul of man' . . . I felt there was enough decency and love around to nourish the gift of hope. There will be many who say that I was foolish, naïve to ever have had such faith in man. Maybe they are right. In any event after Rwanda I lost that optimism.

Fergal Keane, *Season of Blood: a Rwandan Journey*

Some wars and massacres seem primitive: smouldering hostility flares up into mutual killing. Between neighbours this hostility is so common that it can seem to be the human condition. There are Israelis and Palestinians, Greeks and Turks in Cyprus, Armenians and Azerbaijanis, Republicans and Loyalists in Northern Ireland, the group hostilities in India and also in Sri Lanka, the sectarian hostilities in Lebanon, and the Russians and the Chechens. The list could go on and on. There is even a restrained version in Canada. Some of these hostilities are contained. Others flare up into wars or massacres.

We call these hostilities tribal, sometimes thinking of this as metaphorical. The common view is that real tribes are in Africa, where the same tribal hatreds have been fought out in battles since the Stone Age. Calling the conflict in Northern Ireland tribal is a kind of rebuke: you are behaving like primitive tribes in Africa. But this picture is wrong. These other conflicts are tribal in more than metaphor: in Ireland, Yugoslavia and elsewhere they are as literal enactments of tribal hostility as those in Africa. The picture of Africa is wrong too. Some of the tribal divisions are recent creations. The origins of African tribal war and massacre are more complex than the 'ancient hatreds' account allows.

Genocide

What took place in Rwanda in the mid-1990s was not war but genocide. It was committed against the Tutsis by the Hutus. Tutsis tend to be tall and Hutus tend to be short. The Tutsis owned cattle and the Hutus farmed the land. In pre-colonial times, the Tutsis were the ruling tribe and sometimes exploited the Hutus ruthlessly. The dominant status of the Tutsis had been supported by German and then Belgian colonial rule. At the end of the colonial period, the Hutus rose up and seized power, killing many Tutsis.

A legacy of Hutu resentment continued after the Tutsi dominance ended. In the 1960s, after independence, there were outbreaks of mass killing of Tutsis by Hutus. In 1990 the Rwandan Patriotic Front, mainly made up of Tutsi exiles, invaded Rwanda from Uganda. Genocidal killing of Tutsis started in 1994 after Juvenal Habyarimana, the (Hutu) President of Rwanda, was killed in a plane crash. The Tutsis, probably unfairly, were blamed.

Hutu roadblocks were set up and the country was scoured for Tutsis, each ten houses having one man appointed to conduct a systematic search. Tutsis were denounced by their neighbours and then killed. Thousands of their corpses floated down river to Tanzania and Uganda. Perhaps a million people were killed in a few months.

Among the massacres was one at Ntarama, where people sought shelter in the school and in the church. Busloads of soldiers came and killed everyone they could. One woman (whose sister had been killed) took her own son and ran away. She described the desperation to which parents were reduced by the Hutu, who occupied both banks of the river:

> The Interahamwe [Hutu militia] on the Ntarama side ordered us to commit suicide by throwing ourselves into the river. In desperation and in the hope of avoiding an even worse death under the machete, very many people jumped and drowned, including many women with babies strapped to their backs. Knowing the death that awaited them, fathers threw their children into the river as a last gesture of love.[1]

A massacre at Kibeho was seen by a schoolgirl, Yvette. She saw many brutal killings, including a baby killed with a machete and thrown down the toilet. Yvette received two blows which nearly killed her. Later she was interrogated, beaten, raped and made pregnant. She saw many men, women and children thrown alive into a common grave and then being stoned when they asked for water.[2]

Fergal Keane visited Nyarubuye, where about 3,000 people had been killed. Corpses were everywhere, many of them in the church. One dead man had his arms raised against the machete blows. There were decapitated children in classrooms. Among the dead were a mother and her children, who had tried to hide under the school desks. Keane also went to orphanages for children who had seen their parents hacked to death. When asleep, 'some called for dead parents; others screamed out in the grip of some nightmare'. There were 'little boys and girls who had literally died of sorrow, withdrawing from everyone and refusing to eat or drink, until they finally wasted away'.[3]

The Hate Campaign

Propaganda stirred up hatred and fear of the Tutsis. But in some ways the close-up brutality is like a much larger My Lai, and suggests that the human responses were also overwhelmed by some powerful emotional state.

Tribal hostility is the obvious powerful emotion and Rwanda looks like a classic case of traditional tribal hatred erupting into massacre. The emotion is correctly identified, but it is too simple to think of it as either 'traditional' or as just 'erupting'.

The tribal picture needs complicating. The tribes were not sharply divided. They spoke the same language, had a shared culture and there were many marriages between the two tribes. The Tutsis were as much a ruling class as a ruling tribe. Hutus who grew rich and bought cattle became Tutsis. Only during the colonial period did the division become more rigid as identity cards locked people into a tribe for life.

The genocide was not a spontaneous eruption of tribal hatred, it was planned by people wanting to keep power. There was a long government-led hate campaign against the Tutsis. In 1990 the journal *Kangura* published 'The Hutu Ten Commandments', one of which said that any Hutu who married, employed or even befriended a Tutsi woman was a traitor. Another told Hutus to 'stop having mercy on' the Tutsis.[4]

Leon Mugsera, an academic who has a PhD from a Canadian university, said the Tutsis were the accomplices of the Rwandan Patriotic Front, who were 'cockroaches'. He asked about Tutsi families with a son away, possibly with the Front: 'What are we waiting for to decimate these families and these people who recruit for the RPF?' If the system did not punish them, 'we, the people, are obliged to take responsibility ourselves and wipe out this scum.' There was a legend that the Tutsis came from Ethiopia. Mugsera urged they be sent back there, by the river: in other words, dead.[5]

Radio Television Libre des Milles Collines, a Hutu station owned by relatives of the President, poured out propaganda against the Tutsis: they planned to enslave the Hutus; they were dishonest; they should be excluded from business, education and public life. After Habyarimana's plane crash, the radio station urged killing Tutsis: 'The grave is only half full. Who will help us to fill it?' and, 'By 5 May, the country must be completely cleansed of Tutsis.' Children were included: 'We will not repeat the mistake of 1959. The children must be killed too.'[6]

The human responses were overwhelmed in the killers by tribal hatred, but this emotion was itself a product of conscious political manipulation.

The World's Passivity

A fuller account of the genocide also has to ask why the United Nations and the world did not prevent it.

The United Nations had 2,500 men in Rwanda. When the genocide began, ten UN troops from Belgium were killed. UN troops saved each other, but were ordered not to use force to save Rwandan victims. The UN then withdrew all but 270 of its troops. One Rwandan Minister, Marc Rugenera, commented that the UN force 'did very little to help people when the crisis began. They had armoured carriers and tanks. What did they bring these weapons for if they are going to stand by when people are being butchered in front of their very eyes?'[7]

The UN lacked the ability to act without the support of its more powerful members, notably the United States. The American government wanted to avoid a repetition of its unsuccessful intervention in Somalia, in which thirty American troops were killed. President Clinton issued a directive on UN military operations. American support was dependent on demanding financial and military conditions. The operations would also have to be directly relevant to American interests. These conditions excluded American support for UN intervention to stop the genocide.

There is a legal obligation to take action against genocide and the Clinton administration was worried about this. State Department officials were instructed not to use the word 'genocide' about Rwanda. At the United Nations the United States blocked a resolution authorizing the use of up to 5,500 men because of reluctance to involve American troops. Later, 6,800 troops and police were sent, mainly from Africa and after delays caused by arguments over the finances. The Security Council followed the American lead and avoided using the word 'genocide'. The upshot was humanitarian aid instead of effective police action.

Events like those in Rwanda are caused partly by a tribal psychology locally stirred up. They are also caused because the rest of the world has not created the means to prevent them. Outside Rwanda, the international response veered between indifference and a compassion which was not translated into action to stop the killing.

CHAPTER 15

The Tribal Trap

> We lived happily together for many years and now it has come to killing
> each other's babies. What is happening to us?
>> Indira Hadziomerović, mourning in Sarajevo,
>>> *Independent* (8 August 1992)

Our picture of tribal war is of aggression: two groups, say Serbs and
Croats, go for each other in the way two angry men come to blows in an
argument after a car crash. This model is primitive and explains little. As
Indira Hadziomerović said, Yugoslavs had lived together happily for years.
We have to ask how the relationship changed to the point where they could
kill each other's babies.

Tribal conflicts rarely just 'break out'. Hostility is enflamed by the
nationalist rhetoric of politicians. Other groups then feel threatened and
react with their own defensive nationalism. People are pushed into the trap
by politicians. Then, in psychologically deeper ways, the rival groups
become mutually trapped by their responses to each other. This is how
Yugoslavia fell apart.

Tito's Yugoslavia

Yugoslavia was a federation of six republics. There were three small
republics, Slovenia, Macedonia and Montenegro, each on a different edge
of the country. Centre-stage were the three large republics: Serbia, Croatia
and Bosnia-Herzegovina. In these three, ethnic differences were under-
scored by religious ones. Serbia was mainly Orthodox, Croatia was mainly
Catholic, while in Bosnia the largest group was Islamic.

The detail is more splotchy than these smooth generalizations. Serbia
included Kosovo, with a large Albanian majority. Croatia included the
Krajina, which was mainly Serb. There were also Serb and Croatian
minorities in Bosnia.

In President Tito's time, there were Yugoslav patriots. The Yugoslavs had largely liberated themselves from the Germans and Italians. Communism had not been imposed on them by the Soviet army and there was pride in Tito's independence from Moscow. Many felt they were Yugoslavs, as well as Serbs, Croats or Bosnians. There were many marriages across the barriers.

But the divisions between the republics were serious. Tito tried to ensure that power was shared between the different nationalities. The Serbs, who were 40 per cent of the population, were much the largest group. Tito made appointments to ensure that they did not dominate the federal institutions, but to balance this, he gave Serbs positions of importance in other republics such as Croatia. Although Kosovo was part of Serbia, he gave most power to the Albanian majority there. Maintaining this balance was Tito's success, impressive in the light of what followed.

What followed came partly from the weaknesses of Tito's federation, however. The carefully constructed balance aroused resentments. When Tito died in 1980, although there was little support in the republics for full independence, there was nationalist feeling. Serbs felt they were a persecuted minority in Kosovo. Croatians and others resented the influence of Serbs in their republics. Many people wanted more autonomy from the federation. This local nationalism in turn was felt as a threat by minorities.

The imposed federal balance was not sufficiently deep-rooted to survive Tito's death. Although his rule was too liberal for Moscow, he still ran a one-party state with a strong secret police. The democratic habits of tolerance, persuasion and compromise had not had a chance to grow.

After Yugoslavia: Serbia and Croatia

In Kosovo the Serbian minority felt threatened. Kosovo is of great importance to Serbs. The seat of the Patriarch of the Serbian Orthodox Church is there, at Pec. And they still commemorate the Battle of Kosovo, in 1389, when the Serbs were defeated by the Turks on the Field of Blackbirds. Serbs killed then are great martyrs of their Church. Kosovo, finally regained from Turkey, was a symbol of Serbian nationhood.

But, when Tito died, 90 per cent of people in Kosovo were Albanians, who did not accept Serbian domination. In 1981 Albanians in Kosovo demonstrated in support of independence from Serbia. The demonstration was crushed by the federal army and police.

Some Kosovo Serbs resented what they saw as discrimination against them. There were complaints of rapes and of being forced to move. In

1987 the leader of the Serbian Communist Party, Slobodan Milosević, went to hear their grievances and was met by a huge crowd. The police and the crowd clashed, the police using batons, the crowd throwing stones. Milosević told the crowd, 'No one should dare to beat you.' He was treated as a hero. He responded to this with a passionate Serb nationalist speech:

You should stay here. This is your land. These are your houses. Your meadows and gardens. Your memories. You shouldn't abandon your land just because it's difficult to live, because you are pressured by injustice and degradation. It was never part of the Serbian and Montenegrin character to give up in the face of obstacles, to demobilize when it's time to fight . . . You should stay here for the sake of your ancestors and descendants. Otherwise your ancestors would be defiled and descendants disappointed. But I don't suggest that you stay, endure, and tolerate a situation you're not satisfied with. On the contrary, you should change it.[1]

Milosević forced out the incumbent and took over the Serbian presidency. As President, he addressed enormous nationalist rallies, using huge crowds to bully into submission the previously autonomous provinces of Vojvodina and Kosovo. He then looked beyond Serbia. He wanted Serbian rule wherever any Serbs lived. He used intimidation by crowds to replace the government of Montenegro with his own supporters. His speeches alarmed other republics. There was a huge rally to commemorate the six hundredth anniversary of the Battle of Kosovo. Milosević said, 'The Kosovo heroism does not allow us to forget that, at one time, we were brave and dignified and one of the few who went into battle undefeated. Six centuries later, again we are in battles and quarrels. They are not armed battles, though such things should not be excluded yet.'[2]

Milosević aroused fear in Croatia, where moderate nationalism gave ground to a more extreme form, supported by Franjo Tudjman, a former General in the Yugoslav army. Tudjman defended the old pro-Nazi Ustase state, saying it was not the creation of fascist criminals: 'It also stood for the historic aspirations of the Croatian people for an independent state. They knew that Hitler planned to build a new European order.' Tudjman also said, 'Thank God my wife is not a Jew or a Serb.'[3] In the 1990 election, Tudjman ran a strongly nationalist campaign and became President.

Tudjman's new constitution, which ignored the Serbian minority, defined Croatia as the nation-state of the Croats. This alarmed Serbs, who found they had to take loyalty oaths. Some lost their jobs. Some suffered attacks on their houses.

In Krajina, a part of Croatia with a Serbian majority, extreme Serbian nationalism became popular. A Serb assembly declared a referendum on Serbian independence: only Serbs were to vote. Croatian helicopters, sent to stop the referendum, were turned back by Yugoslav army jets. Krajina, armed by Milosević's government, was now out of Croatia's control. The Krajina Serb leaders declared independence. Armed clashes followed. The Yugoslav national army was sent in. Serbia recognized the independence of Krajina and promised help. In clashes, Serbian villagers killed Croatian police. Tudjman said this was war against Croatia, while the Serbian government said Croatia was attacking the entire Serb nation.

The secession of Slovenia, after disputes with the federal government and with Serbia, gave Tudjman the opportunity to declare Croatian independence at the same time. Both countries were recognized by the then European Community. The (mainly Serbian) Yugoslav army entered Slovenia. For two weeks there were minor skirmishes. Then Serbia accepted Slovenian independence and the Yugoslav army invaded Croatia.

For eighty-six days they surrounded, besieged and bombarded Vukovar. When the army finally captured it, they let the women of the town choose to go to Serbia or Croatia. But the men were held, often to be ill-treated or killed. The Yugoslav army then besieged Dubrovnik. They had taken 30 per cent of Croatia by the end of the year. The war then reached a stalemate, with the Croatian army growing stronger. Milosević accepted international mediation. UN peace-keepers were sent and the Yugoslav army withdrew. Serbs and Croats were then to co-operate in the destruction of Bosnia.

Bosnia

In Bosnia, 44 per cent of the population were Islamic, 31 per cent were Serb and 17 per cent were Croat. Relations were often friendly. A family on a holy day might be visited by friends of other faiths. In the 1990 elections, the largest Muslim party was led by Alija Izetbegović, who hoped to get beyond tribal politics:

> By their oppression the communists created this longing among people to express their religious or national identity. Perhaps in four or five years we shall have passed through the minefield to the horizon of civil society! For now, unfortunately, our party *must* be sectional . . . There is a real risk of civil war here; our main aim as a party is to keep Bosnia-Hercegovina together.[4]

Izetbegović's party won the largest number of seats. To hold the country together, he chose to govern in coalition with the major Serb and Croat parties. But there was already a Serbian nationalist movement, parallel to that in Croatia, which wanted to secede from Bosnia and unite with the Krajina Serbs.

By 1991 Milosević was both supplying arms and dictating policy to

Radovan Karadzić, the Bosnian Serb leader. Karadzić, who had been jailed for mortgage fraud, started politics in a Green party and not as a nationalist. In 1990 he had spoken of closeness to Bosnian Muslims, saying there was no need for Serbs to fight for Christianity against Islam. But now, a year later, he was a militant Serb nationalist. He was also, perhaps implausibly, both a poet and a psychiatrist.

The tactics were the same as in Croatia. 'Serb Autonomous Regions' were declared and the Yugoslav national army moved in to support them. In 1992 a Bosnian referendum was held on the question: 'Are you in favour of a sovereign and independent Bosnia-Hercegovina, a state of equal citizens and nations of Muslims, Serbs, Croats and others who live in it?' Karadzić's party, supported by the Yugoslav army, told Serbs not to vote and blocked ballot boxes from areas they controlled. Sixty-four per cent of the electorate, including many Serbs, did vote and answered 'yes' almost unanimously to the question.

On the day of the referendum results, Serbian paramilitary forces tried to take over Sarajevo. They were thwarted by thousands of citizens putting up rival barricades. In April 1992 the European Community recognized Bosnia as an independent state. That day Serbian paramilitaries again tried to take over Sarajevo. They were opposed by between 50,000 and 100,000 demonstrators, who in turn were fired on.

Having failed to take over Sarajevo, Bosnian Serb forces besieged and bombarded it, killing thousands of people. Among many horrors in 1992, three stood out. Shells were fired at the maternity clinic, setting fire to it while 70 pregnant women and 173 babies were asleep inside. A mortar attack on a bread queue killed about 20 people and injured 160. And a busload of children was fired on, killing one three-year-old and another aged fourteen months. As Indira Hadziomerović said, it had come to killing each other's babies. The children's funeral was also the target of a mortar attack.

Other Serbian forces created a reign of terror in eastern Bosnia. There were at least 17 rape camps, where Bosnian women and girls were held for weeks and repeatedly raped. A European Community investigation later estimated that 20,000 women had been sexually violated. Some of the victims were as young as three or four.[5]

In their 'ethnic cleansing', the Serbian forces killed or drove out Muslims. In some areas houses would have the owners' ethnic group written by the door. Those with 'Serb' were untouched, while those with 'Muslim' or 'Croat' would be destroyed. Non-Serbs were sacked from their jobs and told to leave. Fearing for their lives, they were forced to sign away their property. Sometimes Muslims were locked in buildings, which were then burnt down. In Kozarac, 2,500 civilians were killed in seventy-two hours. Serbian tanks shelled the town. When the shelling stopped, loudspeakers promised that those who surrendered would be unharmed. When people emerged, the shelling started again. When the surrender was accepted, a Serb from the town pointed out important Muslims, including the mayor, the police chief and doctors. They were shot or had their throats cut.[6]

Non-Serbs were removed from some places in cattle trucks. Children died when the wagons were left for days in the hot sun. Some Bosnians went to concentration camps. Prisoners in Omarska were put in extremely crowded sheds, where they died of thirst, starvation or asphyxiation. To get water they were forced to sing pro-Serb songs for hours. They were beaten, tortured, mutilated and killed.[7] Some were made, on pain of death, to hit or even castrate each other. In the camp at Keraterm, 150 people were locked in a shed with no food or water. When they cried out for water, the guards shot through the doors, killing or wounding about forty of them. A few days later there were hardly any survivors.[8]

By August 1992 Serb forces had driven out 1.8 million Bosnians. UN relief agencies had at first accepted the refugees through Croatia, but then refused to do this, as it made them accomplices to the ethnic cleansing. The Serb troops then forced the refugees to cross the hazardous ground between the Serbian and Bosnian front lines. Many died on the journey across.[9]

The national army and the other Serb forces captured over half Bosnia in six weeks. The national army was then supposedly withdrawn. Bosnian Serb military operations were put under General Ratko Mladić. Milosević and the Bosnian Serb leaders then presented the conflict as a civil war.

At first the Bosnian Serb military actions were resisted by Bosnian Croatians and by the Croatian army. Bosnia and Croatia made a military alliance. But Izetbegović turned down a proposal for a confederation of Croatia and Bosnia. Then Bosnian Croatian leaders followed Bosnian Serb tactics and declared their own autonomous region. An understanding was reached between Milosević and Tudjman. Bosnian Muslims found themselves driven out again, this time by Croatian ethnic cleansing, which also included massacres and camps where people were tortured and starved to death. Bosnia was to be carved up by an improbable alliance of Serbs and Croats.

Creating a Spiral of Hatred

The war between Serbia and Croatia was not a purely spontaneous explosion of ethnic hatred. The hostility was stirred up by political leaders.

Slobodan Milosević's 'this is your land' speech in Kosovo aroused Serbian passions. It also frightened the Albanians and others who were not

Serbian. It was probably calculated – it turned him from being the embarrassed representative of the unpopular federal government into the champion of Serbian nationalism.

Milosević had been not a nationalist but a Communist. Many observers are sceptical about his more recent nationalism. Warren Zimmermann, the United States ambassador to Yugoslavia from 1989 to 1992, had many long talks with Milosević. Zimmermann saw him as a habitual liar, and described him as driven not by nationalism but by power:

> He has made a Faustian pact with nationalism as a way to gain and hold power. He is a man of extraordinary coldness. I never saw him moved by an individual case of human suffering; for him, people are groups (Serbs, Muslims) or simply abstractions. Nor did I ever hear him say a charitable or generous word about any human being, not even a Serb. This chilling personality trait made it possible for Milosević to condone, encourage, and even organize the unspeakable atrocities committed by Serbian citizens in the Bosnian war.[10]

In contrast to Milosević, Franjo Tudjman's nationalism is genuine and fanatical. In Tito's time he had been jailed for nationalist activities. Warren Zimmermann describes his Croatian nationalist movement as intolerant, anti-Serb and authoritarian, 'together with an aura of wartime fascism, which Tudjman has done nothing to dispel'. Zimmermann describes having lunch with Tudjman and listening to his ministers revile Serbs in racist terms.[11]

These two leaders, from very different motives, stirred up hostility between their peoples. Before they started, attitudes were far less polarized. In Serbia there was a lot of alarm at what Milosević was doing and some impressive opposition. In March 1991, in Belgrade, nearly 100,000 people demonstrated against him and the way his aggressive nationalism was leading to pariah status in the world community, in the style of Saddam Hussein's Iraq. One chant was 'Slobo, Saddam'. The demonstrations were crushed by tanks, but their size showed the scale of the propaganda campaign needed to line up support behind Milosević's nationalism.

The Serbian and Croatian governments used the same techniques of media manipulation. In Serbia the government dominated the television and radio stations. Pressures on independent newspapers were extreme. When *Borba* ran a report critical of the Serbian paramilitary leader Arkan, he arrived with armed men, threatened to 'liquidate' the writer, and made them print an interview with him.[12]

The Croatian government also used its control of the media to stir up fear among the Serbs. One magazine editor described a meeting at which Milosević 'outlined a strategy for provoking ethnic conflict in Croatia', and went on to say that 'a massive media campaign convinced the Serbs in Croatia that they were in danger of a "new genocide" '.[13]

In Croatia, especially during the war in Bosnia, the official media fabricated stories of atrocities against Croats and adopted a highly sceptical attitude towards well-attested stories of atrocities by Croats. Serbian journalists were dismissed, independent papers were shut down and at least one independent journalist was jailed.

In both Serbia and Croatia the media were used to stir up ethnic hostility. In Serbia the Croats were often represented as 'vampires'. Radovan Karadzić described the war in Croatia as a war against a 'vampirised fascist consciousness'.[14] During the rebellion of the Krajina Serbs, one headline in *Politika Ekspres* was 'Protecting Serbs from vampirical Ustase'. One Croatian newspaper, reporting on the killings in Borovo Selo, described the Serbian killers as 'beasts in human form', as 'bearded animals on two legs', and as 'bloodsuckers'.[15]

Slavenka Drakulić saw the stirring up of hostility as a prelude:

> Long before the real war, we had a media war, Serbian and Croatian journalists attacking the political leaders from the opposite republic as well as each other as if in some kind of dress rehearsal. So I could see a spiral of hatred descending on us, but until the first bloodshed it seemed to operate on the level of a power struggle that had nothing to do with the common people.[16]

Increasingly the media became dominated by racist fanatics. Serbian television gave time to Vojislav Seselj, who thought that all the Kosovo Albanians should be killed. One journalist said to Warren Zimmermann, 'You Americans would become nationalists and racists too if your media were totally in the hands of the Ku Klux Klan.'[17]

The Belief Trap

The media spread misinformation, for instance about Serb atrocities in Bosnia. The Sarajevo bread queue massacre was attributed to the Muslims, who were supposed to have stage-managed it as anti-Serb propaganda. It was said that most of the victims were Serbs, and that their bodies had been replaced by corpses of Muslims killed elsewhere.[18]

People assess the plausibility of what they are told in the light of what other information they have. Where nearly all the information they have on a topic comes from distorting sources, they may be trapped inside a system of false beliefs. Information which contradicts that system of beliefs may be rejected as implausible.

The propaganda was so sustained and consistent that much of it was accepted. In 1992 people in Belgrade were asked in a survey to say who had been bombarding Sarajevo from the surrounding hills. Only 20.5 per cent thought it was Serbs, while 38.4 per cent thought the answer was 'Muslim–Croat forces'.[19] Contrary views became hard to believe. In the same year as the survey, one journalist said that Serbian television could by then allow opposition views to be expressed: 'Reality sounds like the blackest anti-Serbian propaganda, and anyone who describes it will frighten people and turn them against him.'[20]

The Trap of Hobbesian Fear

War can result from fear of being attacked as well as from actual attack. Thucydides saw this as the true cause of the Peloponnesian War: 'What made war inevitable was the growth of Athenian power and the fear which this caused in Sparta.'[21]

Thomas Hobbes, who translated Thucydides and also watched civil war break out in England, saw this fear of the power of others as a prime cause of conflict: 'And from this diffidence of one another, there is no way for any man to secure himselfe, so reasonable as Anticipation; that is, by force, or wiles, to master the persons of all men he can, so long, till he see no other power great enough to endanger him.'[22] The Hobbesian trap captures groups as well as individuals. Where two groups are a potential threat to each other, the resulting mutual fear gives each a reason for striking first. And, since each can see that the other has this reason, the circle of fear is reinforced.

Hobbesian fear led to a defensive–aggressive nationalism in the republics near Serbia. The manipulation of ethnic and religious tribalism by Serbian politicians aroused fear in other groups, whose politicians in turn also played on tribalism. The defeated candidate in the 1990 Croatian election said later, 'Milosević's aggressive policy was the strongest propaganda for Tudjman.' (At the time of the Belgrade demonstrations the next year, one student leader urged Milosević to resign: 'If you resign tomorrow, Franjo Tudjman would lose all support within fifteen days. He built his myth on you.')[23] With politicians in both Serbia and Croatia whipping up fear of each other, the trap was harder to escape.

When fighting starts, people are pulled more deeply into the psychological trap. On a flight from London, Slavenka Drakulić (a Croatian) heard a girl, no older than twelve, talking to her friend: 'If we were forced to land in Zagreb, I would have to lie about my Serbian nationality, or those Croats would kill me on the spot.' Slavenka Drakulić comments, 'We are all trapped. The two girls are at war, too, and even if hostilities were to cease instantly, how long would it take for these girls not to be afraid of landing at Zagreb?'[24]

The Trap of the Tribal State

In the former Yugoslavia most people cannot have wanted ethnic conflict. About 40 per cent of all families were ethnically mixed. But ethnic national units seemed the only protection against threats from other groups.

There are pluralist states and tribal states. Pluralist states include, and give equal citizenship to, people with different characteristics such as ethnicity or religion. A tribal state is thought of as the state of a particular people or 'nation', who are marked out by a characteristic such as ethnicity or religion. Pluralist states can develop a kind of nationalism. Although the United States is a pluralist state, there are nationalist emotions, for instance when American hostages are taken. Nationalist movements, however, are usually bound up with the desire to create, defend or enlarge a tribal state.

A tribal state poses no problem if it has clear-cut boundaries and if its territory is occupied only by members of the tribal group. But most territories contain minority ethnic or religious groups. The tribal state is seen as a threat or an insult to the minorities who are not members of the tribe.

In regions of mixed population, believers in the tribal state have to be careful how they advocate it. At a peace conference chaired by Lord Carrington, the Serbian delegation urged that it was painful for Serbs to live under Croatian rule. Carrington responded to this with a plan which gave many cultural and political rights to Serbs outside Serbia. This plan was then rejected by Milosević, partly because it granted the same rights to Albanians inside Serbia.

Milosević pressed for a Serbian tribal state not just where Serbs were in the majority, but wherever Serbs lived, which aroused fear among others living alongside Serbs. In the 1990 elections the defensive reaction of these others was to move towards their own tribal states. Tudjman's victory in Croatia led to a state for the Croatian people only.

Milosević's demand for a Serbian tribal state led to the Croatian defensiveness which elected Tudjman. Tudjman's Croatian tribal state led to the defensive demand by the Serbian minority in Croatia for their own tribal state. Fear is central. The trap of the tribal state is a version of the Hobbesian trap.

CHAPTER 16

The Political Containment of Tribalism

I have no respect for any of these people, Karadzić, Boban or Izetbegović.
Only Tito. He was a killer but look, if you have three wild criminals at each
other's throats, who wouldn't want a policeman around somewhere?
Fahrudin Alihodzić, Bosnian Commander in Travnik,
quoted in Ed Vulliamy, *Seasons in Hell*

Force is the ultimate arbiter and any diplomatic policy that does not rely on
carrots and sticks will not really get you very far. Without a club in the
closet, without a credible threat of force, policy becomes bluff, bluster.
Herbert Okun, UN Special Adviser, quoted in James Gow, *Triumph
of the Lack of Will: International Diplomacy and the Yugoslav War*

To avoid repeating what went wrong in Yugoslavia, we need alternatives to
the trap of the tribal state. Above all, we need to weaken the grip of
Hobbesian fear.

The Soft-edged Nation-state

Often the best way of containing tribalism is to concede to nationalism,
particularly where there is a tribal nation or something close to it. The
former Czechoslovakia provides a model. If the Slovaks want to separate
from the Czechs, both groups will live next to each other more happily
without the tribal conflict generated by the refusal of a divorce. This
applies to other possible cases. If the majority of Scots or of Basques or of
Quebecois really want their own independent state, 'yes' is the answer
which defuses tribal conflict, and 'no' starts the spiral of resentment.

But the tribal state is not usually the best way to grant the demands of
nationalism. The simple case of the tribal nation is rare. More common is
the Russian doll problem: inside one nation is a smaller one wanting to get

out, but inside that second one is a yet smaller one wanting to get out. Inside Yugoslavia, Croatia wants independence. But inside Croatia, the Krajina wants independence. And even in the Krajina, there were non-Serbs who had to be excluded from the independence referendum. Because of the Russian doll problem, any policy of giving independence to groups which want it has to be combined with guarantees for minorities within the new nation-state.

The problem is so common that a standard set of minimum requirements for minorities could be a condition of international recognition. The policy would be one which both favoured nationalism and limited it. Recognition of independent nationhood would be more readily available, but national autonomy would be more restricted. What nations did to minorities within their borders would no longer be regarded as a domestic affair.

In many cases there is no serious possibility of a tribal nation. Shared or disputed territory necessitates some sort of pluralism. We could be more imaginative about the kinds of pluralism which are possible.

Where geographical boundaries are disputed, there is a case for blurring the conceptual boundaries of the nation-state. Northern Ireland, for instance, is like the ambiguous duck–rabbit figure discussed by philosophers. It has usually been seen either as a duck or as a rabbit: 'The six counties belong in the Republic' versus 'Ulster is part of the United Kingdom'. No solution is likely to work unless it takes account of both views. Ideally, a solution would encourage tolerance of ambiguity, a recognition that it is not quite a duck, nor quite a rabbit. The beginnings of this can be seen in attempts to make peace, with proposals for shared power in an autonomous local administration and guarantees of respect for minority rights.

Another step would be to give up the assumption that nation-states must have hard borders: that any piece of territory is either part of one country or of another. Avishai Margalit once proposed that Jerusalem should be the capital both of Israel and of a Palestinian state. If countries can be soft-edged, Northern Ireland could be part of both the Republic and the United Kingdom. Already people can choose citizenship of either country, or dual nationality.

Such an approach obviously raises many questions and problems. Can two independent countries harmonize enough to share a province or a city? What happens when they disagree? The detailed answers will be messy compared to the hard-edged nation-state, but duck–rabbit figures are messy. Traditional policies were made by those who saw the duck trying to twist the figure one way and those who saw the rabbit trying to twist it the other way. The policies were not such a success that messy alternatives should be excluded. The emergence of nation-states with soft edges expresses a policy of adapting states to fit people, rather than making people fit states.

Thomas Hobbes and the United Nations

Thomas Hobbes saw a way out of the trap of mutual fear and violence: an authority strong enough to impose peace and to police it. Hobbes spoke of this as the 'Leviathan', to which we owe our peace and defence: 'he hath the use of so much Power and Strength conferred on him, that by terror thereof, he is inabled to forme the wills of them all'.[1]

Hobbes might have recognized Tito as Leviathan in Yugoslavia. But after Tito some new Leviathan was needed, and in other places threatened by tribal war an international Leviathan may be needed. Some people believe we already have this needed peace-keeping authority in the United Nations, but, in Bosnia as in Rwanda, the UN fell short of Leviathan.

The UN recognized Bosnia in May 1992 when the Serbian attack was just starting. UN units were sent, but the Security Council did not back the use of force. The aim was a negotiated peace. An arms embargo was placed on Yugoslavia, which favoured the Serbs because Bosnia could not then buy arms to defend itself. The Serbs had the Yugoslav national army. UN forces were to deter further attacks and to get food and medical supplies to civilians. As in Rwanda, humanitarian aid took the place of imposing peace.

In Bosnia the humanitarian supplies were not trivial. The effect of lack of medical supplies could be seen in Zepa. Operations, sometimes on children, had to be carried out with a carpenter's saw and without anaesthetic. One field officer working for UNHCR (United Nations High Commission for Refugees) said the supplies saved 100,000 lives. But the no-force policy failed to stop the war. The UN did not arouse Hobbesian terror in the Serbian leaders. It was not the all-powerful sovereign which would impose peace. It responded to aggression with gestures and scolding.

Because the Security Council had not supported force, the UN in Bosnia had to bargain with the Serb forces to get food convoys through. During the siege of Sarajevo, the UN forces could keep the airport open for humanitarian supplies only on Serb terms. These included the UN stopping people trying to escape and confiscating their food.

Denied the use of force, the UN on the ground found its authority endlessly mocked. In 1992 a Serb soldier shot Hakija Turajlić, the Deputy Prime Minister of Bosnia, while he was being carried in a UN vehicle. Repeated ceasefire agreements were immediately broken. At one ceasefire signing ceremony at Sarajevo airport, the agreement was broken so quickly that the signatories had to take cover under the table they had just used.

In 1993 the UN declared six 'safe areas', but the troops of UNPROFOR (the United Nations Protection Force) were allowed to use their weapons only to protect themselves, not to protect the Bosnians. The Serbian forces bombarded the 'safe areas' and captured two of them in 1995, at Srebrenica and Zepa.

Those implementing UN policy sometimes felt shamed by its passivity. One UN spokesman said, 'we have to defend a policy which no one can coherently explain to us'. A British officer with the UN forces wrote a troubled letter about

> how my children will regard our role in this genocidal conflict. How did we stand by and watch the systematic destruction of Sarajevo by Serb artillery? . . . What did we think while we watched entire communities dispossessed and flee into a cauldron of shellfire to die on the streets of some further besieged village of cold and neglect?[2]

One officer found the passive policy too much to stomach. General Morillon led a convoy of vehicles with food, medicine and a few soldiers into Srebrenica, which the Serbs were shelling and were about to capture. The Serbs reduced their fire and held back from taking the town while he was there. The townspeople, who expected to be killed when the town fell, blocked his exit. He decided to stay and raised the UN flag: 'I have now decided to stay in order to calm your anguish and try to save you. I am here, and here I stay.' The Serbs stopped their attack and agreed to allow UN forces to stay in the town and to let supplies in and some refugees out.

After Morillon left, the Serb forces renewed the shelling and killed many people, including children in a school playground. Larry Hollingworth of UNHCR said, 'My first thought was for the commander who gave the order to attack. I hope he burns in the hottest corner of hell. My second thought was for the soldiers who loaded the breeches and fired the guns. I hope their sleep is forever punctuated by the screams of the children and the cries of their mothers.'[3] But the first thought of higher UN authorities was for General Morillon. Two weeks after his defence of Srebrenica, he was dismissed from his Bosnian command.

The Serbian forces under General Mladić captured Srebrenica. They held the women and children of the town in pens. The men were taken for 'questioning' and killed. Dutch UN troops who saw this had no authority to stop it and could only urge the victims not to panic. Mladić spoke of them with contempt: 'Do you think the Dutch are afraid of me? I don't fear them. I am stronger than all of you. They cannot protect you.'[4]

Sometimes Bosnians had a chance to comment on the performance of the UN. When the Secretary-General, Boutros Boutros-Ghali visited him, the Bosnian Vice-President said that Sarajevo was the world's biggest concentration camp: 'People are dying slowly. Old people and children are suffering enormously. All the visits by foreign dignitaries produced hope, but after they left the situation continued to get worse. We hope that after your visit things will become better.' Boutros-Ghali wished Bosnia a Happy New Year and said that the UN had set up a standing committee for peace talks, with six working committees, and had appointed a full-time co-chairman.

At Boutros-Ghali's press conference, Vedrana Bozinović, a young woman who reported for a Sarajevo radio station, said:

> You too are guilty for every single raped woman, for every single murdered man, woman and child . . . We think that you are guilty for our suffering. What do you want before you will do something? How many more victims are needed before you act? Aren't 12,000 enough? Do you want 15,000 or 20,000? Will that be enough?

Boutros-Ghali said the UN wanted peace through negotiation and that ten places in the world were worse off than Sarajevo. Vedrana Bozinović, crying, said, 'We are dying, Mr Ghali, we are dying.' Boutros-Ghali said time was needed for a peaceful solution. Vedrana Bozinović asked, 'How much time?' Boutros-Ghali said, 'I cannot give you a target date.'[5]

Sometimes the UN tried a mild toughness which proved inadequate. In 1995, after new heavy shelling of Sarajevo, the UN gave the Serbs an ultimatum, which was ignored. NATO then bombed a Serb ammunition depot at Pale. The Bosnian Serb army took UN soldiers as hostages. A Serb telephoned the UN and said, 'Three UN observers are now in the site of the warehouse. Any more bombing, they will be the first to go. Understood?'[6]

After the Serb forces took hostages, the UN told NATO to stay away. It allowed Bosnian Serb police to replace the UNPROFOR escorts of its convoys. The UN had promised not to negotiate with hostage-takers. But General Janvier negotiated with General Mladić, obtaining the release of the hostages in return for no more air strikes.

When the Serb forces attacked the safe area of Goradze, bombing the hospital, minor retaliatory air strikes were made. The Serbs took UN hostages and there were telephone negotiations between a Bosnian Serb official and General Michael Rose of the UN. Jovan Zametica spoke to General Rose in a tone which Hobbes did not imagine would be used by people addressing Leviathan: 'Don't mess with us, Mike. Don't fuck with us.'[7]

The powers of the United Nations were limited by what the international community would allow. Suppose Boutros-Ghali had been persuaded of the need to force the Serbian leaders to stop their attack. This would not have been enough. The United Nations has no army of its own. It has to ask individual countries such as Canada or India to supply forces. Overwhelmingly, it needs the support of the United States and the countries of the European Union.

Thomas Hobbes and the International Community

If the United Nations does not get the title, perhaps the international community is the real Leviathan. But the 'international community' is a fiction. The response to UN requests for forces may depend on calculations of national interest or of electoral popularity.

The leaders of the then European Community started with a disastrous decision, taken with their minds half on other things. EC recognition of Slovenia and Croatia in 1991 was one trigger of the war. There were warnings that to recognize the independence of some of the republics without an overall settlement would be dangerous. Lord Carrington said it 'might well be the spark that sets Bosnia-Herzegovina alight'. But the German Foreign Minister, Hans-Dietrich Genscher, pressed for recognition. At first, his only support was from Belgium and Denmark, but, at the final vote, his view prevailed. There were suspicions that Britain had changed sides as part of a deal to obtain an opt-out from parts of the Maastricht Treaty. Avoiding catastrophe in Bosnia seems not to have been the central consideration.

Throughout the war in Bosnia, the leaders of the European Union were unable to agree on any serious measures to defend another European country from being attacked and destroyed or to protect people from the horrors of 'ethnic cleansing'. Europe was not totally unresponsive to the crisis. As well as attempts to arrange peace, there were several European military contributions to the UN forces, but the contingents were small. European, and especially British, lack of enthusiasm forced the UN to abandon plans for a substantial force of 100,000 men. The weaker military presence made decisive intervention harder. European leaders feared reprisals against their small contingents on the ground.

Sometimes the spotlight was turned on the inadequacy of the European response. The US government wanted to end the arms embargo on Bosnia, but this was opposed by Britain and France. President Izetbegović went to the Security Council and made an emotional speech, saying, 'Defend us, or let us defend ourselves.' After his speech, no one spoke. The silence lasted at least a minute. Afterwards, the US ambassador to the UN, Madeleine Albright, said to the British ambassador, Sir David Hannay, 'I'm stunned, stunned. Why didn't you say anything?' She asked the French ambassador the same question.

President Izetbegović's plea to the UN Security Council challenged countries to show where they stood in the face of the worst human catastrophe in Europe since the Second World War. It was a moment which showed in sharp focus the moral quality of governments. It is dismaying to have been represented by an ambassador who, no doubt under instructions, was satisfied with silence. Worse was to come. The press was given an attempted justification: 'The British view was that no questions or diplomatic niceties were required because Mr Izetbegović had been emotional rather than specific about his requirements, and because it was not a proper meeting, simply a chance to hear his views.'[8]

The American response was less inadequate than the European one. The United States opposed the arms embargo and it eventually arranged the Dayton peace agreement. But at first the main concern of the American government was to avoid involvement. Before the 1992 election, the Bush administration wanted the issue played down. George Kenney resigned in protest from the State Department:

> The Bush administration pronouncements on the Yugoslav crisis between February and August exhibited the worst sort of hypocrisy. I know; I wrote them ... My job was to make it appear as though the US was active and concerned about the situation and, at the same time, give no one the impression that the US was actually going to do something significant about it.[9]

The government, not wanting pressure to intervene, discounted reports of atrocities. The Serbian siege of Sarajevo was described as 'all sides' shelling each other. The next year, under the Clinton administration, three other people resigned from the State Department on the same grounds.

There were efforts to arrange a negotiated peace. Lord Carrington, on behalf of the European Union, and later Cyrus Vance and Lord Owen (on behalf of the United States and the European Union) ran peace conferences and proposed peace plans.

Finally the Clinton administration persuaded the parties to accept the Dayton peace agreement, which stopped the war. Anyone must welcome that; but the weakness of all these efforts was the lack of any credible Hobbesian threat. The stronger parties in the negotiations had to be accommodated. The only peace plans which stood any chance of being accepted rewarded Serbian and Croatian aggression. The Serbian leaders, followed by the Croatian leaders, adopted the policy of forcible dismemberment of a state recognized by the United Nations. Some Bosnian Serbs carried out policies close to genocide. And the international community allowed them to gain by these policies. The message will have been noted round the world.

Policing the Global Village

Some ordinary villages are peaceful and well policed. The global village is of another kind. It has feuds and vendettas which often break into violence. All the inhabitants are armed. The part-time police force is amateurish and weak. It is run by a committee of villagers who rarely agree on what it should do. Powerful neighbours sometimes suppress violence by force. Peace will only come to such a village when the rule of law is imposed.

The disaster after Yugoslavia might have been averted in a world which had learnt more from Hobbes. The Serb leaders could have been shifted by credible threats of really strong action. In 1993 Milosević opposed the Vance–Owen peace plan. It was attacked frequently on Serbian television and in April only a third of Serbs supported it. When Milosević thought the United States would intervene if the plan was rejected, Serbian television changed its line and in May two-thirds of Serbs supported it.

The UN in Bosnia never looked like Leviathan, but a substantial force could bring about the Hobbesian effect. In 1995, when a mortar shell killed thirty-seven people in the Sarajevo marketplace, the international outcry led to massive air strikes on Serb positions. The Serb forces then withdrew from round Sarajevo. They became more co-operative in a way that contributed to the Dayton peace agreement. This response to stronger force suggests that the UN would have been more effective from the start if it had come closer to wielding Leviathan's power.

The case of Yugoslavia, like that of Rwanda, suggests that the rule of law will only be imposed by a powerful international police force. It needs the authority to intervene when the law is broken, even without the support of the great powers. This requires something along the lines of a strong and properly funded permanent UN force, together with clear criteria for intervention and an international court to authorize it.

It will be very hard to persuade governments to accept such a proposal, but creating this Leviathan is the only way to impose the rule of law on the world. In a country with the rule of law, people who are attacked call the police, who are strong and come at once. They do not have to persuade strong citizens to form a posse to stop the criminals. Nor do they have to make deals to persuade criminals to let ambulances through to the victims.

If the means to impose the rule of law are not created, the Hobbesian trap will create more horrors like those of Yugoslavia. There has been no adequate response to the challenge of President Izetbegović: 'If the international community is not ready to defend the principles which it itself has proclaimed as its foundations, let it say so openly, both to the people of Bosnia and to the people of the world. Let it proclaim a new code of behaviour in which force will be the first and the last argument.'[10]

CHAPTER 17

The Roots of Tribal Conflict

Only part of us is sane: only part of us loves pleasure and the longer day of happiness, wants to live to our nineties and die in peace, in a house that we built, that shall shelter those who come after us. The other half of us is nearly mad . . . and wants to die in a catastrophe that will set back life to its beginnings and leave nothing of our house save its blackened foundations. Our bright natures fight in us with this yeasty darkness, and neither part is commonly quite victorious, for we are divided against ourselves and will not let either part be destroyed.

Rebecca West, *Black Lamb and Grey Falcon*

A tribal conflict is often viewed from outside as the product of an ineradicable historical enmity. This 'ancient hatreds' view misses more immediate and remediable causes: political manipulation, belief traps and Hobbesian fear.

But the Hobbesian account is not the whole story either. The 'ancient hatreds' account has some truth in it. There are aspects of human psychology to which tribalism has a deep appeal. People are drawn into the tribal trap, as well as pushed into it.

There is a disposition to group conflict. And there are aspects of people's sense of their own identity which make the conflict likely to be between 'tribal' groups.

The Human Disposition to Group Conflict

People identify with one group and feel hostility to another even where they belong to 'minimal groups': ones without any emotionally charged ethnic, religious, or political basis. In the extreme case, group membership is known to be random. In a psychological study of 'prison' role playing, students were assigned randomly to either of two groups: 'prisoners' or 'prison guards'. They identified with their own group and were hostile to the other one. After several days the 'guards' were treating the 'prisoners' so badly that the study had to be called off.[1] Why does hostility develop between even these minimal groups?

One explanation is biological. Some behaviour patterns may have had survival value for genes in an earlier environment. Konrad Lorenz cites the way modern domestic cows and pigs mob people or animals appearing in their midst, which may once have been a defence against wolves. The wolves have gone, but the genetically programmed disposition remains.[2]

Group identification and rivalry may be a similar residue. Darwin's thinking about survival of the fittest was in terms of individual fitness: the capacity of the individual to survive and to reproduce. But the shift to thinking in terms of gene survival makes relevant the genetic similarity between related individuals. For the survival of my genes, saving the lives of several of my family may be more important than saving me. W.D. Hamilton's concept of 'inclusive fitness' combines personal fitness with this kinship component.[3]

Inclusive fitness provides the basis for a biological account of group identification and group hostility.[4] A disposition to protect genetically related people from attacks by others could help gene survival because unrelated individuals may be dangerous. Attitudes of fear and hostility towards other groups could have survival value.

Such a theory needs to explain why the groups which generate identification and hostility are not all kin groups. One possible explanation is that alliances between kin groups give an advantage in conflict.

This account is plausible, but it suffers from a general problem of sociobiology. What are the constraints on such an explanation? Almost anything can be argued to be just what you would have expected to emerge from evolutionary competition: a tendency to feel friendly towards other groups could equally be explained by the advantages of reciprocal altruism. Because these explanations do not predict, but explain after the event, they are too easy. Such genetically programmed dispositions may include group identification and hostility. We will know only when we have ways of testing what now are just plausible stories.

A genetically programmed disposition may explain hostility between minimal groups. But, even if this is so, the biology needs supplementing with psychology. Explanation of group conflict needs to go beyond minimal groups. Why do some groups and not others arouse tribal identification and hostility? People do not identify with being engineers or farmers as they do with their nationality. Why, in the modern world, does tribal conflict focus on religious, linguistic, ethnic or territorial groups, and in particular on nations?

Nationalism

The appeal of nationalism is almost universal. The central idea that each nation (or one particular nation) should govern itself is summed up in Giuseppe Mazzini's slogan: 'Every nation a state, only one state for the entire nation.'[5] Everything depends on how the 'nation' is understood. Where it is understood in a tribal and exclusive way, but (as in Yugoslavia) the population is mixed, the nation-state is a trap.

Nationalists often suppose there is something 'natural' or pre-social about nationality. Nation-states are supposed to reflect deep differences between kinds of people: Swedes differ from Italians in the way the fish of the Baltic are different from those of the Mediterranean. This is at best a simplification: some historians and social scientists emphasize the relative modernity of European nation-states, dating them from around the end of the eighteenth century.

There are various explanations for the rise of nation-states. An agrarian society changed into an industrial capitalist economy. The division of labour called for large economic units, which in turn may have needed central control of public order and defence, together with a standard education system. The dominance of national languages may have come with the decline of Latin as the idea of Christendom faded. National languages may have superseded regional dialects because of the need for communication within large units and for national administration. And the products of printing may have been more profitable in a national market.[6]

If these suggestions are correct, the European states arose not just as a vehicle for a pre-existing national consciousness. In some cases the state may have arisen before there was much sense of nationhood. Eric Hobsbawm quotes a speaker in the first parliament of the new Kingdom of Italy: 'We have made Italy, now we have to make Italians.'[7]

If it is true that the nation-state appeared only recently, perhaps some nations existed before they had their own states. When Englishmen and Frenchmen fought each other at Agincourt, the natural conflict was still English-against-French, and not short-against-tall or peasants-against-lords. And there are now groups, such as the Kurds, who are denied a state but who certainly think of themselves as a nation. Their nationalism is expressed in the belief that they should govern themselves in their own state.

But if already having a state is not essential, what makes a group a nation? The usual conception of the 'nation' is as the group people identify with, the community that they think of as 'us'. Benedict Anderson's idea that nations are 'imagined communities' captures well this psychological component of nationhood. This self-conception of a community as 'us' can be called tribal.

Tribalism is a deeper phenomenon than nationalism. Historically tribalism came first. And nationalism presupposes the idea of a nation, understood in terms of a tribal self-conception. Its central idea is that a nation, so understood, should govern itself.

Tribalism

Tribal consciousness is a matter of a group thinking of itself as an 'us', as a community. But people think of themselves in this way only if they suppose they have distinctive shared characteristics.

These characteristics are of two kinds. There are those which make up the tribal or national self-image, and there are identifying characteristics: those which show someone is a member of the group.

National self-images require the selection of some features rather than others. Slobodan Milosević said that it was never part of the Serbian character to give up in the face of obstacles, to demobilize when it's time to fight. He said that Serbs were brave and dignified. He chose the commemoration of the defeat at Kosovo to say that Serbs were one of the few peoples who went into battle undefeated.

Naturally, the characteristics chosen are usually favourable. We are determined, brave, dignified victors. It is a conceptual feat to maintain that we score so well on these characteristics without seeing our neighbours as vacillating, cowardly, undignified losers.

A student at a university in Northern Ireland told me that her fellow students know each other by first names only. Surnames more readily give away which community they come from, and they want their student life to escape the community divisions. But when friendships are secure the community membership can be revealed and there is a rare chance for stereotypes to be compared in an atmosphere of goodwill. The student mentioned one of the stereotypes she had been taught as a child. The primitiveness of the members of the other community was shown by their having one long eyebrow, rather than two brows with a gap between them. Her friends in the other community reported exactly the same stereotype in reverse.

Usually the identifying characteristics of a tribal or national group are evaluatively more neutral, but they too may contain an element of myth. Typically these features include the territory the group inhabits, some distinct 'ethnic' appearance, and a shared language, religion and culture. All these characteristics carry an emotional charge. One question is why these particular charged features are central to membership of the tribe or nation.

Charged Characteristics, Identity and Respect

Tribal membership and loyalties are linked to people's sense of their own identity. Nietzsche's idea of self-creation has a degree of truth. A person's identity is something not completely given, but is partly created. Some characteristics, including those linked to tribal membership, such as skin pigmentation or other ethnic features, are just given. We do not choose our parents, where we are born or what language we are brought up to speak. We do not choose the religion and culture we absorb as children. But there is also the identity people create for themselves, typically elaborating on, or branching out from, this 'given' identity. This self-creation gives part of the sense people have of their lives being worth while.

Perhaps tribalism is linked to our need to create something coherent out of ourselves and our own lives. If so, its roots go very deep in our psychology. Its elimination may be impossible and, at the least, dauntingly difficult.

Some characteristics we want are lasting ones (these include many which are central to our moral identity). There is a long process of self-creation, which is like a novelist telling a story about a character. The mixture of freedom and constraint is similar. There are open possibilities, but what the character can do depends partly on circumstances and on the other people in the story. There are also limits on how far acting 'out of character' is possible. The story we tell about ourselves, partly by what we do and partly by how we edit the account of our past, is central to our sense of our own identity.

The story is bound up with the places which are its context. To be forced into exile is, among other things, to be excluded from the scenes of earlier parts of the story. The role which places have in our self-creative story makes the emotional pull of territory unsurprising and is one reason why people are more likely to identify with being a Serb or a Croat than with being a builder or a car mechanic. It helps to explain why people respond to someone who says, 'This is your land. These are your houses. Your meadows and gardens. Your memories . . .'

The story is bound up with a few other people. What I did was done with them, or done in response to what they did or said. I still carry their hopes and expectations with me. The values that guided what I have done (and which colour the tone of the narrative) were partly shaped by them. It is not just that particular people shape the content and tone of the story. As we tell it or act it out, we need them to listen. We hope for their recognition of what we are like.

The role of particular people in our self-creative story makes our closeness to them natural. (Of course there are many other, less egocentric, reasons for such closeness.) But this account of the role of people close to us faces a problem parallel to that faced by the sociobiological account of tribalism. Just as the nation, our 'imagined community', is far larger than the group of those we are genetically related to, so it is far larger than the group of people in our personal story.

The relationships which are so important to us, both for our sense of our identity and for other reasons, draw heavily on a shared cultural background. A shared frame of reference, a common history (passed on by a common education), and a shared sense of humour, all create a context in which relationships and identity can flourish. And in turn this cultural context is tied up in obvious ways with a shared language.

It is in the context of a particular culture and language that our created identity is validated by the recognition bestowed by others. So any lack of respect for our culture and language in turn devalues our personal self-respect. In recent times, awareness of the centrality of this has increasingly shaped the way people show respect for the dignity of others. The desire not to use disparaging terms for other groups can have its comic side, and is often dismissed as a product of 'political correctness'. But the concern behind it is part of the growth of one of our central moral resources.

Isaiah Berlin quoted Friedrich Schiller's 'bent twig' theory of national-ism as a reaction to oppression or humiliation, and suggested that the nationalism of Israelis and Palestinians may be so intractably strong because both are reacting against having been victims.[8] One of the strengths of nationalism is the contribution it can make to self-respect. But the strengths and the weaknesses are closely interwoven. Slights to self-respect often help to start the spiral of conflict.

Narrative and the Trap of Vendetta

Tribal or national identity, like personal identity, is constructed partly by means of a story about the past. The narrative used to shape national consciousness can also sharpen conflicts.

Much of the story is made up of relations with other nations, who usually turn out to have behaved terribly. There are narratives of defeat and narratives of victory. Narratives of defeat bring the desire to redress a grievance: the bent twig. Narratives of victory can have a triumphalism which stirs resentment in those on the other side. An obvious case is the Orange parades in Northern Ireland, celebrating the defeat of the Catholics by William of Orange. Both kinds of narrative help the spiral of hostility.

They also contribute to the belief trap. The narrative is the background against which new acts are judged, making it harder to accept the genuineness of gestures of friendship, and making the hostile interpreta-tion more plausible.

The narrative of the Croats emphasizes the stifling nature of Communism, which was seen as a system mainly imposed by Serbs. The narrative of the Serbs emphasizes Croatian fascism, the evils of the Ustase, and the Serbian part in defeating the Croats and their Nazi allies. (After Tito, the Croatian authorities reinforced this by renaming streets after fascist leaders.)

At the time of the Second World War, the Serbs remembered the involvement of the Croatian leader Ante Pavelić in the assassination of King Alexander in Marseilles. Croatians remembered the Serb domination during King Alexander's rule. Before the Second World War, the Serbs and the Bosnian Muslims remembered each other's role in the Second Balkan War in 1913.

The narratives go right back. In 1993 the defeat by Islamic forces at Kosovo was recalled by Serbian soldiers fighting the 'Turks': the Bosnian Muslims. And in 1989 Serbian nationalists dug up what were supposed to be the bones of Tsar Lazar, the Serbian leader killed by the Turks on the Field of Blackbirds in 1389. These bones were carried round Serbia to stir up national feeling before being re-buried.[9] These narratives generate their own growth: the 1990s added new chapters.

For those caught up in the vendetta, validating their narrative can require the destruction of the physical embodiments of the other side's story. When the Serbian forces invaded Croatia, they destroyed many Catholic churches and attacked monasteries. Bosnia was subjected to the same cultural destruction. The Serbian forces surrounding Sarajevo targeted the Oriental Institute, destroying thousands of its Islamic and Jewish manuscripts. They shelled the National Museum and the National Library, destroying over a million books and many thousands of manuscripts and records.[10]

Serb and Croat forces destroyed other Islamic sites in Bosnia, including some of the best Ottoman architecture, going back to the fifteenth century. They wrecked more than 800 mosques, blowing them up, burning them down and covering the sites with new buildings or car parks. They paved over Islamic cemeteries and destroyed libraries which contained documents of the Ottoman Empire. The aim was to obliterate history: to destroy any sign that the Muslims had ever lived there. There was also a cold joke at the expense of the Islamic community: before being destroyed, the mosque at Modrica was used as a slaughterhouse for pigs.[11]

The narrative obsession with history keeps the past alive in the present with terrible vividness. In the Krajina, Tudjman's defence of the Second World War Ustase state will have aroused memories. The Ustase forces used to destroy Serb villages and kill their inhabitants. Their leader, Ante Pavelić, had a policy towards Serbs: 'Kill a third, expel a third, convert a third.' Many Serbs died as the victims of death squads, or in concentration camps such as Jasenovać. In some cases, the villagers were locked in the Orthodox church, which was then burnt down.

One boy of twelve came close to death at the hands of the Ustase. A killing squad led by their closest neighbour had come to murder the family. They escaped because they were out. That boy's son, Milan Babić, led the Krajina rebellion against Tudjman's government. General Adzić, the Yugoslav national army chief of staff, who planned the war against Croatia, had hidden in a tree as a boy, while Ustase troops hacked his parents to death. General Mladić's father was killed by the Ustase. Milan Kovacević, who ran a string of Serbian concentration camps around Prijedor, had himself been born in the Croatian camp at Jasenovać.

It is hard to lecture victims about avoiding hatred. Fikret Alić, who had been tortured and starved in the camp at Trnopolje, could no longer like Serbs:

> I worked to get money for my mother. And now I have nothing, and I hate those people. I never did anything to harm them. I hate Vjeko Zigić, who killed my grandfather and uncle, who had never harmed him. I never saw any difference between Serb or Muslim and anyone. But now I could never look at them or greet them or live with them again. We liked each other for forty-five years, and in the forty-sixth year, we hate each other.[12]

It is impossible for those of us who have not had his experiences to say to Fikret Alić that he should stop hating Serbs. But the developing tragedy is apparent. It would have been impossible to tell Milan Kovacević that he should not hate the Croats for what they did to his family in Jasenovać. We can imagine what some of those who survived his camps in Prijedor may in turn want to do to Serbs.

Slavenka Drakulić writes, 'After the war the role will be reversed and the victims will judge not only the executioners, but their silent accomplices. I am afraid that, as we have been forced to take sides in this way, we – all of us, on both sides – will get caught in that cruel, self-perpetuating game for ever.'[13]

CHAPTER 18

The Capacity to Unchain Ourselves

I was brought up in that harsh, divided landscape of the Northern Irish working class and I came into captivity with all its attendant baggage, good and bad. John McCarthy, from the utterly different background of the English upper class, discovered his own 'people' and baggage. In the circumstances in which we found ourselves physically chained together we both realized an extraordinary capacity to unchain ourselves from what we had known and been.

Brian Keenan, *An Evil Cradling*

The urgent need is for a proper world police force. No thoughts on psychological changes alter this. But, for the further future, we may hope to go beyond containing the effects of tribalism. Perhaps we can start to modify tribalism itself. Political change first, but psychological change as well.

Because tribalism runs so deeply in us, it may be impossible to eliminate. This tells against the Enlightenment hope that national loyalties would fade away. We now see the case for greater sympathy with nationalism, a case based on the contribution national loyalties make to people and their sense of identity. But this makes nations only of instrumental value. They are to be judged by the good and bad contributions they make to the lives of people. In this way the Enlightenment thinkers who kicked nations off their pedestal got it right. A good Enlightenment principle might be: always treat nations merely as a means and never as ends in themselves.

For now, the only realistic option is to accept our tribal psychology as a fact of life. But there is also a long, slow strategy which goes deeper. Perhaps we need not abandon the Enlightenment hope that eventually these tribal loyalties may take second place to a more general humanism. Greater self-consciousness about our psychology may mean that these simple-minded commitments grow into something more complex.

A more sophisticated awareness of how tribal narratives are constructed may slowly erode uncritical acceptance of them. And seeing how modern plural nations differ from tribal nations may weaken the grip of the old narratives. Belief in such ideas as 'Greater Serbia' depends on myths which are unlikely to survive a more critical outlook.

We can also try to make the chapters of the story now being written different from past chapters. The moral resources have a role in this.

Respect and the Bent Twig

Respect for someone's dignity is an affirmation of a fundamental human equality. You may be richer and more powerful than me, and from a different ethnic group or religion. But if you treat me with courtesy and respect, you signal your recognition of my status – that I am as much a person as you are. If, when we meet, you listen as well as talk, you acknowledge that I too have experiences, thoughts and a way of seeing the world, that I too may have something to say worth hearing.

Respect for dignity is one of the great barriers against atrocity and cruelty. To acknowledge our shared moral status makes it harder for us to torture or kill each other. The erosion of the protective barrier creates danger. When one group tramples on the dignity of another, it tramples on its own inhibitions and an Amritsar massacre may not be far off.

The bent twig of tribalism shows the other way in which respect for dignity is a protection against future horrors. The humiliated group is fully aware of the denial of its equal status. Resentment enters the tribal narrative and the desire for vengeance is implanted.

The only escape from the trap of vendetta is awareness of how the stories on both sides were constructed. There has to be some shared recognition of how things have gone wrong and that showing mutual respect is the only way out. In post-apartheid South Africa the fact that Nelson Mandela and other black African leaders resisted the temptation in their turn to humiliate the white minority gave all groups a chance to escape the cycle of revenge. Symbolism matters. The once all-white Springboks were a symbol of apartheid. When President Mandela wore their rugby shirt, a new version of the old story was starting to be written.

Why were black African leaders able to resist humiliating the whites in turn? One, Archbishop Desmond Tutu, had a childhood memory of a rare gesture of respect by a white man, Father Trevor Huddleston. In that society, an uneducated black woman like Desmond Tutu's mother counted for very little.

In the eyes of the world this lovely person was a nonentity. I was standing with her on the hostel verandah when this tall white man, in a flowing black cassock, swept past. He doffed his hat to my mother in greeting. I was quite taken aback; a white man raising his hat to a black woman! Such things did not happen in real life. That gesture left an indelible impression. Perhaps it helped deep down to make me realize we were precious to God and to this white man; perhaps it helped me not to become anti-white, despite the harsh treatment we received at the hands of most white people.[1]

Sympathy and Friendship

Every human gesture or act of generosity across the tribal barriers may lodge in someone's memory and shape their version of the story. In Israel David Grossman remembers how, when over fifty Israelis were killed by Hamas suicide attacks, a Palestinian friend called him from Ramallah and offered to donate blood to the wounded.[2]

Another instance was at a time of sectarian killings in Northern Ireland. A group of workmen going home was held up by masked men, who said that any Catholics should step out. All but one of the group were Protestants. They assumed the masked men were Protestants who intended to kill the Catholic. Seamus Heaney has written about what happened to the single Catholic, torn between fear and loyalty:

> in the relative cover of the winter evening darkness, he felt the hand of the Protestant worker next to him take his hand and squeeze it in a signal that said no, don't move, we'll not betray you, nobody need know what faith or party you belong to. All in vain, however, for the man stepped out of the line; but instead of finding a gun at his temple, he was thrown backward and away as the gunmen opened fire on those remaining in the line, for these were not Protestant terrorists, but members, presumably, of the Provisional IRA.[3]

The killing of the other men makes this a terrible story. But the human gesture by one of the Protestants – the last act of his life – is known through the report of the Catholic he tried to save.

Acts of generosity across the tribal divisions, like those of David Grossman's Palestinian friend or the Protestant worker, must at least complicate the story told in the other community.

A More Complex Identity

The sense of our identity is not static, and as it evolves we may come to see tribal identification in a different light.

Understanding the psychology of tribalism gives us some encouragement to focus on all the other resources we can draw on for our identities. We have more than just our tribal membership. We are mothers and fathers, sons and daughters, brothers and sisters, friends, architects, scientists; we enjoy looking after children; we have our own hairstyles and our own jokes; we are fans of the Grateful Dead, supporters of Liverpool Football Club, mountaineers, vegetarians, amateur photographers, admirers of Tolstoy, lovers of Mozart and of New York.

To have an identity limited to being a Serb or a Croat would be a great impoverishment. Slavenka Drakulić felt this loss during the Yugoslav conflict. She had resisted seeing nationality as the main feature of people and had tried to keep a dialogue going with Serbian friends. But pressures inside Croatia reduced people to the one dimension of nationality: 'The trouble with this nationhood, however, is that whereas before, I was defined by my education, my job, my ideas, my character – and, yes, my nationality too – now I feel stripped of all that. I am nobody because I am not a person any more. I am one of 4.5 million Croats.'[4] Seeing this for the impoverishment it is can help to reduce the grip of tribal psychology.

Tribal hostility can be transcended by a sense of moral identity rooted in other commitments, such as to a religion or a profession, with its own values and standards of conduct. Or it may be rooted in a humanism which looks through tribal membership to the person behind it.

Both of these may be present, as in one doctor in Srebrenica. All medical supplies had run out, and Dr Mujkanović had to do amputations without anaesthetics. When he was asked later what he was most proud of, he said:

> When captured Serbian soldiers entered the hospital, they lay side by side with Bosnian soldiers. They stayed in the same rooms, and they shared the food that Bosnian families brought to the hospital. I guaranteed that nothing happened to them. My greatest satisfaction as a humanist and as a doctor is that they were carried into the hospital on stretchers and left on their legs.[5]

PART FOUR

WAR AS A TRAP

CHAPTER 19

The Trap of the Trenches

Out of the air a voice without a face
Proved by statistics that some cause was just
In tones as dry and level as the place:
No one was cheered and nothing was discussed;
Column by column in a cloud of dust
They marched away enduring a belief
Whose logic brought them, somewhere else, to grief.
W.H. Auden, The Shield of Achilles

What in earlier days had been drafts of volunteers were now droves of victims.
Siegfried Sassoon, Memoirs of an Infantry Officer

Tribalism is central to the psychology of going to war. Another part of our psychology which is often cited in explanation of war is aggression, but other, more neglected, aspects of our psychology may be more important. I hope to replace aggression with the concept of entrapment. At first aggression seems to be at the centre of the psychology of combat, but it explains little and fits only some extreme episodes. Killing in angry retaliation, or the emotional explosions at My Lai, can be called 'aggression'. But the word does not fit most ground combat, and aggression is not the state of mind of those involved in technological warfare.

Aggression is also thought to explain the outbreak of war. Often the first move is an 'act of aggression': an illegal use of force against another territory. It does not follow that the psychological state of aggression is an important cause of war. Richard Nixon worked himself up by watching a film about General Patton before ordering the bombing of Cambodia, but his case is hardly typical.

War is often a trap and going to war is not often an aim of modern political leaders. Usually they find themselves trapped by the implications of policies they have embarked on. And whole groups can be trapped in a spiral of hostility leading to war. Understanding these traps is more important than thinking about how to control aggression.

This chapter is about soldiers trapped in battle: in particular those trapped in the trenches of the First World War. The following chapters will look at how whole communities and their leaders enter, and are held inside, the trap of war.

The Trap

Some soldiers are conscripted. Others enter the army freely, but may find that what they have volunteered for is a trap. In war the moral resources – respect, sympathy and the sense of moral identity – are often neutralized, but, even when they still exist, the trap of war can make them largely ineffective. The First World War is the classic case.

In August 1914 most of the belligerent countries were swept with enthusiasm. In Berlin, when mobilization was announced, the crowd sang the hymn 'Now thank we all our God'. In Britain, too, there was a wave of patriotism. Kitchener had hoped for 100,000 volunteers in the first six months, and for 500,000 in all. There were 500,000 in the first month and nearly 2 million in the first six months.

The Kaiser told German troops, 'You will be home before the leaves have fallen from the trees', and many in Britain thought it would all be over by Christmas. Those who volunteered may not have been quite in the mood of an August Bank Holiday lark, but the euphoria was real. So was the innocence. Neither survived the first two years of trench warfare. After the Battle of the Somme, the view from the trenches was of a seemingly endless nightmare.

In 1916 Joffre and Haig agreed to launch a French and British offensive on the Somme. On the British sector there was a week of massive artillery bombardment on the German lines. Then, on 1 July, the infantry were to attack, under the protection of an artillery barrage in front of them. The bombardment was meant to have killed or driven out the German troops, cut their defensive belts of wire, and destroyed their fortifications. The infantry would have the job of occupying largely undefended positions, so they were to advance across no man's land carrying a heavy load of ammunition, picks, shovels, field telephones and other equipment. The barrage would always be clearing the ground in front of them. One general, seeing the heavily laden men moving up to the trenches, said, 'Good luck, men. There is not a German left in their trenches, our guns have blown them all to Hell.'[1]

The plan failed. The Germans knew the time and place of the attack and, despite the bombardment, most had survived in their deep dug-outs.

The laden British infantry were massacred as they advanced into heavy machine-gun fire and towards thick defensive wires. As Unteroffizier Paul Scheytt saw it, 'The English came walking, as though they were going to the theatre, or as though they were on a parade ground. We felt they were mad. Our orders were given in complete calm and every man took careful aim to avoid wasting ammunition.'[2] On 1 July there were 60,000 British casualties. Over 20,000 men were killed, most of them in the first hour of the attack.

A few battalions were held back when their officers saw it was a massacre, but the majority attacked according to plan. Despite what happened on 1 July, Generals Haig and Rawlinson continued with similar attacks in the following days. The battle lasted until mid-November, gaining about five miles at a cost of 420,000 British and 200,000 French casualties. There were about 450,000 German casualties.

John Keegan compares our present-day emotional response to this slaughter to that aroused by Auschwitz: 'guilty fascination, incredulity, horror, disgust, pity and anger'.[3] At the time, most people back in England were ignorant or uncritical. Among those who did know, Winston Churchill's response stands out. He circulated to the War Cabinet a paper urging abandonment of the whole Somme strategy, arguing that so many had been killed for such little gain. The Cabinet asked Haig to explain his intentions, but the dissident view was defeated, and the King expressed his strong disapproval of Churchill. The Somme deserves its reputation as the extreme case of futile loss. John Keegan mentions incredulity: how can this have happened? Why did soldiers continue to take part?

As Corporal Harry Shaw said, 'Whatever was gained, it wasn't worth the price that the men had paid to gain that advantage. It was no advantage to anybody. It was just sheer bloody murder. That's the only words you can use for it.'[4] If the troops on all sides had been consulted as to whether a battle with such costs should take place, their answer would not be hard to guess. But the costs were not predicted. And, of course, there was no question of the troops being consulted. Some saw that they were trapped. Private W. Hay said, 'You were between the devil and the deep blue sea. If you go forward, you'll likely be shot, if you go back you'll be court-martialled and shot, so what the hell do you do? What can you do? You just go forward . . .'[5]

The trap extended beyond the Battle of the Somme. Many saw that those fighting on both sides had no quarrel with each other. A German soldier, portrayed in Erich Maria Remarque's autobiographical novel *All Quiet on the Western Front*, says, 'Now just why would a French blacksmith or a French shoemaker want to attack us? No, it is merely the rulers. I had never seen a Frenchman before I came here, and it will be just the same with the majority of Frenchmen as regards us. They weren't asked about it any more than we were.'[6] The whole war was a trap.

There were several responses to this. Most of the troops obeyed orders and fought the war. Some had a resigned sense of powerlessness. Some expressed resentment. Some tried to mitigate the conditions by explicit or tacit co-operation with those in the enemy lines. A few got back to England, and either campaigned against the war or at least tried to make people aware of its nature.

Obedience, Resignation and Resentment

It would have been in the interests of the troops on both sides to have agreed to refuse to fight. But such a thing must have seemed impossible to arrange, and to most of them it cannot have seemed an option. The soldiers were not consistent or unanimous in thinking that the war was an outrage. Many oscillated between the official line and a more sceptical view. Refusal to continue fighting by groups would get nowhere unless it spread rapidly. The opposition of the authorities and the lack of unanimity among the troops made this very unlikely.

Most of the time, there was no serious alternative to obeying orders. This was so obvious that very few even considered refusing to continue the battle. A comment of Corporal Joe Hoyles reflects his courage and the army's discipline, but also the inconceivability of any alternative: 'We were in the first wave, and our platoon officer, Fitzgibbon, was away out in front of us. They just mowed us down! People were falling on your right and your left and of course you had to keep going forward.'[7]

Many saw the futility, and the apparent impossibility of stopping the war. In his autobiographical novel, Siegfried Sassoon described his sense of helpless resignation one late summer evening when he walked by the Somme near Albert:

> I leant on a wooden bridge, gazing down into the dark green glooms of the weedy little river, but my thoughts were powerless against unhappiness so huge. I couldn't alter European history, or order the artillery to stop firing . . . a second-lieutenant could attempt nothing – except to satisfy his superior officers; and altogether, I concluded, Armageddon was too immense for my solitary understanding.[8]

Many resented the senior officers and the plans they drew up back at headquarters. The fighting at Passchendaele lasted from the end of July until early November 1917. A very small amount of ground was gained, at a cost of 300,000 British and 200,000 German soldiers killed or wounded. After the first few days of the battle, General Gough came to inspect the remnants of those who had done the first fighting. Seated on his horse, he said, 'Well done, you did your best. I deplore your losses. I am sure you will all want to avenge their deaths so I am making you up with a large draft so that you can return and avenge your comrades.' One soldier shouted angrily, 'You're a bloody butcher.' Gough ignored this and rode off, but after that he was known as 'Butcher Gough'.[9]

Yesterday's Enemies

Sometimes a glimpse of an alternative could be seen. There was occasional fraternization between the lines.

Christmas 1914 was the most spectacular case. Leutnant Johannes Neumann looked from the German lines and saw 'the incredible sight of our soldiers exchanging cigarettes, schnapps, and chocolate with the enemy'. A Scottish soldier produced a football, and with Scottish and German hats marking their respective goals, they played a match, which the Germans won 3–2. 'Us Germans really roared when a gust of wind revealed that the Scots wore no drawers under their kilts – and hooted and whistled when they caught an impudent glimpse of one posterior belonging to one of "yesterday's enemies". But after an hour's play, when our Commanding Officer heard about it, he sent an order that we must put a stop to it.'

In one place the Germans had laid out a Christmas dinner in their trench and pressed the British soldiers to stay and eat with them. The Germans, 'when they declined, dragged them bodily into the trench by their legs'.[10] Lieutenant Cyril Drummond describes another contact. There was a shouted exchange of invitations, and then a German soldier climbed out of his trench and walked over: 'We met, and very gravely saluted each other.' Others came out on both sides and gifts were exchanged. 'One of them said, "We don't want to kill you, and you don't want to kill us, so why shoot?" '[11]

The truce went on in some places for a few days after Christmas. On 30 December Lieutenant J.D. Wyatt wrote:

> Still no war! At about lunchtime however a message came down the line to say that Germans had sent across to say that their General was coming along in the afternoon, so we had better keep down, as they might have to do a little shooting to make things look right!!! And this is war!! This we did, and a few shots came over about 3.30 p.m.[12]

Live and Let Live

Sometimes, without any formal contact, a policy of 'live and let live' grew up. Mutual restraint in firing could save lives on both sides. Edmund

Blunden, worried by the feeble defences in the village of Boesinghe, said that 'our future, in short, depended on the observance of the "Live and Let Live" principle, one of the soundest elements in trench war'.[13] Robert Graves mentions both sides turning a blind eye when they all had to escape a flood, or sometimes when putting up defences: 'Occasionally, it was said, the rival parties "as good as used the same mallets" for hammering in the pickets. The Germans seemed much more ready than we were to live and let live.'[14]

Tony Ashworth, in his study of this tacit co-operation, suggests that these brief arrangements for specific purposes were the start of mutual empathy, which spread to other areas: if we allow the enemy breakfast in peace, they will do the same for us. Their doing so reinforced both the empathy and the use of inaction to communicate across the lines.[15]

One aspect of live and let live was the ritual use of artillery. Lord Reith wrote, 'Funny business this. The enemy throws some shells at our trench. We've got your range accurately you see. No monkey tricks. Home battery replied. We've got yours; trench line and battery position – both. No more nonsense. Live and let live.'[16] In some sectors of the front, regular targets and timing were part of a tacit mutual agreement. The predictability minimized casualties on both sides, while conveying an impression of activity to higher officers.

Robert Axelrod, drawing on Ashworth's work, uses the live-and-let-live policy as an example of a TIT FOR TAT co-operative strategy in prisoners' dilemma.[17] TIT FOR TAT is a policy simple enough to be signalled easily to the other side. It provided a way for both sides to co-operate rationally to minimize the severity of the trap in which they all found themselves.

Live and let live is not a perfect example of prisoners' dilemma. The self-interested case for firing at the enemy (in the absence of co-operation) is a lot weaker than that for confessing in the original prisoners' dilemma. Axelrod says that weakening the enemy would have made it easier to survive in a major battle. There is something to this. But, because of such factors as reinforcements and troop rotation, the advantage of firing seems more speculative and remote than the gain to the prisoner who confesses.

But battalions did stay facing each other for some time, so it was to some degree a repeated prisoners' dilemma, and co-operation was rational. When battalions were changed, those leaving would indicate the tacit understandings to their successors. Firing to hit the enemy was defection, and not doing so was co-operation. Out of TIT FOR TAT emerged the live-and-let-live policy.

The Moral Resources

From time to time the moral resources, notably mutual respect and sympathy, could also be seen. The tacit agreement to live and let live was a moral relationship between the two sides. The respect they had for each other's moral standing in this relationship was sometimes signalled.

When the policy broke down, there could be an explicit apology, like that made by a Saxon unit of the German army for a death in the Christmas truce: 'One of the Dublin Fusiliers was killed one day by a bullet which came from the front of Plugstreet Wood, and the Saxons immediately sent over and apologised, saying it hadn't been anything to do with them, but from those so-and-so Prussians on their left.'[18]

The empathy involved in seeing what the other side would want, for instance an uninterrupted breakfast, was already close to sympathy: hoping they would have it. There were cases where sympathy quite clearly broke through the hard crust of official enmity between the two sides. A writer in a French trench newspaper described French soldiers coming across two Germans supporting a dying friend: 'These three men must have been great friends. The two without wounds had their eyes full of tears and as the wounded man died, one of them leaned slowly across to his brother in distress and embraced him lengthily. Impressed by such misery, and despite the urgency of the moment, the *poilus* stopped, moved.'[19]

Sympathy helped in the mutual restraint which left each side unmolested to collect or attend their wounded. This restraint could turn into something more. Private Moodie remembered shouting to the Germans to fetch their wounded:

> At first they seemed very dubious and would only show their helmets but we promised not to shoot and a man who wore the Iron Cross advanced boldly to our entanglements and proceeded to assist a wounded man. Another followed and, amidst our cheers, they carried him off. Before going, the first man saluted and said, 'Thank you, gentlemen, one and all. I thank you very much. Good day.' The incident quite upset me for a time and I wished that we might all be friends again.[20]

Because thinking based on prisoners' dilemma is so influential now, it is easy to see how reciprocal self-interest contributed to the restraint. It was, of course, a motive. Soldiers at risk of being wounded themselves have an interest in medical attention and rescue being unimpeded.

But their motives probably went beyond this. There is sympathy for a fellow soldier in agony, even if he is on the other side. Moral identity may have played a part: a sense of honour is bound up with a tradition of chivalry. And there was mutual respect, particularly evoked when the other side was seen to take risks to rescue their wounded. Mere self-interested calculation does not explain the cheering on the one side and the courtesy on the other. And the result of such chivalry could be such uncalculating thoughts as Private Moodie's wish that 'we might all be friends again'.

In such episodes, the moral resources can be glimpsed, but the trap was so powerful that they were relatively ineffective. Their influence was local. Some shots were not fired. Some wounded men were saved. But mutual respect and sympathy were powerless to stop the war.

The Response of the Authorities

The authorities were determined to keep the trap in place. With them a Christmas truce was predictably unpopular. Lieutenant Cyril Drummond said:

> But of course the war was becoming a farce and the high-ups decided that this truce must stop. Orders came through to our Brigade, and so to my own battery, that fire was to be opened the following morning on a certain farm which stood behind the German support line . . . We sent someone over to tell the Boches, and the next morning at eleven o'clock I put twelve rounds into the farmhouse, and of course there wasn't anybody there. But that broke the truce.[21]

In 1915 the authorities on both sides gave orders that there was to be no Christmas fraternization, but there were some local truces, including at least one football match and a meeting in no man's land at which chaplains from both sides said prayers. The French and Germans sang carols across to each other. At one meeting in no man's land, the Germans said that they had to fire but would fire high, which they did. The authorities intervened to stop the contacts and Major-General Cavan issued a memo deploring one of the episodes: 'Large parties of unarmed Germans were the first to appear but this is no excuse, and I regret the incident more than I can say.'[22] Official disapproval never quite extinguished the contacts – there were Christmas truces in 1916 at Loos and in 1917 at Oppy.

It was not only at Christmas that the authorities discovered fraternization and tried to stamp it out. At Givenchy in 1916 a German officer and about twenty men came out of their trench, some calling things like, 'Good morning, Tommy, have you any biscuits?' and inviting the British troops out to join them. The two British officers there ordered that they were not to be fired on. Shouted remarks were exchanged and both sides returned to their lines. When more senior officers heard about the incident, the two officers were put under arrest because the enemy had not been fired on. The officers marched under arrest towards the Battle of the Somme.[23]

Some of the more thoughtful officers reflected on the implications of all this. Colonel W.N. Nicholson wrote:

> it is a commentary on modern war that commanders should fear lest the

soldiers on each side become friendly. Our soldiers have no quarrel with 'Fritz', save during the heat of battle, or in retaliation for some blow below the belt. If whole armies fraternized politicians on both sides would be sore set to solve their problems. Yet it is possible that if there had been a truce for a fortnight on the whole trench line at any time after the Battle of the Somme the war might have ended – and what would mother have said then?[24]

The authorities hated live and let live and instituted a system of 'raids' aimed at killing or capturing enemy soldiers in their own trenches. In raids, there was no chance of tacit co-operation or of pretence. Edmund Blunden wrote, 'the word "raid" may be defined as the one in the whole vocabulary of the war which most instantly caused a sinking feeling in the stomach of ordinary mortals'. He describes an order to Colonel Grisewood to raid a very strongly fortified place in the dark and without preparation. Grisewood refused and 'another battalion was forced to lose the lives which ignorance and arrogance cost'. After another such raid, a general asked a sentry what he thought of the attack. The sentry replied, 'Like a butcher's shop.'[25]

Those running the war kept their troops inside the trap by enforcing terrifying penalties. Refusal to fight risked the death sentence. Hundreds were executed, often for forms of 'cowardice', which would now be recognized as psychiatric disorders resulting from the experience of war.

Robert Graves describes being appointed a member of a court martial to try an Irish sergeant charged with 'shamefully casting away his arms in the presence of the enemy'. Maddened by an intense bombardment, he had thrown down his rifle and run away with the rest of his platoon. Graves knew about the secret order that made death the mandatory punishment for cowardice, regardless of medical excuses. He revolted against taking part in this: 'If I refused, I should be court martialled myself, and a reconstituted court would sentence the sergeant to death anyhow. Yet I could not sign a death-verdict for an offence which I might have committed myself in similar circumstances.'[26] Graves was able to evade the dilemma, as another officer was willing to take his place. He was lucky in this. Usually, the authorities had in their trap not only those who displayed 'cowardice', but also those who had to take part in their court martial and execution. And, admirable as Robert Graves's revulsion was, the Irish sergeant did not escape the death the authorities had arranged for him.

The Larger Trap

Fraternization and the live-and-let-live policy grew partly out of sentiment and partly out of rational co-operation to reduce the horrors of entrapment. But these efforts could not stop the war, nor could they stop battles or even raids.

Perhaps, as Colonel Nicholson thought, a two-week truce along the whole line might have ended the war. If the truce had been combined with extensive flooding, and the troops on both sides had started to rescue each other, peace might have been even more likely; but, with things as they actually were, the authorities on both sides were able to succeed in *their* tacit co-operation against any outbreak of peace.

The possibility of public opinion turning against the war may have seemed a better hope. Certainly, some of those who went home from the trenches either wounded or on leave tried to educate people about what the war was really like. Propaganda had created a bellicose climate in which returning soldiers were more readily honoured as heroes than listened to. In *All Quiet on the Western Front*, Erich Maria Remarque described the strain of going back to Germany on leave. Attempts to say what the front was like simply made no impact on the confidence of patriotic civilians that things were *really* quite different. His old headmaster lectured him about strategy and dismissed Remarque's thought that the war was rather different from what people thought. Remarque's father asked about the front: 'he is curious in a way that I find stupid and distressing; I no longer have any real contact with him . . . I find I do not belong here any more, it is a foreign world.'[27] The same was true on the Allied side. Robert Graves described the alien climate he found in 1916 after he was wounded: 'England looked strange to us returned soldiers. We could not understand the war madness that ran wild everywhere, looking for a pseudo-military outlet. The civilians talked a foreign language; and it was newspaper language. I found serious conversation with my parents all but impossible.'[28] The outer guards of the trap were civilians on both sides who believed what they read in the newspapers.

CHAPTER 20

The Home Front

It is not true that the public didn't know what was going on. Everyone could see parents opening their doors to those zinc coffins or having their sons returned to them broken and crippled. Such things weren't mentioned on radio or television, of course, or in the newspapers . . . but it was plain for all to see . . . What kind of people are we, and what right have we to ask our children to do the things they had to do there? How can we, who stayed at home, claim that our hands are cleaner than theirs? . . . The machine-gunned and abandoned villages and ruined land are not on their consciences but on ours. We were the real murderers, not they, and we murdered our own children as well as others.

A. Golubnichaya, on the Soviet war in Afghanistan,
in Svetlana Alexievich, *Zinky Boys*

Immanuel Kant said that war breaks out easily where a state is under an absolute monarch. Such a ruler does not lose by a war, but goes on enjoying the delights of his table or sport: 'He can therefore decide on war for the most trifling reasons, as if it were a kind of pleasure party.' Kant said that peace is more likely if those who will suffer its miseries have to consent to war.[1] The wars of twentieth-century dictators support Kant's gloomy view of absolute power, but he may have been optimistic about the results of government by consent. He did not foresee how people can be manipulated, how they can be drawn into intellectual and emotional traps.

Being trapped can be a complex, and sometimes mutual, affair. Soldiers like Erich Maria Remarque and Robert Graves may be trapped in a war because the public 'at home' supports it. That public may be the victims of ignorance and misinformation spread by their leaders and by the media. Journalists may find it hard to tell the whole truth, and in turn may feel trapped, mainly by the authorities, but also by the way news organizations respond to the public mood. Even the government can sometimes feel trapped by what people expect.

The wartime mood is important. The heightened emotions of war spill over into the civilian world. Anticipation of a war can excite even those opposed to it: 'I am worried about myself. I firmly oppose war in the Gulf yet I find myself excited by the prospect. Am I sick, or are there thousands like me? What can we do about it?'[2] Winston Churchill noticed similar feelings in himself on the brink of the First World War. He wrote to his wife, 'Everything tends towards catastrophe and collapse. I am interested, geared up and happy. Is it not horrible to be built like that? I pray to God to forgive me for such fearful moods of levity. Yet I wd do my best for peace, and nothing would induce me wrongfully to strike the blow.'[3]

Heightened emotional intensity among civilians at the outbreak of war may not last. But war is then sustained by changing beliefs and attitudes. This creates an intellectual trap.

Rival Narratives

Beliefs can cause wars. Crusades are fought to defend or propagate a set of religious or political beliefs, but genuine crusades are rare. War shapes belief in the great cause more often than the other way round. It shapes conflicting beliefs about who was the aggressor and which side is committing barbaric atrocities. These accounts reinforce the conflict.

Usually there is little overlap between the rival narratives. The Japanese attack on Pearl Harbor is widely seen in the West as a classic case of unprovoked aggression, but the Japanese account at the time explained it as a response to military and economic encirclement by the Americans, British, Chinese and Dutch. In 1943 the Greater East Asia War Enquiry Commission reported that 'the arrogant Anglo-Saxons, ever covetous of securing world hegemony according to the principle of the white man's burden' tried 'to stifle Nippon to death'. Encirclement meant that 'the only paths that lay ahead of her were suicide or annihilation. Nippon chose to rise in self-defence.'[4]

The story is often supported by historical analogies. Neville Chamberlain was naïve when he made the Munich agreement with Hitler, but the lesson of Munich has been too widely and too crudely applied. Countries have gone to war partly because Nasser or Saddam Hussein is 'another Hitler', without much critical attention being given to this thought. As a war goes on, the accounts become more emotionally charged and the beliefs more extreme.

Virtually all the information on which the charged narratives of war are based comes from news reports: in 1914 from newspapers, now mainly from television. Since 1914 we have grown more aware of how fragmented and unreliable this news is.

Censoring the News

Wartime governments have more than one motive for withholding the true picture. Of course, there are genuine military reasons. Journalists reporting from a war are subject to censorship of information to avoid helping the other side, but this spills over into other kinds of censorship.

Governments are reluctant to discourage allies or to boost the morale of the enemy by admitting that things look bad. In December 1963 Robert McNamara, the US Defence Secretary, told President Johnson that the Vietnam War was going badly. He called the situation 'very disturbing' and said that current trends were most likely to lead to a Communist-controlled state. But, speaking to the press, he said, 'We reviewed the plans of the South Vietnamese and we have every reason to believe they will be successful.' Many years later, McNamara called this comment 'an overstatement at best' and reflected on his lack of candour:

> Perhaps a senior government official could hardly have been more straightforward in the midst of a war. I could not fail to recognize the effect discouraging remarks might have on those we strove to support (the South Vietnamese) as well as those we sought to overcome (the Vietcong and North Vietnamese). It is a profound, enduring, and universal ethical and moral dilemma: how, in times of war and crisis, can senior government officials be completely frank to their own people without giving aid and comfort to the enemy?[5]

Such 'overstatements' contributed to the lack of proper debate which, in the early stages, eased the slide into the American disaster in Vietnam.

Governments also want to keep their own public committed to the war. In Britain in the First World War this was the main function of the newly created Ministry of Information. In a document published in 1918 about its work, this was accepted: 'Propaganda is the task of creating and directing public opinion. In other wars this work has not been the function of government.' But 'in a struggle which was not of armies but of nations, and which tended to affect every people on the globe, this aloofness could not be maintained'.[6]

Sometimes leaders know that an informed public would see the human cost of a war as too great, so the facts are carefully filtered. In 1917 the Prime Minister, David Lloyd George, went to a dinner at which the returned journalist Philip Gibbs described the Western Front. Lloyd George later said, 'Even an audience of hardened politicians and journalists was strongly affected. If people really knew, the war would be stopped tomorrow. But of course they don't know and can't know . . . The thing is horrible beyond human nature to bear and I feel I can't go on with the bloody business: I would rather resign.'[7]

Whistle-blowing: Ronald Ridenhour

It is not only governments who suppress information. Some military people feel that their profession can only do its job if the public are kept from knowing the reality. One colonel wrote about Vietnam, 'We in the military knew better, but through fear of reinforcing the basic antimilitarism of the American people we tended to keep this knowledge to ourselves and downplayed battlefield realities.'[8]

Soldiers returning from war practise their own self-censorship. They can be reluctant to shock and horrify innocent people. One Soviet soldier back from Afghanistan said, 'We're invited to speak in schools, but what can we tell them? Not what war is really like, that's for sure . . . I can't very well tell the schoolkids about the collections of dried ears and other trophies of war, can I?'[9] This gentleness about mentioning war's horrors allows people to feel more comfortable about their support for it.

Some are prepared to become whistle-blowers. Ronald Ridenhour was not at My Lai, but had fought with several soldiers who were. When he found out about the massacre, he thought he would be a participant if he did not expose it. He wrote an account and sent it to his Congressman, President Nixon and other political leaders. The White House ignored his letter, but his Congressman, Mo Udall, pushed for an investigation.

Ronald Ridenhour believed that those who carried out the massacre should be brought to justice, but he also saw that the responsibility was not theirs alone:

> We were kids, 18, 19 years old . . . Here are these guys who had gone in and in a moment, in a moment, following orders, in a context in which they'd been trained, prepared to follow orders . . . The extraordinary few somehow did withstand it. But we shouldn't – our society shouldn't be structured, so that only the extraordinary few can conduct themselves in a moral fashion.

He saw that the policy-makers who created 'search and destroy' missions and 'free fire zones' must have foreseen that many civilians would be murdered: 'These people should have been on trial.'[10]

The whistle-blowing was only partially successful. Lieutenant Calley was convicted, but the thoughts about policy-makers were not followed up. President Nixon's response to the whistle-blowing was to suggest a secret investigation of Ronald Ridenhour and to single out Lieutenant Calley for a pardon. This may have been based partly on a judgement about public opinion.

Reporting the News: the Public as Part of the Trap

Censorship is not the only thing stopping journalists from reporting the full reality of a war. They may also be trapped by their own psychological defences. Victoria Brittain reported for the London *Times* on Vietnam. Later another journalist asked her why she had written what she was told, instead of what she knew. She accepted that she should have given less space to official briefings and more to the human horrors of the war. She thought about why she had not done this:

> Visiting orphanages and refugee camps was a wretched way to spend the day. The kids clung to any passing person like leeches, demanding a moment of fleeting attention or affection, and the repetition of their stories by women uprooted from their village by the US B-52 bombers which had killed their neighbours, relations and at worst their own children, was numbing. To protect your own sanity, you switched off.[11]

Above all, reporters may find themselves trapped by what people will accept. Good journalists know how to talk to their public. They know that people find easiest what fits their expectations. Kate Adie, reporting in 1993 for BBC Television on the war in Yugoslavia, felt the pressure of this: 'At home, viewers like to identify with one side. Where are the good guys? Who are the bad guys? And when you're trying to report something like Yugoslavia where everybody's up to something, nobody's totally good, nobody's totally bad, then you lose out with viewers.'[12]

People committed to a war do not want to hear things which call in question its justification, its success, or its methods. Newspapers may lie because they dare not say what people do not want to hear. British newspaper proprietors of the First World War sometimes saw this clearly. Lord Rothermere said to J.L. Garvin, 'You and I, Garvin, we haven't the pluck of those young lieutenants who go over the top. We're telling lies, we know we're telling lies, we daren't tell the public the truth, that we're losing more officers than the Germans, and that it's impossible to get through on the Western Front.'[13]

Those who report things that people do not want to hear risk being stigmatized as enemy sympathizers. In the Vietnam War, Harrison Salisbury of the *New York Times* reported accurately from Hanoi that civilian targets were hit. The Pentagon called him 'Ho Chi Salisbury of the Hanoi Times'. The *Washington Post* said he was Ho Chi Minh's new weapon. William Randolph Hearst Jr likened his reports to the broadcasts of Lord Haw Haw and other traitors in the Second World War.[14]

Other worries about the public also tone down the reality of war. Some photographs seem simply too horrible to use. Among pictures from Cambodia rejected by Associated Press were one of a smiling soldier eating the liver of a Khmer Rouge fighter he had killed, one of decapitated corpses being dragged along and one of a human head being lowered by the hair into boiling water.[15] Many of us are relieved to be protected from such images, but, when we support a war, we lack a full grasp of what it is we agree to.

Reporting for BBC Television on killings in Bosnia, Martin Bell ran into the 'good taste' guidelines for family viewing before nine o'clock in the evening. Bodies and blood were excluded, as was anything which would upset people. Once he sent film of fighting between Muslims and Croats. There were extraordinarily beautiful scenes of battle in the snow-covered landscape. But the rushes also showed the costs of the combat: the stacked bodies of captured Croatians who had been tortured and killed, followed by pictures of their mourning mothers and widows. The good-taste guidelines excluded all this. What was left in the report was 'apparently heroic pictures of camouflage-clad figures blazing away at the ruins'. And 'even the ruins seemed picturesque, being sunlit at this season against the snow. It was about as close to reality as a Hollywood action movie.'

Writing later (as 'a fierce BBC loyalist', proud to work for the BBC as 'a force for truth and freedom in the world') Martin Bell was concerned about such reporting:

> In our anxiety not to offend and upset people, we were not only sanitising war but even *prettifying* it, as if it were an acceptable way of settling disputes, and its victims never bled to death but rather expired gracefully out of sight. But war is real and war is terrible. War is a bad taste business.[16]

News Manipulation: the Case of the Gulf War

The authorities do not always stop at the 'filtering' kind of censorship. They may go on to create a version of the war which may have little basis in fact. One case of this was the Gulf War.

Saddam Hussein's use of television was apparent. Part of his strategy was to rely on American reaction against what he anticipated would be heavy casualties in Baghdad. He gave CNN a special protected line to the outside world, and allowed CNN correspondents to stay when others were expelled. He also used television for cruder kinds of propaganda. Among those held hostage in Iraq were children, some of whom were made to appear on television with Saddam so that he could talk to them about how well they were being looked after. And, contrary to the Geneva Convention, captured pilots from coalition countries were shown. Some were severely bruised. They made obviously coerced statements saying the war against Iraq was criminal.

Saddam ruled by blood and terror. There were Stalin-like show trials, followed by executions. Children were encouraged to inform on their parents, and men were made to take part in the execution of their sons and brothers. People were terrified to express any criticism of Saddam. Every newspaper had a photograph of him on the front page every day. Saddam was always the first item on the television news. He would go out to meet members of the public and ask them who they had to thank for their prosperity. Their predictably fulsome answers would take up much of the news.[17]

There was also news manipulation on the other side. One instance came from Kuwait. Two women told a Congressional hearing in Washington that Iraqi troops in Kuwait had taken dozens of babies, perhaps more than a hundred, from incubators in a hospital and left them to die. One of the women claimed to have buried forty newborn babies killed in this way. The story was presented again, more elaborately, to the United Nations Security Council and it was used as an argument for war by President Bush.

Later it was found that five of the seven 'witnesses' in the UN presentation had used false names without indicating this. One was the daughter of the Kuwaiti ambassador in Washington. The women had been sent to testify by Hill and Knowlton, a public relations firm which was paid $10 million to present the Kuwaiti case. After the war the allegations were not supported by doctors in the hospital.[18] Since there were many real Iraqi atrocities in Kuwait, it is odd that this fake one was thought necessary. It was disturbingly easily accepted and exposed only after its work had been done.

It was widely (though perhaps not correctly) held that support for the Vietnam War had been undermined in the United States by the television coverage of the horrors. Those running the Gulf War took no chances. The *New York Times* described how the manipulation of the news began with 'a decision by the Administration's most senior officials, including President Bush, to manage the information flow in a way that supported the operation's political goals and avoided the perceived mistakes of Vietnam'.[19]

On television the air attacks on Iraqi targets were presented like computer games. There was praise for 'smart bombs' guided by radar and lasers, which gave them extraordinary accuracy in hitting military targets rather than nearby civilians. After the war, a spokesman for the US air force said that the smart bombs were less than 9 per cent of what was dropped on Iraq. The remainder was dropped from old-fashioned bombers with an accuracy rate of about 25 per cent.[20]

Those concerned to 'manage the information flow' hoped for not too many detailed reports from Baghdad. Correspondents were urged to leave, and those working for the largest American newspapers were withdrawn. President Bush himself telephoned American editors to persuade them to recall their teams.

What the public would accept was part of the trap in which journalists found themselves. In Britain some Conservative Members of Parliament pressed the Foreign Secretary to persuade the broadcasting organizations to remove their correspondents from Baghdad. One referred to the BBC as the 'Baghdad Broadcasting Corporation'. In the United States, Peter Arnett, who stayed in Baghdad to report for CNN, was subjected to similar attacks to those Harrison Salisbury had experienced in Hanoi. Arnett too was likened by one critic to Lord Haw Haw. He was attacked by General Schwarzkopf for reporting on civilian buildings which had been hit.[21]

These attacks intensified when the news to be reported was the destruction by an American missile of an underground shelter at Al Amiriya in Baghdad. Two or three hundred civilians, including many women and children, were burnt to death. The scenes on television showed what is sometimes the reality behind the computer-game simulations. Some people would have liked this news to have been suppressed. There were telephone complaints in the United States to CNN and in Britain to the BBC and ITN.[22]

The massacre of retreating Iraqi troops at Mutla Ridge also raised questions about reporting the unwelcome reality of war. There was some debate in Britain when the *Observer* published Kenneth Jeresky's photograph of the head of an Iraqi soldier. The man's hair was burnt. His eyes had gone from their sockets. His nose and mouth were charred and burnt. The picture showed something between a face and a skull. Some felt that this was taking the showing of horror too far. No American newspaper would take the picture.

Others felt it was important to show the reality of the war. Alex Thomson, who reported the war for Channel Four News, took this view: 'What happened below Mutla Ridge was not some genteel matter of military burial with people being laid out under blankets with their rifles across them, it was people being cut to ribbons and burned alive as they tried to save themselves.'[23] The television pictures of the massacre are said to have influenced President Bush's decision to stop the war before the public pleasure in victory turned into revulsion.[24]

Throughout the war censorship was used to keep anxiety or bad news about coalition forces from the home public. Photographers were not allowed to show the coalition dead.[25] Stephen Sackur, covering the war for BBC Radio, asked how many of the seventeen British servicemen who died during the ground offensive were killed by Iraqi fire. He was told that details of casualties could not be made public.[26] One brigadier briefed troops about an expected tank battle. He said they would hear their horribly burnt friends screaming in agony. They would never forget the experience and would have nightmares for the rest of their lives. Simon Clifford, reporting for provincial newspapers in Britain, wrote up the briefing, but these parts were deleted by the censors at the Forward Transmission Unit.[27]

A system was set up for reporters with the coalition forces, under which they were given official help and would share the information between them (the 'pool' system). Life was made difficult for those who did not join. One of them, Robert Fisk of the *Independent*, was told, 'You're not allowed to talk to US Marines and they're not allowed to talk to you.' French television reporters risked their lives filming the fighting at Khafji. They broke no security guidelines, but their tape was confiscated: they were not in the pool.

Those who did join the pool were supposed always to be escorted. Members of the pool were under severe restrictions on talking to soldiers. With the US forces, a Public Affairs Officer was always present. Gary Matsumoto, reporting for NBC, noted the effect of his PAO on the soldiers interviewed. The PAO would stare right into the soldier's eyes. He would 'stretch out a hand holding a cassette recorder, and click it on in the soldier's face. This was patent intimidation . . . which was clear from the soldiers' reactions. After virtually every interview, the soldier would let out a deep breath, turn to the PAO, and ask, "Can I keep my job?" '[28]

Stanley Cloud, the chief of *Time*'s Washington bureau, later said, 'it is membership in that pool that gave the Pentagon the opening to control everything we did in the Gulf War'. He also said:

> They figured out a way to control every facet of our coverage. They restricted our access to a point where we couldn't do any of our own reporting. They fed us a steady diet of press conferences in which they decided what the news would be. And if somehow, after all that, we managed to report on something they didn't like, they would censor it out . . . It amounted to recruiting the press into the military.[29]

Stephen Sackur remembered a colonel announcing to the British army pool that the ground offensive had begun, but that they would not be allowed to report on it for some time: 'I'd go back to sleep, if I were you.'[30]

Some members of the pool felt that pressure to identify with their units was a threat to their identity as objective reporters. Deborah Amos, of National Public Radio, commented: 'They'd say things to me like we want you out there at least two weeks before the ground war because we want you to bond with your unit. I didn't want to bond with my unit. I wanted to report on my unit.' Pool reporters wore military uniform, which Deborah Amos again saw as an erosion of her independent identity: 'There was something insidious about us having their clothes and I kept saying this over and over again. It makes it harder to remember who you are when you're in their clothes.'[31]

From outside, Robert Fisk described the 'almost fatally blurred' relationship between the pool and the army. Pool journalists were given small American flags taken from the cockpits of jets which had bombed Baghdad. The colonel presenting the flags said the reporters were warriors, too. They depended on soldiers for protection, and also for advice and news. 'So dependent have journalists become upon information dispensed by the Western military authorities in Saudi Arabia, so enamoured of their technology, that Press and television reporters have found themselves trapped.'[32]

Tribalism

Tribal hostility can develop quickly. Only a month after the outbreak of the First World War, Robert Bridges, the Poet Laureate, wrote to *The Times*:

> Since the beginning of this war the meaning of it has in one respect considerably changed, and I hope that our people will see that it is primarily a holy war. It is manifestly a war between Christ and the Devil . . . There was never anything in the world worthier of extermination, and it is the plain duty of civilised nations to unite to drive it back into its home and exterminate it there.[33]

Events since 1914 have made us less comfortable with the word 'extermination'. Was the Poet Laureate advocating only the extermination of an abstraction, the German aggression? Or was he urging the extermination of the soldiers who made up the German army? The moral blurring helped to sustain public support while the trapped rival armies slaughtered each other.

There is the same disturbing note in other First World War propaganda. At the time of a campaign to intern Germans in Britain, one cartoon was headed 'A Clean Sweep'. It showed Britannia as a housewife with a broom, sweeping up piles of small figures marked 'Germans'. A sign said: 'To the Concentration Camps'. There was a caption in which Mrs Britannia said, 'It has to be done: so I might just as well do it first as last – and so get rid of all the dangerous microbes.'[34]

As part of the same campaign Horatio Bottomley said, 'I call for a vendetta – a vendetta against every German in Britain – whether "naturalized" or not . . . You cannot "naturalize" an unnatural abortion, a hellish freak. But you *can* exterminate him.' He urged that naturalized Germans should be made to wear a distinctive badge and not be allowed out after dark. Their children should be excluded from schools. And he further supported this treatment of Germans by encouraging fantasies of them being stripped of protective dignity. After the war, 'If by chance you should discover one day in a restaurant you are being served by a German waiter, you will throw the soup in his foul face; if you find yourself sitting at the side of a German clerk, you will spill the inkpot over his foul head.'[35]

Despite the hysteria, some people kept the human decencies alive. At New College, Oxford, lists of members killed in the war were put up under the heading 'Pro Patria'. Three of the German soldiers killed in 1914 had been at the college. In 1915, a visiting American wrote to the *Morning Post*, disgusted that the three Germans were on the list. Warden Spooner replied that 'the Germans had done no disgraceful act in fighting for their own country' and that one had 'died in the act of carrying in a wounded comrade'. Spooner suggested that 'to carry on a spirit of hate against those who passed into another world can make us neither better patriots nor better men'. (Later, the philosophy tutor H.W.B. Joseph persuaded the college to erect a permanent memorial: 'In memory of the men of this College who coming from a foreign land entered into the inheritance of this place and returning fought and died for their country in the War 1914–1919'.)[36] But such exceptions to the tribal climate were rare.

The Second World War was far from being a mere tribal conflict, but, in the Pacific war especially, attitudes on the home front were highly tribal, and at times racist.

On the Japanese side, some held a belief in their own racial superiority. A year before the war, the politician Nakajima Chikuhei said that there were superior and inferior races in the world and that it was the sacred duty of the leading race to lead and enlighten the inferior ones. Because the Japanese were racially pure descendants of the gods, they were 'the sole superior race in the world'.[37]

When war came, so did racist stereotypes of the Americans and British. A Japanese novelist said he was 'itching to beat the bestial, insensitive Americans to a pulp'. One publication described the 'bestial' enemy as demons, devils, fiends, monsters, and as 'hairy, twisted-nosed savages'. Another urged extermination: 'Beat and kill these animals that have lost their human nature! That is the great mission that Heaven has given to the Yamato race, for the eternal peace of the world!' Another magazine said of the Americans, 'the more of them are sent to hell, the cleaner the world will be'.[38]

Racism was not just Japanese. In the United States, the Japanese were called 'yellowbellies', 'yellow bastards' and 'yellow monkeys'. Admiral Halsey, of the US Navy, said he was 'rarin' to go to get some more monkey meat'. In Britain Sir Alexander Cadogan, Permanent Secretary at the Foreign Office, wrote in his diary of the Japanese as 'beastly little monkeys'. The Australian General Sir Thomas Blamey said of the Japanese soldier that 'he is a sub-human beast', and 'a cross between the human being and the ape'.

There were worse forms of dehumanizing. Sir Thomas Blamey said, 'we have to exterminate these vermin'. The journalist Ernie Pyle said, 'out here I soon gathered that the Japanese were looked upon as something subhuman and repulsive; the way some people feel about cockroaches or mice'. He described some Japanese prisoners: 'They were wrestling and laughing and talking just like normal human beings. And yet they gave me the creeps, and I wanted a mental bath after looking at them.' Car stickers showed rats with Japanese faces. *The Nation* contrasted the manly death of the typical American soldier with the way Japanese soldiers died like cornered rats. The flame throwers used to attack Japanese positions were advertised in the *New York Times* with a picture of an attack captioned 'Clearing Out a Rat's Nest'.[39]

The tribal loyalty evoked by war can spill over into tribal hatred. Anti-Japanese racism in Allied countries led some to attitudes which at other times might have appalled them. An American submarine commander was honoured for an action in which he sank a Japanese ship and spent more than an hour massacring the survivors. A report in *Time* magazine of another American massacre of Japanese survivors in lifeboats provoked a letter of moral criticism, which was published. Many of the replies to that letter claimed that Japanese atrocities justified the massacre. One reader wrote of 'killing a helpless rattlesnake'. Another had 'thoroughly enjoyed' reading about the slaughter. Another said that a 'good old American custom I would like to see is nailing a Jap hide on every "backhouse" door in America'.[40]

Racism influenced attitudes towards policy. Admiral Halsey urged 'the almost total elimination of the Japanese as a race'. The chairman of the War Manpower Commission suggested 'the extermination of the Japanese in toto'. Polls suggested that more than 10 per cent of Americans supported the 'annihilation' or 'extermination' of the Japanese as a people. A poll in December 1945 found that more than one-fifth of Americans regretted that many more atomic bombs were not used before Japan had a chance to surrender.[41]

The mutual racism of the Pacific war was an extreme case. But the tribalism of the home front is important in most wars. Official propaganda, fed to people often too willing to believe, distorts their judgement and weakens their powers of criticism. As Erich Maria Remarque and Robert Graves found, the resulting view of the war may bear little relation to its reality. The home front in Germany was 'a foreign world' and in England they 'talked a foreign language'. The official version of events creates tribal solidarity and the mind-set to go with it. On the home front tribalism and belief combine to sustain the trap of war.

CHAPTER 21

The Stone Has Started to Roll: 1914

The war was an unprecedented disgrace to the human intellect . . . The contrast between the success of modern European minds in controlling almost any situation in which the elements are physical bodies and the forces physical forces, and their inability to control situations in which the elements are human beings and the forces mental forces, left an indelible mark on the memory of everyone who was concerned in it.

R.G. Collingwood, *An Autobiography*

Because war causes so much death and misery, it can only be justified by showing that the alternative will bring greater horrors. But, typically, the attempt to make this case is casual and impressionistic. Consider other life-and-death decisions. Where someone's terminal illness has become a nightmare, family and doctors may give careful and often painful thought to withdrawing life support. The decision about one person's life is taken very seriously. This is in sharp contrast to the slack thinking when the decision is about war.

This is partly because, for most people, the outbreak of war is experienced passively. It comes like the outbreak of a thunderstorm. Only a few people in governments take part in the discussions. Negotiations break down: an ultimatum is issued. The rest of us turn on the television news and find ourselves at war. Often even the leaders who take the decisions are trapped in a war most of them do not want. 1914 was like that.

1 THE OUTBREAK OF FOUR WARS

June 28, 1914 was the fourteenth wedding anniversary of Archduke Franz Ferdinand of Austria. He visited Sarajevo so that he and his wife, side by side, could inspect the troops. His assassination on that day was the start of five weeks during which Europe stumbled into war. The inadequate thinking behind the decisions of those weeks started with the assassination itself.

Half a dozen schoolboys planned the killing. The shot was fired by Gavrilo Princip, who was an admirer of Nietzsche, liking to recite passages from *Ecce Homo*. A passionate nationalist, he hoped the assassination would start a nationalist revolution. In 1912 he had volunteered to fight in the First Balkan War, but had been rejected because he was too small. Later he said that in Sarajevo, 'I had little to do with people at all. Wherever I went, people took me for a weakling . . . and I pretended that I was a weak person, which I was not.' He told an interviewing psychiatrist that he had wanted to die for his ideals and had 'wanted to avenge the nation. The motives: revenge and love.'[1]

The way his group reached the decision to carry out the assassination was described by one of them, Borijove Jevtić. Allowance should be made for their ignorance of just how important their act was to be. Even so, there is something disappointing about the quality of their deliberation, something hasty about their reasoning:

> Only four letters and two numerals were sufficient to make us unanimous, without discussion, as to what we should do about it. They were contained in the fateful date, 28 June [the date of the Serbian defeat by Turkey, in 1389 in Kosovo at the Field of Blackbirds]. How dared Franz Ferdinand, not only the representative of the oppressor but in his own person an arrogant tyrant, enter Sarajevo on that day? Such an entry was a studied insult. 28 June is a day engraved deeply in the heart of every Serb . . . That was no day for Franz Ferdinand, the new oppressor, to venture to the very doors of Serbia for a display of the force of arms which kept us beneath his heel. Our decision was taken almost immediately. Death to the tyrant![2]

On a ridiculously simple view of history, the decision resulting from these thoughts ruined the rest of the twentieth century. If there had been no assassination, there would have been no First World War. The Russian Revolution, Nazism and the Second World War can all be seen as coming from the First World War. But the assassins can hardly be held responsible for all this. And it would be harsh to hold them solely responsible even for the outbreak of war in 1914.

Who or what was responsible? Answering this question starts with an analysis of the events between the assassination on 28 June and the German invasion of Belgium on 3 August. In those thirty-six days, a political murder by a group of teenagers was turned into a world war. This happened in stages as four different wars broke out. The first war was between Austria–Hungary and Serbia. That led to a war between Russia and Germany, which led to a war between Germany and France, which in turn led to a war between Britain and Germany.

Austria–Hungary and Serbia

On 23 July Austria–Hungary responded to the assassination by issuing an ultimatum to Serbia. It demanded the suppression of propaganda and subversion against Austria–Hungary and the purging of those who had taken part in them, the tightening of border controls, the dissolution of a Serbian nationalist organization, the arrest of named officers, and Austro-Hungarian participation in the inquiry into the assassination.

On hearing the details of the ultimatum, Sazonov, the Russian Foreign Minister, said, 'C'est la guerre européene.' He also said to the Austro-Hungarian ambassador, 'You are setting fire to Europe!'[3] The British Foreign Secretary, Sir Edward Grey, said it was 'harsher in tone and more humiliating in its terms than any communication of which we had recollection addressed by one independent Government to another'.[4]

It was meant to be tough. A meeting of the Austro-Hungarian Council of Ministers had been virtually unanimous in agreeing that 'such stringent demands must be addressed to Serbia, that will make a refusal almost certain, so that the road to a radical solution by means of a military action should be opened'.[5] Count Leopold Berchtold, the Austrian Foreign Minister, told the German ambassador that it would be 'very disagreeable' to him if the Serbs accepted the ultimatum.[6] Having waited twenty-five days before issuing the ultimatum, Austria–Hungary demanded a reply in forty-eight hours.

The ultimatum was tough partly as a result of German encouragement and pressure. The German ambassador told Berchtold that an action against Serbia was fully expected and that 'Germany would not understand' if they neglected this opportunity.[7] In Berlin it was indicated that 'we would agree to any method of procedure which they might determine on there, even at the risk of a war with Russia'. The Austrian ambassador said, 'Here every delay in the beginning of war operations is regarded as signifying the danger that foreign powers might interfere. We are urgently advised to proceed without delay and to place the world before a *fait accompli*.'[8] Austria–Hungary probably thought that backing from Germany would deter Russian intervention in support of Serbia.

The Serbian reply to the ultimatum on 25 July accepted nearly all the demands, but objected to Austro-Hungarian participation in the inquiry into the assassination. Austria–Hungary then broke off diplomatic relations.

On 27 July in an attempt at peacemaking, Sir Edward Grey spoke to Lichnowsky, the German ambassador in London. Saying that he had urged moderation on Russia, he asked Germany to persuade Austria to accept Serbia's reply to the ultimatum. Lichnowsky put this in a telegram to Theobald von Bethmann Hollweg, the Chancellor, who passed it on to the Kaiser. On 28 July the Kaiser said that the Serbian response contained 'the announcement *orbi et urbi* of a capitulation of the most humiliating kind and as a result, *every cause for war* falls to the ground'.[9] On the 30th, Bethmann Hollweg cabled Vienna: 'We are, of course, ready to fulfil the obligations of our alliance, but we must decline to be drawn wantonly into a world conflagration by Vienna, without having any regard paid to our counsel.'[10] At the same time, however, the German Chief of Staff, General Helmuth von Moltke, was telling the Austrian army not to risk any further delay in mobilizing.

Berchtold himself hoped that a declaration of war would lead to Serbia submitting without a fight. On 28 July Austria–Hungary declared war on Serbia. (As the Austrian ambassador had already left Belgrade, the declaration of war was sent by telegram and the Serbian Prime Minister at first thought it was a hoax.)

On 29 July the British ambassador was told that Bethmann Hollweg had passed on the British proposal that Austria should accept the Serbian response, but had been told 'that it was too late to act upon your suggestion as events had marched too rapidly'.[11]

Russia and Germany

On 24 July, the day after the Austrian ultimatum, the Crown Prince of Serbia appealed to the Tsar: 'We cannot defend ourselves. Therefore we pray Your Majesty to lend help as soon as possible. Your Majesty has given so many proofs of your previous goodwill and we confidently hope that this appeal will find an echo in your generous Slav heart.'[12] The previous year Russia had failed to support Serbia in a crisis. Both honour and credibility made it important not to back away again.

On the 25th, Russia responded to the Austrian bullying of her ally by partial mobilization. There was an emotional exchange of telegrams between the Tsar and the Serbian Crown Prince. On 27 July the Tsar cabled, 'Your Royal Highness is not deceived, in turning to me in this extraordinarily difficult moment, in the feelings which I cherish for you and also in my heartfelt affection for the Serbian nation.' He talked of averting the horrors of a new war, but said that, 'if, contrary to our most upright wishes, we have no success, Your Highness may rest assured that under no circumstances will Russia remain indifferent to Serbia's fate'. On the 29th the Crown Prince replied that he was 'deeply moved' by the Tsar's telegram, which 'fills our soul with the hope that the future of Serbia is assured', and said that the Serbian 'sentiments of deep gratitude . . . will be preserved in the souls of all Serbians as something sacred'.

Germany had the impression that Russia would not get much support from her ally, France. On 29 July Germany warned that further Russian mobilization would compel German mobilization. The response of Russian ministers was to propose immediate general mobilization, but the Tsar hesitated. On 30 July it was clear that Austria would not suspend action against Serbia, and Russia announced a general mobilization. The Kaiser sent the Tsar a telegram saying that peace depended on Russia halting its mobilization. The Tsar showed his Foreign Minister the telegram and said, in an agitated voice, 'He is asking the impossible . . . If I agreed to Germany's demands now, we should find ourselves unarmed against the Austrian army which is mobilized already. It would be madness.'[13]

On 31 July Germany declared a state of 'imminent danger of war' and threatened general mobilization unless Russia suspended 'warlike measures'. On 1 August Germany declared war on Russia and announced general mobilization.

Germany and France

On 31 July Germany sent an ultimatum to France, demanding French neutrality in a war between Germany and Russia, together with the handing over to Germany of the fortresses of Toul and Verdun while the war lasted, as a guarantee. Germany demanded that France should accept these humiliating terms within eighteen hours.

German plans for war were based on the need to avoid having to fight on two fronts, against both Russia and France. The Schlieffen plan (named after the general who devised it) was to attack France at once and to win victory in the West before turning to Russia.

German mobilization was a threat to France. On 1 August France also mobilized.

The diplomatic efforts to avoid war turned into farce. (I take this account from Barbara Tuchman's book *The Guns of August*.) On the day France and Germany mobilized, Sir Edward Grey made another attempt to keep the peace. He telephoned Lichnowsky, the German ambassador, and offered to keep France neutral if Germany would stay neutral with respect to France and Russia. Lichnowsky misunderstood the proposal. He thought Grey was offering to keep France neutral in a war between Russia and Germany, provided Germany did not attack France. He sent a telegram to this effect to Berlin.

On 1 August Germany invaded Luxemburg, claiming this was necessary to protect railway communications against a possible French attack. On 2 August Germany sent an ultimatum to Belgium, demanding passage through the country for troops invading France, which was refused.

In the late afternoon of 1 August, shortly before the invasion of Luxemburg was due to begin, Lichnowsky's telegram, with the misunderstood version of Grey's offer, reached the Foreign Office. Bethmann

Hollweg, together with his Foreign Minister, hurried with it in a taxi to the palace.

The Kaiser read Moltke the telegram, and said that the army should all march to the east, as they could now fight against Russia only. Moltke had spent years preparing to implement the Schlieffen plan. He foresaw the chaotic results of adopting the Kaiser's sudden improvised change of strategy, and simply refused to accept it: 'Your Majesty, it cannot be done. The deployment of millions cannot be improvised. If Your Majesty insists on leading the whole army to the East it will not be an army ready for battle but a disorganized mob of armed men with no arrangements for supply. Those arrangements took a whole year of intricate labour to complete and once settled it cannot be altered.'[14]

The Kaiser grudgingly allowed himself to be persuaded by Moltke. He then sent a telegram to England, in another attempt to negotiate French neutrality, but he saw that the invasion of Luxemburg would undermine this diplomatic move. Without asking Moltke, he also ordered a telephone message to be sent, followed by a telegram, cancelling the invasion. Moltke went back in despair to the General Staff, and refused to sign the written version of the order to halt the invasion. The telephone call had arrived too late, and the invasion had gone ahead at seven o'clock as planned. At seven-thirty, the invading army was caught up by cars from Germany ordering them back, saying that a mistake had been made. But it was too late, as news of the invasion had been sent round Europe. The invasion was completed on 2 August and, on 3 August, Germany declared war on France and invaded Belgium.

British Entry

Britain and France had developed a military understanding against a possible threat from Germany, but there had been ambiguity about what was agreed. In one letter to the French, the British government had said they were not committed to anything by taking part, but substantial joint military plans were made. In 1911 Lord Esher, of the Committee of Imperial Defence, told the Prime Minister that the plans had 'certainly committed us to fight'.[15]

In 1912 a naval agreement between the two countries secretly committed Britain to guard the French coast from attack by the Channel, leaving the French navy free to go to the Mediterranean. But Sir Edward Grey wrote a letter to the French ambassador, saying each country was free to decide whether to use force in support of the other, and that the naval agreement was 'not based upon an engagement to cooperate in war'.[16] One of Germany's central aims was to keep Britain neutral if war broke out, and the divided and ambiguous British attitude encouraged them to hope for this.

At weekends Sir Edward Grey liked to escape to Itchen Abbas for some fishing. Fifteen years before, in his book on fly-fishing, he had written of the oppressiveness of the hard pavements of London on hot summer days:

> Happily it is possible to get away, if not to home, at any rate to some country retreat at the end of the week, and to combine the best of dry fly fishing with this on Saturday ... The earliest trains leave Waterloo, the usual place of departure for the Itchen or the Test, either at or just before six o'clock in the morning ... At some time between eight and nine o'clock, you step out of the train, and are in a few minutes among all the long-desired things ... You are grateful for the grass on which you walk, even for the soft country dust about your feet.[17]

On Saturday 25 July the situation looked serious enough for Grey to postpone the fishing. He spent most of the day in London trying to arrange international mediation to avert war. On Sunday, by then at Itchen Abbas, he had invitations sent to Germany, France and Italy to attend a conference with Britain. But next day, the 27th, Germany turned down the invitation. Grey then tried his approach through Lichnowsky to persuade Germany to urge restraint on Austria–Hungary, two days later receiving the rebuff that 'events had marched too rapidly'.

Both France and Russia pressed Britain to stand firmly with them, arguing that this would make Germany back down and so be the best way to prevent war. Grey was reluctant to accept this. He did not want to give Russia a reason for being tough. And he was under pressure from Cabinet members hostile to getting entangled in war. Pressure the other way came from other Cabinet members, who were supported by Foreign Office officials and by the Conservative opposition.

Pressure also came from Paul Cambon, the French ambassador. After failing to persuade Grey to fight beside France, he appealed to British honour:

> All our plans are arranged in common. Our General Staffs have consulted. You have seen all our schemes and preparations. Look at our Fleet! Our whole Fleet is in the Mediterranean in consequence of our arrangements with you and our coasts are open to the enemy. You have laid us wide open! ... Et l'honneur? Est-ce que l'Angleterre comprend ce que c'est l'honneur?[18]

On 2 August the Cabinet agreed to naval defence of the French coast, and that violation of the neutrality of Belgium would be grounds for war. On 3 August Britain gave Germany an ultimatum to this effect. The same day Germany invaded Belgium.

The Sense of Defeat

As war closed in, statesmen and diplomats felt a sense of failure and defeat.

Sir Edward Goschen, the British ambassador in Berlin, presented the final British ultimatum to the German Foreign Secretary. He then called on the Chancellor, who was 'very agitated', and had obviously not expected war with Britain. Goschen reported him as saying that the ultimatum was terrible:

> just for a word – 'neutrality', a word which in wartime had so often been disregarded – just for a scrap of paper Great Britain was going to make war on a kindred nation who desired nothing better than to be friends with her. All his efforts in that direction had been rendered useless by this last terrible step, and the policy to which, as I knew, he had devoted himself since his accession to office had tumbled down like a house of cards.[19]

Bethmann Hollweg's predecessor as Chancellor, Prince von Bülow, corroborated this picture in a rather histrionic description of a visit to him in the Chancellor's Palace after the outbreak. He noticed the anguish in Bethmann Hollweg's eyes:

> For an instant we neither of us spoke. At last I said to him: 'Well, tell me, at least, how it all happened.' He raised his long, thin arms to heaven, and answered in a dull, exhausted voice: 'Oh – if only I knew!' In many later polemics on 'war guilt' I have often wished it had been possible to produce a snap-shot of Bethmann Hollweg standing there at the moment he said those words. Such a photograph would have been the best proof that this wretched man had never 'wanted war'.[20]

Lichnowsky, the German ambassador in London, had breakfast on 2 August with the Prime Minister. He urged that Britain should not side with France, saying that Germany was far more likely to be crushed than France. Asquith wrote to Venetia Stanley that 'he was very agitated, poor man, & wept . . . He was bitter about the policy of his Government in not restraining Austria & seemed quite heartbroken.'[21]

The German ambassador in St Petersburg, Count Pourtalès, was in a similar state when he took the Declaration of War to the Russian Foreign Minister. Agitated, he twice asked Sazonov whether Russia would accept the German ultimatum. Sazonov later described the scene as Pourtalès presented the Declaration of War:

> Pulling out of his pocket a folded sheet of paper, the ambassador repeated his request for the third time in a voice that trembled. I said that I could give no

other answer. Deeply moved, the Ambassador said to me, speaking with difficulty, 'In that case my Government charges me to give you the following note.' . . . After handing the note to me, the Ambassador, who had evidently found it a great strain to carry out his orders, lost all self-control and leaning against the window burst into tears. With a gesture of despair he repeated: 'Who could have thought that I should be leaving St Petersburg under such circumstances!' In spite of my own emotion, which I managed to overcome, I felt sincerely sorry for him. We embraced each other and with tottering steps he walked out of the room.[22]

As evening fell on 3 August, Sir Edward Grey famously said, 'The lamps are going out all over Europe; we shall not see them lit again in our lifetime.'

2 CONFUSION AND COMMUNICATION

How were these diplomats and statesmen unable to avert what so many of them saw as a disaster?

The first layer of explanation cites their confusions and misunderstandings. Some had ambiguous intentions. They misperceived each other and miscalculated each other's responses — they were sleepwalking into war.

Ambiguous Intentions

Where governments want to avoid war, and their aims are sufficiently compatible for agreement to be reached, there is a chance of peace. This chance is reduced where the aims are less coherent. A government divided or confused about its own aims may itself act irrationally and make it harder for other governments to respond to its policies.

The British government did not want war, but it was divided over the way to peace. Was it to avoid entanglements with France? Or was it to deter Germany by a firm commitment to France? This division mirrored public opinion. The government was held back by the anti-war wing of the Liberal Party and was urged not to let France down by the Conservative opposition. The government's muddle over aims was expressed by Lord Esher, who said that Britain was certainly committed to fight, and Sir Edward Grey, who said to the German ambassador that Britain had no obligations to France in the event of a European war and wanted to preserve 'an absolutely free hand'.[23] France had the impression that they could rely on the Royal Navy, while Germany had the impression that Britain would remain neutral.

The German government's aims contained a greater ambiguity, which is reflected in the views of more recent historians, who disagree over whether the German leaders aimed at a European war.

Fritz Fischer, arguing that Germany aimed at war, cited German pressure on Austria to give Serbia an unacceptable ultimatum. Some German leaders saw war as inevitable and necessary, and only pretended to co-operate with peace efforts. Helmuth von Moltke thought of war in racial terms and considered it inevitable. He wrote, 'a European war is bound to come sooner or later, and then it will, in the last resort, be a struggle between *Teuton and Slav*. It is the duty of all states who uphold the banner of German spiritual culture to prepare for this conflict.'[24] Moltke wanted to have the inevitable war soon, before Russia and France were properly prepared.

Other German leaders were prepared to risk war, but hoped it could be localized. Bethmann Hollweg told the German ambassador in Vienna that Germany was concerned only to 'enable the realization of Austria–Hungary's aim without at the same time unleashing a world war, and should this after all prove unavoidable, to improve as far as possible the conditions under which it is to be waged'.[25] By late July a localized war looked less possible and Bethmann Hollweg put pressure on Austria to accept mediation. One observer in Berlin contrasted Moltke pushing for war with Bethmann Hollweg's efforts to 'apply the brakes with all his energy'.[26] Bethmann Hollweg was defeated. In the first month of the war he said to a friend, 'for five years I have worked that this insane war could be avoided. This work and hope have shattered in my hands.'[27]

The Kaiser was on both sides of the debate. Like Moltke, he believed in inevitable racial conflict: before the crisis he had written of 'the imminent struggle for existence which the Germanic peoples of Europe (Austria, Germany) will have to fight out against the Slavs (Russians) and their Latin (Gallic) supporters'. But in the July crisis, he thought that the Serbian response to the ultimatum removed the grounds for war at that time.

The Kaiser was the ultimate authority, but he was weak and rather dim. His marginal comments on diplomatic documents and in letters during the crisis are petulant. The Serbs were 'Orientals, therefore liars, tricksters, and masters of evasion'. Another comment on the Serbs was 'Just tread hard on the heels of that rabble!' He called one of Grey's attempts to mediate 'a tremendous piece of British insolence'. A marginal note on Grey said, 'Common cur!' and another on the English said, 'That mean crew of shopkeepers has tried to trick us with dinners and speeches.'[28] At times he thought of his position in grand terms: in 1910 he said that he ruled 'as an instrument of the Lord'.[29] In the summer of 1914 one of his friends noticed that he was 'more nervous than usual'. During the July crisis he was in the dangerous state of being very anxious to show that he was not weak. Gustav Krupp met him on 6 July and thought it was almost pathetic how the Kaiser kept saying, 'I shall not chicken out.'[30]

The German government's lack of coherence influenced their response to Grey's peace proposals. There was certainly some deception: Germany had planned in advance to express surprise when the Austrian ultimatum was delivered. The German Foreign Minister passed on Grey's request to Austria for an extension of the time limit on the ultimatum only after it had expired. And he sent on some later British peace proposals, telling the Austrian ambassador that Germany *does not identify itself* with these propositions, that on the contrary it advises to disregard them, but that it must pass them on, to satisfy the English Government'.[31] Bethmann Hollweg commented, 'If we rejected every attempt at mediation the whole world would hold us responsible for the conflagration and represent us as the real warmongers. That would also make our position impossible here in Germany, where we have got to appear as though the war had been forced on us.' A message was sent to London that 'we have immediately initiated mediation in the sense desired by Sir Edward Grey'.[32]

Germany encouraged Austria to be tough and yet claimed to want peace. If the German government had been unambiguously aiming at peace throughout the crisis, war would have been unlikely. Some German leaders wanted war and all of them were willing to risk a major war; but some, like Bethmann Hollweg, hoped that war could be limited to Austria–Hungary and Serbia. There was no coherence. Between the Kaiser, Bethmann Hollweg and Moltke, no one was fully in charge and policy was being run in part by supporters of war. The hope for peace was that German policy was also partly run by people half against war. This was not enough.

Chinese Whispers and Blind Man's Buff

The story is one of governments' mutual misperceptions and repeated miscalculations about each other's responses. There were too many governments for them all to understand each other. The communications were like a children's game of Chinese whispers: Britain sent messages to Austria through Germany and hoped they would be heard undistorted.

The misperceptions made the moves of each country like blind man's buff. Berchtold wrongly thought an Austrian declaration of war might avoid all military action by forcing Serbia into instant submission. On 31 July the Austro-Hungarian Chief of Staff said, 'We are not clear whether Russia is only threatening so we must not let ourselves be distracted from our action against Serbia.'[33] The German government, alarmed by Russia's partial mobilization, wrongly thought the way to deter further steps was to threaten their own mobilization. Germany, again wrongly, thought that France would not support Russia.

The story was the same between Britain and Germany. Things were complicated by the interpretation of secret intelligence. The second secretary at the Russian embassy in London, Benno von Siebert, was passing information to the German Foreign Office. In 1914 documents from this source reached Bethmann Hollweg, which showed that Britain and Russia were negotiating a naval agreement which would tie Britain into supporting a Russian landing in Pomerania. An account appeared in the German press and the question was raised in the House of Commons. Grey replied that no unpublished agreements existed which committed Britain to participate in a European war. Bethmann Hollweg took this to be a lie and felt betrayed by Grey.

There was also the lack of clarity. Grey's unclear offer to keep France neutral if Germany would stay at peace with both Russia and France was interpreted by Lichnowsky as more of a concession. Sometimes clarity was not even an aim of British policy. One minister expressed the thought that 'if both sides do not know what we shall do, both will be less willing to run risks'.[34] This ambiguity disastrously allowed the German government to count on British neutrality.

Even if all the governments had wholeheartedly wanted to avoid war, it would take an optimist to bet that peace would survive so much muddle and confusion.

3 THE MILITARY TRAPS

Confusion and ambiguity would have mattered less in a world prepared for peace, but the statesmen were inside a series of military traps created by their preparations against attack.

The Mobilization Trap and Military Drift

Governments often make military arrangements which drift out of their control. This was a key feature of 1914.

Moltke saw the partial Russian mobilization as forcing mobilization on Austria and Germany:

> she puts Austria in a desperate position and shifts the responsibility to her, inasmuch as she is forcing Austria to secure herself against a surprise by Russia . . . but she knows perfectly well that Germany could not remain inactive in the event of a belligerent collision between her ally and Russia. So Germany, too, will be forced to mobilize.[35]

Bethmann Hollweg echoed this in a warning on 29 July to the Russian Foreign Minister: 'further continuation of Russian mobilization measures would force us to mobilize, and in that case a European war could scarcely be prevented'.[36]

In Russia on the other hand, the Chief of Staff, General Yanushkevich, was extremely concerned to move from partial mobilization to full mobilization. He cited 'the extreme danger that would result for us if we were not ready for war with Germany'. He said that, once this had been ordered, 'I shall go away, smash my telephone and generally adopt measures which will prevent anyone from finding me for the purpose of giving contrary orders.' On 30 July, the Tsar was persuaded of the danger of inadequate preparations for an apparently inevitable war, and ordered general mobilization. The Foreign Minister told Yanushkevich, 'Now you can smash your telephone.'[37]

A.J.P. Taylor, in a characteristically provocative comment, said the outbreak of the First World War was caused by the rigidities of the railway timetable. Because 'mobilization' was a matter of sending large numbers of troops long distances by rail, neither Russia nor Germany would be safe if they waited. Only by mobilizing before it was clear the other side had done so could either avoid starting the war at a disadvantage.[38] This is obviously an exaggeration, but there is something to Taylor's point. By their military arrangements governments had locked themselves into a position where war was hard to avoid. Joint planning with France, undertaken without sufficient clarity about its consequences, meant that the British government was trapped between war and dishonour. The Schlieffen plan made it hard for Germany to leave France alone and switch German troops to the east.

The impression of politicians sleepwalking into war comes partly from the fact that they often had little idea of the extent to which they were trapped. The Russian Foreign Minister, Sazonov, had no idea of the risks of mobilization. He said to the German ambassador, 'Surely mobilization is not equivalent to war with you either. Is it?' (The ambassador was more realistic, and replied, 'Perhaps not in theory. But . . . once the button is pressed and the machinery of mobilization is set in motion, there is no stopping it.')[39]

It is possible that war with France and Britain would have been avoided if the Kaiser had been strong enough to impose on Moltke his own preference for sending the army to the east. The way in which he yielded to Moltke, together with Moltke's refusal to sign the order cancelling the invasion of Luxemburg, shows the degree to which the army had escaped from political control. If the military men had not felt free to push their own policies, war might on this occasion have been avoided. If the Kaiser's advice to Austria had been taken, the Serbian response to the ultimatum would have been accepted, but it was the military viewpoint expressed by Moltke which prevailed. When the conflicting pieces of advice arrived, the Austrian Foreign Minister, Berchtold, asked, 'Who actually rules in Berlin, Bethmann or Moltke?'[40]

The Arms Race as a Hobbesian Trap

Mobilization was the final step: the arms race, of which it was the culmination, was a deeper cause of the war. Thucydides on the Peloponnesian War is again relevant: 'What made war inevitable was the growth of Athenian power and the fear which this caused in Sparta.' Sir Edward Grey echoed this:

> More than one true thing may be said about the causes of the war, but the statement that comprises most truth is that militarism and the armaments inseparable from it made war inevitable. Armaments were intended to produce a sense of security in each nation – that was the justification put forward in defence of them. What they really did was to produce fear in everybody.[41]

Claims of inevitability may be too strong. Some arms races have not ended in war. Michael Howard has cited the long Anglo-French naval arms race between 1815 and 1904, and Paul Kennedy has cited the European arms race of the late 1880s and early 1890s.[42] Nor did the Cold War arms race lead to war.

An arms race need not destabilize peace. Each side could be concerned only with deterring the other, and perhaps the nuclear danger made the arms race of the Cold War a case in point. But arms races often have psychological effects which make war more likely. Even where their intention is to deter, the aim may be misperceived as aggressive. Preparing for war may create a jittery climate which makes it more likely. Thucydides and Sir Edward Grey were right to cite the psychological effects of an arms build-up – the fear caused in Sparta, and the fear in 1914 all over Europe.

In 1898 Germany had seven first-class battleships to Britain's thirty-eight. The German government responded to economic pressure and started a major naval construction programme under Admiral Tirpitz. After twenty years of economic depression, industrialists liked the idea of regular orders for ships and the Navy League was founded by Alfred Krupp to press for the policy. In the twelve years to 1908 arms expenditure nearly doubled. In Britain similar economic pressures helped to sustain the arms race. MPs representing shipbuilding towns on the Tyne and the Clyde pressed for more naval orders.

There were also political pressures behind the German arms programme. The government was worried about growing support for the radical policies of the Social Democrats and military strength was seen as helping build up patriotism as an alternative. In the 1890s Tirpitz had supported a bigger navy because 'the great patriotic task and the economic benefits to be derived from it will offer a strong palliative against educated and uneducated Social Democrats'. Bülow, who was Chancellor in the early stages of the build-up, took the same view, urging 'a policy which appeals to the highest national emotions' and the need to 'keep the non-Socialist workers away from Social Democracy'.[43]

In 1904 Britain responded to growing German naval strength by building Dreadnought battleships, the first of which was launched in 1906. In Germany Tirpitz increased the rate of shipbuilding through a Naval Law passed in 1908. In both countries public pressure to compete in the arms race was partly the result of manipulation. From the 1880s Admiral Fisher used his influence with journalists to create public pressure for a strong navy. Tirpitz created a News Bureau in the Navy Office for the same purpose, and helped with pro-naval campaigns by the Navy League and others. In both countries the navy lobby helped to create public pressure, which took on a life of its own as a force behind the arms race.

Because it was building at a faster rate, Germany was on the way to surpassing Britain as a naval power. Tirpitz's plan was long-term: 'it was always clear to me . . . that the First Navy Law did not create the final, full fleet.'[44] In 1899 he discussed plans for forty-five battleships with the Kaiser.

Tirpitz saw the risk of alarming Britain into a pre-emptive strike and hoped that a quick dash would give Germany enough lead to deter a British attack. But he saw there would be a 'danger zone' before such a lead was established: 'the fleet construction had to be done as quickly as possible in order to shorten the danger zone'.[45] As the Chancellor, Bülow, put it, 'in view of our naval inferiority, we must operate so carefully, like the caterpillar before it has grown into the butterfly'.[46] Looking back, Tirpitz thought it had been a question of 'our keeping our nerve, continuing to arm on a grand scale, avoiding all provocation, and waiting without anxiety until our sea power was established and forced the English to let us breathe in peace'.[47] This was a miscalculation.

British naval planners became anxious that the Germans might secretly be building at an even faster rate than they had admitted. By 1912 Britain planned to have eighteen Dreadnoughts and the Admiralty was worried that Germany might have as many as twenty-one. To meet this threat, the British programme was expanded in 1909. In fact, by 1912, Germany had only nine Dreadnoughts to the British fifteen.[48]

An arms race creates a climate in which a conciliatory gesture can seem weak. Even after the war, Tirpitz ascribed British concessions on the Baghdad Railway and Portuguese colonies to the growing power of the German fleet. Sir Edward Grey saw British motives differently:

> It was I who negotiated and initialled the last versions of those two Agreements. The whole transaction was in my hands, and I *know* that the growth of the German Fleet had nothing whatever to do with my attitude. The sole motive was a desire to show that we were ready to meet German aspirations, wherever we could reconcile them with British interests and

engagements. The challenge of the German Fleet was making it more difficult, and not more easy, to be conciliatory.[49]

In 1911 Grey appealed for an end to the arms race, but this in turn was misperceived as a sign of weakness. The German naval attaché said, 'Grey's surrender is due to the Navy Law alone and the unshakeable resolution of the German nation not to allow any diminution of this important instrument.'[50] Bethmann Hollweg took the same view and briskly rejected Grey's proposal.

In 1913 German military expansion switched to the army. The pattern was repeated. This time France and Russia joined the arms race with Germany in response to a perceived threat. A series of international crises, in 1908, 1911 and 1913, created a climate where peace seemed fragile. This, with the arms race, made people think that war was inevitable, or at least overwhelmingly likely.

The arms race caused concern in Germany as well as in neighbouring countries. Some Germans worried that a later war might be worse than an earlier one. Germany's military build-up made it harder to pass up the opportunity to have the 'inevitable' war, while Germany was still stronger than Russia. Two weeks before war broke out the German Foreign Minister expressed the feeling of being trapped by Russia's future build-up: 'Then she will crush us on land by weight of numbers, and she will have her Baltic fleet and her strategic railways ready. Our group meanwhile is getting steadily weaker.'[51]

These concerns encouraged preventive war as a way out of the trap. Looking back in 1919, Bethmann Hollweg said, 'Lord, yes, in a certain sense it was a preventive war. But only if war was hanging over our heads, if it had to come two years later much more dangerously and inevitably, and if the military said today war is still possible without defeat, but no longer in two years.'[52]

In March 1914 the *Frankfurter Zeitung* said, 'Broad circles of the population have allowed themselves to be seized by a nervousness which offers the armaments enthusiasts and war fanatics the fertile soil into which to put the seeds of new army increases.'[53] People were trapped. The arms race caused fear, which in turn fuelled the arms race.

Military Alliances as a Hobbesian Trap

Muddle, misperception and military drift were some of the immediate causes of the war. The arms race was a deeper cause. But further explanation is needed. Why did the international situation produce the arms race?

It was assumed that countries pursued their national interests and that war was legitimate in support of vital interests. On these assumptions, each country had to plan against being attacked. Although most governments did not want war, they were in a prisoners' dilemma, where individual pursuit of national self-interest made it hard for them collectively to avoid the worst outcome.

National self-interest required alliances, both as deterrence and in case deterrence failed, but the resulting system of alliances, which were intended to deter war, turned out to be a trap. It was absurd that a supposed Serbian insult to Austria should result in almost every country in Europe going to war with each other. In Hobbesian fashion, the defensive alliances of one country were often seen as a threat by others.

The growth of German military power led Russia, France and Britain to form an alliance to contain what was seen as a threat. But this 'containment' was seen in Germany as 'encirclement'. In 1913 *Der Tag* wrote of the position of Germany: 'Enemies all round – permanent danger of war from all sides.'[54] In one of the Kaiser's notes on a document dated 30 July 1914, he wrote that 'the famous *encirclement* of Germany has now become a complete fact . . . The net has been suddenly thrown over our head, and England sneeringly reaps the most brilliant success of her persistently prosecuted purely *anti-German world policy*.'[55] Germany saw the growing Russian support for Serbia against Austria as a threat. Bethmann Hollweg later said, 'It was the preparation for the World War which the Russian rulers believed necessary in order to become masters of the Dardanelles.'[56] Bethmann Hollweg told his son that it was pointless to plant new trees on his estate near Berlin, as 'in a few years the Russians would be here anyway'.[57]

When Bethmann Hollweg received the Russian documents about secret negotiations for a naval alliance with Britain, his belief in encirclement was reinforced. In a diary entry on 4 July his closest friend, Kurt Reizler, wrote of a conversation with him: 'The secret news of which he informs me provide a shattering picture. He considers the Anglo-Russian negotiations for a naval convention, landing in Pomerania, as very serious, the last link of the chain.'[58]

The final Hobbesian twist was that defence seemed to require attack. On 3 August 1914 Bethmann Hollweg wrote, 'wedged in between East and West, we had to make use of every means to defend ourselves'. Of the violation of Belgian neutrality, he wrote that it was 'not intentional violation of international law, but the act of a man fighting for his life'.[59]

4 THE PSYCHOLOGICAL TRAPS: THE MIND-SET OF 1914

The deepest parts of the trap were psychological. Why did governments feel they had to prepare against attack? Why were the alliances so rigid that the assassination of an Archduke dragged the whole of Europe into war?

And why were national aims pursued with so little regard for the danger of war? For answers we need to go behind politicians to the people they represented. We need to look at the mental climate of the time: at what James Joll called 'the unspoken assumptions'. They were assumptions of minds deeply shaped by a tribal nationalism.

War and Nationhood

In many countries there was a strand of public opinion which saw willingness to go to war as essential to nationhood. In Britain the Foreign Office official Sir Eyre Crowe urged the government not to back down: 'The theory that England cannot engage in a big war means her abdication as an independent state.'[60] This remark was almost precisely echoed by Bethmann Hollweg: 'We cannot bear Russia's provocation, if we do not want to abdicate as a Great Power in Europe.'[61] He said later that it would have been self-castration for Germany not to have supported Austria–Hungary.

Cambon, the French Foreign Minister, commented, 'It is false that in Germany the nation is peaceful and the government bellicose. The exact opposite is true.' This is supported by something Bethmann Hollweg said to Cambon: 'Don't you think that there is a public opinion in Germany which is easy to influence in questions in which patriotism and self-interest combine? At any rate be fair enough to admit that I seek to arouse it as little as I try to follow it.'[62]

In both Britain and Germany there were supporters of a more internationalist outlook. In Germany the Social Democrats were hostile to militarism, and in Britain many supporters of the Liberal government were unenthusiastic about war, but even in most of them a submerged nationalism surfaced when war broke out.

In Germany, Bethmann Hollweg persuaded the Social Democrats' leaders to stop opposing the government by saying that opposition would help both the war party in Russia and the war party in Germany. SPD supporters in the country were won over by the ploy of making Russia appear to be the aggressor. When it was reported that Russian patrols had entered German territory, the SPD press fell into line behind the government. Most Social Democrats shared the nationalist indignation at the incursion.

In Britain Grey carried nearly all the Cabinet with him in support of going to war and the decision was popular in the country. Asquith, out at dinner, could hear the crowds cheering the King at Buckingham Palace: 'One could hear this distant roaring as late as 1 or 1.30 in the morning. War or anything that seems likely to lead to war is always popular with the London mob.'[63] Bertrand Russell walked through cheering crowds near

Trafalgar Square: 'During this and the following days I discovered to my amazement that average men and women were delighted at the prospect of war.'[64]

Social Darwinism

Nationalism was reinforced by the belief in a Darwinian struggle for survival, with the race or nation being the unit taking part in the struggle. Nations unwilling to fight would go under.

Not all those influenced by Darwin accepted that struggle was inevitable. Some stressed more co-operative methods of survival,[65] but the combative version, Social Darwinism, had more impact.

In England Social Darwinism was supported by Karl Pearson, who said that the nation should be 'kept up to a high pitch of external efficiency by contest, chiefly by way of war with inferior races, and with equal races by the struggle for trade routes and for the sources of raw materials and food supply'.[66] Lord Salisbury divided nations into the living and the dying: 'the living nations will gradually encroach on the territory of the dying and the seeds and causes of conflict among civilised nations will speedily appear'.[67]

In Austria a strong supporter of a preventive war was the Chief of the General Staff, Franz Baron Conrad von Hoetzendorf. Even after the war, he asserted its Social Darwinist inevitability:

> Philanthropic religions, moral teachings and philosophical doctrines may certainly sometimes serve to weaken mankind's struggle for existence in its crudest form, but they will *never* succeed in removing it as a driving motive in the world . . . It is in accordance with this great principle that the catastrophe of the world war came about inevitably and irresistibly as the result of the motive forces in the lives of states and peoples, like a thunderstorm which must by its nature discharge itself.[68]

In Germany Social Darwinism was often taken up in the form propounded by the Englishman Houston Stewart Chamberlain. His book, *The Foundations of the Nineteenth Century*, advocated the self-assertion of the German race when freed of its Jewish elements. It was published in German in 1899 and had been through ten editions by 1912. It influenced the Kaiser's thoughts about racial struggle. The Kaiser wrote to Chamberlain in 1901, thanking his 'companion in battle and ally in the struggle of the Germans against Rome, Jerusalem, etc.' for showing the way 'that must be followed for the salvation of the Germans and thus the salvation of mankind'.[69]

Social Darwinism influenced the naval arms race. Hunold von Ahlefeld was the director of the Imperial Shipyards at Kiel and one of those who pressed for naval expansion. In a letter to Tirpitz in 1898, he wrote, 'The "struggle for survival" is raging between individuals, provinces, parties, states. The latter are engaged in it either with the force of arms or with economic means; there is nothing we can do about this, except to join in. He who doesn't will perish.'[70]

Tirpitz was himself a Social Darwinist and saw the naval arms race as part of the struggle for survival. During the war he was a member of the right-wing Vaterlandspartei and afterwards sat in the Reichstag for the Deutschenationale Volkspartei. In 1922 he told Rudolf Hess of his sympathy for Nazi aims. At the time of the arms race, he was worried about 'going under' in the struggle: 'The development of Germany into an industrial nation is irreversible, like a law of nature ... collisions and conflict points will grow with other nations, therefore power, sea power, is essential if Germany is not to go under swiftly.'[71]

The Social Darwinist conception of the arms race is also apparent in Bethmann Hollweg's rebuff to Grey's proposal to end it:

> The old saying still holds good that the weak will be the prey of the strong. When a people will not or cannot continue to spend enough on its armaments to be able to make its way in the world, then it falls back into the second rank ... There will always be another and a stronger there who is ready to take the place in the world which it has vacated.[72]

In a climate influenced by Social Darwinism and by a fatalistic pessimism about preserving peace, some people were drawn to the idea of war. This was particularly so in Germany. One right-wing journalist wrote in praise of 'a fresh and uninhibited war'. Another said that 'war is the only remedy to cure existing illnesses'.[73] In 1913 one journalist wrote that 'war is beautiful. Its noble grandeur raises man high above earthly, daily things', and looked forward to the 'happy and great hour of a struggle'. The previous year, the views of Dr Schmidt-Gibichenfels ('We Teutons in particular must no longer look upon war as our destroyer ... at last we must see it once more as the saviour, the physician') had been described in the press as a 'masterpiece of the ethic of war'.[74]

National Honour

Why were the bonds between allies so rigid that the whole of Europe was dragged into war?

Behind Social Darwinism was the idea that nation-states were the units of evolutionary selection. There was an idea of the 'nation' almost as a person and central to this was national honour. Talk of national shame and dishonour, and thoughts about nations living, dying, or engaging in self-castration, all reflected this.

Thinking in terms of the emotions, the health, the life and death of an imaginary people called 'Germany' or 'Britain' contributed to the outbreak of war. It turned attention away from what war would mean for the emotions, the health, and the lives and deaths, of real people.

National honour was used to provoke war with Serbia. One Austrian minister said the ultimatum about to be presented made such demands that 'no nation that still possessed self-respect and dignity could possibly accept them'.[75]

Allies were locked together through their commitments: Russians would have felt dishonoured by failure to give Serbia support, or by the Tsar brushing aside the appeal to his 'generous Slav heart'. The Russian Foreign Minister later said capitulation to German and Austrian demands would have been 'a thing that Russia would never forgive to the Tsar, for it would cover with shame the good name of the Russian people'.[76] The Russian government was in a trap, where one exit led to dishonour and the other to war. Something similar held for each bond between the various countries in the two alliances.

For Germany, its commitment to Austria was a matter of honour. Moltke said that not to give support 'would be violating in ominous fashion the deep-rooted feelings of fidelity which are among the most beautiful traits of German character'.[77] Bethmann Hollweg later said that the only way war could have been avoided was by a rapprochement with England, but that 'after we had decided for a policy with Austria, we could not desert her in that crisis'.[78]

The question of honour was also taken seriously in Britain. When, at the last minute, Bethmann Hollweg proposed British neutrality if Germany and France went to war, Grey was shocked: 'Did Bethmann Hollweg not understand, could he not see that he was making an offer that would dishonour us if we agreed to it? What sort of man was it who could not see that? Or did he think so badly of us that he thought we should not see it?'[79] In his reply to Bethmann Hollweg he said, 'to make this bargain with Germany at the expense of France would be a disgrace from which the good name of this country would never recover'.[80]

In the Foreign Office, Sir Eyre Crowe wrote that in making the alliance with France 'a moral bond was being forged', raising the honourable expectation that in a just quarrel 'England would stand by her friends'.[81] The Conservative Party pressed the British government to be firm in the same terms: 'Any hesitation in now supporting France and Russia would be fatal to the honour and to the future security of the United Kingdom.'[82]

These thoughts were central to Grey's thinking. As he later wrote, 'The real reason for going into the war was that, if we did not stand by France and stand up for Belgium against this aggression, we should be isolated, discredited, and hated; and there would be before us nothing but a miserable and ignoble future.'[83] A few days after war had broken out, the Prime Minister, Herbert Asquith, said in the House of Commons that Britain was fighting 'in the first place to fulfil a solemn international obligation which, if it had been entered into between private persons in the ordinary concerns of life, would have been regarded as an obligation not only of law but of honour, which no self-respecting man could possibly have repudiated'.[84]

In our own time, there is scepticism about possible hypocrisy when politicians cite honour to support foreign-policy decisions, but perhaps, in 1914, the idea of national obligations of honour had widespread and genuine support. In the course of arguing that, if war broke out, Britain also had self-interested reasons for entering on the side of France and Russia, Michael Howard makes an aside about British public opinion which may be more widely relevant. He says that the self-interested reasons applied, 'leaving any consideration of honour, sentiment, or respect for treaties on one side'. He then adds, 'and let us remember that that generation of Englishmen did *not* leave them on one side but regarded them as quite central'.[85] It is hard to assess claims about the moral climate of earlier times, but, to some of us, knowledge or memories of people of that generation, together with much that was written at that time, may give Michael Howard's comment the ring of truth.

If so, part of the trap was created by the prevailing moral outlook, by the view that war was less bad than a betrayal of trust. Sometimes, looking back at the people of that time, it is possible to see in many of them a wonderfully uncynical belief in the moral law. To think of their rectitude and integrity may suggest that, in our more disenchanted time, we have lost something important. But there is another side to this. Those qualities of rectitude and honour were part of the innocence, part of the trap that led to the trenches.

The ease with which governments, with public support, could do the honourable thing was partly a matter of their having so little grasp of what the full consequences would be.

Missing the Scale of the Crisis

As we look back, the statesmen seem too small for the scale of the events they tried to control, and for the scale of the catastrophe they tried to prevent. This is partly because we can see the enormity of the First World War, while they, hoping it would be over by Christmas, had no conception of it. Military people were not immune to this blindness. A few months into the war General Sir William Birdwood said, 'What a real piece of luck this war has been as regards Ireland – just averted a Civil War and when it is over we may all be tired of fighting.'[86]

Sir Edward Grey saw that war would be a disaster and tried harder than most to avoid it. He expressed his fear of it:

> The possible consequences of the present situation were terrible. If as many as four great powers of Europe – let us say Austria, France, Russia and Germany – were engaged in war, it seemed to me that it must involve the expenditure of so vast a sum of money and such an interference with trade, that a war would be accompanied or followed by a complete collapse of European credit and industry. In these days, in great industrial states, this would mean a state of things worse than that of 1848, and, irrespective of who were victors in the war, many things would be completely swept away.[87]

But even this sombre prediction, of economic collapse and of things being worse than 1848, seems puny by contrast with what was in fact to happen.

This was a crisis whose full dimensions were not seen by those caught up in it. They were entangled in a web of each other's ambiguities, misperceptions and confused intentions. They were also in a trap created by military planners who were not under proper control, by military alliances and by public opinion. At a deeper level they were psychologically trapped. Part of the psychological trap was the Hobbesian mutual fear caused by the arms race.

It was also a trap created by the bizarre interaction of different strands of prevailing beliefs: in some a nationalistic Social Darwinism, in others a morality which made an absolute of honour. What these very different beliefs had in common was the way they stunted the moral imagination. Instead of attention being directed to people and what war would do to their lives, it was turned to the abstraction of the nation. The survival of the nation in the evolutionary struggle, the refusal to accept an insult to the nation, the avoidance of the nation being humiliated or dishonoured, seemed of supreme importance. Nations as imaginary people were put before the real people who made them up.

The political and psychological traps combined with this inadequate mode of thinking to cause the statesmen collectively to bring about the disaster. It was a disaster unwanted, certainly by most of them, and probably by all of them. What Bethmann Hollweg said to the Prussian Cabinet on 30 July could perhaps have been said by any of them: 'The great majority of the peoples are in themselves peaceful, but things are out of control and the stone has started to roll.'[88]

CHAPTER 22

Sliding Out of the Trap: 1962

Don't ask who lost or who won. Mankind won. Human reason won.
Nikita Khrushchev

The man-made catastrophe of 1914 dwarfed any previous disasters, but 1914 would have been utterly surpassed by the nuclear catastrophe which was narrowly averted in 1962. The two superpowers, the United States and the Soviet Union, nearly went to war. The causes of this contained some of the ingredients of 1914: accident, misjudgement, national egoism and pride, the Hobbesian traps of an arms race and of competitive military alliances. Together the superpowers averted war in 1962, partly because of the sobering effects of nuclear weapons and partly because they had learnt lessons from the earlier disaster. There are now, in turn, things to be learnt from 1962.

1 FIFTEEN DAYS IN OCTOBER

On 14 October 1962 Major Rudolf Anderson flew a U2 aircraft over Cuba and brought back photographs of missile sites and missile components. The next day the photographs were interpreted. On 16 October President John Kennedy was told.

Two days later Kennedy met the Soviet Foreign Minister, Andrei Gromyko, but did not say what he knew. Gromyko told him that no Soviet missiles would go to Cuba. The same assurance had been given to Kennedy in other personal messages sent by the Soviet leader, Nikita Khrushchev. Kennedy was angered by the Soviet move and by the deception.

On the day Kennedy was told about the missiles, the first meeting took place in the White House of the Executive Committee of the National Security Council, or 'Ex-Comm'. At first, a majority of its members supported an air strike against the missile sites. Kennedy was sure that the United States could not accept the missiles in Cuba.

Ex-Comm continued to meet throughout the crisis. The central issue was between an air strike and a blockade of Cuba. Adlai Stevenson, the US ambassador to the United Nations, made a third proposal: in exchange for Soviet withdrawal of the missiles, the United States would withdraw its own missiles from Turkey and Italy, and give up its Cuban naval base at Guantanamo Bay. This met with strong opposition. (Stevenson had already made his case against an air strike with elegant understatement: 'To start or risk starting a nuclear war is bound to be divisive at best.'[1]) Kennedy chose the blockade.

On Monday 22 October, Kennedy made a broadcast about the missiles and announced (as an initial step) a blockade, or 'quarantine'. Ships bound for Cuba would be stopped and searched. Those carrying offensive weapons would be turned back. Any nuclear missile launched from Cuba against any Western country would be treated as a Soviet attack on the United States, calling for full retaliation.

Many Congressional leaders criticized the response as far too weak. Some senators strongly urged an air attack or an invasion. Kennedy had indicated that even the blockade was risky, that the Soviet side expected the blockade would not include Russian ships because this would mean war: 'So, we may have the war in the next 24 hours.'[2]

Khrushchev reacted angrily to the broadcast. He ordered work on the missile sites to be speeded up. He also ordered Soviet ships to ignore the blockade and to stay on course for Cuba. The Soviet government accused the United States of piracy, illegality and of 'assuming the right to demand that states should account to it for the way in which they organize their defence, and should notify it of what their ships are carrying on the high seas'. It said that the Soviet government 'firmly repudiates such claims', and warned of the danger of nuclear war. Khrushchev wrote to Kennedy that his measures were a serious threat to peace.

On Wednesday 24 October the first Soviet vessels approached the quarantine line. Anastas Mikoyan, the Soviet First Deputy Premier, took it on himself to reverse Khrushchev's order. Some of the ships slowed down or changed course. When the news came through to Ex-Comm, Dean Rusk whispered to McGeorge Bundy, 'We are eyeball to eyeball and the other fellow just blinked.'[3]

But the crisis continued to escalate. American Strategic Air Command was put on 'Def/Con 2' level of alert, indicating readiness for war. Some Soviet ships kept on course. Khrushchev threatened to sink American ships if they stopped Soviet ones. The next day, Thursday, a Soviet tanker was intercepted and allowed to go on without being boarded. On Friday another Soviet ship was stopped and boarded. It had no missiles and was allowed to continue.

The same day Fidel Castro authorized his forces to fire on American aircraft. On Saturday 27 October a U2 was shot down over Cuba. The pilot, again Major Rudolf Anderson, was killed. Another U2, said to be on a routine 'air sampling' flight, strayed into Soviet airspace. Soviet fighters took off, but did not succeed in intercepting it. Khrushchev received a message from Castro, saying that an American attack on Cuba (probably an air strike, but possibly an invasion) was imminent. Castro said that, in the event of an invasion,

> the Soviet Union must never allow the circumstances in which the imperialists could launch the first nuclear strike against it. I tell you this because I believe that the imperialists' aggressiveness is extremely dangerous and if they actually carry out the brutal act of invading Cuba in violation of international law and morality, that would be the moment to eliminate such danger forever through an act of clear legitimate defence, however harsh and terrible the solution would be, for there is no other.[4]

Khrushchev interpreted this as urging him to make a pre-emptive nuclear strike against the United States.

Between Thursday and Saturday, as these naval, air and diplomatic events intensified the crisis, two possible solutions started to emerge.

The first was removal of the missiles in exchange for an American promise not to invade Cuba. On Friday, Aleksander Fomin, a senior Soviet intelligence officer, outlined this plan to the television reporter John Scali. He asked Scali to find out whether the United States would be interested in it. The American Secretary of State, Dean Rusk, gave Scali a message for Fomin, expressing serious interest.

That evening Kennedy received a long and conciliatory personal letter from Khrushchev. The letter expressed deep emotional revulsion against war:

> Should war indeed break out, it would not be in our power to contain or stop it, for such is the logic of war. I have taken part in two wars, and I know that war ends only when it has rolled through cities and villages, sowing death and destruction everywhere ... If people do not display wisdom, they will eventually reach the point where they will clash, like blind moles, and then mutual annihilation will commence ... You and I should not now pull on the ends of the rope in which you have tied a knot of war, because the harder you and I pull, the tighter this knot will become. And a time may come when this knot is tied so tight that the person who tied it is no longer capable of untying it, and then the knot will have to be cut.[5]

Khrushchev proposed a solution along the lines which Fomin had mentioned.

The other proposal was for the withdrawal of Soviet missiles from Cuba and of American missiles in Turkey. This was suggested by Bruno

Kreisky, the Austrian Foreign Minister, and by Walter Lippmann in his column in the *Washington Post*. Late on Friday night the President's brother, Robert Kennedy, secretly met Anatoly Dobrynin, the Soviet ambassador. Dobrynin queried the American response to the missiles, drawing a parallel with the missiles in Turkey. Robert Kennedy consulted the President and reported back that he was willing to 'examine favourably the question of Turkey'.

On Saturday 27 October Kennedy received a tougher letter from Khrushchev, proposing the Cuba–Turkey missile exchange. At the Ex-Comm meeting at which this letter was discussed, the Joint Chiefs of Staff said the blockade had not worked. They proposed an air strike on Cuba on the Monday, to be followed by an invasion. This view did not prevail and Kennedy wrote back to Khrushchev. The letter was couched as a reply to the earlier, more friendly letter. It accepted the proposals in the earlier letter for withdrawal of the missiles in exchange for an American undertaking not to invade Cuba, and said that 'the effect of such a settlement on easing world tensions would enable us to work toward a more general arrangement regarding "other armaments", as proposed in your second letter'.

Kennedy's Press Secretary, Pierre Salinger, described the mood after the Ex-Comm meeting broke up that Saturday night. If there was no Soviet response that night or early next morning, they were going to discuss military escalation. 'As I walked out of the White House, I was handed a sealed envelope, and I was told to give it to my wife and to tell her that the next day, if I disappeared . . . she was to open this envelope which would tell her where to take my children and herself to be safe.'[6]

Late that Saturday evening Robert Kennedy again met Dobrynin. He said the US government knew that work on the missile bases had been speeded up, and that they took the shooting down of Major Anderson very seriously. The United States needed a commitment by the next day that the missiles would be removed. If the Soviet Union did not remove the missiles, the United States would do so. Robert Kennedy describes himself as having indicated that 'I was not giving them an ultimatum but a statement of fact'. Robert Kennedy and Dobrynin also worked out a deal, not to be made public, whereby the Cuban and Turkish missiles would be withdrawn in exchange for each other. Dobrynin sent this proposal to Moscow.

Robert Kennedy went back to the White House:

> The President was not optimistic, nor was I. He ordered twenty-four troop-carrier squadrons of the Air Force Reserve to active duty. They would be necessary for an invasion. He had not abandoned hope, but what hope there was now rested with Khrushchev's revising his course within the next few

hours. It was a hope, not an expectation. The expectation was a military confrontation by Tuesday and possibly tomorrow.[7]

The Soviet leaders were highly alarmed by what they heard from Dobrynin, and decided to accept the deal and pull their missiles out of Cuba. Because of the urgency they replied on Sunday over the radio. Khrushchev's speechwriter, Fyodor Burlatsky, has described how the reply was prepared at Khrushchev's dacha outside Moscow: 'When the letter was finished, a man was dispatched with it to drive very quickly to the radio station. He was told to have it for transmission before three o'clock. They were very nervous.' One of the lifts in the Moscow Radio building was kept free to take the letter.[8]

It was still morning in Washington when Moscow Radio broadcast Khrushchev's agreement to withdraw the missiles. Dobrynin also brought the message, together with best wishes from Khrushchev to President Kennedy and his brother. That afternoon the dismantling of the missiles began. There were a few further unfriendly exchanges about which weapons were to go and about the American commitment not to invade Cuba, but the crisis was over.

The next month, Khrushchev wrote in a letter to Kennedy, 'The knot we are now untying has been tied rather tightly, almost to the limit.'[9] What aims led two governments, fully aware of what nuclear war would be like, to usher each other so close to the precipice?

2 BLIND MOLES

Soviet and American Aims

Why did the Soviet government decide to send missiles to Cuba? The dominant motive was to deter the United States from attacking the island. They thought that missiles could tip the balance of power more in the Soviet direction and they feared losing prestige and influence if Castro fell.

There was reason to fear an American invasion of Cuba. The US government wanted to bring down Castro and had cut off oil supplies and other trade. Speaking later of their meeting together in Vienna, Khrushchev claimed that Kennedy had compared what the United States might do to Cuba with the Soviet treatment of Hungary. The United States had supported the unsuccessful 'Bay of Pigs' invasion by anti-Castro Cubans and contingency plans were made, under the code name 'Operation Mongoose', for an invasion by American forces. The American government was not committed to these plans, but their discovery was not reassuring.

Another Soviet aim was to reduce the American nuclear lead. Khrushchev later wrote, 'In addition to protecting Cuba, our missiles would have equalized what the West likes to call "the balance of power". The Americans had surrounded our country with military bases and threatened us with nuclear weapons, and now they would learn just what it feels like to have enemy missiles pointing at you.'[10] Or, as Khrushchev put it to the Soviet Defence Minister, Rodion Malinovsky, 'Why not throw a hedgehog at Uncle Sam's pants?'[11]

In the dangerous world of the Cold War and the nuclear arms race, Khrushchev's secret move was an alarming gamble. His adviser Fyodor Burlatsky says he thought deception was normal in political relations with a possible adversary.[12] He had a poor grasp of the probability of detection and of the likely American reaction. But his motives were deterrent rather than aggressive. These aims then combined with a similarly non-aggressive set of American aims to bring the world as close as it has been to disaster.

In the Kennedy administration there was agreement on the urgency of having the missiles removed. This has obscured differences about the possible reasons for their intense concern, of which there were several. Missiles so close, which could hit American targets so quickly, were a new level of threat. President Kennedy, speaking to the Joint Chiefs of Staff on 19 October, said that when the missiles became operational, 'We're going to have this knife stuck right in our guts.'[13] It would be more dangerous if control over the missiles passed to Castro. The extra nuclear threat could tip the balance of power towards the Soviet Union. Accepting the missiles would be to lose a round in the Cold War, with a resulting loss of American prestige. Both the fear of a nuclear attack from Cuba and loss of American prestige would make the presence of the missiles intolerable to American public opinion.

There were reasons to doubt whether the missiles in Cuba really changed the strategic balance. Robert McNamara said, 'I don't believe it's primarily a military problem. It's primarily a domestic political problem.'[14] He also said afterwards that Khrushchev was behind in missiles by about seventeen to one: 'Do you think an extra forty-three missiles in Cuba, each carrying one warhead, would have led him to think he could use his nuclear weapons? No way! Khrushchev had created a *political* problem, not a military problem.'[15]

Some members of Ex–Comm felt there was a greater nuclear threat to the United States. Some also supported the Monroe doctrine, that there should not be intervention in the Americas by powers from other parts of the world. This doctrine has obvious appeal to the United States, but is not much of a reply to the Soviet argument that their missiles in Cuba were exactly parallel to American missiles in Turkey.

The central weakness of the American case was that there was no convincing reply to this equivalence. President Kennedy saw this. He said of the Soviet proposal to remove the missiles from Cuba in exchange for American missiles being removed from Turkey that 'to any man at the

United Nations or any other rational man, it will look like a very fair trade'.[16] Theodore Sorensen, who wrote the speech Kennedy made in his broadcast, later said that Kennedy's worry about the equivalence shaped the speech: 'It was precisely for that reason that there was so much emphasis on the *sudden* and *deceptive* deployment. Look at that speech very carefully; we relied very heavily on words such as those to make sure the world didn't focus on the question of symmetry.'[17]

But the missiles caused a genuine defensive anxiety. One estimate quoted by Robert Kennedy was that, if the missiles were fired, they would kill 80 million Americans. And worries were justified about what would happen if control passed to Castro. His letter seeming to advocate a Soviet first strike supports American concern.

Two governments, each with (mainly) reasonable and defensive aims, found themselves pulling on the rope tightening the knot of war. Like the leaders of 1914, they were mutually trapped. In 1962 the trap was created partly by the two sides mistaking each other's intentions, partly by the arms race and partly by the political competition of the Cold War.

Confusion and Communication

One problem was technological: communication in those days was slow. Khrushchev's proposal of 26 October took seven hours to reach Washington. The Soviet ambassador, Anatoly Dobrynin, later described what happened when the embassy wanted to send urgent messages about the crisis to Moscow: 'We called Western Union. From Western Union a black man rode a bicycle, came to our embassy. We gave him the cables. And he, at such a speed – and we tried to urge him on – rode back to Western Union where the cable was sent to Moscow.'[18]

But primitive technology is not the whole story. The telephone existed. With the help of interpreters, conversations could have taken place if the two leaders wanted them. (When President Kennedy was discussing the time–lag in communication, Llewellyn Thompson said Kennedy could always telephone, but this was not followed up.)[19] As in 1914, the problem of communication was partly caused by lack of clarity about intentions.

American intentions towards Cuba were unclear – even if they were peaceful, they could be misinterpreted. The armed forces had contingency plans for an invasion. A Senate resolution sanctioning the use of force if necessary against Cuba was passed on 20 September by 86 votes to 1. At a news conference on 29 August, Kennedy rejected an invasion, saying, 'I'm not for invading Cuba at this time.'[20] Those close to Kennedy say there was no intention of acting on those plans. Robert McNamara has said, 'I can state this categorically, without qualification, and with the certainty that I am speaking not only of my own knowledge, but of my understanding –

and I think it was complete – of the mind of President Kennedy . . . I can state unequivocally that we had *absolutely no intention* of invading Cuba.' But rejecting an invasion 'at this time' at least left room for concern about future intentions. And McNamara admitted with hindsight that the contingency plans could reasonably have been interpreted by Cubans as evidence that an invasion was intended: 'If I had been a Cuban I might have thought that.'[21]

Military Drift

On both sides there were signs that the armed forces were drifting out of control.

Major Anderson's U2 was shot down on the orders of Soviet commanders in Cuba. Soviet units had orders that, for missiles to be fired, there had to be both an American attack and orders from Moscow, but there are Soviet standing orders 'to fire on any aircraft that flies overhead in wartime'. Local generals had twenty minutes to decide whether or not to fire on the U2. They tried to contact the Soviet commander in Cuba, but did not succeed. General Georgy Voronkov gave the order to fire. When criticized for this later by Khrushchev, he cited the standing orders.[22]

On the American side, some risks came from military slip-ups. A missile was launched from Vandenberg Air Force Base in California as part of a planned programme of tests, without thought about how the Soviet Union might interpret this. On 28 October the North American Air Defence Command was told that a nuclear missile from Cuba was about to hit Tampa. When no nuclear explosion happened in Tampa, it was discovered that a radar operator had inserted a test tape simulating a Cuban attack.

Another danger came from the military preference for independence of action. One senior officer wanted to impose his own stamp on policy. General Power, the Commander-in-Chief of the Strategic Air Command, had to send the signal to his units to go into 'Def/Con 2', the state of alert appropriate to readiness for war. Normal procedure was to send the signal in code. Without authorization, General Power sent an uncoded signal, intending Soviet detection. He is said to have wanted to 'rub the Soviets' noses in their nuclear inferiority'.[23]

General Power's embellishment of policy was an exception. The greater danger in this crisis was that military priorities would influence policy in directions that would risk nuclear war. Among some military leaders there was a preference for massive air attack and invasion over Kennedy's more cautious approach.

The quick, decisive action has military appeal. On 19 October, after a meeting between Kennedy and military leaders, the tape recorder was running after the President left the room. It caught General David

Shoup's inarticulate anger at Kennedy's caution: 'He finally got round to the word "escalation". That's the only goddam thing that's in the whole trick. Go in . . . and get every goddam one. Somebody's got to keep them from doing the goddam thing piecemeal. That's our problem. Go in there and friggin' around with the missiles. You're screwed. You're screwed, screwed, screwed. Some goddam thing, some way, that they either do the son of a bitch and do it right, and quit friggin' around . . . once you do it you can't fuck around and go take a missile out. You can't fiddle around with the SAM sites. You got to go in and take out the goddam thing that's going to stop you doing your job.'[24]

General Maxwell Taylor is reported as saying then that he 'did not share McNamara's fear that if we used nuclear weapons in Cuba, nuclear weapons would be used against us'.[25] The Joint Chiefs of Staff formally recommended an air strike, and, even after Khrushchev's broadcast message agreeing to remove the missiles, they sent a memorandum saying that the statement was an attempt to 'delay direct action by the United States while preparing the ground for diplomatic blackmail'. They still thought that, unless there was irrefutable evidence that the missiles were being dismantled, there should be an air strike next day followed by an invasion.[26]

The Joint Chiefs of Staff believed the CIA report that there were only 10,000 Soviet troops in Cuba. In fact there were 43,000 and they were equipped with tactical nuclear warheads, which, with Khrushchev's approval, were moved closer to their delivery vehicles in anticipation of an American attack. In an invasion tactical nuclear weapons might well have been used against Americans, with the likelihood of an American nuclear response. Even without the use of nuclear weapons, the Russians and Cubans would have suffered a bloody defeat. Years later Robert McNamara was at a conference with Gromyko, Dobrynin and other leading Soviet policy-makers at the time of the crisis. He says that they 'expressed utter disbelief that we would have thought that, in the face of such a catastrophic defeat, they would not have responded militarily somewhere in the world. Very probably the result would have been uncontrolled escalation.'[27] The greatest danger of the crisis was that political decision-makers would be swayed by the advice of confident and apparently knowledgeable military chiefs.

The Arms Race as a Hobbesian Trap

The crisis was caused partly by the American lead in the arms race, one aspect of which influenced Khrushchev particularly. Kennedy had campaigned for election on a promise to eliminate the 'missile gap', a supposed Soviet lead. There was no missile gap, but Kennedy ordered a large build-up of intercontinental ballistic missiles. Robert McNamara announced in June 1962 that the United States would soon be able, if attacked, to destroy the remaining Soviet missiles as well as other targets. Every Soviet missile would be the target of an American one. McNamara intended deterrence rather than first-strike capacity. But this posture also meant that an American first strike which destroyed Soviet missiles would escape retaliation.

Robert McNamara later said that the American expansion was to meet a Soviet expansion anticipated by the CIA, which did not materialize. As with the naval arms race between Britain and Germany before 1914, each side thought it had to run to keep up. McNamara's own account of the thinking behind the American build-up gives a clear view of the mechanism of the trap. The time-lag for producing missiles was about seven years, and so the 1961 decisions were based on estimates of what the Soviet Union would have in 1968: 'And we based our estimates on what we called the "worst case" estimate. And therefore, we based it on capabilities . . . That was why the forces developed as they did – and it was very dangerous, for both of us, because it led to this constant imbalance, which you might well have interpreted as showing signs of aggression.'[28]

After the CIA's imaginary future Soviet lead, it was Khrushchev's turn to see things as worse than they were. He saw the new situation as a threat of a first strike. The hope of frustrating this was one reason for sending missiles to Cuba.[29] Khrushchev's later account of why he sent the missiles in secret is startling. He hoped the Americans would discover them only after they were ready to strike and thought that the Americans would be deterred from attacking them by the probability that some of them would survive to retaliate.[30]

What if the missiles were discovered before they were ready to use? Khrushchev veered between hoping this would not happen and seeing that, if it did, he would have entered a trap. In September, hearing about the progress of the missiles, he said, 'Soon hell will break loose.' An aide said, 'I hope the boat does not capsize, Nikita Sergeyevich.' Khrushchev said, 'Now it's too late to change anything.'[31]

This was one way in which the crisis resembled the prelude to the First World War. Khrushchev's more hopeful thoughts followed those of Admiral Tirpitz exactly. There would be a danger zone when Britain might make a pre-emptive strike, but, as German naval strength increased, Britain would be deterred from reacting by inability to destroy the German navy. Like Tirpitz, Khrushchev miscalculated.

The misjudgement was part of a general over-optimism. Khrushchev's response to Cuban anxieties about an American pre-emptive strike was to say, apparently without irony, that 'in case that happened, he would send the Baltic Fleet to Cuba and that he would still defend us.'[32] Soviet–American mutual perception had a distinct flavour of 1914.

As well as being trapped in the arms race, the two governments were caught up in its political equivalent: the contest for prestige. Neither wanted to lose a round in the Cold War.

Soviet motives for protecting Cuba were similar to the 'domino theory' later used to justify American support for South Vietnam. Khrushchev thought the loss of Cuba 'would gravely diminish our stature throughout the world, but especially in Latin America. If Cuba fell, other Latin American countries would reject us, claiming that for all our might the Soviet Union hadn't been able to do anything for Cuba except to make empty protests to the United Nations.'[33]

This belief was mirrored on the American side. Douglas Dillon, the Treasury Secretary, argued for an air strike:

If we allow the offensive capabilities presently in Cuba to remain there, I am convinced that sooner or later and probably sooner we will lose all Latin America to Communism because all credibility of our willingness to effectively resist Soviet military power will have been removed in the eyes of the Latins.[34]

It is hard to avoid conflict when each side sees any climbdown as the fall of the first Latin American domino.

The Public as Part of the Trap

Their political system allowed the Soviet leaders to be relaxed about criticisms from their own public, although they did try to calm anxiety. In the middle of the crisis Khrushchev and other leaders went to the Bolshoi:

I suggested to the other members of the government: 'Comrades, let's go to the Bolshoi Theatre this evening. Our own people as well as foreign eyes will notice, and perhaps it will calm them down. They'll say to themselves, "If Khrushchev and our other leaders are able to go to the opera at a time like this, then at least tonight we can sleep peacefully." ' We were trying to disguise our own anxiety, which was intense.[35]

In the United States politicians had to take more notice of public opinion. Robert McNamara said several times that the missiles did not pose a military problem but a political one. Part of the political issue was 'the problem of dealing with our domestic public'.[36]

American public opinion was part of the trap in which Kennedy found himself. The political climate was aggressively hostile towards Cuba. During the crisis Senator Richard Russell thought Cuba should be invaded and nuclear war risked:

The time is going to come, Mr President, when we're going to have to take this step in Berlin and Korea and Washington D.C., and Winder, Georgia, for the nuclear war. I don't know whether Khrushchev will launch a nuclear war over Cuba or not. I don't believe he will. But I think that the more we temporize, the more surely he is to convince himself that we are afraid to make any real movement and to really fight.

Kennedy's response was that to invade would be to gamble on the missiles in Cuba not being fired: 'The fact is that that is one hell of a gamble.'[37]

Before the crisis many demands had been made in Congress for military action against Cuba. In a Congressional debate before the crisis one attitude was expressed by a Democrat from South Carolina: 'It is as simple as the ABC's. If you give the military the word to go ahead, and we can blockade Cuba. You say, "You cannot do it, you may bring on a rain of missiles." If you are afraid to die now, you will be afraid to die two years from now ... If blockading Cuba brings on war, let our boys die for America.'[38]

The political climate favoured tough policies of standing up to the Soviet Union. Having won the election partly by playing on fears of a Soviet missile lead, it would have been hard for Kennedy to accept these Soviet missiles so close to home. Kennedy's adviser McGeorge Bundy later suggested that public opinion about the missiles had been central: 'our public simply would not tolerate them so close to us. So the first premise of our discussion was that a policy must be found which leads to the removal of those missiles.'[39] When the crisis was over, there were newspaper attacks on Adlai Stevenson, accusing him of having advocated a Caribbean Munich. Kennedy gave Stevenson a lot of private support. Stevenson said, 'That's fine, but will he say it publicly?' When this was reported to Kennedy, he did not feel able to give public support, saying, 'Just tell Adlai to sit tight and everything will subside.'[40]

A case can be made that public opinion created the crisis. The warnings against Soviet missiles in Cuba were not mainly made because of anxiety about the military balance. At one point Kennedy said, 'Last month I said we weren't going to [allow it]. Last month I should have said that we don't care. But when we said we're *not* going to, and then they go ahead and do it, and then we do nothing, then I would think that our risks increase.'[41] Afterwards Theodore Sorensen suggested that 'the President drew the line precisely where the Soviets were not and would not be; that is to say, if we had known that the Soviets were putting forty missiles in Cuba, we might under this hypothesis have drawn the line at one hundred, and said with great fanfare that we would absolutely not tolerate the presence of more than one hundred missiles in Cuba'.[42] The warnings Khrushchev defied were given by Kennedy because he needed to show a combative public that a line was being drawn somewhere.

At the height of the crisis, the President talked to his brother Robert about how bleak things looked, but said that he had had no choice but to respond toughly. Robert Kennedy replied, 'Well, there isn't any choice. I mean, you would have been, you would have been impeached.' The President agreed: 'Well, I think I would have been impeached.'[43] This may not have been meant literally, but it expressed something real about the way policies of compromise were constrained by public opinion. There was a circle. To get elected, Kennedy had needed to feed this opinion with talk of a missile gap, but he in turn was trapped by the climate he had helped to create.

3 THE GUNS OF AUGUST AND THE MISSILES OF OCTOBER

The other side of the crisis is the way the two governments managed to slip out of the trap. They did not pull tight the knot of war. In this they succeeded, but they also nearly failed.

The misinterpretation of each other's intentions, the military drift and the trap of the arms race were all reminiscent of 1914. On the American side, there was acute awareness of this parallel. Barbara Tuchman's *The Guns of August* had been published that year. In one Ex-Comm meeting, George Ball saw the dangers of entrapment in terms of 1914: 'We all, of course, remember the guns of August, where certain events brought about a general situation which at the time none of the governments involved could avoid.'[44] Robert Kennedy ended his memoir of the crisis with an allusion to Bethmann Hollweg's despairing 'Oh – if only I knew' in reply to Bülow's question about how the war happened.

President Kennedy had also read *The Guns of August*. During the crisis he talked to Robert Kennedy about the German, Russian, Austrian, French and British leaders of 1914. He said they seemed to tumble into war through 'stupidity, individual idiosyncrasies, misunderstandings, and personal complexes of inferiority and grandeur'. He said, 'I am not going to follow a course which will allow anyone to write a comparable book about this time, *The Missiles of October*. If anybody is around to write after this, they are going to understand that we made every effort to give our adversary room to move. I am not going to push the Russians an inch beyond what is necessary.'[45]

The Dialogue: Taking Time

One lesson from the poor communications of 1914 was to have clear priorities and to send clear signals. Another, equally important, was to take time. In 1914 the rebuff to Grey that 'events had moved too rapidly' for his peace proposals to be accepted was a symptom of the mutual pressure created by ultimatums and deadlines. A slower pace might have softened fixed positions.

That the doves would prevail in 1962 was not a foregone conclusion. The hawks argued that a fast response was needed: delay would allow the missiles to be hidden and they might come to be seen as a *fait accompli*. Most of all, time should not be given for them to be made operational. 'Mr Acheson said that Khrushchev had presented the United States with a direct challenge, we were involved in a test of wills, and that the sooner we got to a showdown the better. He favoured cleaning the missile bases out decisively with an air strike.' But at the same meeting where Dean Acheson urged speed, Dean Rusk took the other view: 'The US needed to move in such a way that a planned action would be followed by a pause in which the great powers could step back from the brink and have time to consider and work out a solution rather than be drawn inexorably from one action to another and escalate into general nuclear war.'[46]

Some of the reasons for a quick decision were valid, but hindsight shows the value of taking time. The first response to the crisis by both Kennedy and Khrushchev was anger. Kennedy was angry at being deceived and at the sudden new threat. Khrushchev was angered by the peremptory tone of Kennedy's broadcast.

The prevailing mood of Ex-Comm at first was for military action. Kennedy at first assumed that an American strike on at least the missile sites was inevitable: 'Maybe we just have to take them out . . . I think we ought to, beginning right now, be preparing to. Because that's what we're going to do *anyway*. We're certainly going to do number one. We're going to take out these missiles.'[47] Khrushchev's first response to the blockade was to reject compromise and to threaten to sink American ships. We can be glad that both sides took time for a more considered view.

Dean Rusk defended the blockade because it 'provides a brief pause for the people on the other side to have another thought before we get into an utterly crashing crisis'.[48] President Kennedy saw the importance of this. After most of the Soviet ships had turned back, the first of the rest to cross the blockade line was a tanker, the *Bucharest*. Kennedy postponed a decision on stopping it until evening, and then let it go through, explaining that he did not want to rush Khrushchev: 'We don't want to push him to a precipitous action – give him time to consider. I don't want him put in a corner from which he cannot escape.'[49]

Later during the crisis, when Major Anderson was shot down over Cuba, there was danger of an instant but risky response. The contingency plan for an immediate air strike against the missile sites had almost unanimous support; but Kennedy delayed the decision for further thought.[50]

One of the benefits of taking time was that, on both sides, the closeness of nuclear war meant that anger was replaced by fear.

Checking Military Drift

The Soviet and American leaders were not crazy: both sides wanted to avoid a nuclear war. The danger was of a third world war starting through the muddle and military drift which had helped to start the first one.

The Soviet leadership was aware of the danger. When the Soviet forces had shot down the U2 over Cuba, Marshal Malinovsky sent a telegram: 'You hastily shot down the U.S. plane; an agreement for a peaceful way to deter an invasion of Cuba was already taking shape.'[51] Khrushchev ordered that no nuclear weapons were to be used in Cuba without specific orders from Moscow. His attitude has been described by his son Sergei:

> He believed that while the events were fully controlled by the leaders of the two governments, the threat of war was practically nonexistent. But as a man who lived through two wars, and knew what could happen in situations when troops were tense, and located very close to one another, an unexpected decision, an unexpected shot, for example, could lead to loss of control over events.

When news of the U2 came in, he 'was very upset and considered it a big mistake on our part'.[52]

One lesson some of the Kennedy administration had learnt from *The Guns of August* was not to allow military drift. Kennedy himself was worried about the use of nuclear weapons by American forces in Turkey and Italy. He ordered that specific orders were to be sent underlining the need for presidential authorization.

The Defence Secretary, Robert McNamara, insisted on controlling the way the navy carried out the blockade. He saw Admiral Anderson the day before the first Soviet ship was due to reach the quarantine line. He asked how the ship was to be stopped, and the Admiral said they would hail it. McNamara asked whether this would be in English or Russian, and what would happen if they did not understand or did not stop.

He later recounted the Admiral's response:

> 'We'll send a shot across the bow,' he said.
>   'Then what, if that doesn't work?'
>   'Then we'll fire into the rudder,' he replied, by now clearly very annoyed.
>   'What kind of ship is it?' I asked.
>   'A tanker, Mr Secretary,' he said.

'You're not going to fire a single shot at anything without my express permission, is that clear?' I said. That's when he made his famous remark about how the Navy had been running blockades since the days of John Paul Jones, and if I would leave them alone they would run this one successfully as well. I rose from my chair and walked out of the room, saying this was not a blockade but a means of communication between Kennedy and Khrushchev; no force would be applied without my permission; and that would not be given without discussion with the President. 'Was that understood?' I asked. The tight-lipped response was 'Yes.'[53]

The Kennedy administration succeeded almost entirely in keeping the armed forces under political control, but it was even more important to stop the political decisions themselves being taken over by supposed military necessities. If Kennedy had played the Kaiser to an American Moltke, the outcome could have been very different.

The leaders on both sides had to contain military pressures for harder policies. Khrushchev later said that he had been much criticized by the military for not taking a tougher line.[54] Kennedy had to resist strong military pressure for an attack on Cuba. This unanimous view of the Joint Chiefs of Staff was strongly urged by their chairman, General Maxwell Taylor, as well as by General Curtis LeMay, Air Force Chief of Staff. And for some even the Russian promise to withdraw their missiles did not change their view. Robert McNamara described the time after the crisis when President Kennedy had the Chiefs of Staff to the White House to thank them for their support: 'There was one hell of a scene. LeMay came out saying, "We lost! We ought to just go in there today and knock 'em off!"'[55]

Not Pulling on the Rope

Where both sides are in a trap, the ideal response is for both explicitly to acknowledge this. They can then turn escape from the trap into a shared project.

In the missile crisis there was no explicit joint acknowledgement that both sides were trapped. Perhaps the nearest anyone came to saying this to the other side was Khrushchev's reference to not pulling on the rope of war. But both sides did come to see they were trapped and they adjusted their behaviour accordingly. One change was in tone of voice. Khrushchev, in particular, moved away from the angry tone of his threat to sink American ships. His letter about his experience of war rolling through villages and cities had a conciliatory and human tone which changed the atmosphere. And Kennedy moved from the toughness of his broadcast to a willingness to compromise. He was looking for a way out of the trap and chose to respond to Khrushchev's conciliatory letter and to ignore the other one.

Khrushchev was concerned to make concessions where possible and not to raise the temperature of the crisis. At one point he said, 'We cannot liquidate the conflict, if we don't give some satisfaction to the Americans and acknowledge that we have R-12s there . . . We must not be obstinate.'[56] And, when pressure on Berlin was proposed as a response to the blockade, he said he could 'do without such advice . . . we had no intention to add fuel to the conflict'.[57]

At the American end, it was important not to give the Soviet government the impression that an American nuclear attack was imminent, so that self-defence would require a pre-emptive nuclear strike. General Power's uncoded signal raising the alert level could have given this impression, as could the entry into Soviet air space of the 'air sampling' U2. American preparations to strike against Cuba could have suggested that control of policy had shifted towards the military. Another possible source of this danger came from the arrest of a Western double agent in Soviet intelligence, Colonel Oleg Penkovsky. When he was arrested, he sent the telephone signal for an imminent Soviet attack. Any intensified American alert in response could have raised Soviet alarm about an attack.[58]

Kennedy was anxious to avoid unnecessary challenges to the Soviet leaders. He was concerned not to specify in the proclamation of the blockade that the prohibited weapons were from the Soviet Union, because to do so might be 'more challenging'. For the same reason he said that a Soviet ship refusing to allow Americans aboard should be disabled, but not then boarded: 'it would be better . . . to let that boat lie there disabled for a day or so, not to try to board it and have them reopen machine-guns and have 30–40 people killed on each side'. Kennedy was also concerned to avoid failure of communication between American and Soviet ships, giving orders that every ship policing the blockade must have on it someone who spoke Russian.[59]

At one point Kennedy said that the removal of missiles in Turkey as an exchange would be the only offer that made sense, 'the point being to give him some out'.[60] Dean Rusk later mentioned Sun Tzu's book, *The Art of War*, in which he warns against completely surrounding an enemy, who will fight harder without an escape route. (Rusk could have cited the ultimatums of 1914 as a case of forgetting this.) The doves were influenced by the need not to surround Khrushchev completely. Wanting a peaceful solution, and not wanting to trigger a Soviet first strike, suggested not pushing too hard. It was important to leave Khrushchev an exit from the trap.

4 MIND-SETS OF ENTRAPMENT AND ESCAPE

In 1914 the unspoken assumptions included some rather crude tribal thinking about nation-states, both personifying them and thinking of them as engaged in a Social Darwinist struggle. There was also a simple-minded morality which made an absolute of honour. None of this was present in 1962. There was also, unlike 1914, the sobering effect of the prospect of nuclear war. But it was not inevitable that this would stop war. The thinking in 1962 was also limited by dangerously crude assumptions, this time influenced by the 'realism' of rational choice theory.

Hawks and Doves as Psychologists

On the American side the Ex-Comm meetings were dominated by the debate between hawks and doves. The military case for tougher American policies was put by General Maxwell Taylor. Other hawks included the former Secretary of State, Dean Acheson, as well as Douglas Dillon and the Assistant Secretary of Defence, Paul Nitze. Among the doves were Robert McNamara and the Secretary of State, Dean Rusk, together with the Under-Secretary of State, George Ball. Robert Kennedy and the President were also doves.

Among the hawks there was talk of a tougher interpretation of the blockade and of an invasion of Cuba, but the dominant view saw an air strike as most effective. Although it would probably not eliminate all the missiles, only a few would be likely to survive. They also saw an air strike as a signal to Khrushchev that the United States meant business. Such a move, as General Taylor put it later, would 'have really shaken Khrushchev'.[61]

The doves thought an air strike was too risky. They were concerned about nuclear retaliation against the United States (either from the Soviet Union or from remaining missiles in Cuba) and about other Soviet responses, perhaps against Berlin or against American missiles in Turkey. Robert McNamara thought there was at least a fifty–fifty chance that an American attack on Cuba would lead to a Soviet military response elsewhere.

The hawks also wanted to avoid nuclear war, but thought it was a much lower risk than the doves supposed. The hawks thought the Soviet Union was in a very weak position and would back down. General Taylor later said that he had never worried much about the final outcome because 'I was so sure we had 'em over a barrel'.[62] This view was shared by some strategic theorists. Thomas Schelling was at a Harvard–MIT arms control seminar on the night of the President's television broadcast, which the participants watched: 'I remember after the speech we were left with a sense of gloating; we just couldn't imagine how Khrushchev could have done such a dumb, blundering act, and we knew that we had him on this one and the only question was how bad a fall we were going to give him.'[63]

The hawks' optimism that the risks were very low was based on confidence that it would be irrational for the Soviet Union to make a military response. Douglas Dillon later said, 'If we'd struck at the bases, they'd have acted rationally and stayed put, I think, around Berlin and elsewhere. The Russians are rational. They're not like Khomeini or Quaddafi.' He had also thought American military superiority meant there would be no Soviet military response even to an invasion.[64] Paul Nitze also thought American strategic superiority meant that the risk of a Soviet response against Berlin was small: 'Not infinitesimal, because you can never tell what people like the Soviets will do, and therefore you could well imagine that some irrational act could take place. But it seemed to me that it would have to be an irrational act, a totally irrational act.'[65]

The hawks were also confident that the crisis would not get out of control. Douglas Dillon afterwards referred to the doves being 'so irrationally fearful of nuclear war', and said, 'I don't understand . . . why people worried so much about one limited, conventional action leading to nuclear war. The idea is preposterous!'[66]

The doves placed much more emphasis on uncertainty and human fallibility. They thought that Khrushchev, backed into a corner and under domestic political pressure, might not behave according to predictions derived from theorizing about rational choice. Dean Rusk, looking back on the crisis, said:

> I've met and worked with a good many people whose names are in the history books or in the headlines. I have never met a demigod or a superman. I have only seen relatively ordinary men and women groping to deal with the problems with which they are faced. One must always remember that element of human fallibility. Now, that is also underlined by the fact that in a crisis of this sort, you can never know all that you need to know. And that's true of both sides. And it's particularly true about how human beings will react to the situations in which they find themselves.[67]

The doves and hawks also differed over how acceptable they found even a low risk of nuclear catastrophe. Robert McNamara later estimated that the risk of retaliation by missiles which survived an air strike, or of a Soviet response in Berlin or Turkey, might be quite low. But '*any* of these routes could lead you into disaster. We should not accept even a small risk of any of them, therefore, if we could avoid it.'[68]

Hindsight suggests that the hawks were over-confident in their predictions of Soviet 'rationality'. They thought that anxieties about nuclear war were the result of the doves' relative inexperience in managing crises. But getting used to nuclear diplomacy may dull the perception of real risks. Perhaps the same is true of strategic theory. In view of what we now know about control over the missiles in Cuba, the gloating about the crisis by members of the arms control seminar seems grotesquely misplaced.

Those confident about the rationality of Soviet responses too readily assumed that the policy-makers were fully in command. The shooting down of the U2 suggests the Soviet army was not under complete control. And, while the missiles capable of reaching the United States remained, at least in theory, under Khrushchev's control, the Soviet commander in Cuba was allowed to use tactical nuclear missiles on his own initiative in the event of an American invasion. This would probably have led to an American nuclear response against the Soviet Union.

Even where the policy-makers were in control, things might have been more complex than rational choice theory suggests. It leaves out such things as the emotional response to being humiliated. An air strike might not have carried the same risk of immediate nuclear war as the invasion, but it would have had its own less immediate dangers. Sergo Mikoyan, the son of Anastas Mikoyan, thought it would have led to a Soviet response. He knew Khrushchev well: 'I think I understand his nature and his perception of the prestige of our country. For both reasons, in my opinion, we could not swallow an air strike without a very strong reply. I do not know where or how, but I do not think we would do nothing.'[69]

Rational choice theory leaves out the effect of other emotional pressures on decisions. Robert Kennedy noticed this in members of Ex-Comm: 'Some, because of the pressure of events, even appeared to lose their judgement and stability.' Their decision could mean the destruction of the human race: 'That kind of pressure does strange things to a human being, even to brilliant, self-confident, mature, experienced men. For some it brings out characteristics and strengths that perhaps even they never knew they had, and for others the pressure is too overwhelming.'[70] If this could happen to the Americans, it could also happen on the Soviet side. The trust of the hawks was in rationality. The emphasis placed by the doves on human fallibility was itself more rational.

Imagination and Morality

Both hawks and doves saw nuclear war as unacceptable. But the doves' caution about even a low risk may have come from greater imaginative awareness of what it would be like. Both Khrushchev and Kennedy were emotionally responsive to its enormity.

Khrushchev said that, when he first found out what nuclear weapons could do, he could not sleep for several days. And the world wars had clearly marked him. There is a ring of sincerity to his remarks about his experience of war rolling through cities and villages sowing death and destruction. He said that going to the Bolshoi was not only to reassure the public, but also 'to disguise our own anxiety, which was intense'. And his speech-writer said that, when the leaders at the dacha sent the message about withdrawal to be broadcast, they were 'very nervous'.

The same feeling emerged on the American side. As the Soviet ships drew close to the blockade line, a Soviet submarine was reported to be with them and the plan was that it should be ordered to surface. Robert Kennedy describes President Kennedy: 'His hand went up to his face and covered his mouth. He opened and closed his fist. His face seemed drawn, his eyes pained, almost grey. We stared at each other across the table.' A little later the news came through that the twenty Soviet ships closest to the line had stopped or turned round. 'Everyone looked like a different person. For a moment the world had stood still, and now it was going around again.'[71]

After one Ex-Comm meeting, President Kennedy said to Pierre Salinger, 'Do you think the people in that room realize that if we make a mistake, there may be 200 million dead?'[72] Soon after taking office Kennedy and several members of his administration had spent an afternoon being briefed by experts on the full effects of a nuclear war. Dean Rusk said, 'It was quite an experience. And when we got through with it, President Kennedy asked me to come back to the Oval Office with him, and as we got to the door he looked at me with a strange little look on his face, and he said, "And we call ourselves the human race." '[73] Values are shaped by such emotional responses. It is striking that at least three of the doves on Ex-Comm (Rusk, McNamara and the President) had attended that briefing.

Some of the doves were drawn to think about the moral aspects of the alternative policies and found themselves drawing on values that went back further. Dean Rusk argued that a sudden air strike 'had no support in law or morality'.[74] His emphasis on the fallibility of predictions came from his Protestant beliefs:

You're dealing with human beings, and as a Presbyterian, I think that all human beings have feet of clay, and that one can't play games with this sort of thing . . . The first question of the Westminster Shorter Catechism is 'What is the chief end of man?' And during the Cuban missile crisis although I hadn't thought of the Westminster Shorter Catechism since I had memorized and recited it as a small boy, driving through the streets of Washington I suddenly realised that this first of these questions 'What is the chief end of man?' had become an operational question before the governments of the world. And that was a sobering thought.

Dean Rusk took the relevance of morality for granted:

> Moral and ethical considerations play a very important part, even though
> people don't wear these things on their shirtsleeves or put these things into
> official memoranda. They play an important part. People act in reference to
> their basic moral commitments, and they are likely to come to the fore when
> situations become critical.[75]

George Ball opposed an unexpected strike like Pearl Harbor, as 'not
conduct that one expects of the United States'. Robert Kennedy took up
Ball's concern for the moral identity of the United States: 'I think George
Ball has a hell of a good point . . . I think it is a question of . . . what kind
of country we are . . . We've fought for 15 years with Russia to prevent a
first strike against us . . . Now, in the interest of time, we do that to a small
country. I think it's a hell of a burden to carry.'[76] In his account of the
crisis, Robert Kennedy says, 'we spent more time on this moral question
during the first five days than on any other single matter . . . We struggled
and fought with one another and with our consciences, for it was a
question that deeply troubled us all.'[77]

Not everyone thought the moral discussion was relevant. Some of the
hawks were impatient with it. Paul Nitze in a later interview said, 'we had
these everlasting debates on the morality of a big country attacking a small
country, and so forth'. Nitze took the view that discussion should have
concentrated on plans rather than morality:

> Most of the discussion in those early days was way up at the level of morality
> and this kind of thing, and not on the issue of who does what, with what, to
> whom, and when . . . I was so annoyed at the failure of the main discussions to
> deal with who-does-what-with-what-to-whom-when, it wasn't really a plan-
> ning session, it seemed to me to be rather a sophomoric seminar.[78]

Behind this impatience is the unquestioned assumption of the contrast
between morality and the factors that bear on who is to do what to whom.
One legacy of the idea of a moral law whose commands and prohibitions
are absolute, regardless of consequences, is the assumption that morality
cannot realistically be applied to practical decisions. There is a link
between the statesmen of 1914 and the hawks of 1962. Those who led their
countries into the First World War made an absolute out of a morality of
national honour, regardless of the human consequences of obeying such a
morality. They opted for obeying the dictates of what they took to be
morality. The hawks of 1962 shared the absolutist view of morality, but
drew the opposite conclusion: that it was irrelevant to practical politics.
They were left with a calculation of national self-interest, carried out

without imaginative awareness of what was really at risk. Like the men of 1914, they missed the scale of the crisis.

The naïve contrast between concern with morality and concern with practical consequences is one of the disastrous legacies of the idea of the moral law. Justifiable doubt about the moral law leads to scepticism about any moral restraints on political action. This is one source of the history of brutal 'realism' on the part of statesmen and soldiers which goes back at least to the Melian dialogue. The 'sophomoric seminar' on morality would have had the contempt of the Athenian spokesmen too.

Values and Compromise

The deal between Kennedy and Khrushchev is at first sight one which leaves neither of them looking particularly impressive. Khrushchev had to make what was widely seen as a humiliating climbdown. And Kennedy, in order to defend his reputation for toughness, had to deceive the public about the existence of the deal. As McGeorge Bundy later put it, 'The President himself decided not to make a public trade, but undertook to get them [the missiles in Turkey] out, which was hard work. It involved a lot of secret, delicate negotiations. We needed to be very careful about our own public opinion.'[79] Stevenson, one of the heroes of the crisis, took the criticism of those who disapproved of 'appeasement'. Kennedy, an early supporter of a deal, was publicly silent.

In the middle of the crisis, Kennedy had to make a deal which would satisfy both sides, while not losing face by being the one to propose compromise. The concealment continued after the crisis. Robert Kennedy's memoir says that Dobrynin asked him about the Turkish missiles. He refused any deal, but said that 'it was our judgment that, within a short time after this crisis was over, those missiles would be gone'.[80] Dobrynin says that it was Robert Kennedy who pursued the missile exchange, and that there was an explicit deal. In Robert Kennedy's diaries, on which the memoir was based, it was portrayed as an explicit deal. Theodore Sorensen, who edited Robert Kennedy's memoir, has said that, to keep the deal a secret, he suppressed this.

Khrushchev's climbdown was spelt out in his remarks to an emergency meeting of the Presidium on Sunday 28 October. He said, 'Now we found ourselves face to face with the danger of war and of nuclear catastrophe, with the possible result of destroying the human race. In order to save the world, we must retreat.'[81] It was not such a bad reason for a climbdown.

Kennedy's deception and Khrushchev's climbdown are not the stuff of conventional heroism. But, in the nuclear age, such heroism is outdated. Through climbdown and deception they avoided war. After the crisis, Khrushchev wrote to Kennedy that 'we had to step over our pride, both you and we, in order to reach this agreement'.[82] This stepping over pride was what the statesmen of 1914 had not been able to do to their sense of national honour. The humiliating climbdown, the necessary deception, and stepping over one's pride: they should each have their honoured place in a modern account of the political virtues.

CHAPTER 23

Ways Out

We may insist as much as we like that the human intellect is weak in comparison with human instincts, and be right in doing so. But nevertheless there is something peculiar about this weakness. The voice of the intellect is a soft one, but it does not rest until it has gained a hearing. Ultimately, after endlessly repeated rebuffs, it succeeds. This is one of the few points in which one may be optimistic about the future of mankind.

Sigmund Freud, *The Future of an Illusion*

There are some patterns discernible in crises like those of July 1914 and October 1962. The contrasting events of those two months suggest some guidelines to help leaders escape the trap of war. These include clarity in policy and in communication, together with firmness in preventing military drift. Escaping the trap means taking time for considered and cautious responses. It means awareness of fallibility. It means avoiding provocation and using a tone of voice which does not inflame the crisis. Most of all, it requires remembering the opponents' self-respect: a willingness to leave them an exit without humiliation.

In other words, the model is 1962, not 1914. Or at least, 1962 after the first reckless gamble and the first angry response were over. And one improvement on 1962 would be the explicit and public recognition by both parties that they were together in a trap and had to work with each other to get out of it. This recognition did dawn on both sides during the crisis. But, in such a case, a joint statement about a shared problem could transform the atmosphere.

The links between the two crises show that lessons can be learnt from history. It was lucky that Kennedy and some others had read *The Guns of August*. Things could have been different. Some less simple books on 1914, such as those of Fritz Fischer, might have been less helpful. And not all Presidents can be relied on to have read any books on 1914. The lessons Kennedy and others learnt from 1914 were good ones about how not to handle a crisis.

But the lessons of 1914 and of 1962 go beyond the month of crisis. It is necessary to go behind the two crises to the deeper Hobbesian trap which created them: the trap of rival military alliances and the arms race.

1 ESCAPING THE HOBBESIAN TRAP: POLITICS

The central trap of war is Hobbesian fear: 'the growth of Athenian power and the fear which this caused in Sparta'. The response to the fear is to seek allies and to build up armaments. Build some Dreadnoughts. Close the missile gap. The other side is alarmed in turn and the first twists of the spiral have begun.

Consider the dollar auction.[1] A dollar bill will go to the highest bidder, even if the bid is far less than a dollar. But, if you are the second highest bidder, you have to pay what you bid and you get nothing for it.

A low bid, say five cents, seems worth putting in. As the only bidder, you will make ninety-five cents. If someone trumps your bid, you lose only five cents. The gamble looks good and so you bid. Your bid is trumped by a ten-cent bid. It looks worth going to fifteen: you will still make eighty-five cents rather than lose five. The logic of this sends the bidding up on both sides. If you bid ninety-five cents, your rival has reason to bid a dollar: better break even than lose ninety cents. But you then have a reason for bidding a dollar and five cents: better lose five cents than ninety-five. Trying to escape with the smaller rather than the larger loss traps you both into ever bigger bids.

An arms race can be a trap like the dollar auction. Investing in some weapons to dominate an opponent may seem a good investment. When he has responded, it may seem worth paying to be a bit ahead. Both sides may be in a trap which neither dares be the first to leave. But the dollar auction threatens only bankruptcy, while an arms race threatens the 1914 outcome.

The Hobbesian and the Co-operative Solutions

The Hobbesian trap of mutual fear suggests the Hobbesian solution. To police the global village, we could create Leviathan. We could all agree to submit to the power of the strongest. In the world after the Cold War, the emerging approximation to Pax Americana is a bit like this. But the Hobbesian solution has always been a second best. There is no justice in an inequality of power based on mere strength. The power may be used altruistically and wisely. It may also be used selfishly and at whim. And there are dangers in giving anyone total power.

Alternative solutions are based on co-operation. In game theory, one case is the emergence of TIT FOR TAT as a co-operative strategy in Axelrod's tournament. It is obviously encouraging that co-operation can be a rational strategy for self-interested players in a series of repeated prisoners' dilemmas. But the Axelrod result has its limitations. It depends on the rules of that particular tournament. In some others TIT FOR TAT does not win. And, in the real world of international relations, not all conflicts have the structure of rewards and penalties which would make them prisoners' dilemmas. Nor are real prisoners' dilemmas always repeated with the same contestants.

One lesson to take from game theory to the real world is the importance of rigging the context in which international conflicts take place. Things should be rigged so that co-operation is easy and is rewarded.

Often it is better to find ways of escaping from a prisoners' dilemma than to keep repeating it in the hope that co-operation will emerge. The dollar auction, a good model of an arms race, is one where carrying on bidding is incompatible with co-operation. The only way to co-operate is to agree to leave the game. The obvious proposal is to share the current loss equally. Both can escape where both see that this is the way out. But, where both sides agree to leave the game, why should each trust the other not to renege on the agreement? Again, some rigging seems necessary to penalize those who cheat and reward those who do not.

The lesson about rigging the contest in favour of co-operation, whether within the game or in leaving it, raises further questions. Who is to rig the international environment to favour co-operation?

Where groups remain self-interested, the co-operative solution is always in danger of sliding back into the Hobbesian one. One obvious answer to the question about rigging is Hobbesian. The rules of the game, and the rules governing jointly leaving the game, might be imposed by the strongest power or group of powers. But there is the familiar worry about the justice of rules imposed in this way. Also, if all that backs the rules is strength and power, they lack moral authority. Where they can be broken without penalty, there will be no reason to respect them. The Hobbesian solution is an imposed peace. Beneath the surface, there is still a warring state of nature. If there are limits to the strength, reach or permanence of Leviathan, those will be the limits of the peace.

From Hobbes to Kant: from Force to Authority

Can we escape from Hobbesian reliance on the brute power of the strong? In many countries, people obey the law for reasons which go beyond the fear of punishment. They see the law as having some moral authority, which comes partly from the fact that, in a decent society, most laws are roughly just approaches to regulating conflicts of interest or outlook. The authority also comes partly from the fact that, in a democracy, legislators are answerable to those who have to obey the laws.

Immanuel Kant, in *Perpetual Peace*, saw that a Hobbesian state of nature holds between nations. He wanted an international equivalent to the civil constitution which keeps the peace between individuals. As well as noticing the international state of nature, Kant went further than Hobbes in three ways. He thought of a co-operative rather than an imposed solution. He saw the possibility of something between world government and a world of completely independent states. And he saw the need for a world order to be based on authority rather than mere force.

The constitution Kant proposed in order to eliminate war was co-operative rather than Hobbesian. He thought peace would be most secure under a single world state, but he saw that nations want their own states. So, as the best substitute for a world state, he advocated a federation of nation-states. The federation would not seek power for itself, but would combine a permanent peace with protecting the freedom of each state.

The federation would limit national independence while falling short of a world government. States would give up their freedom to wage war. Apart from that, they would be independent. Kant's proposal was a forerunner of modern experiments in limited national independence. His federation has echoes in the European Union, with its partial pooling of sovereignty. His idea of a world authority with limited scope can be glimpsed in the partial policing of the world by the United Nations.

Kant's account of the decision by a state to join the federation hovers between Hobbesian self-interest and morality. His account of the motives which influence international relations is grim: 'the depravity of human nature is displayed without disguise in the unrestricted relations which obtain between the various nations'; but the fact that states do make (often spurious) appeals to morality in justification of war shows that 'man possesses a greater moral capacity, still dormant at present, to overcome eventually the evil principle within him'. And Kant does think that doing what brings about peace is morally obligatory: 'reason, as the highest legislative moral power, absolutely condemns war as a test of rights and sets up peace as an immediate duty'.[2]

This suggestion of a moral basis is the biggest departure from Hobbes. It moves from an international order based on force to one based on authority. A Hobbesian imposed peace is only as secure as the strength and permanence of the dominant power allow it to be. But a generally acceptable moral basis would give an international order an authority it would otherwise lack. It might support co-operation with reasons, making it less likely to slide back into dependence on Hobbesian power.

But such a moral basis has pre-conditions. One is that it has some kind of democratic authority. Another is that it has to be possible for states not to act always in a narrowly self-interested way. Transcending the Hobbesian solution requires both democracy and transcending the Hobbesian psychology.

Democracy as a Source of Authority and as a Safeguard

From Pax Romana to Pax Americana, there have been periods of relative international peace imposed by a dominant power. But a more stable and more acceptable solution depends on a world order which is recognized as having some moral authority. One condition of this is that the world order should be freely accepted by countries rather than imposed on them.

The other condition is that the governments agreeing to the world order on behalf of their countries should be broadly democratic. Where national leaders come to power through military coups, there is a real question about whether deals those individuals sign with each other, supposedly on behalf of their countries, are at all binding on anyone. In the world as it is, many countries are not democracies and yet we still need a peaceful world order. Undemocratic countries have to be included in the agreements, but this should be recognized as a second best. A world order so created can still have some moral authority as mankind's attempt at world peace, even if it is reduced by the arbitrary power of some of those agreeing to it. This is roughly the basis of the partial moral authority of the United Nations.

There is a different argument linking world peace with democracy. Democracies may be more pacific than dictatorships. Leaders outside democratic control are less concerned about the potential victims of war. In a democracy, the government has to please those who will bear war's human cost. Kant understood this difference. He quoted a Bulgarian prince who rejected another ruler's offer that the two of them should have a duel instead of there being a war: 'A smith who possesses tongs will not lift the glowing iron out of the coals with his own hands.'[3]

Although democracy is often a restraint on going to war, it is not always effective. Germany in 1914 was partly democratic. And the mood in the democracies was enthusiastic when war was declared. Fear of war may be counterbalanced by an ugly excitement, often fanned by propaganda. And, in 1962, the American public were part of the trap in which Kennedy found himself. One worry in a democracy is a cycle of mutual reinforcement between the public and political leaders. Politicians are tempted to win elections by promising more Dreadnoughts or by inventing missile gaps, thereby creating traps for themselves when in office.

2 ESCAPING THE HOBBESIAN TRAP: PSYCHOLOGY

Co-operation to escape war is easier between democracies. It is easier if states are subject to some degree of international authority. But the restraining effects of democracy and international authority depend on the psychological climate. Escaping from the Hobbesian traps, like unchaining ourselves from tribalism, calls for the use of politics and psychology together.

To blame 1914 entirely on some combination of Bethmann Hollweg, Moltke, Berchtold, Sazonov, Poincaré, Grey and others is too simple. The ecological niche of statesmen is the population of their country. The mood of the public both influences who reaches the top and shapes the choice of policies. An adequate understanding of the trap of war starts with leaders, but has to go behind them to public opinion. ('I would have been impeached.')

This applies to understanding the period during a war as well as before it. The trap in which Erich Maria Remarque and Robert Graves found themselves was partly maintained by public satisfaction with the war: by Remarque's uncomprehending old headmaster and by the parents Graves could not talk to about the war. The climate of opinion conditions everything.

In 1914 the outlook included tribal nationalism and Social Darwinism. Other aspects of the climate of the time were the beliefs countries held about each other, a concern with national honour, and some deeper, Hobbesian, 'unspoken assumptions'.

Belief

People in different countries become mutually trapped by their beliefs about each other. In 1914 what people in Moscow, Paris and London saw as 'containment' of Germany was seen in Berlin as 'encirclement'. And often the belief trap is reinforced by government misinformation, as happened on both sides before the Gulf War.

There is no quick way out of a belief trap. Modern communications are some help. Government propaganda is less likely to be believed by a population with access to broadcasts from other countries. But the most fundamental protection from belief traps is the scepticism appropriate to official information and to the partisan national narrative. This all-important scepticism comes partly from a culture in which critical habits of mind are cultivated, and partly from awareness of the historical role of beliefs in causing war. So it grows only slowly.

Honour and National Pride

The psychological trap of 1914 was partly created by what were seen as the demands of honour and national pride. Austrian leaders could create a war with Serbia by offering terms intended to make it 'impossible for a state with any self-respect and dignity to accept them'. Russia could be brought to support Serbia by wanting not to 'cover with shame the good name of the Russian people'. It was hard for Britain to escape war without betraying commitments to France. The claims of honour urged by some statesmen ('Est-ce que l'Angleterre comprend ce que c'est l'honneur?') found a response in others: an obligation 'not only of law but of honour, which no self-respecting man could possibly have repudiated'. Countries were thought of as people and as subject to similar moral claims. For the statesmen, and for many of those they represented, the personal sense of moral identity was bound up with the expectation that their nations would act honourably.

Seeing national honour and pride as part of the trap may encourage the growth of a more complex sense of moral identity. Where they are necessary to avoid disaster, the willingness to compromise or to back down, even to break a commitment, can be seen in a new light. Paradoxically, both Khrushchev and Kennedy could have been proud of the fact that 'we had to step over our pride, both you and we, in order to reach this agreement'. Stepping over their pride was stepping together out of the trap, taking mankind with them.

Hobbesian Self-interest and the Moral Imagination

At a deeper level people are trapped by the limitations of their view of the world. The 'unspoken assumptions' of 1914 played their part in the disaster of that summer. And some of the unspoken assumptions of 1962 made the escape narrower than it need have been.

One common feature of the July crisis of 1914 and of the early stages of the Cuba crisis was a psychology of group self-interest. This psychology generalizes far beyond those two crises. It was the psychology of the Athenians in the Melian dialogue and is at the heart of most group conflict. If we hope to escape being trapped into war, we need to transcend this Hobbesian psychology.

Those who think their country is engaged in a Hobbesian contest normally make the same assumption about other countries. Their interpretations and predictions about those other countries assume policies are rational means to pursue national self-interest. This can limit the imagination in dangerous ways. In 1962 the hawks on the Ex-Comm thought the risk of nuclear war was very low because 'we had 'em over a barrel'. The Soviet Union was politically in a weak position and was militarily weaker than the United States. Because the rational Soviet response would be not to retaliate, it was a good bet for America to carry out an air strike or an invasion.

This thinking left out military drift, for instance by the Soviet commander in Cuba authorized to use tactical nuclear weapons on his own initiative. It left out the sense of wounded national pride. ('I knew Khrushchev very well . . . and his perception of the prestige of our country

. . . we could not swallow an air strike without a very strong reply.') It is not always rational to assume a calculating rationality on the part of other groups.

The Hobbesian outlook of the hawks meant that they wanted do pursue a policy based only on self-interested calculation. This generated impatience with 'sophomoric seminars' on morality. General acceptance of this amoralism would make impossible the Kantian transition to an international order based on authority rather than power. The idea of authority is based on non–Hobbesian values. A purely Hobbesian outlook can only generate a commitment to an international order which is conditional on its continuing to be in a nation's self-interest.

One reason for a contemptuous dismissal of morality as something to be taken seriously by statesmen is widespread scepticism about the existence of a moral law. On this topic, Kant's outlook has been losing ground. Because the outlook is so poor for reviving a defensible version of the moral law, let alone a version which would also gain widespread acceptance, those of us who hope for an international order based on something other than force must hope that there is some middle way between Kant and Hobbes.

In a particular society a moral code may emerge without a belief in a moral law. It is likely to come partly from self-interested agreements. But, as we have seen, a moral code which protects the weak will need additional resources, notably the human responses and the sense of moral identity. An international order which is to have any authority other than pure self-interest is also going to need the moral resources. In particular, it will need sympathy, supported by imagination.

In 1914 it was imagination that was so lacking in the sleepwalking statesmen who missed the scale of the crisis. It was lacking in the crowds in the capitals of Europe who cheered when war was declared. Perhaps neither the statesmen nor the crowds of 1914 can be blamed for failing to imagine the utterly unprecedented slaughter which was to follow.

In 1962 it was possible to imagine something of the human catastrophe just over the precipice. And, strikingly, in those who practised or advocated restraint, the role of the imagination was visible. Khrushchev's memories of war rolling through cities and villages sowing death and destruction were important. His efforts to escape from the trap were given an emotional charge by his being able to imagine something of what failure might mean. On the American side, the imagination of Kennedy, McNamara and Rusk had been charged by the traumatic briefing on the full effects of nuclear war.

Sometimes, apparently rational self-interested strategies turn out (as in the prisoners' dilemma or the dollar auction) to be self-defeating. This may look like a defeat for rationality, but it is not. Rationality is saved by its own open-endedness. If a strategy of following accepted rules of rationality is sometimes self-defeating, this is not the end. We revise the rules to take account of this, so producing a higher-order rational strategy. This in turn may fail, but again we go up a level. At whatever level we fail, there is always this process of standing back and going up a further level.

These revisions take place within a system of thought where goals are taken for granted. National leaders act in the interests of their own countries, even if in the long run this is best served by some co-operation with other countries or even some generosity towards them.

But rationality can be more open-ended still. People can question their goals, as well as their means of pursuing them. Sometimes national goals pursued by leaders are seen not to correspond with what the people the leaders represent really care about. (This is the political equivalent of the personal reappraisal which takes place when someone who has lived for making money comes to think such a life is too driven or too narrow.)

In international relations, starting to question the goal of national self-interest can be the result of imagining the human implications of, for instance, the use of nuclear weapons, even if used only against people on the other side. Here the imagination encourages a move from game theory to philosophy. The goal of making sure that our side gets as much advantage as possible over theirs may come to seem less important. Those on the other side are still people. Why should their interests matter less? The slow growth of such scepticism about the adversarial stance between human groups is, in the long run, the best hope for peace.

In 1962 Kennedy and Khrushchev did well in escaping from the trap, but the deep lesson of the Cuba crisis, the importance of escaping from the ruinous and dangerous Cold War, was not taken seriously at the time by anyone capable of acting on it.

The end of the Cold War in the late 1980s partly reflected the growth of a less adversarial psychology. It was not in the interests of the Soviet Union when Mikhail Gorbachev withdrew the forces which had imposed Communism on a reluctant Eastern Europe. The balance of power tilted heavily in favour of the West. And, because it was hard to stop self-determination at the Soviet frontier, the further consequence was the destruction of the Soviet Union itself. Of course it is not clear that Gorbachev anticipated all this. And his decision may have been influenced by the burden of the arms race on the ossified Soviet economy. But, however mixed Gorbachev's motives, his decision was still to lose the conflict in order to end it. In doing so, as he said to the West, he had 'deprived you of an enemy'. He was, we may hope, a forerunner of a period in which other statesmen will put shared values before Hobbesian group self-interest. Although it took a quarter of a century, eventually the deepest lesson of the Cuba crisis was acted on.

Gorbachev's decision can also be seen as the eventual breakthrough into world politics of something once confined to people trapped and remote from power. It was the success, delayed by three-quarters of a century, of the attitude expressed by the German soldier at Christmas in 1914: 'We don't want to kill you, and you don't want to kill us, so why shoot?'

The voice of the intellect is a soft one, but it does not rest until it has gained a hearing. Given our recent history, it is a bit early for optimism. But Freud may have been right that ultimately the voice of the intellect succeeds in being heard. If so, perhaps a time will come in which one may be optimistic about the future of mankind.

PART FIVE

BELIEF AND TERROR:
STALIN AND HIS HEIRS

CHAPTER 24

In Those Years

In those years only the dead smiled,
Glad to be at rest:
And Leningrad city swayed like
A needless appendix to its prisons.
It was then that the railway-yards
Were asylums of the mad;
Short were the locomotives'
Farewell songs.
Stars of death stood
Above us, and innocent Russia
Writhed under bloodstained boots, and
Under the tyres of Black Marias.

Anna Akhmatova, '*Requiem*'

War killed an average of over a hundred people an hour through the twentieth century. Stalin's policies are not far behind this.

Numbers are disputed. One estimate is that, in the seventy years after 1917, the Soviet regime killed 61,911,000 people.[1] Another estimate puts the deaths for 1937–8 at over a million executed and a further 2 million who died in the camps, these figures being part of an overall 20 million who were killed in the whole Stalinist period.[2] Another estimate (ascribed to a KGB report to Khrushchev) is that 7 million people were killed in six and a half years between January 1935 and June 1941.[3] Yet another estimate is that 9.5 million people were killed in the decade of the 1930s.[4]

These estimates cover wider and narrower periods and use different methods of assessment. Here it is not necessary to try to decide between them. A very rough idea is enough. Stalinist deliberate killing was on a scale surpassed only by war.

Many were executed, often in mass executions. Some died in compulsory movements of population, which in effect were often mass murder. Others died in deliberately created famine, or working on huge slave-labour construction projects, or as the result of their treatment in the camps.

The mass executions were at pits. Excavations have revealed layers of victims. They were shot from behind and pushed into the pit. A group of bodies would be covered in sand and another group would be shot and pushed in on top. Then more sand, and so on until the pit was full with about 150 bodies. There were many regions where this happened and each region has hundreds of pits.

Population movements and deliberate famine were used to destroy the kulaks in the early 1930s. 'Kulaks' were peasants classified as 'bourgeois', though the criteria for this were vague. In 1930 the Central Committee of the Communist Party decided to shift 'from a policy of restricting the exploiting tendencies of the kulaks to a policy of liquidating the kulaks as a class'.

Whole communities were driven from their homes and left in some inhospitable place, like a stony hillside without water. Sometimes the people dumped down were forbidden to grow grain crops. Alexander Solzhenitsyn described one of these expulsions. In 1930, 10,000 families were sent on a journey over the ice of the Vasyugan river. Many, especially children, died on the journey. The survivors were left, with no food or tools, on bits of land in the middle of marshes. The paths back were guarded with machine-guns. Everyone died.[5]

Peasants who were not deported were forced into collective farms. In the Ukraine an effort was made to crush both Ukrainian nationalism and the peasants at the same time.[6] The collective farms were set impossible quotas for grain production. All other food was forcibly removed and villages were blockaded to prevent food coming from outside. People swelled up with starvation. They ate birds, rats, mice, worms and weeds. And finally, in large numbers, they died. This deliberate famine killed 4–6 million people.[7]

Many died during slave labour on the construction of the Baltic–White Sea Canal. The prisoners were set a daily norm. In extreme cold they had to break up two and a half cubic yards of granite and move it a hundred yards in a wheelbarrow. One work supervisor described the results:

At the end of the workday there were corpses left on the work site. The snow powdered their faces. One of them was hunched over beneath an overturned wheelbarrow, he had hidden his hands in his sleeves and frozen to death in that position. Someone had frozen with his head bent down between his knees. Two were frozen back to back leaning against each other . . . At night the sledges went out and collected them. The drivers threw the corpses onto the sledges with a dull clonk.[8]

In 1966 Solzhenitsyn spent a day by the canal, which he estimated had cost a quarter of a million lives. In eight hours only two barges carrying logs passed. The huge slave-labour projects were major islands in the system of prison and labour camps which Solzhenitsyn has described as an archipelago stretching over the Soviet Union.

People could be arrested for nothing: some were denounced by jealous neighbours, others were arrested to fulfil some quota. The secret police chief, Yezhov, sent one official a telegram saying, 'You are charged with the task of exterminating 10,000 enemies of the people. Report results by signal.' The reply was a numbered list of those who had been shot.[9]

Certain things made arrest almost inevitable. Stubborn religious commitment was one. A clear expression of dissent was another. In 1934 Osip Mandelstam was arrested for writing a poem about Stalin. The version known to the authorities was about 'the Kremlin mountaineer, the murderer and peasant-slayer', with his 'cockroach whiskers'. Such opposition led to a nightmare, which started with arrest at night and then the process of interrogation.

Torture was often part of the interrogation. The authorities hoped to make Brigade Commander Rudolf Pintsov confess to having wanted to turn his tanks against the government at a parade in Red Square. Their efforts included pouring water into him to bursting point and pushing needles under his nails. They scraped skin off his back with a grater and then poured turpentine on it.[10] One woman in prison complained about a friend who had incriminated her. After seeing him she was remorseful for having been critical, because she understood why he had done it: 'How could I? How could I? Today I had a confrontation with him and I saw not a man, but live raw meat.' Stalin encouraged torture. In a note to Yezhov he wrote, 'Can't this gentleman be made to tell of his dirty deeds? Where is he – in a prison or a hotel?' He gave orders about the interrogation of those accused in the 'Doctors' Plot': 'beat, beat and beat again'.[11]

The interrogation, even without full-blown torture, could affect people's minds. When Mandelstam was arrested, one of his friends telephoned someone she knew in the secret police. He said, 'Let's hope they don't drive him out of his mind – our fellows are very good at it.' Released after his first arrest, Mandelstam had hallucinations. The doctor refused to arrange a psychiatric examination: 'What do you expect me to do? They're always in this state when they come "from there".'[12]

One way of extracting confessions was the 'conveyor': continuous questioning, for days on end, carried out by relays of interrogators. This, together with days of standing up with no sleep, almost always worked. Sleep deprivation and interrogation under bright lights helped to disrupt Mandelstam's mind.

After 'confession' and sentence, there was the train journey to the camps in hugely overcrowded cattle trucks. In the camps many would die from cold and exhaustion. They were starved: at one camp the prisoners ate the week-old corpse of a horse, covered with flies and maggots.

One of the grimmest camps was Vorkuta, inside the Arctic Circle. During the two months of total darkness each year, the centigrade temperature sank to sixty degrees below zero. The walls of the mines were running with water which turned to ice. The prisoners worked in shifts round the clock. Day and night were indistinguishable.

A Pole, Bernard Grzywacz, has described the life of the Vorkuta prisoners:

> We had a quota we had to fulfil, and what food we got depended on how far we met it. In more than eleven years I never met it once. Fights broke out. We were all starving. The lucky ones got jobs on the surface. The guards decided who was too weak to go down the mines by getting us to strip and face the walls: the ones whose buttocks were shrivelled with starvation were kept above ground. In snow storms we had to link arms for the walk back to barracks, and hold on to a rope. Any man who fell out was shot. If he didn't die then, he soon did, from the cold. The guards had a way of testing if anyone was feigning by bashing their skulls in with a sledgehammer.[13]

Many in the camps were tortured. Some had salt water sprayed in their throats and were left in a box all day to be tormented by thirst. In the punishment cells at Solovki, people had to sit all day trying to keep their balance on poles set too high for their feet to reach the ground. Anyone who fell was beaten up, or tied to a beam and rolled down 365 steep steps. Another practice at Solovki was to tie a prisoner to a tree, naked among a cloud of mosquitoes.[14]

The numbers of people killed go beyond our normal understanding. And the same goes for the cruelty of it all. Those of us who have not lived through it can have only a very remote imaginative grasp of what it was like. But, as with the Nazi atrocities, one question which strikes nearly everyone is how people can have done these things. Nadezdha Mandelstam wondered about this: 'The only really strange thing is that all this was done by people, the most ordinary sort of people . . . How can we understand it or explain it?'[15]

CHAPTER 25

The Trap of Terror

What has been already mentioned is as conducive as anything can be to preserve a tyranny; namely, to keep down those who are of an aspiring disposition, to take off those who will not submit, to allow no public meals, no clubs, no education, nothing at all, but to guard against everything that gives rise to high spirits or mutual confidence; nor to suffer the learned meetings of those who are at leisure to hold conversation with each other; and to endeavour by every means possible to keep all the people strangers to each other.

Aristotle, Politics

In the years of the terror, there was not a home in the country where people did not sit trembling at night, their ears straining to catch the murmur of passing cars or the sound of the elevator.

Nadezhda Mandelstam, Hope Against Hope

How can so many people have allowed a minority to impose such things on them? They were frightened. Most Soviet citizens knew what was in store for those who stepped out of line. And they were kept divided from each other to prevent mutual support in resistance.

Terror and Atomization

Stalin did not start Soviet terror. It went back to the earliest days of the Revolution. In August 1918 Lenin wrote to the Bolsheviks of Penza that the kulak rising there must be crushed without pity:

1.) Hang (and I mean hang so that the *people can see*) *not less than 100* known kulaks, rich men, bloodsuckers.
2.) Publish their names.

3.) Take *all* their grain away from them.

4.) Identify hostages as we described in our telegram yesterday.

Do this so that for hundreds of miles around the people can see, tremble, know and cry: they are killing and will go on killing the bloodsucking kulaks. Cable that you have received this and carried out [your instructions]. Yours, Lenin.

P.S. Find tougher people.[1]

Stalin brought the terror to a new pitch and made it universal.

Osip and Nadezhda Mandelstam went to Maly Yaroslavets, a town where many had been arrested. Arriving at night, they found the town in darkness, with no street lights or lighted windows. Nadezhda Mandelstam thought keeping the lights off might have come from an animal instinct to hide in the dark. There was relief when people saw the Mandelstams were no threat: 'We had to knock on windows to ask the way, and each time a fear-contorted face peered out. But when we simply asked the way, the faces were at once transformed and wreathed in smiles.'[2]

Society was atomized as never before. Resistance was paralysed by lack of trust. People could not combine against the terror because things said to more than a few would be heard by an informer. Only a few people very close were entrusted with the quietly spoken criticisms. As Mandelstam wrote in his Stalin poem, 'ten steps away no one hears our speeches'.

The terror fed on itself. Fear led some to establish their own credentials by informing on others. Those who did nothing might still be denounced by those arrested and put under pressure to name 'accomplices'. People were denounced by enemies or by those who wanted their jobs or houses.

Even a hint of stepping out of line could bring drastic retribution. Solzhenitsyn tells a story about applause. At the end of a Party conference in Moscow Province, a tribute to Stalin was called for. Everyone stood and clapped wildly, for three minutes, then four, then five. The clapping became more painful. It was a kind of physical embodiment of the trap people were in. Who would dare to be the first to stop? The Secretary did not dare, as his predecessor had been arrested, and the NKVD men were there watching. The painful applause went on past ten minutes, with everyone trapped in it. Among those on the platform was the director of a paper factory. After eleven minutes of applause, he sat down, followed by everyone else. That night, he was arrested. He was given ten years on some pretext, but his interrogator told him never to be the first to stop applauding.[3]

People feared for their families. In interrogation a husband would be told his wife had been arrested and was being interrogated in the room next door, from which a woman's screams could be heard. Other pressure was applied through the family: children were taught that it was their duty to inform on parents who showed signs of dissidence. Pavlik Morozov was held up as a hero in Soviet school textbooks for denouncing his parents.

Despite the pressure, people sometimes showed solidarity with the victims. Nadezhda Mandelstam earned money by working in a textile factory, where the workers knew she was a political victim. They kept a place for her in the cafeteria and gave her food and moral support. During a night shift, two men took her away from her machine to the personnel section. 'Seeing us go by, other workers switched off their machines, and began to follow us . . . I sensed that this was a way of saying goodbye to me – the workers knew only too well that people were often taken straight from the personnel section to the secret police.' The support may have influenced the interrogators. 'That night they decided to let me go, perhaps because of the workers who had gathered outside in the yard.' After the night shift, many workers came to her house and talked. They gave her money and advised her to leave.

Terror, the Leadership and the Show Trials

The terror was not only imposed on ordinary people. The Party leaders had most reason to be terrified. Lenin's original Politburo of 1917 contained, apart from himself and Stalin, six other people: Trotsky, Kamenev, Zinoviev, Bukharin, Rykov and Tomsky. Stalin had Trotsky assassinated in Mexico. He had Kamenev, Zinoviev, Bukharin and Rykov shot. Tomsky committed suicide when about to be arrested. Like the leaders of the French Revolution, most of the leaders of the Russian Revolution were themselves swallowed up, with the difference that in this case the swallowing was all arranged by the single survivor.

Throughout the 1930s 'spies', 'terrorists', 'saboteurs' and 'wreckers' were arrested, forced to 'confess' and then put through show trials. Stalin himself played a role behind the scenes. In a letter to Molotov in 1930 he suggested the content of some of the confessions: 'By the way, how about Messrs. Defendants admitting their mistakes and disgracing themselves politically, while simultaneously acknowledging the strength of the Soviet government and the correctness of the method of collectivization? It wouldn't be a bad thing if they did.'[4]

The leaders were not exempt from these trials. In 1934 the Leningrad Communist leader Kirov was murdered, perhaps on Stalin's instigation. Among those arrested for the murder were Kamenev and Zinoviev. They 'confessed' their 'moral responsibility' for the murder, saying it could have been encouraged by their political views. Their trial was in secret, with Andrei Vyshinsky as prosecutor. They were sentenced only to prison, although they were later shot. A huge purge, including other trials, followed.

Pyatakov and Radek, who were both senior in the Party, were among a group who 'confessed' to Trotskyite sabotage. Vyshinsky, again prosecuting, concluded his speech:

> The victims may be in their graves, but I feel that they are standing here beside me, pointing at the dock, at you, accused, with their mutilated arms, which have mouldered in the graves to which you sent them! I am not the only accuser! I am joined in my accusation by the whole of our people! I accuse these heinous criminals who deserve only one punishment – death by shooting!

The accused were scarcely more fortunate in their defence lawyer, Ilya Braude. His 'defence' included saying: 'First of all, Comrade Judges, the Counsel for Defence is a son of his country. He, too, is a citizen of the great Soviet Union, and the great indignation, anger and horror which is now felt by the population of our country, old and young, the feeling which the Prosecutor so strikingly expressed in his speech, cannot but be shared by Counsel.' He continued:

> All the facts have been proved, and in this sphere the Defence does not intend to enter into any controversy with the Procurator. Nor can there be any controversy with the Procurator concerning the appraisal of the political and moral aspects of the case. Here, too, the case is so clear, the political appraisal made by the Procurator is so clear, that the Defence cannot but wholly and entirely associate itself with that part of his speech.[5]

Unsurprisingly, after such a trial, all were found guilty. Most were sentenced to be shot and those given lighter sentences were later killed in custody. Even those at the top of the Party knew the kind of justice and punishment that could await them.

In 1938 came the most spectacular trial. Twenty-one people were accused of espionage, wrecking and conspiracy to destroy the Soviet Union. They included Bukharin, Rykov and Krestinsky, who had all been members of Lenin's Politburo, and Yagoda, the NKVD chief who had been behind the previous show trials. Vyshinsky was again prosecutor. Again, Ilya Braude appeared for the defence, representing an accused doctor. Preparing for the trial, Braude had to rehearse his own role with Vyshinsky. During interrogation before the trial the accused had 'confessed' their crimes. They had also been persuaded to implicate each other in their confessions.

There is a powerful eye-witness account of the trial by Fitzroy MacLean in his book *Eastern Approaches*. When proceedings opened, most of the accused stuck to the plan and pleaded guilty. But when it was Krestinsky's turn, he pleaded not guilty. The judge adjourned the court for twenty minutes. When the trial resumed Krestinsky stuck to his position. Vyshinsky asked him to account for the confessions he had made before the trial. He said, 'I was forced to make them. Besides, I knew that if I said then what I say now, my statement would never reach the heads of the Party and of the Government.'

Many years later, Krestinsky's claim about being forced to confess was supported by Anna Anatolevna Rozenblum, who at the time had been head of the medical unit in the Lefortovo prison. She said, 'From the interrogation Krestinsky was brought to us in the medical unit in an unconscious state. He had been severely beaten, his entire back was one large wound, all battered and bruised. He was in the medical unit, if I remember correctly, for about three days in a very serious condition.'[6]

After Krestinsky's continued defiance, there was a two-hour adjournment. This was not enough to make him change his mind. However, the overnight adjournment was successful. The next day Krestinsky appeared, and, as Fitzroy MacLean noted, 'at once the change was obvious'. Krestinsky confirmed everything in his confession, and had even learnt up an explanation for his claims of the previous day:

> Yesterday, influenced by a feeling of false shame, and by the atmosphere of the court, and by my state of health, I could not bring myself to tell the truth and admit my guilt before the world. Mechanically, I declared myself innocent. I now beg the court to take note of the statement which I now make to the effect that I admit my guilt, completely and unreservedly, under all the charges brought against me, and that I accept full responsibility for my criminal and treacherous behaviour.[7]

Yagoda pleaded guilty, but tried to deny some aspects of the charges. When he was asked about how he had come to confess things he now denied, he asked to be excused from answering that question. The implications of this were obvious. There was also the irony that Yagoda had arranged the confessions in previous trials. An adjournment was put to use and Yagoda returned a broken man, prepared to admit anything.

A central aim of the trial was to discredit Bukharin, who had been a colleague and friend of Lenin, and was a Marxist theorist. In earlier days he had been thought of as a more leading figure than Stalin. He was by far the most impressive of the accused, and behaved as such throughout the trial. He fully confessed to a plot against the Soviet government, but in a way that caused maximum discomfort to the prosecution case. He treated Vyshinsky as an equal or as an inferior, sometimes making fun of him. He cross-examined witnesses and dominated them.

Bukharin denied the detailed charges (such as being a foreign spy) and frustrated the prosecution's presentation of him as a self-interested criminal. Even the use that could be made of a day when the court was not in session was of no avail. Bukharin returned to the next session showing signs of strain, but unbowed and still capable of embarrassing references to Vyshinsky's Menshevik past.

He admitted the 'conspiracy' only in the most general way. He gave a political account of it, as being based on criticisms of Stalin's policies. The conspirators had been critical of the speed of industrialization, of the way the collectivization of agriculture had been carried out, and of the liquidation of the kulaks. They had wanted a system more like a liberal democracy, with different political parties. This account of a coherent political opposition to Stalin was not what had been planned.

In his final speech before verdict and sentence, Bukharin combined a destructive analysis of the details of the prosecution's case with a general admission of guilt and an acceptance that the death penalty would be justified. He said that their opposition to the regime led them into acts of banditry, but that they also had a commitment to the Soviet Union, which pulled the other way, leading them to confess. Not to confess would leave him dying for nothing, but his repentance and confession would contribute to another moral triumph of the Soviet Union. 'My own fate is of no importance. All that matters is the Soviet Union.'[8]

At the end of his own closing speech Vyshinsky surpassed himself:

> Our country only asks one thing: that these filthy dogs, these accursed reptiles, be wiped out. The weed and the thistle will grow on the graves of these execrable traitors. But, on us and our happy country, our Glorious Sun will continue to shed His serene light. Guided by our beloved Leader and Master, Great Stalin, we will go forward to Communism along a path that has been cleansed of the sordid remnants of the past.[9]

The accused were all found guilty. Three were sentenced to imprisonment. All the eighteen others, including Bukharin, Rykov, Krestinsky and Yagoda, were sentenced to death and shot the next day. Vyshinsky had served Stalin well. But even he was humiliated, perhaps as a reminder of his utter dependence on his leader. Stalin made him identify personally the corpses of those who had been shot.

Those running the show trials knew the precariousness of their own positions. This was the meaning of Yagoda's fate. Vyshinsky must have been frightened in case his performance as prosecutor did not give satisfaction. It was closely monitored. Fitzroy MacLean described a chilling moment during the trial: 'a clumsily directed arc-light dramatically revealed to attentive members of the audience the familiar features and heavy drooping moustache peering out from behind the black glass of a small window, high up under the ceiling of the court-room'.[10]

Cat and Mouse

Vyshinsky was not alone among Stalin's associates in being bullied and humiliated. Nikita Khrushchev remembered Stalin's amusement at humiliating people. In front of others, Khrushchev was made to dance the Gopek: 'I had to squat down on my haunches and kick out my heels, which frankly wasn't very easy for me. But I did it and I tried to keep a pleasant expression on my face. As I later told Anastas Ivanovich Mikoyan, "When Stalin says dance, a wise man dances." '[11]

Stalin enjoyed playing a cruel game of cat and mouse. He did this even with Marshal Voroshilov, who was enough of a friend to address him by the familiar form of 'you'. Of the five who had been Marshals in 1935, Voroshilov was one of the two not to have been shot. In a discussion of naval policy after the war, Voroshilov held a minority view. Stalin, who came in at the end of the discussion, said, 'I don't understand why Comrade Voroshilov wants to weaken the Soviet Navy.' The leaders then went to sit at little tables to watch a film. No one would sit with Voroshilov. When the lights went up after the film, Stalin put his hand round Voroshilov and said to the NKVD (later KGB) chief, Beria, 'Lavrenty, we really should take care of Voroshilov. It's not as though there are many old Bolsheviks like him around. We must look after him.'[12]

In cat and mouse, the mouse often did not survive. Stalin took those, like Yagoda, who had operated the system of the rigged trial followed by execution, and forced them into the trap they had set up. In this there was grim humour, as well as some covering of tracks. Yagoda's trial and execution were partly orchestrated by his successor, Yezhov. Later it was Yezhov's turn to be destroyed. The game of cat and mouse began.

The game was slow. A commission was set up to investigate the NKVD and its report was critical. Many of Yezhov's colleagues were accused of conspiring to kill Stalin and were shot. Yezhov was replaced by Beria as head of the NKVD, but was allowed to remain as Commissar of Water Transport. He was present at a meeting to decide on a new Central Committee.

Stalin did not chair the meeting, but sat in a corner at the back. When Yezhov's name was put forward, there was some support. Then Stalin walked to the front. He asked Yezhov questions about his links with colleagues who had been shot, and then asked, 'Did you want to kill Stalin? Top officials of the NKVD are plotting, but you, supposedly, are not involved. You think I don't see anything? Do you remember who you sent on a certain date for duty with Stalin? Who? With revolvers? Why revolvers near Stalin? Why? To kill Stalin? And if I hadn't noticed? What then?'

Stalin went on to accuse Yezhov of arresting innocent people and covering up for guilty ones. 'Well? Go on, get out of here! I don't know, comrades, is it possible to keep him as a member of the Central Committee? I doubt it. Of course, think about it . . . As you wish . . . But I doubt it!'[13] Yezhov was arrested a few days later. About a year afterwards he was shot.

'My Knees Began to Knock'

Some of Stalin's associates believed in the terror they were imposing, but what comes across mainly is their own terror, their sense of finding themselves in a nightmare. Hypnotized with fear, they sometimes seem to have been sleepwalking through the things they were ordered to do.

Some of these must have been repugnant even to the hardest of them. Lazar Kaganovich had made his reputation with Stalin by his ruthlessness in the collectivization. He was responsible for huge numbers of deaths both in the deportation of the kulaks and in the purges. He was in charge of the reconstruction of Moscow and of building the Moscow Metro. Despite being Jewish, he stayed in office through the whole Stalin period, but he had to implement policies based on Stalin's anti-Semitism, such as refusing Jews promotion in the Party. He had Trashunov, a Kiev newspaper editor, dismissed for being Jewish. When Kaganovich's wife, Maria, attacked him: 'Have you no sense, no compassion, no feelings for one of your own? He is your people, not Stalin,' he replied, 'I am doing what I have to do. My God is Stalin.'[14]

Soviet leaders were too terrified even to speak in defence of members of their families. Kaganovich would not defend his own brother Mikhail. Stalin told him on the telephone that Mikhail was accused of sabotage and of plotting with the Nazis and asked him if Mikhail should be arrested. Knowing his own fate was also at stake, he said, 'If it's necessary, arrest him.' Mikhail shot himself in a lavatory during his investigation. Lazar later claimed to have given him the gun and suggested suicide. Soon after the arrest, Mikhail's wife Anya had sent Lazar a note pleading for help: 'He is the son of Moisev, as you are.' Lazar's reply was a single sentence: 'I have only one brother – Joseph Stalin – and forget about the voice of blood.'[15]

The same paralysis hit Stalin's closest colleague, Vyacheslav Molotov, whose wife, Polina, was arrested. Polina had been close to Nadezhda, Stalin's second wife, who had killed herself after Stalin publicly insulted her at dinner. That night Polina had walked out of the dinner with her. Stalin waited sixteen years. In the late 1940s Polina was arrested, with other Jews with Zionist links, for 'treason against the motherland'. She was imprisoned for a year and then exiled until after Stalin's death.

Molotov was there when her arrest was proposed. Stalin read out the accusations. Years later, Molotov remembered his fear: 'At the session of the Politburo when he read out the material on Polina Semenovna supplied by the security people, my knees began to knock.'[16] All the others voted for Polina to be arrested. Molotov abstained, and did not speak. He had to break the news to his frantic and desperate wife.

Describing the episode in his old age, he seemed still to be hypnotized by Stalin and unable to say clearly and directly that Polina had done nothing wrong. And he seemed to think of the affair mainly as an episode in his relationship with Stalin:

> What did they accuse her of? Of connections with a Zionist organization and with Golda Meir, the Israeli ambassador. Security charged that they sought to make the Crimea a Jewish autonomous region . . . They had good relations with the great Jewish actor Mikhoels . . . Security found he was an alien element. Of course, she should have been more fastidious in choosing her acquaintances. She was removed from office but for some time was not arrested. Then she was taken into custody and summoned to the Central Committee. A black cat had, as they say, crossed our path. Relations between me and Stalin cooled.[17]

Several years after Polina's arrest, an Israeli Communist asked Molotov how he could have acquiesced in his wife's arrest. He replied, 'Because I am a member of the Politburo and I must obey Party discipline . . . I submitted to the Politburo, which had decided that my wife must be put away.'[18]

Stalin's Death

Stalin's death fits Aristotle's thought that 'a tyrant is of all persons the man who can place no confidence in friends, as every one has it in his desire and these chiefly in their power to destroy him'. Some of Stalin's colleagues certainly had reason to hope for his death. He was preparing another purge and had also indicated that he was thinking of removing Beria from his post as head of the secret police. The night before his stroke, he had kept his colleagues up until four in the morning. He had said that some of the leadership thought they could get by on their past merits. Some of them may have been chilled by his further remark that 'they are mistaken'.

All the next morning Stalin did not appear. His staff started to worry at midday, but they knew better than to enter his room unless they were sent for. They first went in at eleven o'clock that night and found Stalin on the floor, conscious but unable to speak. They called Malenkov and Beria, but Malenkov would not come without Beria. At three in the morning, Beria arrived and said Stalin was only sleeping. Under Beria's instructions, no doctors were called. Beria and other leaders came back at nine a.m. The doctors followed.

Beria had delayed medical help for perhaps a whole day after the stroke had occurred and it seemed clear that Stalin could not live. Khrushchev described Beria at the bedside: 'Beria started going around spewing hatred against him and mocking him. It was simply unbearable to listen to Beria.' But Stalin regained partial consciousness and pointed to something on the wall. Stalin's daughter noted how Beria changed: 'Beria stared fixedly at those clouded eyes, anxious even now to convince my father that he was the most loyal and devoted of them all, as he had always tried with every ounce of his strength to appear to be.'[19] Khrushchev says that Beria then 'threw himself on his knees, seized Stalin's hand, and started kissing it. When Stalin lost consciousness again and closed his eyes, Beria stood up and spat.'[20]

Stalin's Trap and Socrates

Stalin's Russia was a trap, in which even those running the system were caught. The leaders were trapped by fear of Stalin and even he was trapped by his fear of their desire to be rid of him. Everything he had to eat or drink had to be tasted by one of his colleagues first. Beria's behaviour at his death showed that his fear was only partly paranoia.

In view of the numbers of people whose lives Stalin turned into a nightmare, it is hard to have much sympathy for Stalin himself, but his life gives striking support to what Socrates said about the life of an immoral person not being enviable. His bitterness, paranoia and fear make it hard to imagine anyone else wanting to be Stalin. He was described as 'sickly suspicious' by Khrushchev, who wrote, 'He could look at a man and say, "Why are your eyes so shifty today?" or "Why are you turning so much today and avoiding looking me directly in the eyes?" . . . Everywhere and in everything he saw "enemies", "double-dealers" and "spies".'[21] Khrushchev noticed how terribly lonely he was, and how he needed people round him all the time: 'When he woke up in the morning, he would immediately summon us, either inviting us to the movies or starting some conversation which could have been finished in two minutes but was stretched out so that we could stay with him longer.'[22]

Milovan Djilas saw Stalin close up and saw he had trapped himself: 'He became himself the slave of the despotism, the bureaucracy, the narrowness, and the servility he imposed on his country. It is indeed true that no one can destroy another's freedom without losing his own.'[23]

In *The Republic*, Socrates talks about what makes a leader of a populist party become a dictator. He quotes a legend that anyone who tastes human flesh becomes a wolf:

Doesn't the same thing happen to a champion of the people? Suppose the masses are more or less totally under his thumb and he feels no compunction about shedding the blood of a fellow citizen; suppose he trumps up the usual charges against someone, takes him to court and murders him, thereby eliminating a human life; suppose on his tongue and in his unholy mouth is the taste of the blood of a kinsman, and he turns to demanding banishment and death . . . Isn't it unalterably inevitable that this man will next either be assassinated by his enemies or change into a wolf instead of a human being – that is, become a dictator? . . . His enemies might not be able to arouse enough hostility against him to have him exiled or executed, so they start to try to find a secret way to assassinate him . . .

And some – they'll have to be the bravest – of those who helped him on his way and who are in positions of power will speak their minds to him, as well as to one another, and will criticize what's going on . . . So a dictator has to eliminate the lot of them – or else relinquish power – until there's no one of any value left among either his friends or his enemies . . . He has to keep a sharp eye out, then, for anyone with courage, self-confidence, intelligence or wealth. He has no choice in the matter: he's bound to treat them as enemies and to intrigue against them, until he's purged the community of them. That's the nature of his happy state.

They never have any friends, then, throughout their lives: they can only be masters or slaves. Dictatorial people can never experience freedom and true friendship.[24]

CHAPTER 26

Belief: Ends and Means

Macbeth's self-justifications were feeble – and his conscience devoured him. Yes, even Iago was a little lamb too. The imagination and the spiritual strength of Shakespeare's evildoers stopped short at a dozen corpses. Because they had no *ideology*.

Alexander Solzhenitsyn, *The Gulag Archipelago*

Lady Astor, on a visit to Moscow in December 1931, had the rare honour of being received by the new Leader. During their conversation she asked a question no one else would have dared:

'How long will you keep killing people?'

Stalin's interpreter froze. But the Boss insisted on hearing the question and, without a pause, as though he had been expecting a question like that, replied to the naïve lady that 'the process would continue as long as was necessary' to establish communist society.

Anton Antonov-Ovseyenko, *The Time of Stalin: Portrait of a Tyranny*

Stalin's rule was the powerful modern version of the ancient practice of tyranny. The comments of Socrates and Aristotle need no adaptation when applied to the Soviet terror, but there is more to the Stalinist atrocities than terror. What distinguishes the Soviet terror from its predecessors is the role of an ideology, or system of beliefs. No doubt the beliefs were in part a mask for the interests of those in power, but it is a simplification to see Soviet Marxism in this Marxist way. As Solzhenitsyn said, it was ideology which suspended the moral restraints which held back even Macbeth and Iago.

Faith in Stalin

In the early Soviet period, the great cause was to build a socialist society in which people would no longer exploit each other and where everyone would flourish. This ideal must have seemed far distant, but there was faith that the Soviet Union, led by the Party, was journeying towards it. Throughout the Stalinist period, and beyond, there were still believers. Sometimes they denied the horrors. Sometimes they accepted them, either as regrettable blemishes or else as necessary for a greater good. According to their system of belief, the workers needed to be led by the Party. There was a Stalinist embellishment to this: the Party in turn needed to be led, and Stalin was wise enough to do this.

Many also accepted the religious cult of Stalin, expressed by a Lithuanian writer:

> I approached Stalin's portrait, took it off the wall, placed it on the table and, resting my head on my hands, I gazed and meditated. What should I do? The Leader's face, as always so serene, his eyes so clear-sighted, they penetrate into the distance. It seems that his penetrating look pierces my little room and goes out to embrace the entire globe . . . With my every fibre, every nerve, every drop of blood I feel that, at this moment, nothing exists in this entire world but this dear and beloved face.[1]

Milovan Djilas later remembered his own intellectual version of this:

> Among us Communists there were men with a developed aesthetic sense and a considerable acquaintance with literature and philosophy, and yet we waxed enthusiastic not only over Stalin's views but also over the 'perfection' of the way he formulated them. I myself referred many times in discussions to the crystal clarity of his style, the penetration of his logic, and the aptness of his commentaries, as though they were expressions of the most exalted wisdom.[2]

Some of the admiration for Stalin was based on his unpretentious personal style, which contrasted favourably with that of leaders such as Mussolini. In 1930 he looked over a story for publication in *Pravda* and wrote, 'I have deleted what it says about "Stalin" as the "vozhd of the Party", the "leader of the Party" and so on. I think such laudatory embellishments can only do harm.' As his seventieth birthday approached, he told Malenkov not to think of presenting him with a star, and on his birthday he expressed anger at finding he had been given the title of Generalissimo of the Soviet Union. People spoke of 'the exceptional modesty of Comrade Stalin' and of his being 'totally devoid of vanity'.[3]

However, Stalin's image of modesty seems to have been carefully cultivated. His letter about the story in *Pravda* was revealed to a meeting by his personal assistant Mekhlis. Stalin also revised his own *Short Biography* in some striking ways. Khrushchev reported that he changed the sentence 'Stalin is the Lenin of today'; his revised version read, 'Stalin is the worthy continuer of Lenin's work, or, as it is said in our Party, Stalin is the Lenin of today.' At another point he inserted the sentence: 'Although he performed his task as leader of the Party and the people with consummate skill and enjoyed the unreserved support of the entire Soviet people, Stalin never allowed his work to be marred by the slightest hint of vanity, conceit or self-adulation.'[4]

This careful self-presentation worked well and faith in Stalin, for many, lasted right up to the end of his life. Many people were in tears at the news of his death. Even victims of the system often retained their faith, assuming that Stalin himself could not possibly know about the terrible things done in his name. One imprisoned old Bolshevik kept her faith during her years in the camps. In 1961 she told the Party Congress, 'All the time I defended Stalin, whom the other prisoners and inmates and exiles cursed. I said to them, "No, it's not possible that Stalin would allow what is happening in the Party. It's not possible." '[5]

Ethics, Omelettes and Eggs

Marxism stresses that people can be deformed by an economic and social system. This is a problem for revolutionaries: those who make a better society will themselves bear the marks of the old system. One response is to try to reshape humanity. There was an influential image of society as a factory, in which people were to be remodelled. In his book *The Economics of the Transition Period*, Nikolai Bukharin used the phrase 'the manufacturing of Communist man out of the human material of the capitalist age'. In his copy, Lenin underlined this phrase, and wrote 'exactly!' in the margin.[6]

These views about means were inspired by the goal of a socialist society liberated from oppression and exploitation, but the system of beliefs included more than this. Underneath the political beliefs were philosophical ones. Any large human project on the scale of the Soviet one raises questions about ethics: about the limits of what may be done to individuals in pursuing the project. The ideology included scepticism about ethics itself.

Marx believed he had discovered scientific laws governing human society and thought that effective political action would be based on those laws, rather than on moral values. He believed that morality was a disguise for class interests and he showed a tough contempt for ethical ideas about equal rights and fair distribution. In the *Critique of the Gotha Programme* he wrote that he had aimed

> to show what a crime it is to attempt, on the one hand, to force on our Party again, as dogmas, ideas which in a certain period had some meaning but have now become obsolete verbal rubbish, while again perverting, on the other, the realistic outlook, which it cost so much effort to instil into the Party but which

has now taken root in it, by means of ideological nonsense about right and other trash so common among the democrats and among the French Socialists.[7]

('What a crime it is'? It was not a legal crime. Even in this over-confidently 'realistic' social-science outlook, ethical concepts have a habit of slipping in.)

The 'realistic outlook' towards 'nonsense about right and other trash' supported Soviet policies. Optimism about changing people led to a ruthless consequentialism which discouraged moral constraints. When the end is as large as changing human nature, all necessary means may seem acceptable. And the image of the factory makes sympathy for the 'human material' seem irrelevant.

In the years after the Revolution, publications like *Red Terror* carried discussions of whether torture was permissible from the Marxist standpoint. The answer seems to have been 'yes'. If torture is acceptable, it is hard to imagine what is not. The belief system included a commitment that the end was so good that absolutely nothing should be allowed to stand in the way of the most efficient means to reaching it.

There was indifference to the individual people who might be destroyed by the new policies. This view came from Lenin, who had written in 1908 that the Paris Commune had failed because of the 'excessive generosity' of the proletariat, who 'should have *exterminated its enemies*' instead of trying 'to exert moral influence on them'.[8] In 1917, when Lenin opposed the abolition of capital punishment for deserters at the front, Trotsky quoted him as saying, 'Nonsense, how can you make a revolution without executions? . . . It is a mistake, impermissible weakness, pacifist illusion, and so on.'[9]

One phrase caught the individual's unimportance relative to the great project and was spread around the world by an American journalist, Walter Duranty, an admirer of Stalin who reported for the *New York Times*. In 1932 he published in the paper a poem called 'Red Square', which included the lines:

> Russians may be hungry and short of clothes and comfort
> But you can't make an omelette without breaking eggs.

This first use of the phrase was used only to justify shortages. Duranty, later trying to discredit reports of mass starvation in the terror famine, wrote, 'to put it brutally – you can't make an omelette without breaking eggs'.[10] The phrase was to be used frequently by Stalin's supporters.

It is hard to be sure how far, and in how many people, these ruthless beliefs were genuinely accepted. Some will profess an official ideology because of the rewards of conformity or because of the penalties for dissidence. This must have been true of people at every level of the Soviet hierarchy.

It may seem that for the Soviet leaders, who knew most about the reality behind the stage-set, the ruthless consequentialism was a front for self-interest. But this could be combined with a genuine belief in the unimportance of the victims. Stalin himself believed that individual victims were unimportant: in the longer historical perspective they would be forgotten. Once, signing lists of people to be executed, he said to Molotov and Yezhov: 'Who's going to remember all this riff-raff in ten or twenty years' time? No one. Who remembers the names now of the boyars Ivan the Terrible got rid of? No one . . . The people had to know he was getting rid of all his enemies. In the end, they all got what they deserved.'[11]

Probably some of the other leaders were genuine believers. Years after Stalin was safely dead, Lazar Kaganovich still defended ruthless consequentialism to his American nephew:

> you must think of humanity as one great body, but one that requires constant surgery. Need I remind you that surgery cannot be performed without cutting membranes, without destroying tissues, without the spilling of blood? Thus, we must destroy whatever is superfluous. These are unpleasant acts, granted, but we do not find any of this immoral. You see, all acts that further history and socialism are moral acts.[12]

CHAPTER 27

Stalinism and the Moral Resources

What happened in Stalin's time to the moral resources? It was an inhospitable climate, both for human responses and for the sense of moral identity. The climate was partly one of fear, but it was also created by the belief system.

Much of the propaganda for the belief system was designed to undermine human responses towards the victims: to oppose respect or sympathy for those Stalin thought of as 'all this riff-raff'.

The Erosion of Respect

The victims were stripped of their protective dignity; as elsewhere, the cold joke flaunted the lack of respect. The cattle cars transporting prisoners to the camps were not labelled as prisoner transport, but had other words chalked on the side by the guards. One phrase had a grim humour: 'perishable goods'.

Stalin liked the cold joke. The main road round Vorkuta can be seen on the map to be exactly the shape of a skull. The chief architect of Vorkuta says this was no accident, but was Stalin's 'Satanic joke'.[1] Sometimes Stalin made a cold joke in his writing: 'It is now ridiculous and foolish to discourse at length on dekulakization. When the head is off, one does not mourn for the hair.'[2]

When he wanted to put pressure on those in charge of the interrogators at the time of the 'doctors' plot', Stalin said to Beria: 'Tell Ignatiev that if he doesn't get full confessions out of them, we'll reduce his height by a head.'[3] Some cold jokes have a history, usually of bloody times. In the French Revolution, Hébert defined the guillotine as something which shortens someone's height by a head. Queen Elizabeth I of England also used the phrase as a contemptuous threat.

The removal of protective dignity went beyond the cold joke. The victims were derided by comparisons with animals and other non-human forms of life. Vyshinsky's references in the show trials to 'filthy dogs' and 'reptiles' were part of a way of thinking which went back to Lenin. In *How to Organize Competition*, Lenin advocated on-the-spot executions of 'parasites'. This was justified by 'one general aim: the *cleansing* of the Russian land of any harmful insects, swindler-fleas, wealthy bugs and so on and so on'.[4]

Sympathy and the Mildest Form of Betrayal

Nadezhda Mandelstam noted that kindness needs to be cultivated, and that some times are unfriendly to this:

> For our generation, kindness was an old-fashioned, vanished quality, and its exponents were as extinct as the mammoth. Everything we have seen in our times – the dispossession of the kulaks, class warfare, the constant 'unmasking' of people, the search for an ulterior motive behind every action – all this has taught us to be anything you like except kind.

Many people did nothing positively cruel themselves, but fear made them look away and say nothing. Solzhenitsyn noticed how common this was:

> The mildest and at the same time the most widespread form of betrayal was not to do anything bad directly, but just not to notice the doomed person next to one, not to help him, to turn away one's face, to shrink back. They had arrested a neighbour, your comrade at work, or even your close friend. You kept silence. You acted as if you had not noticed.[5]

When the Mandelstams travelled escorted by three armed soldiers, people found it easier to look away. Osip Mandelstam whispered that 'with a crowd like this they could do anything to a prisoner – shoot him down, kill him, torture him – and nobody would interfere'. Throughout the journey, Nadezhda Mandelstam never succeeded in catching anyone's eye. Self-preservation often required this refusal of sympathy. Sometimes the climate seemed too harsh for kindness to survive. Solzhenitsyn asked, 'How could one possibly preserve one's kindness while pushing away the hands of those who were drowning? . . . And when you add that kindness was ridiculed, that pity was ridiculed, that mercy was ridiculed . . .'[6]

But in some people kindness persisted, and was shown even when it took courage to do so. Some sheltered fugitives and helped the families of prisoners. When the Mandelstams went into exile, there were women who broke the rules and raised money for them: 'In periods of violence and terror people retreat into themselves and hide their feelings, but their feelings are ineradicable and cannot be destroyed by any amount of indoctrination.' This was true of many people in Strunino. Prisoners passed through in nightly trainloads, sometimes throwing out notes. Anyone finding an addressed note would post it. It was forbidden to give the prisoners things, but when a train stopped everyone tried to throw in food or tobacco. Nadezhda Mandelstam's landlady managed to throw in a piece of chocolate. Such acts were a message to those inside, who were stripped of everything and anonymously transported to the horrors of the camps, that there were people outside who cared.[7]

Hardness

Sympathy was replaced by hardness in those who carried out the policies. During Stalin's terror famine, ruthless consequentialism was used to discredit sympathy for the victims, as one who took part testified:

> With the rest of my generation I firmly believed that the ends justified the means. Our great goal was the universal triumph of communism, and for the sake of that goal everything was permissible – to lie, to steal, to destroy hundreds of thousands and even millions of people, all those who were hindering our work or who could hinder it, everyone who stood in the way. And to hesitate or doubt about all this was to give in to 'intellectual squeamishness' and 'stupid liberalism', the attribute of people who 'could not see the forest for the trees' . . . With the others, I emptied out the old folks' storage chests, stopping my ears to the children's crying and the women's wails.[8]

The authorities deliberately encouraged this hardness. Party members were told to act

> without whimpering, without any rotten liberalism. Throw your bourgeois humanitarianism out of the window and act like Bolsheviks worthy of Comrade Stalin . . . *Don't be afraid of taking extreme measures*. The Party stands four-square behind you. Comrade Stalin expects it of you. It's a life and death struggle; better to do too much than not enough.[9]

Hardness was sometimes expressed in choice of language. In those times there was much news which, if it had to come at all, called for gentleness and the human voice, but it was often broken with bureaucratic coldness. Andrei Sakharov's Uncle Ivan died from malnutrition in a prison hospital. Sakharov's Aunt Zhenya did come to hear of this: one of her letters to her husband was returned, marked 'Addressee relocated to the cemetery'.[10] The same bureaucratic language was used to break the news of Osip

Mandelstam's death to Nadezhda: 'I took a few books from our bookcase, sold them in a second-hand bookstore and spent the proceeds on the first and only food package I was able to buy for him. It was returned "because of the death of the addressee".'[11]

Belief in hardness went all the way up and the names assumed by many of the Bolshevik leaders suggest that it was part of their self-image. Dzhugashvili became Stalin: man of steel. Rozenfeld became Kamenev: man of stone. Skyrabin became Molotov: the hammer. These assumed names now seem ludicrous. A democratic politician who changed his name to 'Man of Steel' would, one hopes, have his political career finished by the laughter. But the hardness of these leaders was no joke.

Stalin seems to have seen himself as hard by nature. After the death in 1908 or 1909 of his first wife, Yekaterina, he said, 'This creature softened my heart of stone. She died and with her died my last warm feelings for people.'[12] This hardness made it possible for Stalin to introduce the death penalty for children as young as twelve. It enabled him to initial long lists of death sentences, including the names of people he knew. On lists of people about to be tried, he could write 'shoot all 138 of them'. On one day in December 1938 Stalin and Molotov signed for the shooting of 3,167 people. After such days, the two of them sometimes went to a film together.[13]

Moral Identity: Turning into Wood

Sometimes an intuitive resistance held people back from participation in the Stalinist atrocities. Self-interest might support joining in, but revulsion worked against it. Solzhenitsyn described this:

> It would be hard to identify the exact source of that inner intuition, not founded on rational argument, which prompted our refusal to enter the NKVD schools . . . People can shout at you from all sides: 'You must!' And your own head can be saying also: 'You must!' But inside your breast there is a sense of revulsion, repudiation. I don't want to. *It makes me feel sick.* Do what you want without me; I want no part of it.'[14]

Those who did participate had to overcome this revulsion as well as their sense of moral identity. The system of beliefs had its own resources to discredit the values once central to people's moral identity. Nadezhda Mandelstam described how 'Thou shalt not kill' was identified with 'bourgeois' morality: 'A number of terms such as "honour" and "conscience" went out of use at this time – concepts like these were easily discredited, now the right formula had been found.' She noticed that people were going through a metamorphosis: 'a process of turning into wood – that comes over those who lose their sense of values'.[15]

The Case of Bukharin

Nikolai Bukharin was torn between beliefs which called for hardness and his own, very different, emotional nature. In theory he accepted a ruthless consequentialism. But to be hard and to look through individual people were alien to his feelings and to his natural personal style. He had a sense of humour not based on the cold joke. He read poetry. He admired Mandelstam's poems and helped to have them published. He was also a good friend. When Mandelstam was hungry becuse the authorities deprived him of work, Bukharin helped to arrange a flat, ration cards and money for him. Nadezhda Mandelstam wrote that Osip Mandelstam was indebted to Bukharin for all the bright spells in his life.

Bukharin's theoretical commitment to a hard version of consequential-ism was linked to the idea of society as a factory for re-shaping humanity.[16] In theory he was against moral restraints. In 1914 he wrote, 'there is nothing more ridiculous . . . than the attempt to make Marx's theory an "ethical" theory. Marx's theory knows no other natural law than of cause and effect, and can admit no other such law.' He said that 'ethical rhetoric' was 'something which we need not take seriously'. In 1924 he said that what he believed in was 'not the categorical imperative of Kant and not a Christian moral commandment, but revolutionary expediency'. In 1925 he criticized people who 'very often replace sober reasonings with moral ones, which have nothing to do with politics'.[17]

Despite his advocacy of tough amoralism, Bukharin's opposition to the brutal treatment of the peasants gives a glimpse of different, almost Tolstoyan, values. He urged that backwardness 'is not the peasant's "guilt", but his misfortune'. The Bolsheviks were competing 'for the soul of the peasant', who should not be approached with 'disgust and contempt', but 'seriously with love'. And he opposed coercing the peasant into Communism with 'an iron broom, pushing him with the kicks of war communism', saying 'we do not carry out experiments, we are not vivisectionists, who . . . operate on a living organism with a knife'.[18]

Hardness did not come easily to Bukharin. He found it natural to speak to opponents in a personal tone and was disappointed when they did not reciprocate. In April 1929 Stalin secured the Party's condemnation of Bukharin's 'Rightist Deviation', and used savage language against Bukharin in doing so. Bukharin protested against the tone, reminding Stalin of their friendship. But Stalin did not respond warmly: 'Bukharin has mentioned personal correspondence with me. He has read out a few letters that show that although we were personal friends yesterday we now differ from each other in our policies . . . I think all this wailing and moaning isn't worth a brass farthing.'[19]

Bukharin hoped that friendship would continue even after such rebuffs and despite deep political disagreements. During New Year's Eve, 1930, Bukharin, Rykov and Tomsky went uninvited to Stalin's flat in the Kremlin, taking bottles of wine and hoping to renew their friendship. Stalin invited them in, but their hopes for the friendship proved optimistic. (Though in one direction the friendship could still be drawn on. In 1932, after Stalin's wife killed herself, memories made their old flat too painful for him and it was Bukharin who changed flats with Stalin.)

Even when campaigned against as a traitor, Bukharin still expected ordinary human responses from those who knew him. He thought that they must know the kind of person he was and see through the charges. He telephoned Stalin about the absurdity of the accusations. Stalin said, 'Nikolai, don't panic. We'll sort things out . . . We don't believe you're an enemy. But as you've been implicated by Sokolnikov, Astrov, Kulikov and other double-dealers, who have admitted to being wreckers, we have to look into it calmly. Don't worry!' Bukharin replied, 'How can it even be thought that I am an accomplice of terrorist groups?' Stalin said, 'Take it easy, Nikolai, take it easy. We'll sort it out.'[20]

Bukharin's trust in the human response to a personal appeal was again shown in a letter which he sent to Voroshilov. In this long letter to 'Dear Kliment Yefremovich', he strongly denied the charges against him, and ended: 'Forgive this confused letter: a thousand thoughts are rushing around inside my head like wild horses and I have no strong reins. I embrace you because I am clean.'

But Voroshilov knew the way things were going. Sending a copy of his reply to Stalin, he wrote:

> To Comrade Bukharin. I return your letter in which you permit yourself to make vile attacks on the party leadership. If you were hoping by your letter to convince me of your complete innocence, all you have convinced me of is that henceforth I should distance myself from you as far as possible, regardless of the outcome of your case. And if you do not repudiate in writing your foul epithets against the party leadership, I shall even regard you as a scoundrel. K. Voroshilov.

Yet again Bukharin was surprised and disappointed that the human appeal met with the hard response: 'Comrade Voroshilov. I have received your *appalling* letter. My letter ended with "I embrace you". Your letter ends with "scoundrel". What is there to write after that?'[21]

Despite his dislike of ruthlessness towards the peasants, and his preference for the human response and personal tone of voice, Bukharin never quite rid himself of the earlier, tough version of consequentialism.

The letter to Voroshilov included a chilling remark about the execution of Zinoviev and Kamenev: 'I'm terribly glad the dogs were shot.' This residue of ruthless consequentialism may explain in part his willingness to 'confess' in court. Fitzroy MacLean and other Western observers had puzzled discussions about the confessions. The defendants were clearly in full possession of their faculties: their statements were not learnt by heart; they were closely reasoned and apparently spontaneous; yet their content was unbelievable.

Bukharin was later said not to have been tortured. His confession can be explained partly by threats against his wife and baby son, but this may not be the whole story.

There is the view, suggested by Arthur Koestler in *Darkness at Noon*, that Bukharin was persuaded to confess as a last service to the Party. Roy Medvedev contests this, making the point that threats against his family are sufficient explanation, and citing Bukharin's earlier statement that he would never slander himself, as Zinoviev and Kamenev had done.[22]

But this statement does not fit with Bukharin's own past. He had previously been willing to slander himself on what seem to have been consequentialist grounds. He had admitted 'errors' at the Party Congress in 1934. He had been quick to see the Nazi danger. In a 1934 speech, he had quoted *Mein Kampf* on Hitler's intention to take land from Russia, as well as Japanese generals on their designs on Siberia. Apparently because of the need for unity against these threats, he had been willing to abase himself at the Congress.

In that 1934 speech he (rightly) admitted having opposed the liquidation of the kulaks as a class, but he described this as 'opposing every new stage of the broad socialist offensive, failing to comprehend its historical inevitability and drawing conclusions which could only be construed as anti-Leninist'. He said that his policy would have led to counter-revolution and the restoration of capitalism. 'Comrade Stalin was entirely correct in speaking out so eloquently, making brilliant use of Marxist-Leninist dialectics, against many of the theoretical premises of rightist deviation which I myself had previously formulated.'[23] It is unlikely that Bukharin can have believed much of this. Unless he was already in terror of Stalin, the likely explanation is that he accepted this loss of face for the sake of Party unity against the Nazi threat.

His sacrifice in 1934 lends some support to Koestler's conjecture that Bukharin was following the same course at his trial. Although he pleaded guilty, his refusal to admit any of the details of Vyshinsky's case against him, and his display of intellectual superiority, contrasting with the leaden performance of the prosecutor, shows that threats had not turned him into a mere puppet. Even his guilty plea was something of a formality. He pleaded guilty to 'the sum total of crimes committed by this counter-revolutionary organization, irrespective of whether or not I knew of, whether or not I took a direct part in, any particular act'. He may have thought that this formal plea of guilty would be enough to save the lives of his wife and child. Having seen that Stalin would have him dead anyway, he had to decide whether to co-operate further.

Bukharin's sense of his own moral identity was bound up with an idea of individual sacrifice to the cause of the kind he had shown in 1934. Since he was not prepared to say just anything the prosecution wanted, there is reason to take seriously his own account of why he confessed. In his final statement at the trial, he said:

> For three months I refused to say anything. Then I began to testify. Why? Because while in prison I made a revaluation of my entire past. For when you asked yourself: 'If you must die, what are you dying for?' – an absolute black vacuity suddenly rises before you with startling vividness . . . And, on the contrary, everything positive that glistens in the Soviet Union acquires new dimensions in a man's mind. This in the end disarmed me completely and led me to bend my knees before the Party and the country.[24]

This account omits the threats against his family. And Bukharin was certainly aware of the parts of Stalin's regime which were not positive and glistening. But the reference to the need for something to die for does not sound like something he had been told to say. Vyshinsky and the interrogators were not known for their interest in thoughts about moral identity.

Bukharin clearly cared about his posthumous reputation. Just before his arrest he wrote a letter to a future generation of Party leaders. His wife Anna learnt it by heart and years later passed it on to the intended recipients. In it he said that he was never a traitor and had never wanted to restore capitalism. He was a victim of the NKVD, which was 'seeking to satisfy the pathological suspiciousness of Stalin'. He was certain that 'the filter of history will inevitably wash the filth from my head'. But in the letter he also reiterated his commitment to consequentialist cruelty: 'I bow my head, but not before the proletarian scythe, which is properly merciless but also chaste . . . the wonderful traditions of the Cheka have gradually receded into the past, those traditions by which the revolutionary idea governed all its actions, justified cruelty towards enemies.'[25]

Bukharin cared about the survival of the Soviet Union against the Nazi threat. He also had a strong sense of his own moral identity, which he both displayed and defended in his destruction of Vyshinsky's (and so Stalin's) case, but his moral identity was bound up with the view that the individual should be sacrificed for the good of the Party and the state. He turned his inevitable death into an example of that sacrifice.

CHAPTER 28

The Working of the Belief System

> But above all else we must impress on our memory the overriding rule that whatever God has revealed to us must be accepted as more certain than anything else. And although the light of reason may, with the utmost clarity and evidence, appear to suggest something different, we must still put our entire faith in divine authority rather than in our own judgement.
>
> René Descartes, *Principles of Philosophy*

Beliefs were central to what happened under Stalin. Beliefs were invoked to deaden human responses. Beliefs about morality being bourgeois eroded the sense of moral identity, easing the process of 'turning into wood'. To understand Stalinism it is necessary to look more closely at the workings of its system of beliefs.

How Beliefs Form Systems

A belief is not held in isolation, but is part of a system. Frank Ramsey said that a belief is 'a map of neighbouring space by which we steer'.[1] Our beliefs about the world hang together, like a mental map of a city too large to be fully known. Some parts of the mental map are sharp and detailed, others are hazy. There may be vagueness or mistakes about how some regions join up, and some parts of the map may be inconsistent with others; but, despite these defects, the map does not show a series of isolated streets, but a system of streets.

All our beliefs have links to neighbouring ones. I believe the pills the doctor prescribes will cure my illness. This is bound up with my beliefs that the doctor is competent and knows the current evidence. My expectations of the medicine are vulnerable to changes in these other beliefs. More generally, if I abandon my present belief in scientific medicine, or my expectation that evidence from the past is a fairly reliable guide to the future, my confidence in the pills will also be undermined.

This confidence rests on beliefs bound up with other parts of my whole system.

It is too simple to think we can decide whether a belief is true or false just by comparing it with the bit of the world to which it corresponds. If the pills do not work, my beliefs will obviously need revising. But there are alternative revisions. I can decide that the doctor is less good than I thought. Or maybe some chemical peculiarity of mine interfered with the treatment. Or the pills may not have been prepared properly. At the other extreme, I can give up my good opinion of modern medicine, or even of the scientific methods on which it is based. In the middle range of responses, I can decide that this drug or this illness is less well understood than I had thought.

This element of free play in interpreting evidence can be exploited by someone determined to cling to a belief. No matter how absurd, any belief *can* be preserved if you are prepared to make sufficient adjustments to the rest of the system. The flat earth can be preserved if you are prepared to postulate a radically different physics, and to explain away satellite pictures as a conspiracy or as the result of distortions of light in space. Someone may have a belief, say in Creationism, which conflicts with the evidence. If this belief is a rigid part of their system, everything else can be skewed to fit. Philip Gosse argued against the fossil evidence for evolution that perhaps God had arranged fossils to look as if evolution had happened.

One model of a system of beliefs is a kind of wire frame sometimes used as a children's toy. The frame is made of many bits of rigid wire. The joints where the bits of wire meet can be adjusted to different angles. You can choose the shape of any bit of the frame, provided you allow the rest of the frame to bend and twist to accommodate it. The belief you want to preserve at all costs is the bit you hold rigid, letting this determine the shape of the rest of the frame.

Systems do not only contain beliefs about what the world is like and about what is desirable. Some beliefs are about the acceptability of other ones, and are used to adjudicate between them. They could be called structural beliefs. They are like the load–bearing walls of a house. When a structural belief is given up, there are likely to be changes throughout the system. Some structural beliefs are about plausibility. For instance, it is sometimes held that, where two beliefs are both compatible with the evidence, the simpler explanation should be treated as more plausible.

Appeals to authority are a different kind of structural belief. Descartes's claim that divine authority is always a better guide to truth than human reason is one instance, but it has secular equivalents. Some people treat their opinions on science or economics as a religion. They have Beliefs rather than beliefs. Their systems characteristically contain Beliefs which are treated as extremely rigid. And such Beliefs are often based on appeals to authority. In an actual religion the authority may be the Pope, the Church or the Bible, but there are also political religions.

The British Communist Debate on the Second World War

The Stalinist belief system had its own fixed points and holding them rigid caused large deformations in the rest of the system. For some believers this had a heavy cost in moral identity. They might have to sacrifice even core beliefs which had made them Communists.

The working of the Stalinist belief system can be seen in the debate over the Second World War which took place in the Communist Party of Great Britain in 1939. The verbatim record of this debate, kept for many years in Moscow, was published in Britain in 1990.[2] Although the belief system may not have operated in exactly the same way in its British and its Soviet adherents, a high degree of similarity seems likely. And, since the most the participants had to fear was the loss of their Party positions or membership, the British debate gives a glimpse of the belief system working independently of Stalinist terror.

Most members of a Communist Party like the British one had joined for altruistic reasons. The pressures on them, though far less strong, worked in opposite ways from those in the Soviet Union. Membership demanded time and hard work and also carried a social stigma. It could lead to the loss of a job and to blacklisting by the security services. In a comparison unwelcome to both groups, some British Communists were stubborn, non-conforming idealists who in the Soviet Union would have been dissidents.

In the 1930s anti-fascism was one of the strongest motives for joining the Communist Party. As the Nazi threat grew, the response of most democratic politicians was unimpressive. In Britain and France some of those on the right seemed to think accepting Hitler was a price worth paying to avoid Communism. British and French neutrality allowed Franco, backed by Hitler and Mussolini, to win the Spanish Civil War. Hitler was allowed to occupy the Rhineland and to annex Austria. The Munich Agreement was signed. Appeasement made it understandable that people doubted the will and ability of liberal democracy to stop Hitler. To many, Stalin was the best anti-Nazi hope.

Those who joined the Communist Party because they were against Nazism were presented with a problem by the Nazi-Soviet Pact of 1939. Stalin's approach to Britain and France for a military alliance had been rebuffed. In these circumstances, the non-aggression pact with Hitler in August could perhaps be defended as an attempt to ward off the Nazi threat, or at least to buy time. But this line of argument is no defence of the rest of what Stalin did: the secret agreement to divide up Poland, the German-Soviet Friendship and Border Treaty agreed in September,

Stalin's later attacks on Britain and France for starting the war, and his loyal support of Hitler against Britain and France right up until Hitler's attack on the Soviet Union.

True to its anti-Nazi beliefs, the British Communist Party blamed Hitler for the outbreak of the war. It published a statement, drawn up by the General Secretary, Harry Pollitt, supporting 'all necessary measures to secure the victory of democracy over fascism'.

Stalin, not wanting the world Communist Parties to upset his alliance with Hitler, took a different view. In a conversation on 7 September with the Comintern leader Georgi Dimitrov, Stalin said that it would not be bad if Poland ceased to exist. He said the war was imperialist on both sides. 'We would like them to have a really bad fight and weaken each other.' He rejected the contrast between fascist and democratic states and said that it would not be bad if Britain was undermined by Germany.[3] In the light of Stalin's views, the Comintern also decided that the war should be opposed as an imperialist one on both sides. Dave Springhall, of the Central Committee of the British Party, was in Moscow, but was excluded from the meeting which took the decision. He was given the message to convey to London.

In London the Central Committee debated how to respond. To many members, the Comintern decision was shattering. It demanded that they should back away from their deep commitment to oppose Nazism. It required them to treat Nazi Germany and those it attacked as morally equivalent. Worse still, it required them to work for Britain's military defeat by Nazi Germany. Springhall was asked to clarify the proposed new Party line. The questioner asked whether they should 'work not only against our own bourgeoisie but for their military defeat'. Springhall replied, 'Yes, that is correct.'[4]

The responses to these demands are a case study in how a belief system can be skewed. They are also a case study of Stalinism and moral identity. People varied. Some, at least for a time, stood up for their anti-Nazi beliefs, including Harry Pollitt, William Gallacher and J.R. Campbell. Others in the debate, especially Rajani Palme Dutt, William Rust and Dave Springhall, obediently fell into line. Palme Dutt's contributions bring into sharp focus the process of 'turning into wood'.

The Fixed Point: Faith in the Soviet Union

Most of those on the Central Committee had a firm belief in the reliability and good judgement of Moscow. During the debate, John Gollan mentioned the claim in *Pravda* that Poland had tried to embroil the Soviet Union and Germany in a war against each other. He said, 'I think the statements are correct else they would not be in *Pravda*.'[5] This kind of faith exerted a strong pull in the direction of Soviet policies.

Where there were reasons for doubting Soviet policies, something had to give. For most people, even the doubters, belief in the Soviet Union was the fixed point in their system. It was the doubts which gave. Forty years after the debate one of the participants, Ted Bramley, said that he had 'suppressed doubts and voted for the change', citing the fact that his 'respect for the International, led by Dimitrov, was enormous'.[6]

Other doubters reacted similarly. Peter Kerrigan supported the change of policy, despite being 'flabbergasted, quite frankly, when the Soviet Union marched into Poland'. He said, 'what has been one of the main things which has helped me to change my basic line on this question? It is the fact that I have always justified the Soviet Union in every action that the Soviet Union has taken.' He thought that 'anything the Soviet Union is involved in means that we must give support', and said, 'I believe basically I must accept the thesis because I am convinced that the Soviet Union under no circumstances will ever do anything that is against the interests not only of the Soviet people but of the people of the whole world.'[7]

Others favoured giving immediate support without requiring reasons. James Shields said of Soviet actions that 'in every action they take which we uphold and which we should uphold, it is far better for us, whether or not we understand the reasons or the implications in every move, to immediately come out and support that move without first of all weighing up the pros and cons'.[8]

The Party's philosopher, Maurice Cornforth, gave the most striking expression of the view that the rest of the system should be adjusted to preserve the fixed belief in Soviet policies. He accepted that 'a line so contradictory to what we had been saying inevitably shakes one up' and that it had been 'something of a surprise and something of a shock'. He admitted that 'perhaps it sounds rather silly in some ways' to support the Soviet Union while still thinking over the issue. His response was, 'I personally have got that sort of faith in the Soviet Union, to be willing to do that, because I believe that if one loses anything of that faith in the Soviet Union one is done for as a Communist and Socialist.' He went on to say that 'a socialist state, I believe, in that position can do no wrong, and is doing no wrong, and this is what we have to stick to, so these are the reasons why personally I commenced to turn political somersaults, because that is what it means'.[9]

Rabbits in Front of a Snake: the Appeal to Authority

The belief system was partly based on authority. William Cowe said the International was 'an unrivalled political authority and guide', which he had often 'blindly followed'.[10] While the Central Committee waited for

Springhall to return with instructions from Moscow, Pollitt described them as 'like a lot of rabbits in front of a snake, wondering whether we are on the right or wrong line'.[11] Ted Bramley remembered how the Party had changed its position on conscription, 'where all comrades were for the line until we were told it was wrong', and how 'Comrade Dutt was the one who changed very quickly after hearing the proposed changes.'[12]

When Pollitt had written the Party statement in support of the war, Dutt had complimented him on it as one of the best things he had written. After the message from Moscow, Dutt saw things quite differently:

> The American Party and its leadership has adjusted itself. The Belgian Party adjusted itself. We have to go through the same thing here, and the difficulty that we have come up against here is that a group of important leading comrades have taken a position of full opposition to the line decided by the International. And when that happens it is necessary to fight and to make no apologies for it . . . We want unity but we want that on the basis of the line.

In a system even partly based on authority, reasons have a diminished role in determining beliefs. Dutt was against the British Party doing any independent thinking about the line: 'Don't imagine that we are taking any decision that we are going to improve on by putting our own ideas in.' He held up for admiration leaders of other Communist Parties who had instantly obeyed the order to reverse their position: 'Take the position of Comrade Browder, leading a Party of 100,000 who took a direct position corresponding to ours on 3 September in a full statement from the Central Committee of the Party. When it was clear that a different character of the line would be needed, he gives it and leads the opposite line.'

It was Dutt again who gave the most explicit expression of the extent to which the belief system was under the sway of external authority. Criticizing Pollitt and others for standing by their own opinions, he said, 'Comrades, a Communist has no private opinions. That is, he has no sanctum of private opinions that he is going to hold apart from the collective thinking and the collective decisions of our movement.'[13]

Skewing Other Beliefs to Maintain the System

Most of the Central Committee felt the need to continue believing in the rightness of Soviet policy and to accept the views required to obey the authority of the Communist International. It was necessary to skew other beliefs in the system to fit these fixed points: four things would help this project. If democracy and fascism were not importantly different, this would make the fight against Hitler a less worthwhile cause. If the British Empire was as bad as Nazi Germany, this would have the same result. If

Germany was very weak, this would make a Nazi victory unlikely and so less worth worrying about. And if Britain and France were the most dangerous aggressors, this would make it more important to oppose them than to oppose Nazi Germany. Each of these beliefs ran counter to the evidence, but the debate shows members of the Central Committee straining to persuade themselves and each other that all four were true.

The relative unimportance of the difference between fascism and democracy was asserted by Dutt, who claimed that the basic antagonism in the world was between imperialism and the Soviet Union: 'That basic antagonism covers every other. All the particular phases of imperialist conflict, fascism and democracy and the rest of it, are phases in relation to that basic antagonism.'[14] Springhall used Chamberlain's refusal of a military pact with the Soviet Union to support Soviet belittling of the difference between 'so-called democratic countries' and fascist ones, agreeing that 'there was little to choose between Hitler and Chamberlain'.[15]

The moral equivalence of British colonialism and Nazi Germany was also supported. Idris Cox said, 'It is not a question of how many have been put into concentration camps in Nazi Germany, but there are even worse cases of oppression and ill-treatment in our own colonies under British imperialism.'[16] The same thought about British oppression of colonial people led Hymie Lee to say it would be 'a tremendous advantage to them and to us too if this imperialism was defeated'.[17]

In 1939 it was difficult to argue that Nazi Germany was weak. In the previous three years Hitler had occupied the Rhineland, taken over Austria, faced down Britain and France to take part of Czechoslovakia and successfully invaded Poland. Despite all this, Dutt said, 'German fascism had been compelled to amend itself in such a way that it abandoned its offensive leadership against the Soviet Union'.[18] Some members of the Central Committee, including J.R. Campbell, warned that this was a mistake, but William Rust dismissed Campbell's worries, saying, 'in his anxiety to make our flesh creep at the dread prospect of letting in Hitler's fascism, we get a duly distorted picture of the actual situation, because the plain fact is not the power of Germany but the weakness of Germany'.[19]

It was equally difficult to support the view that, in October 1939, Britain and France were more of a threat than Nazi Germany, but efforts were made. William Rust played down the seriousness of the Nazi threat and of the British and French response to it: 'both sides have no particular desire to get at one another because their chief desire is to get at the Soviet Union'.[20] Idris Cox said, 'The danger to the Soviet Union arises now from a military strengthening of British Imperialism. Therefore British Imperialism and not Nazi Germany in this new situation is the chief menace to the Soviet Union.'[21] Dutt thought that Germany was so weak that it was 'desperately searching' for peace, and that now Britain and France were 'the leaders of world reaction', whose 'real fear is how not to defeat

Germany too severely, in such a way as to let loose the real people's revolution or socialist revolution in Germany'.[22] When the preservation of other beliefs drives someone to ascribe *this* fear to Britain and France in 1939, something has gone badly wrong.

Self-Deception, Awareness and Denial

Dutt wanted the members to vote for the new line, but was critical of those who would do so just out of obedience. He did not want the independent thought which might reject the line, but he did want them to think about it in order to convince themselves: 'Communist discipline is not a mechanical robot discipline. The duty of a Communist is not to disagree but to accept ... The votes we want you to cast, we want you to cast on the basis of conviction, clearly, definitely, on the basis of conviction.'[23]

The degree of self-deception needed for all this was evident to those who opposed the new policy. Harry Pollitt commented on the changed view of Nazi Germany: 'I don't envy the comrades who can so lightly in the space of a week, and sometimes in the space of a day, go from one political conviction to another.' His own sense of moral identity was acute. He described his defence of the new policy to miners in the Forest of Dean: 'I spoke better than I have ever spoken in my life and I despised myself.' He knew he could keep the Party leadership by going with the tide: 'It would be very easy for me to say I accept and let us kiss and be friends and everything in the garden would be lovely. But I would be dishonest to my convictions. I would be dishonest to what I want to do. Smash the fascist bastards once and for all.'[24]

Years later, another opponent of the change, J.R. Campbell, looked back on the great pressures towards self-deception: 'If you didn't live through that time you can't understand what the pressures were to convince ourselves that the line of the International and Soviet Union was right, as we had done previously over the Moscow trials.'[25]

The speeches by Pollitt, Campbell and Gallacher showed they were not self-deceived about the change of policy, but even they had limited resistance to the pressures. Gallacher said that he was 'seething through and through with disgust', but that, 'If I have to speak in the House of Commons, you can rely upon it that whatever I say will be on the line of the Party.' At the next meeting a few weeks later Pollitt and Campbell made statements repudiating their previous views and unreservedly accepting the new line.[26]

Even those who originally voted for the new policy understood in some degree the self-deception required. Dave Springhall made a plea for understanding for the Nazi-Soviet pact in terms which showed awareness that something needed explaining:

They should understand that the Communist Party in the Soviet Union has to carry out complicated manoeuvres. In this respect Dimitrov spoke about the photos of Stalin and Ribbentrop shaking hands and went on to emphasise that the Soviet Union at all times in its policy was 'serving the interests of both the Soviet people and those of the international working class, which of course had basically the same interests'.[27]

There was a mixture of denial and awareness. Perhaps Dutt's vehemence betrayed a sensitive spot when he described the view that 'because the Soviet Union has turned its policy . . . everyone has got to turn' as an 'absolute foul slander'. There was also some awareness of deviousness in his references to 'a problem of a transition, a problem of the past statements and condemnation of the Party', and to the need to guard against 'the sudden volte-face'.[28]

Some of those who followed Dutt were more innocent. They presumed the new Party line must be right, but struggled with the difficulty of grasping the reasons behind it. William Cowe said, 'I don't think there is a member of the Central Committee, from Comrade Dutt, who opened the discussion, to the most unenlightened member, who can now come forward and say that he can state a 100 per cent case for this thesis in the sense of developing all the arguments, being able to produce all the solutions to the problems that naturally do arise.'[29] Ted Bramley worried about the new Soviet view that the distinction between fascism and democracy was unimportant. He concluded that the Soviet Union must have thought that Britain, France and Poland wanted war: 'In trying to find the explanation, this is the only place where I can find it comes.'[30]

The British Communist debate shows how, even without fear, the rigidities of Belief can bring about self-deception and skew interpretations of reality. It is a glimpse of Stalinism without terror. But even in the Soviet version, terror was not the whole story. There, too, pressure was put on truth by Belief.

CHAPTER 29

Stalinism, Truth and Moral Identity

For the sake of what idea was it necessary to send those countless trainloads of prisoners, including the man who was so dear to me, to forced labour in eastern Siberia? M. always said that they always knew what they were doing: the aim was to destroy not only people, but the intellect itself.

Nadezhda Mandelstam, *Hope Against Hope*

Under Stalin, the pressure on people to betray their values was enormous. As well as the fear of being denounced by others, there was the pressure to inform. Not to denounce someone's transgression was to put oneself at risk. There was the pressure to participate in the applause for the official version of events. As Solzhenitsyn put it, 'Every wag of the tongue can be overheard by someone, every facial expression observed by someone. Therefore every word, if it does not have to be a direct lie, is nonetheless obliged not to contradict the general, common lie.'

For those with children, this was a special problem. There were two responses, both corrosive of the sense of moral identity. Some chose to make it easier for their children by keeping up the lie in front of them all the time. The alternative was to tell them the truth, which was dangerous: 'you had to instill into them from the start that the truth was murderous, that beyond the threshold of the house you had to lie, only lie, just like papa and mama'.[1] Those of us who have not lived under such pressures should not be too quick to condemn those who compromised to survive.

Some people resisted. And some did not.

Praise from Maxim Gorky

Self-deception sometimes made it easier to yield and betray. One of the saddest cases was the later career of Maxim Gorky. In 1934, with other authors he had a book published on *The White Sea–Baltic Stalin Canal*. The writers had been taken on a boat trip on this canal, built by slave labour and costing a quarter of a million lives. Under the eyes of the project's leaders, prisoners gave the required answers to the writers' questions about the reforming effects of their work and the concern with which they were treated. The book praised the project: 'Criminals are the result of the repulsive conditions of former times, and our country is beautiful, powerful and generous, and it needs to be beautified.' Gorky himself applauded the success of the difficult task of re-education: 'Human raw material is immeasurably more difficult to work with than wood.'[2]

Gorky also went to the camp at Solovki, which was specially prepared for his visit. Prisoners were sent away or given proper clothes. The poles were removed from the punishment cells. Now prisoners reading newspapers were sitting on benches. An avenue of fir trees to the Children's Colony was put down. ('Planted' is not the word. The trees, needed only for a few days, had no roots.) The children looked happy, each on a separate cot with a mattress. One fourteen-year-old boy bravely told Gorky that everything was false and offered to tell him the truth. Gorky listened alone to the boy for an hour and a half and then left in tears. The boy said he had told Gorky everything: the sacks they had to wear, prisoners in place of horses pulling the carts, the pole torture, being rolled down the stairs, being made to spend all night in the snow and being exposed to the mosquitoes.

It is not hard to guess the fate of the boy. It is harder to guess what combination of fear, self-interest and self-deception lay behind Gorky's comments in the Visitors' Book:

> I am not in a state of mind to express my impressions in just a few words. I wouldn't want, yes, and I would likewise be ashamed, to permit myself banal praise of the remarkable energy of people who, while remaining vigilant and tireless sentinels of the Revolution, are able, at the same time, to be remarkably bold creators of culture.[3]

George Orwell's Fear

Countless ordinary people chose, like Gorky, to participate in the lies; they did so out of fear or self-deception. The belief system gave support to lying. This was partly a matter of ruthless consequentialism. If the end justifies torture and mass killing, surely scruples about lying can be overcome. More interestingly, the belief system included scepticism about objective truth.

George Orwell was one of the first to see the importance of this. While Orwell was famously an opponent of Stalinist lies, it was a piece of anti-Communist propaganda which triggered his reflections on objectivity. In democratic countries, some of Franco's supporters in the Spanish Civil

War claimed that the fascists were saving Spain from a Communist dictatorship. Part of this was the claim that the Soviet Union had sent an army to Spain.

Orwell wrote:

> Now, there was no Russian army in Spain. There may have been a handful of airmen and other technicians, a few hundred at the most, but an army there was not. Some thousands of foreigners who fought in Spain, not to mention millions of Spaniards, were witnesses of this. Well, their testimony made no impression at all upon the Franco propagandists, not one of whom had set foot in Government Spain . . . This kind of thing is frightening to me, because it often gives me the feeling that the very concept of objective truth is fading out of the world.

Orwell reflected that if Franco stayed in power such statements might be taken as history, as might equivalent ones on the other side if fascism was defeated. Previous historians often had been biased and sometimes had lied, but they had believed that 'the facts' existed and were more or less discoverable:

> what is peculiar to our own age is the abandonment of the idea that history *could* be truthfully written . . . The implied objective of this line of thought is a nightmare world in which the Leader, or some ruling clique, controls not only the future but *the past*. If the Leader says of such and such an event, 'It never happened' – well, it never happened. If he says that two and two are five – well, two and two are five. This prospect frightens me much more than bombs.[4]

On the claims about a Soviet army in Spain, Orwell cited the thousands of foreigners who fought in Spain as contrary witnesses. Their testimony is relevant but limited. It is hard to prove a negative statement of broad scope. Since no one on the ground can see the whole of Spain, there is no such thing as 'witnessing' that a Russian army is not in the country.

Orwell was not quite accurate but he was largely right. The story was a huge exaggeration rather than a total falsehood. There were Russian planes on the Republican side, flown by Russian pilots. And Russian tanks, driven by Russians under the command of General Dmitri Pavlov, defended Madrid against Franco's army. But the numbers involved were fewer than two thousand, rather than the half million cited in the propaganda.

On the general issue, it is hard to fault Orwell's worry. Scepticism about objective truth has been one of the themes of modern intellectual life, from Nietzsche at the end of the nineteenth century to 'postmodernists' at the end of the twentieth. It has also been the theme of much political life. Philosophers treat the intellectual version with justifiable condescension, but Orwell was right to fear the political version. Stalin's Soviet Union is a good place to see why.

The Abandonment of Objective Truth

In a famous passage Karl Marx suggested either that the practical results of beliefs were the criterion of truth, or else that their practical results were more important than whether they were true:

> The question of whether human thinking can pretend to objective truth is not a theoretical but a *practical* question. Man must prove the truth, i.e. the reality and power, the 'this-sideness' of his thinking in practice. The dispute over the reality or non-reality of thinking that is isolated from practice is a purely *scholastic* question.[5]

These obscure comments do not clearly deny the attainability of objective truth, but they hardly suggest that aiming for it is important. And, to use Marx's own criterion, their practical result was to encourage the subordination of truth to political strategy. In the Soviet Union these priorities could be seen in fields ranging from biology to the law.

In biology Lamarck's view that acquired characteristics could be inherited seemed more Marxist than Mendelian genetics. Lamarckism would allow human improvements brought about by social changes to be passed on genetically. Lamarck's view did not fit with the evidence, but the interpretation was skewed to fit the belief system. Trofim Lysenko said that Lamarckism was correct: the genes of plants and animals were changed by their environment. He applied this view to agriculture, dismissing the idea of improving plants or animals by selective breeding as fascist. Better go against the evidence than not be against 'fascism'.

Stalin had opinions on biology which Lysenko and his subordinates dutifully endorsed: 'Stalin's teachings about gradual, concealed, unnoticeable quantitative changes leading to rapid, radical, qualitative changes permitted Soviet biologists to discover in plants the realization of such qualitative transitions that one species could be transformed into another.'[6] Stalin had shown how to turn apple trees into orange trees. Lysenko in turn had Stalin's support. In 1948, on Stalin's orders, Mendelian genetics was condemned by the Central Committee and biologists had to follow Lysenko's Lamarckian orthodoxy. The slide away from truth-directed science had disastrous results in agriculture. It was also humanly disastrous. Biologists who disagreed were shot or imprisoned.

Something similar happened in the law. In his reshaping of the legal system, Andrei Vyshinsky drew on scepticism about truth. In the book for which he won the Stalin Prize, *The Theory of Legal Evidence in Soviet Law*, he gave a new account of evidence, giving great weight to confessions made by the accused.

He argued that absolute truth cannot be established: there is only relative truth. In a trial no evidence is certain. So, in finding someone guilty and punishing them, we are acting on an approximate hypothesis. In interrogation and trial, finding the truth is replaced by the aim of finding the most plausible approximation. Vyshinsky thought this justified a more freewheeling approach to evidence: 'The defendants' statements in state crimes are inevitably regarded as the main evidence, the most important, crucial evidence.'[7] As evidence is relative and approximate, the interrogator has scope to use his own judgement, 'basing his conclusions not only on his own intellect but also on his Party sensitivity, his moral forces and on his character'.[8]

The attack on objective truth was an intellectual and human disaster, but it encountered little opposition.

Where Were the Philosophers?

Many things philosophers think about have no political content. But philosophers also have the social role of contributing to a climate of clear and rational thinking. The attack on the idea of objective truth calls for philosophical questions and analysis. When all this was going on, where were the philosophers?

From the time of Lenin, the climate had been unfavourable to independent thought. Lenin himself had criticized Russia's intellectuals: 'the intellectuals, the lackeys of capital, who think they're the brains of the nation. In fact, they're not its brains, they're its shit.'[9]

The leaders of the Party accepted Marx's belief that he had discovered 'scientific' laws of social development. So they thought most philosophical questions had been shown to be pointless, or else had been answered. Leon Trotsky, when he was still a Soviet leader, made use of the image of the factory in arguing that free philosophical discussion was unnecessary:

> Objections to the effect that the 'dogmatization' and 'canonization' of dialectical materialism prevent the free development of philosophical and scientific thought do not deserve serious attention. No factory can work without basing itself on a definite technological doctrine. No hospital can treat its patients if the physicians do not base themselves on the established teachings of pathology.[10]

The 'factory' outlook was to create opportunities for people prepared to engage in this version of applied philosophy. But for real philosophers things were less easy. There were strong pressures on those who did not think Marxist 'established teachings' were as well based as pathology. How did they respond?

At least one philosopher was a participant in Stalin's crimes. Nadezhda Mandelstam wrote of him:

> There was also Glukhov, whose name should be recorded for posterity. This man had received a medal for his part in the deportation of the kulaks, and had also been awarded a doctorate for a dissertation on Spinoza. He performed his duties in quite open fashion, summoning students to his office and instructing them whom they should get up and denounce at meetings, and in what terms.[11]

Reading Spinoza is compatible with moral disaster.

Did philosophers question the attack on objective truth? The answer is understandable but sad. Like nearly everyone else, they did not speak out because they were afraid. They had a special problem because Stalin, in his irascible way, was interested in philosophy. He wrote a chapter on 'Dialectical Materialism' in *The History of the CPSU: Short Course*. The person whose philosophical views had most influence was Stalin himself.

Stalin asked his assistant to assemble a library of books for him and he put philosophy first on the list of subjects to be included. He then appointed the philosopher Jan Sten to be his tutor. Sten must have thought that he had a chance of influence not given to any philosopher since Aristotle taught Alexander the Great. He drew up a programme to teach Stalin about Kant, Hegel, Fichte, Schelling, Feuerbach, Plekhanov, Kautsky and F.H. Bradley. In the tutorials, Stalin sometimes asked questions like 'What's all this got to do with the class struggle?' or 'Who uses all this rubbish in practice?'

Despite his impatience, Stalin persevered with the subject enough to think of himself as a philosopher. In 1930 he gave a philosophical lecture to an institute of professors, which is summarized in the minutes:

> We have to turn upside down and dig over the whole pile of manure that has accumulated in philosophy and the natural sciences. Everything written by the Deborin group has to be smashed. Sten and Karev can be chucked out. Sten boasts a lot, but he's just a pupil of Karev's. Sten is a desperate sluggard. All he can do is talk. Karev's got a swelled head and struts about like an inflated bladder. In my view, Deborin is a hopeless case, but he should remain as editor of the journal so we'll have someone to beat. The editorial board will have two fronts, but we'll have the majority.

After this philosophy lecture there were questions. Unsurprisingly, they were undemanding. One was, 'What should the Institute concentrate on in the area of philosophy?' Stalin replied:

To beat, that is the main issue. To beat on all sides and where there hasn't been any beating before. The Deborinites regard Hegel as an icon. Plekhanov has to be unmasked. He always looked down on Lenin. Even Engels was not right about everything. There is a place in his commentary on the Erfurt Programme about growing into socialism. Bukharin tried to use it. It wouldn't be a bad thing if we could implicate Engels somewhere in Bukharin's writings.[12]

It would be a nightmare for any philosophy tutor to give tutorials to Stalin. And a tutor might be depressed at being described as a desperate sluggard by the most famous person he had taught. But things got worse. Jan Sten was later described as a lickspittle of Trotsky and executed.

Socrates and a few others might have ignored this kind of threat. But, although the silence of most philosophers was not heroic, in that climate it was perhaps not surprising.

Truth and Moral Identity

The abandonment of objective truth as a legal goal was disastrous for those whose lives were destroyed by their 'confessions'. The abandonment of objective truth in biology was disastrous for harvests. But these consequences, each so costly in lives, were not the full extent of the disaster.

Abandoning the commitment to truth has drastic implications for moral identity. The crucial point comes when casualness about what you say to others slides into casualness about what you say to yourself.

In the first stage abandonment of truth is superficial. What is said to other people is determined in ways largely independent of its truth: by the needs of propaganda or by some other consequentialist calculation. The lie is strategic: a private grip on truth is retained.

This strategic phase runs into the problem of the old saw, 'Oh what a tangled web we weave, when first we practise to deceive.' Truths are interwoven. Tearing out one from the fabric of the others leaves jagged edges and patching the hole with a lie may only convince if neighbouring truths are tampered with too. Further effort to improve matters needs more complex fabrication and the awkward frontier with truth grows longer.

Liars in private life have limited resources to deal with these problems. They give evasive answers. They prevent certain people from meeting. They give the improvised explanation. Private lying is limited partly by the insecurity of these strategies. Liars in power have more scope: even in a democracy they use propaganda and can invoke 'national security' to keep information from the public. In an authoritarian society there is much more power to defend the small lie by massively churning out the larger one. It is like printing money to get out of a financial crisis. There is a short-term gain for the authorities, who avoid being immediately found out. But the long-term cost of this propaganda inflation is that the official belief system grows ever further out of touch with reality, and so hard to support without yet more coercion and lying.

Paradoxically, concern for moral identity can impel people uncomfortable with their lies to start believing them. Stalin's letters to Molotov give the impression that he did believe in the 'conspiracies' for which he was having so many executed. Perhaps this was not only his paranoia; some residual sense of moral identity may have encouraged self-deception about the fraudulent charges.

The tension involved in conscious deception of others can lead to self-deception and denial. Then the liar crosses the crucial boundary to the second stage of the abandonment of truth. Evidence is not just doctored for other people's consumption, it is defensively interpreted to shore up weak points in the person's own belief system, as in the British Communist Party's debate on the Hitler–Stalin pact. The boundary is crossed when the consciously manipulative approach of Palme Dutt ('When it was clear that a different character of the line would be needed, he gives it and leads the opposite line') shifts to Ted Bramley's attempts to believe that Stalin felt threatened by Poland and its allies: 'In trying to find the explanation, this is the only place where I can find it comes.'

Anyone's beliefs match the world at best roughly. Even those who aim for truth will have incomplete and partly incorrect information. It is hard to escape bias. Everyone has perceptual and intellectual limitations. (These are the truisms hugely exaggerated in the case for scepticism about objective truth.)

Those whose thinking is not truth-directed are in a worse position. By rigging the interpretation of evidence for their own consumption, they open up an additional gap between their beliefs and the world. As the gap grows wider, more things need explaining away. At some level, people may be aware of having defended their belief system at the price of compromising on truth. This price is a further investment in the beliefs, making them harder to give up next time something needs explaining away.

Self-deception can become a self-perpetuating cycle. External pressures may not have been the only ones J.R. Campbell had in mind when he said, 'you can't understand what the pressures were to convince ourselves that the line of the International and Soviet Union was right, as we had done previously over the Moscow trials'.

A sense of moral identity restrains support for atrocities: 'I am not someone who would support mass murder.' The restraint depends on the jarring incompatibility between mass murder and the kind of person one is prepared to be. But the cycle of self-deception blocks this. When mass murder is sufficiently reinterpreted, people can support it with an unimpaired sense of moral identity.

Truth and moral identity are linked. As self-deception feeds on itself, there is less and less to stop beliefs about one's moral identity becoming systematically false. The growth of such a delusional system is a personal moral disaster. It can also be a political disaster.

The link between truth and moral identity can function the other way. Moral identity can prompt people not to give up on truth. Milovan Djilas, a believing Communist who looked hard at what Stalin was really like, later spoke and wrote publicly both about Stalin and about the system: 'I had to follow that road, even if my steps were confused and indecisive. Otherwise I would not remain a man in my own eyes. For if I know something with certainty and I am convinced of its truth, how can I deny it, hide it from my closest friends; from the world and from myself?'[13]

CHAPTER 30

Mao's Utopian Project

The greatest horror of the Cultural Revolution – the crushing repression which had driven hundreds of thousands of people to mental breakdown, suicide and death – was carried out by the population collectively. Almost everyone, including young children, had participated in brutal denunciation meetings. Many had lent a hand in beating the victims.

           Jung Chang, *Wild Swans: Three Daughters of China*

But it is no accident that, in a human spectacle as rich in hope and tragedy and evil as Mao's China and its aftermath, I see also not only the story of twentieth-century communism . . . but also much that in an important sense is true or could be true of humanity as a whole.

           Jiwei Ci, *Dialectic of the Chinese Revolution*

The true heirs of Stalin were not the Soviet leaders who followed him. They had no large political scheme beyond keeping the Soviet Union afloat. For huge Stalinist projects of reshaping society, one has to turn to Mao Zedong in China and to Pol Pot in Cambodia. Which features of Stalinism were distinctively Russian or Soviet? Which were the likely result of any social engineering on that scale? Comparison of the Soviet, Chinese and Cambodian experiences gives clues.

In 1949, when Mao stood on the Gate of Heavenly Peace in Beijing and proclaimed the People's Republic of China, many Chinese felt a wave of optimism. There had been civil war since the 1930s, only interrupted by some joint resistance during the horrendously bloody Japanese occupation. Their hope was that China might now be united and peaceful.

Many thought a planned socialist economy might eliminate poverty. Mao and his colleagues were widely trusted. In the two-year retreat in the mid-1930s known as the Long March, the Communist army and its leaders had shown great strength in the face of daunting obstacles and had refused to exploit the people along their route. Now the Communists were in power, they set out to raise standards of health and literacy. They improved the status of women, ending child marriages and the practice of binding women's feet. There were reasons to see the new government as both determined and idealistic.

But in the first twenty years of Mao's rule China experienced two of the century's great man-made catastrophes: the Great Leap Forward and the Cultural Revolution.

The Great Leap Forward was an ambitious plan to involve everyone in producing vast quantities of steel and food. It caused mass starvation. Famine was familiar in China. Civil war and rivalries between warlords had resulted in millions of armed men criss-crossing the country and taking the food from peasants. But the famine caused by the Great Leap Forward was on a new scale. Between 1958 and 1962 it killed 20–30 million people.

The Cultural Revolution was an attempt by Mao to hold on to power and to defeat his opponents, but it was also intended to revive the revolutionary spirit of ordinary people. For several years after 1966, it created a climate of fanaticism and fear, an oppression without previous parallel. Most of the people of China were involved, as persecutors or victims or both, in its cruelties.

Why were the hopes of 1949 so soon followed by these disasters?

The Great Leap Forward and the Famine

In 1957 Mao said that in fifteen years the Soviet Union would overtake the United States in production of steel, and that China would overtake Britain. There were few grounds for either claim, but Mao held a view sometimes called 'voluntarism': he had great faith in what huge numbers of ordinary people could do when they willed something collectively.

Every family was encouraged to make a backyard steel furnace, to double the country's steel production in one year. Zhisui Li was Mao's doctor and also part of his political entourage. He recalled his first visit with Mao to one of the makeshift furnaces: 'The fire was going full blast, and inside were all sorts of household implements made of steel – pots, pans, doorknobs and shovels – being melted down to produce what Zeng assured Mao was also steel.' Dr Li did not know whether the steel was any good, but wondered about using the furnaces 'to melt steel to produce steel, to destroy knives to make knives'.[1]

Much of the melted-down steel was unusable and many who would have gathered in the harvest were diverted into the steel project, making worse an already serious food crisis.

The other part of the Great Leap Forward was the hugely ambitious programme for increasing grain production. Peasants had been made to form co-operatives. Animals were collectivized, with the result that peasants neglected them or sometimes worked them to death. Mao thought the energies of the peasants would be released if the co-operatives were amalgamated into huge communes of about 50,000 people. In 1958 this was done, and all private ownership of land was abolished. Mao expected the combination of science and the release of energy to result in enormous harvests.

Mao's version of 'science' was heavily influenced by Soviet orthodoxy. All Chinese biology and agriculture was based on the work of Lysenko, and Western-trained biologists had to repudiate Darwinian views. The agricultural plan for the Great Leap Forward was drawn up by Mao himself and gave prominence to some of his own views. He was an enthusiast for deep ploughing and for planting seed close together. (Mao explained his belief in close planting: 'with company they grow easily, when they grow together they will be comfortable'.)[2]

Propaganda claimed that China had overtaken the United States in wheat production. A poster was produced showing one of the triumphs of close planting with children apparently standing on top of a crop dense enough to bear their weight. (They were actually on a concealed bench.)[3] As with the steel project, Mao's plans for harvests had no basis. His optimistic view that his policies had resulted in China being awash with surplus food led to the doubling of China's grain exports between 1958 and 1961. By 1960, even in villages close to Beijing, many peasants were dying and others were too weak to plant or harvest crops. In Henan people died of starvation while state granaries had enough grain to feed everybody. It became common to eat the flesh of dead family members. Still the official belief in an abundant harvest kept the granaries shut.

Mao was not used to being contradicted. Afraid of not pleasing him, senior officials pressed junior ones for results. They in turn reported what was wanted, making utterly fantastic claims about production. Mao went by train to look at the harvests. Dr Li was one of the Party:

> The scene along the railroad tracks was incredible. Harvest time was approaching, and the crops were thriving. The fields were crowded with peasants at work . . . 'Good news reporting stations' were being set up in communal dining halls, each station competing with nearby brigades and communes to report – red flags waving, gongs and drums sounding – the highest, most extravagant figures.

But one evening Dr Li was told the reality. They were seeing an opera staged for Mao: furnaces had been built on a strip on each side of the railway. In Hubei the peasants were ordered to remove rice plants from far-away fields and transplant them along Mao's route to give the impression of a wildly abundant crop. 'The rice was planted so closely together that electric fans had to be set up around the fields to circulate air in order to prevent the plants from rotting.'4

Fear, Truth and the Imperial Court

Tiananmen Square in Beijing was created by Mao as an enormous space for rallies. It would eclipse Red Square in Moscow. On the west side is the Stalinist architecture of the huge parliament building. On the east side is another Stalinist building, which houses an exhibition of the Chinese Revolution. The architecture on the north side is different: the Gate of Heavenly Peace, leading into the Forbidden City, from which in imperial days ordinary people were excluded.

The symbolism must have been intended. The declaration of the People's Republic was from the top of the gate. Next to the once forbidden city was now the new open square with room for thousands to meet, and with the parliament along one side housed in the 'Great Hall of the People'. The government was no longer to be cut off from the people but belonged to it.

But things did not turn out as intended. From the north-west corner of Tiananmen Square, running up the west side of the Forbidden City, are the park and lakes of Zhongnanhai. Since 1949 Zhongnanhai has housed the political leaders of the People's Republic. Walled off and guarded by soldiers, it is as much a forbidden city as its predecessor was.

Inside Mao lived the life of an Emperor beside his swimming pool or in his huge, specially made bed. There he kept up his reading, being provided with a steady supply of books, often about Emperors of China. There he also kept up his sex life, being provided with a steady supply of young women. His vanity demanded flattery, as a great philosopher and poet as well as a great leader. He was concerned about the sort of legend he would leave behind him. When he discovered that some of his entourage were recording his conversations, part of his anger was at the thought of a 'black' record to be used after his death against him, in the way Khrushchev's revelations discredited Stalin.

Like Stalin, Mao was lonely and craved conversation. He was not intimate with the other leaders and had no friends. He would talk to his young, uneducated bodyguards, often about their girlfriends, but he wanted to talk about philosophy and Chinese history. He encouraged Dr Li to read on those topics and had long conversations with him at night. Again like Stalin, and for reasons Socrates would understand, Mao was very suspicious. His food was tested for poison and then given to tasters. When he visited Sichuan, he did not swim in the pool built for him because he was afraid it was poisoned. Sometimes he would insist on moving because of worries that villas he lived in had been poisoned.

Mao was skilled at manipulating his court. All his staff had to talk to him about each other and to repeat conversations they had with each other. They were threatened with 're-education' on some labour project if they held back. And the knowledge they gave him about each other could in turn be used for manipulation and threats.

It was hard to tell Mao anything he did not want to hear. Disagreement could anger him. When he wanted to swim in the Yangtze, its currents and whirlpools made his advisers warn Mao it was very dangerous. He swore at them and bullied them until they said the opposite. When Mao did swim without incident, he was encouraged in his belief about doing the apparently impossible: 'There is nothing you cannot do if you are serious about it. Remember, when you face something unfamiliar, don't oppose it right away . . . Comrade Wang Renzhong opposed my swimming before, but then he switched his position and made serious preparation for the swimming. That is the right attitude.'[5]

Mao did not want to hear reports of famine, which he thought were being spread by rich peasants who did not want to hand over grain. His response was a drive against 'grain concealment', which resulted in purges and many suicides. Some who denied there was any grain were beaten or tortured. Some were left naked to freeze to death in the snow. Some were buried alive. The 1959 harvest was at least 30 million tonnes less than the previous year's, but officials found it prudent to report large increases.

Peng Dehuai, the Minister of Defence, sent reports from the country about the danger of starvation. In 1959, at a meeting of leaders at Lushan, Peng spoke up against Mao's denials of famine. He followed this up with a politely worded letter to Mao. At a later meeting Mao dismissed Peng's criticisms. The two men had an angry confrontation. Peng said Mao was being like Stalin, sacrificing people to impossible production targets. Peng was condemned as 'an anti-Party element' and 'a right opportunist'. He had to write a self-criticism and was put under house arrest. (In the Cultural Revolution he was to be tortured and killed.)

Mao's policies needed corrective feedback, but most people were too frightened to give it.

The Cultural Revolution

The Great Leap Forward damaged Mao's reputation. He decided to become the theorist of the revolution and made Liu Shaoqi the head of state.

The new regime relaxed the collectivization policy. It also allowed people to wear different clothes instead of the uniform Mao suits. There was more artistic and intellectual freedom. Western ideas were again discussed in universities. Responsibility for the famine began to be investigated.

Mao fought back, passionately encouraged by his wife, Jian Qing, and a few associates. Lin Biao, the Minister of Defence, produced a little red book of *Quotations from Chairman Mao* for everyone in the army. Mao ordered that all schoolchildren should study the book. The relative pluralism of Lui Shaoqi was threatened by the emerging cult of Chairman Mao.

Mao intended to purge the leadership and the Party. In 1966 he criticized Liu Shaoqi in a widely distributed essay called 'Bombard the Headquarters – My Big-character-poster'. He supported student criticism of the authorities at Beijing University. In many colleges and schools, Maoist student groups of Red Guards started to denounce their teachers and Party officials. Mao, wearing their uniform, presided over huge Red Guard rallies in Tiananmen Square.

In fomenting the Cultural Revolution, Mao's aim was partly to defeat his rivals in the leadership, but he also believed that those in authority were in danger of getting out of touch with the uneducated and the peasants. (Given his record over the famine, this has obvious ironies.) Re-education through labour was partly a threat used to make people obey, but it was also linked to a real belief in learning from the peasants.

Mao had a restless energy and a genuine dislike of things becoming rigid and fossilized. When he asked Dr Li to investigate how the Cultural Revolution was going in Beijing, he said, 'A thousand people will die this time, I think. Everything is turning upside down ... I love great upheavals.'[6] Mao believed especially in the energy of the young: 'The young and the uneducated have always been the ones to develop new ideas, create new schools, introduce new religions. The young are capable of grasping new situations and of initiating change, brave enough to challenge the old fogies.'[7] At the huge rallies of Red Guards, Mao encouraged the young to tear up the existing society and start again.

Sometimes the Cultural Revolution met with resistance. In Shanghai the Red Guards demanded that *Liberation Daily* should carry their own *Red Guard Battle News*. When this was refused, the Red Guards occupied the newspaper's offices and shut it down for a week. More than a million people demonstrated against the occupation outside the building. It was only after appealing for support from workers' organizations that the Red Guards won and the paper was made to carry their supplement.[8] But the Red Guards rarely met effective opposition.

Traditional Chinese culture was attacked. The influence of 'Confucius and Co' was to be eliminated. The Red Guards destroyed most of the temples in China. In people's houses, books and works of art were destroyed. Libraries were wrecked and books burnt.

To attack the old society was to attack people as well as temples and books. The teenage Red Guards felt licensed to carry out acts of great cruelty. At the age of fifteen, Zhai Zhenhua led eight other girls who were also Red Guards to the home of Xiuying, a woman in her late forties who had been a landlord and was said not to love Chairman Mao. When the Red Guards searched they found nothing incriminating and Xiuying refused to talk to them.

Zhai Zhenhua ordered the other girls to beat her: 'As soon as they started to strap her with their belts, she slid down onto the floor with her back against the wall and from then on hardly moved. Her eyes never looked up. Before we left, we grabbed some of her belongings at random to turn over to our headquarters.' The next day another girl in the Red Guards casually mentioned that Xiuying was dead. A few days later, Zhai Zhenhua went on another raid. She first saw the victims, a couple, lying on the floor with their eyes closed and looking badly beaten. The woman's face still seemed to have an unyielding expression and Zhai Zhenhua beat her savagely. When the woman seemed unconscious, Zhai Zhenhua worried that she too was dead, and was relieved that a bucket of water revived her for more beating.[9]

All this had Mao's support. In a letter to the Red Guards, he wrote:

The action of the Red Guards expresses their indignation at, and accusation of, the exploitation and oppression of the workers, peasants, revolutionary intellectuals, and revolutionary parties by the landlords, capitalists, imperialists, revisionists and their lackeys. It fully justifies any rebellion against the reactionaries. I am firmly behind you.[10]

'Bombarding the headquarters' meant personal disaster for Mao's successor as head of state, Liu Shaoqi. He was dragged from his house and his wife was humiliated by being made to dress up as a grotesque parody of a capitalist. He himself was 'struggled against'. Dr Li saw him with his shirt torn open, being pulled around by the hair, his head forced near the ground, being slapped in the face and kicked: 'I could not bear to watch. Liu Shaoqi was already an old man by then, almost seventy, and he was our head of state.'[11] He was then forced into self-criticism before 10,000 students in the Great Hall of the People. In an echo of Stalin, Mao listened to this from behind a curtain. But then Mao emerged on the stage and walked back and forth, waving to acknowledge the thunderous reception. He did not look at Liu Shaoqi. The expression of disfavour was clear.

Liu Shaoqi had diabetes. He now developed pneumonia and was refused all medicine. On the orders of Mao's wife, he was kept alive so that the Ninth Party Congress in 1969 would have a 'living target'. At the Congress he was denounced as a traitor and enemy agent. He was then allowed to die in agony.

Other leaders were also attacked. Governors of provinces and mayors of cities, including Beijing, were humiliated. 'Class enemies' were a target. Having parents who were landlords or 'rich peasants' imposed a hereditary stigma which nothing could remove. One slogan used was 'Dragons beget dragons; phoenixes beget phoenixes; rats beget rats.'[12]

Hostile treatment was given to anyone in any kind of authority: teachers were particularly singled out. In 1970, aged thirteen, Anchee Min was head of her school's Little Red Guards. One teacher in particular (whose name literally means 'Autumn Leaves') had given her encouragement and kindness. Anchee Min was told to denounce Autumn Leaves as an American spy. When Anchee Min found the accusation of spying unbelievable she was told Autumn Leaves was like a wolf in sheep's clothing who killed without leaving any trace of blood. She had been educated in the United States and was poisoning the children's minds.

Autumn Leaves was dragged before 2,000 people. Her arms were twisted behind her and a notice put round her neck saying that she was a spy. She was forced to bow to Mao's portrait and beg his forgiveness.

When, in tears, she refused to confess that she was a spy, Anchee Min was brought on to denounce her. Autumn Leaves looked at Anchee Min and, saying she wanted her to be honest, asked whether she really thought she was an enemy. Anchee Min found it terrible to look into her eyes:

> They had looked at me when the magic of mathematics was explained . . . When I won the first place in the Calculation-with-Abacus competition, they had looked at me with joy; when I was ill, they had looked at me with sympathy and love. I had not realized the true value of what all this meant to me until I lost it forever that day at the meeting.

Anchee Min was almost unable to denounce her teacher. But the Party Secretary reminded her of a story Mao wrote about the mistake of being merciful to a beautiful snake. She was encouraged by the shouted slogans. She remembered her duty to be merciless to Mao's enemies. In tears herself, she blurted out the accusations: 'Yes, yes, yes, I do believe that you poisoned me; and I do believe that you are a true enemy! Your dirty tricks will have no more effect on me! If you dare to try them on me again, I'll shut you up! I'll use a needle to stitch your lips together!'[13]

Hardness

Some people recoiled from all this cruelty. Young men ransacking an old couple's house found boxes of precious French glass. When the old man begged them not to destroy the glass, one of the group hit him in the mouth with a club, leaving him spitting out blood and teeth. The students smashed the glass and left the couple on their knees crying. One schoolboy in the group did not take part again: 'deep in my heart I knew I could not continue to do this kind of thing. Perhaps I was born with a soft heart. I couldn't stand seeing other people suffer, bleed, or weep. I found it hard to face those defenceless "targets of revolution".'[14]

Such responses were discouraged and people learnt to overcome automatic responses of sympathy.

Dr Li treated everyone, regardless of class. Mao told him, 'We don't object to humanitarianism in its entirety. We are simply opposed to practising humanitarianism on the enemy.'[15] When it came to sympathy, Mao himself had something missing. Dr Li spoke of him as devoid of human feeling, love, friendship or warmth. He described sitting next to Mao at a performance when a child acrobat slipped and was seriously hurt. The child's mother was distraught and the crowd aghast. Mao did not ask after the child, but carried on laughing and talking.[16]

Mao discouraged gentleness. At a mass rally he asked one Red Guard what her name was. When she said 'Bin-bin', meaning 'gentle', he replied disapprovingly, 'Be violent.' One seventeen-year-old boy, fending off criticism as he beat up a kneeling and bloodstained woman, quoted Mao: 'Mercy to the enemy is cruelty to the people!'[17]

Dignity and Humiliation

The human response most spectacularly overcome was respect for dignity. Humiliation was the main tool of the Cultural Revolution. People were paraded through the streets with degrading slogans on placards worn round their necks. They were made to wear dunce's caps and their hair was cut in grotesque ways.

The dunce's cap displays the cold joke again. Some of those who ran the Cultural Revolution had long been practitioners of the cold joke. In 1946 Kang Sheng had been inspecting land reform in Gansu and Shanxi provinces. His hostility to 'leniency' for landlords had encouraged people to behead them or bury them alive. One landlord's name was the word for 'cow'. Kang Sheng's joke was to order him to have an iron ring put through his nose and to be led by his son through the streets on a rope.[18]

One cold joke was to turn people into involuntary clowns. The first act of violence Zhai Zhenhua took part in during a home raid was against a painter:

the two of us stood on stools to cut his hair. We were impatient and not interested in doing a good job, so we left tufts and scratches here and there. When his scalp showed clearly, two other Red Guards took brushes soaked in some black ink the painter had and painted his head and face. Having transformed this dignified man into a clown, we were satisfied.[19]

For some the indignities were unbearable. Many killed themselves. The humiliations were also cruel to those close to the victims. Jung Chang describes the response of her grandmother to the tormenting of her daughter (Jung Chang's mother), who was among those paraded through the streets wearing dunce's caps and humiliating placards. They were made to go down on their knees and kowtow to jeering children, and to bang their foreheads loudly on the pavement. When Jung Chang's grandmother first heard of this she fainted. When she came round, tears ran down her face as she asked, 'What has my daughter done to deserve this?'[20]

It could be hard for children to bear what was done to their parents. Xiaoyu saw the humiliation of her mother on a platform in a crowded Beijing sports arena: 'Hung around her neck on a piece of thin wire was a large iron sign that read "I am the cursed wife of XX". Her neck was bowed by the heavy sign, and the wire was visibly cutting into her neck. Her head was splotched with bald spots.' When she refused to confess her guilt, she was kicked and she fell down. 'The leader of the Rebels stepped on her back and shouted, "You are dead! You are dead!" My brother and I could not bear to watch, and we ran from the meeting.'[21]

These cruelties had unprecedented mass participation. As Jung Chang saw, the crushing repression which drove so many to mental breakdown or suicide was carried out by nearly everyone. In this way, Mao's China was qualitatively different from Stalin's Soviet Union. It is hard to be sure why. Perhaps the traditions of Chinese culture made people more conformist or more susceptible to propaganda than Russians. Perhaps a part was played by the ugly psychology of a crowd in the presence of a scapegoat. Participants may have felt the grim fascination of seeing people publicly stripped of their dignity. Reflective and honest Chinese might later have echoed the thought, 'I loved it in strange and troubling ways.'

The Pressure to Believe

The pressures and propaganda made people take on the outlook of the regime. The pressures were felt in personal as well as in public life. As in Stalin's Soviet Union, fear imposed orthodoxy even inside families. Parents said nothing which might raise doubts in their children. It was safer for children to conform.

People feared stepping out of line even in their thoughts. A caption under a huge photograph of Mao's mother said that she had been very kind and had often given food to the poor. Jung Chang realized this meant Mao's parents had been rich peasants, now denounced as class enemies: 'Why were Chairman Mao's parents heroes when other class enemies were objects of hate? The question frightened me so much that I immediately suppressed it.' People felt guilty about such thoughts. Mao decided that grass and flowers were bourgeois and would have to go. Jung Chang blamed herself for feeling sad to see the plants uprooted: 'In fact such feelings frightened me . . . I tried to suppress them and acquire the correct way of thinking. I lived in a state of constant self-accusation.'[22]

In a lecture in 1951 Michael Oakeshott said that the expression 'political education' had fallen on evil days. He spoke of its association with a softening of the mind 'by force, by alarm, or by the hypnotism of the endless repetition of what was scarcely worth saying once'.[23] No doubt Oakeshott had in mind the political education promoted by Hitler and Stalin. But 1951, the year of Oakeshott's lecture, saw the start of a massive campaign of 'Thought Reform' aimed at Chinese intellectuals. Oakeshott's comments exactly fit this campaign, except that endless repetition was not the only technique used to instil what was scarcely worth saying once.

Thought Reform was an attempt to get inside people's minds and restructure their system of beliefs. It put them under strong physical and psychological pressure to repudiate their beliefs and accept new ones. Physical pressure included standing continuously, in handcuffs and chains, with no sleep for days. The psychological pressure included humiliation: having to eat with your mouth in the bowl like a dog and urinating only when others unzip your trousers. There were endless denunciations and demands to confess crimes.

One Westerner accused of crimes described the result of Thought Reform:

> You are annihilated . . . exhausted . . . you can't control yourself, or remember what you said two minutes before. You feel that all is lost . . . From that moment, the judge is the real master of you . . . You have to get rid of and denounce all your imperialist thoughts, and you must criticise all of your own thoughts, guided by the official . . . 'I did this, I am a criminal.' If you doubt, you keep it to yourself. Because if you admit the doubt you will be 'struggled' and lose the progress you have made . . . You begin to believe all this, but it is a special kind of belief. You are not absolutely convinced, but you accept it – in order to avoid trouble – because every time you don't agree, trouble starts again.[24]

The 1951 campaign of Thought Reform lasted a year and was directed mainly at universities. It put academics under pressure to make humiliating self-criticisms in front of their students and in the press.

Professor Chin Yueh-lin was a Harvard-trained philosopher who specialized in formal logic. His written confession, published in 1952, is full of self-criticism for having followed 'the decadent philosophy of the bourgeoisie' and having 'played the game of concepts'. Chin Yueh-lin had to apologize for his logician's concern for the validity of arguments:

I disseminated the purely technical viewpoint in logic . . . I only tried to teach logic from the formalistic viewpoint, as for instance I was only concerned with the correctness of the reasoning without caring about the truthfulness of the premises. My mistaken viewpoint of education for the talented led me to think highly of Wang Hao, who even now is serving the interests of American imperialism by being connected with an American university.

Particular apologies had to be made for subjecting the official system of belief to philosophical criticism: 'When Comrade Ai Ssu-ch'i lectured in Tsinghua, I even tried to argue with him.' The self-abasement was extreme: 'I am now close to sixty and I am a criminal for having sinned against the people.'

But now, as a result of having read Mao's essay 'On Practice', Chin Yueh-lin had been converted: 'The old philosophy, being metaphysical, is fundamentally unscientific, while the new philosophy, being scientific, is the supreme truth . . . the mission of the Philosophy Department lies in the training of propaganda personnel for the dissemination of Marxism-Leninism.'[25]

Conformity and Belief

Most people did not experience the nightmare of Thought Reform, but the same pressure to believe pervaded the whole of life. Party members met weekly in groups for 'thought examination', which often included insistent demands for self-criticism. And even outside the Party there were strong pressures towards orthodoxy.

There may be a general human disposition to conform in belief. This is one interpretation of a classic psychological study by Solomon Asch. A group of six people were shown a line and asked to say which of three other lines was the same length. Each group had one genuine participant and five people who had previously been briefed to select one of the wrong lines. All or most of the others' answers would be given before the question was put to the one genuine participant. A large number gave the group answer rather than the one their own observation presumably suggested.[26]

With Asch's study there is a question about those who conformed, against the evidence of their own experience. They may privately have kept to their own opinion, only outwardly agreeing with the majority. Private disagreement behind public conformity is familiar, it avoids bother in everyday life. Under Stalin and Mao it was a way of avoiding re-education, slave labour or death. On this interpretation, Asch's results are unexciting.

The study is interesting because of the alternative interpretation. Those who conformed may genuinely have changed their opinion, or have wobbled about it. This account suggests a disposition to pure conformity of outlook, independent of the advantages of external display. This disposition may seem both irrational and powerful because it overrides strong countervailing evidence. If Asch's results do reflect a genuine change of opinion, this is striking, but to say that those who conformed were irrational is too quick, and misses one of the most interesting implications.

In recent philosophy there has been a growing awareness of the gap between the abstract principles proposed by philosophers and the ways in which people actually think. The kind of rationality admired in the theory of knowledge is an idealization. In the real world people have to act on beliefs often based on fragmentary and unreliable evidence. There may be little time to think through the logical consequences of beliefs, or to test them for consistency. One response to the gap between abstract rationality and how people actually think is to see everyday thinking as inadequate, but another view has been gaining ground. While abstract rationality is a useful heuristic ideal, it may be a criticism of philosophers that they have not done more also to develop standards of 'minimal rationality', ways of thinking which are attainable.[27]

Conformity of belief has obvious limitations. There is an ideal, particularly in philosophy and science, of sceptical enquiry. To take things on trust goes against this ideal. But independent thinking arises against a background of conformity. It is impossible to investigate everything personally. A scientist who overthrows accepted ideas first has to learn enough science to do so, and this means taking on trust a lot of what is said in the textbooks. Checking it all would take many lifetimes. The growth of scientific knowledge depends on people being able to build on the work of others. This needs some conformist willingness to believe the majority of other respected investigators. A degree of (at least provisional) conformity is an uninspiring but necessary intellectual virtue.

People taking part in Asch's study find their own perception of the lines apparently contradicted by how all the other participants seem to see them. In ordinary life we know that our own senses and judgements are fallible. It is often reasonable to revise an opinion in the light of the reports of other people. In the experimental situation, with no reason for thinking the others are lying, it can be rational to give some weight to their judgements as a possible correction. A lot depends on how big the discrepancy between the lines is. The charge of irrationality is based on the idea that the revised judgement goes against all the evidence. The over-simplification in this is to exclude the judgements of the others from the relevant evidence.

On the 'genuine change of opinion' interpretation, Asch's results do suggest a deep tendency towards conformity, but some tendency to conform (as well as some tendency not to) is built into rationality. Mao's China, with its waves of intolerant mass belief is a reminder of the dangers of intellectual conformity. As far as possible, conformity should be provisional. It should be a preliminary to scepticism and to the willingness to look for evidence which may change beliefs. These, the basic intellectual virtues, are also a protection against mental slavery to people like Mao.

A Moral Wasteland

Indoctrination into the belief system could transform the sense of moral identity. One student took part in denouncing a senior teacher, who was made to 'confess' her crimes. They forced garlic into her mouth and then made her swallow garlic mixed with shoe polish. They filled her mouth with leaves and mud. But their beliefs saved them from feeling morally tarnished: 'At that time, it never occurred to me that we were being vicious. On the contrary, we felt justified and heroic because of our firm class stand.'[28] Part of the Maoist project was the deliberate construction of a new moral identity. To do this it was necessary to destroy people's previous sense of who they were and to make sure there was no room for it to grow back.

The Cultural Revolution was an unprecedentedly intrusive assault on any moral identity other than the permitted one. The house of Jung Chang's parents was raided (this was before the arrest of her father and the interrogation which drove him insane). Her father was forced to burn the books which had been a large part of his life, and which he had bought with all his spare money. In this destruction there is an echo of something William James said about the effect on a writer of his book in manuscript being destroyed: 'a sense of the shrinkage of our personality, a partial conversion of ourselves to nothingness'.[29] Jung Chang's father cried as he threw them into the flames: 'It was agonized, broken, and wild, the weeping of a man who was not used to shedding tears. Every now and then, in fits of violent sobs, he stamped his feet on the floor and banged his head against the wall.' After the bonfire 'something had happened to his mind'.[30]

One way of preventing the growth of any alternative sense of identity was to obliterate any private space in which this might happen. To an unprecedented degree, personal life was invaded by the political. The new priorities were expressed in 1958 by the *China Youth Journal*: 'the dearest people in the world are our parents, yet they cannot be compared with Chairman Mao and the Communist Party . . . Personal love is not so important: therefore women should not claim too much of their husbands' energy.'[31]

The new moral identity was bound up with total commitment to the Revolution, interpreted with a puritan narrowness about other values. Everything should be sacrificed for the Revolution. This included personal life, which could have nourished other values, and any sense of moral identity which might have restrained the manufactured hostility to 'class enemies'. Mercy to the enemy was cruelty to the people, something to be ashamed of. And cruelty to actual people left those who took part feeling justified and heroic because of their firm class stand.

Jung Chang said that Mao ruled by getting people to hate each other: 'Mao had managed to turn the people into the ultimate weapon of dictatorship. That was why under him there was no real equivalent of the KGB in China. There was no need. In bringing out and nourishing the worst in people, Mao had created a moral wasteland and a land of hatred.'[32]

Utopia and the Reshaping of Humanity

Mao thought of himself as a philosopher. He wrote two articles, 'On Practice' and 'On Contradiction', trying to work out a distinctively Chinese version of Marxism. He urged Dr Li to study Engels's *Dialectic of Nature*, saying that philosophy might do him good as a physician. Mao had absorbed the Marxist system of belief and his thinking took place within it. He showed no sign of being genuinely puzzled by philosophical questions. He had no knowledge of other systems of thought and was never troubled by the question of whether his set of categories and beliefs were more defensible than alternative ones. He thought it adequate to dismiss non-Marxist thought on the grounds of its class origins.

Like Stalin, Mao brushed aside moral restraints. His amoralism was reinforced by his reading of history. One Emperor he admired was Qin Shihuangdi. Although tyrannical and cruel, he had increased China's political and economic power. Qin Shihuangdi had been hated for killing Confucian scholars and burning the classic books. Dr Li quotes Mao as saying he had killed the scholars 'only because they got in the way of his efforts to unify China and build the Chinese Empire. And he only killed 260 Confucian scholars. Where was the great tragedy in that?'[33]

Mao applied this large-scale approach to his own time. He believed that of the 600 million people in China, there were about 30 million enemies of the people. His view was simple: 'We have so many people. We can afford to lose a few. What difference does it make?' He applied the same thinking to the atomic bomb. He made a speech saying that he was willing to lose 300 million Chinese people in atomic war. This would be half the population, but would be no great loss as the country could always produce more people.[34]

This combination of large-scale thinking and lack of moral restraints enabled Mao to aim for the total reconstruction of life in China, not just of the economy and agriculture. Mao saw the Chinese people as a tabula rasa, which pleased him: 'A blank sheet of paper has no blotches, and so the newest and most beautiful words can be written on it, the newest and most beautiful pictures can be painted on it.'[35]

Mao loved upheavals and the whole world was to be turned upside down. The smashing of the temples and the burning of the books were only part of the destruction of the country's culture. Traditional songs were banned. Feasts and weddings were discouraged. Traditional religious festivals and rituals were forbidden. The ploughing over of ancestral tombs symbolized the repudiation both of the past and of the family. As the *China Youth Journal* said, 'The framework of the individual family, which has existed for thousands of years, has been shattered for all time . . . We must regard the People's Commune as our family and not pay too much attention to the formation of a separate family of our own.'[36]

Mao believed in the total reconstruction of human life. Ruthlessly, he transformed society and all its institutions. Conflict and upheaval were to keep the new China from rigidity and fossilization. With unsurpassed thoroughness, he set out to transform the people who made up the society. Even their inner lives, their beliefs and emotions, were to be made to fit with the theory. And those who resisted would be outcasts: humiliated, enslaved, 're-educated' or killed.

Jung Chang, who saw some of the consequences of Mao's theories at close quarters, reflected on them:

> In the days after Mao's death, I did a lot of thinking. I knew he was considered a philosopher, and I tried to think what his 'philosophy' really was. It seemed to me that its central principle was the need – or the desire? – for perpetual conflict. The core of his thinking seemed to be that human struggles were the motivating force of history and that in order to make history 'class enemies' had to be continuously created *en masse*. I wondered whether there were any other philosophers whose theories had led to the suffering and death of so many.[37]

CHAPTER 31

Overturning the Basket: Cambodia

The Khmer methods do not require a large personnel, there are no heavy charges to bear because everyone is simply thrown out of town. If we may take the liberty of making a comparison, the Khmers have adopted the method which consists in overturning the basket with all the fruit inside; then, choosing only the articles that satisfy them completely, they put them back in the basket. The Vietnamese did not tip over the basket, they picked out the rotten fruit. The latter method involves a much greater loss of time than that employed by the Khmers.

Khmer Rouge official, *Prachachat*, 10 June 1976, quoted in
François Ponchaud, *Cambodia Year Zero*

The Khmer Rouge overturned the basket when they captured Phnom Penh. The people who lived there, including the old and the ill, women and children, were simply thrown out of town. One couple gave away their baby, who they knew would not survive the journey. Mercy was shown to no one:

I shall never forget one cripple who had neither hands nor feet, writhing along the ground like a severed worm, or a weeping father carrying his ten-year-old daughter wrapped in a sheet tied round his neck like a sling, or the man with his foot dangling at the end of a leg to which it was attached by nothing but the skin.[1]

Sometimes a family was told that if they did not leave their house a grenade would be thrown into it. One of the Khmer Rouge described what they did: 'We went to Phnom Penh to search for enemies hidden there, and drive the people out . . . We were told to tell people to leave for three days, and that then they could return. We were told to shoot people who refused. Our group shot 2 or 3 families north of Daeum Thkou market.'[2]

For two days without respite the staff at the French hospital of Calmette were made to operate on Khmer Rouge wounded. Afterwards everyone, including the patients, was thrown out and the medicine cupboards were smashed with rifles. In other hospitals, too, patients had to go, whether in their bandages or pushed on hospital beds with drips still attached. Murray Carmichael, an anaesthetist, described the ruin of his team's work for patients: 'We taught them to walk again, put them on traction and got some unity into their bones. The Khmer Rouge told them to leave in ten minutes. These people have no compassion, no humanity. They are just here to do it their own way and it's nasty.'[3]

People in towns were evacuated, including nearly 2 million in Phnom Penh. Some of the refugees were made into an example. One morning twenty young men with long hair were arrested and shot before the other refugees. Another time a man tried to argue about something: 'The Khmer Rouge cut off his head before my eyes and left the body lying in the road. Nobody dared to touch it for fear of reprisals.'[4] Perhaps 10,000 died during the evacuation of Phnom Phen.

Those marched into the countryside faced near-starvation. Sometimes they were reduced to eating snails or the banana stems usually fed to pigs. In Battambang a lot of rice was produced, but it was kept for the Khmer Rouge. The evacuated people had only the bran, which caused many to die of food poisoning. In 1976 there was a good rice harvest, but it was put in state storehouses instead of being given to the famine-stricken peasants.

The evacuees also faced disease through lack of sanitation and lack of filtered water. Many died of malaria, dysentery or fever. On the march, one hot and thirsty seven-year-old boy drank from a pond by the road. 'An hour later he was taken with dreadful stomach pains which nobody could relieve. He died during the night.' The Khmer Rouge killed anyone among the evacuees suspected of having worked for the previous government. On a farm near Phnom Thom a whole company of soldiers was massacred with their wives. The children cried as they watched, and were told not to cry over enemies: 'if you don't stop we'll kill you too'.[5]

Many were set to work. Propaganda on the radio suggested that before dawn the worksites resounded with the joyful cries of the peasants going to work: 'The earth may be hard as stone and the sun may burn, but nothing can stop the ardent war of production which consumes like a flame.'[6]

The work was indeed gruelling. There was a compulsory twelve-hour working day, which could extend to fifteen hours. Sometimes people were worked to death: 'We didn't have any oxen so we formed a team of eight men to pull the plough. Several of my comrades, exhausted by this work, began spitting blood and died.'[7]

The American Bombing and the Khmer Rouge Victory

In 1969 the Khmer Rouge numbered only about 4,000. By 1975 their numbers were enough to defeat the government forces. Their victory was greatly helped by the American attack on Cambodia, which was carried out as an extension of the Vietnam War. In 1970 a military coup led by Lon Nol, possibly with American support, overthrew the government of Prince Sihanouk, and American and South Vietnamese troops entered Cambodia.

One estimate is that 600,000 people, nearly 10 per cent of the Cambodian population, were killed in this extension of the war.[8] Another estimate puts the deaths from the American bombing at 100,000 peasants.[9] From 1972 to 1973, the quantity of bombs dropped on Cambodia was well over three times that dropped on Japan in the Second World War.

The decision to bomb was taken by Richard Nixon and Henry Kissinger and was originally justified on the grounds that North Vietnamese bases had been set up in Cambodia. The intention (according to a later defence by Kissinger's aide, Peter W. Rodman) was to target only places with few Cambodians: 'From the Joint Chiefs' memorandum of April 9, 1969, the White House selected as targets only six base areas minimally populated by civilians. The target areas were given the codenames BREAKFAST, LUNCH, DINNER, SUPPER, SNACK and DESSERT; the overall programme was given the name MENU.' Rodman makes the point that SUPPER, for instance, had troop concentrations, anti-aircraft, artillery, rocket and mortar positions, together with other military targets.[10]

Even if relatively few Cambodians were killed by the unpleasantly named items on the MENU, each of them was a person leading a life in a country not at war with the United States. And, as the bombing continued, these relative restraints were loosened.

To these political decisions, physical and psychological distance made their familiar contribution. Roger Morris, a member of Kissinger's staff, later described the deadened human responses:

> Though they spoke of terrible human suffering reality was sealed off by their trite, lifeless vernacular: 'capabilities', 'objectives', 'our chips', 'giveaway'. It was a matter too of culture and style. They spoke with the cool, deliberate detachment of men who believe the banishment of feeling renders them wise and, more important, credible to other men . . . They neither understood the foreign policy they were dealing with, nor were deeply moved by the bloodshed and suffering they administered to their stereotypes.[11]

On the ground the stereotypes were replaced by people. In the villages hit by bombs and napalm, peasants were wounded or killed, often being burnt to death. Those left alive took refuge in the forests. One Western observer commented, 'it is difficult to imagine the intensity of their hatred towards those who are destroying their villages and property'.[12] A raid killed twenty people in the village of Chalong. Afterwards seventy people from Chalong joined the Khmer Rouge.

Prince Sihanouk said that Richard Nixon and Henry Kissinger created the Khmer Rouge by expanding the war into Cambodia. The Khmer Rouge themselves understood this: one of them said that the villagers would

> sometimes literally shit in their pants when the big bombs and shells came . . . Their minds just froze up and they would wander around mute for three or four days. Terrified and half-crazy, the people were ready to believe what they were told . . . That was what made it so easy for the Khmer Rouge to win the people over . . . sometimes the bombs fell and hit little children, and their fathers would be all for the Khmer Rouge.[13]

The Origins of the Expulsion from the Cities

Why did the Khmer Rouge drive people out of the cities? Several different reasons were given: one was fear of renewed American bombing; another was the difficulty of transporting food to feed the large population of a city like Phnom Penh. Although these reasons may have played a part, they were not the whole story. Many of those in Phnom Penh were refugees who would have left when the war stopped, and there were stocks of rice unused and rotting after the Khmer Rouge victory. Rice was sent to China in exchange for weapons. Other towns and even villages were emptied, without the pretext that they had populations too large to feed.

A more important reason given was the destruction of the power of enemies of the Revolution. In a speech in July 1975 Pol Pot spoke of the need to 'eliminate saboteurs who attempt to destroy our revolution'. The slogan was 'Dry up the people from the enemy'. One Khmer Rouge journal said that the evacuation of Phnom Penh had saved the Revolution from subordination to private property. After the evacuation, 'the bourgeoisie have nowhere to go. They have been forced into carrying out manual labour as peasants.'[14] Driven out into the country, people were easier to control and would find it harder to create any unified opposition.

Most fundamentally, the Khmer Rouge wanted to sweep away city life itself in favour of a redesigned rural society. City people were seen as workshy and immoral exploiters. As one Khmer Rouge political official said, 'The city is bad, for there is money in the city. People can be reformed but not cities. By sweating to clear the land, sow and harvest crops, men will learn the real value of things. Man has to know that he is born from a grain of rice!'[15] Those driven out of the cities were called the 'new people', a sign of their status as people to be transformed.

Maoism and Beyond: the Year Zero

Sweeping away city life meant that under the new regime 95 per cent of people lived and worked on collective farms. The economy was to be totally reconstructed around agriculture. There was a nationalist agricultural myth that by means of intensive irrigation the old Angkor Kingdom had enabled Cambodia to have a second annual harvest in the dry season. The Khmer Rouge believed this and intended to repeat the project. In a spirit of Maoist voluntarism, irrigation and agriculture were to be transformed by the hard work of huge numbers of people.

The Khmer Rouge, like Mao, wanted to re-create the whole of life and so set out to destroy the whole of the traditional culture. It was 'Year Zero': a totally fresh start to history. The 1976 *Four-Year Plan to Build Socialism in All Fields* said, 'Continue the struggle to abolish, uproot, and disperse the cultural, literary and artistic remnants of the imperialists, colonialists, and all of the other oppressor classes.'[16]

This meant the elimination of traditional musical instruments. Furniture had to go. The traditional houses on stilts were replaced by rows of bungalows. Eliminating Western influence meant the destruction of medicines, gramophone records and especially books. Books from the French Far Eastern School were burnt and François Ponchaud saw several trucks filled with books go past the French Embassy. 'I also saw the books from the cathedral library burning on the lawn.' Foreign influence was to be eliminated in a policy of determined total independence. International food relief was refused and the country was completely sealed off.

Private property, markets and money were all to be eliminated. The Khmer Rouge's ultimate concern was the purity of the society. As one document put it, 'if we use money it will fall into the hands of individuals . . . If the money falls into the hands of bad people or enemies, they will use it to destroy our cadres by bribing them . . . Then in one year, ten years, twenty years, our clean Kampuchea will become Vietnam.'[17]

Religion was to be eliminated. One early order from the Central Committee was for the destruction of Phnom Penh's Christian cathedral. The traditional marriage ceremony was abolished, as were all other Buddhist ceremonies, and temples were destroyed or profaned. The Khmer Rouge overturned statues of Buddha, often smashing them or urinating on them.

The idea of the family was attacked. People who were allowed to stay in their villages had to share everything, down to pots and pans. Communal meals for hundreds of families together were compulsory. Many families were split up, with men and women being forced to sleep in segregated communal dormitories.

The 'new people' had to be re-educated. The inhabitants of Prek Sangkar were watched carefully – anyone showing signs of discontent was 'constructed' through criticism at the evening meeting. Failure to reform meant being sent up the mountain for a week of hard labour. Children were taught to spy on the 'new people', who retreated into defensive silence. They were told that to hide anything about themselves would be punished by death: 'Everything must be clear between us, everyone must know everyone else as well as the image of his own face reflected in a mirror.'[18]

It was not only 'new people' who were targets. Factory workers and peasants were also put under psychological pressure to develop the approved outlook. In one factory the workers met in groups twice a day for education and self-criticism. Questions included, 'Are you in step with the revolution yet?', 'Are you still thinking about private property?' and 'Do you still miss your wife and children, have you given them up completely yet?'[19]

Despite their fierce spirit of national independence, the Khmer Rouge leaders saw themselves as Maoists. In 1957 a committee was set up to decide Party policy. Pol Pot later said, 'Comrade Mao [Zedong's] works and the experience of the Chinese revolution played an important role at that time . . . particularly under the guidance of Comrade Mao [Zedong's] works, we have found a road conforming with the concrete conditions and social conditions in our country.' Khmer Rouge documents often speak of their 'Great Leap Forward'. Pol Pot visited China in the early stages of the Cultural Revolution and was impressed. Two months after the capture of Phnom Penh, he visited Mao. Later Pol Pot described Mao's thought as a 'brilliant beacon' for revolutionaries. He said Mao was the most eminent teacher since Marx, Engels, Lenin and Stalin, and that in the Cambodian Revolution, 'we have creatively and successfully applied Mao [Zedong's] thought'.[20]

The influence of Mao's ideas on the Khmer project of reconstruction is clear. The wild optimism about agriculture was inspired by the voluntarist view that a huge effort by large numbers can overcome almost any obstacle. Voluntarism also said that political commitment mattered more than technology or skills. The Party's Four-Year Plan said, 'technology is not the decisive factor; the determining factors of a revolution are politics, revolutionary people, and revolutionary methods'. Pol Pot himself said, 'Formerly to be a pilot required a high school education – twelve to fourteen years. Nowadays, it's clear that political consciousness is the decisive factor.'[21]

As under Mao and Stalin, people were classified according to their origin. There were three categories. Those with 'Full Rights' were middle to poor peasants and workers: they had voting rights. People who were lower middle class or richer peasants were 'Candidates': allowed to say what they thought but not to vote. Capitalists and members of non-Cambodian minorities were 'Depositees': they were excluded from meetings and all civic activity. The old class divisions were to be eliminated: the forced exodus meant that people who were not peasants either died or in effect became peasants.[22]

The book burnings and attacks on temples were part of the Maoist idea of a total transformation of society. Attacks on religion and the family were the same as in China, as was the use of re-education to bring about fundamental changes of attitude.

The Khmer Rouge went further than the Chinese Revolution had done. Mao had not swept away all cities; nor had he tried to eliminate money; nor had he so thoroughly sealed off his country from foreign contact.

The Khmer Rouge and the Calculation of Consequences

As with the social experiments of Stalin and Mao, the case for all this was a consequentialist one. It was thought acceptable to destroy things people valued, such as the family, religion and the traditional culture. It was thought justifiable to kill so many and to put such pressure on those left alive. The belief was that these things would further the Revolution, which in turn would produce a state 'overflowing with harmony and happiness'.[23]

As with the policies of Stalin and Mao, the huge human costs were much more obvious than the benefits which were supposed to make them all worth while. Once again the causal links between present misery and future benefits were obscure. At the very least, the consequentialist calculations were wildly out.

As so often with social engineering, those doing the calculations of happiness became so immersed in means ('the Revolution') that they lost their grip on ends. The Khmer Rouge leaders had little feel for what other people really cared about. Pol Pot, introducing the Four-Year Plan, explained why one day in ten was to be set aside for leisure:

> Should the people rest, or not? According to our observations, working without any rest at all is bad for the health. There's not enough food for people to work all the time; and leisure increases one's strength. If a person doesn't rest, he gets very ill. It is a strategic objective to increase the strength of the people. Therefore, leisure must be considered to be basic.[24]

The Martian quality of these remarks is one clue to how things went so wrong.

But the greatest distortion in the Khmer Rouge's planning was the fact that, as far as they were concerned, many of the people in the country simply did not count.

Purity and the Fruit Basket

There was a lot of talk of 'purification', with political 'enemies' being likened to causes of disease. One report, probably by Pol Pot, said:

> there is a sickness inside the Party ... We cannot locate it precisely. The illness must emerge to be examined ... we search for the microbes without success. They are buried. As our socialist revolution advances, however, seeping more strongly into every corner of the Party, the army and among the people, we can locate the ugly microbes.[25]

The idea of tipping over the basket and only putting back fruit known not to be rotten was a shift to an initial presumption of guilt. Many revolutions, including the French, the Russian and the Chinese, have been obsessed with the elimination of 'traitors', but usually individuals or groups have been selected to be purged. The model of tipping up the basket goes a stage further by presuming that people are 'rotten fruit' unless they are specially selected as being sound.

Frequent emphasis was placed on the need for drastic measures to protect the purity of the Revolution from contamination by the rotten fruit. On the radio and at meetings the slogans echoed the theme: 'What is infected must be cut out', 'What is rotten must be removed', and 'It isn't enough to cut down a bad plant, it must be uprooted.'

Bertolt Brecht once mocked the moralizing exhortations of the Communist government in East Germany: if the people did not do better the government would dismiss the people and elect a new one. The Khmer Rouge leaders did not care if they were out of step with popular opinion. One early document brought Brecht's joke grimly to life. Discussing the state selling produce at a profit, the document says that this may be unpopular: 'There is a little friction with the people, but we can abandon the people, there is no problem.'[26] Some Khmer Rouge killed people because it was better to kill an innocent person than to leave an enemy alive. Another slogan was 'One or two million young people are enough to make the new Kampuchea!'[27] The rest could be dispensed with.

The Human Responses

When the Khmer Rouge captured Phnom Penh, François Ponchaud spent the first night talking to the newly arrived soldiers: 'Visibly, no ideology had yet made much of a dent in their reactions, which were those of the peasants we had known before. They hated nobody and had no very clear idea what they were fighting for.'[28]

But this innocence could be changed. Ith Sarin, who spent nine months with the Khmer Rouge, described the impersonal dedication they had to show to the group: 'The Organization continually guides them to try to get rid of "personal traits", individualistic aspects which they denounce as "reactionary traits", that in order to attain the highest, one must hold firm "an overall image" of the principle of collectivity.'[29]

In Mao's Cultural Revolution it was respect for dignity which suffered most: humiliation stood out from other forms of cruelty. Under Pol Pot, too, victims had their dignity trampled on and the cold joke played its familiar role. Those who did not respond to re-education and punishment were killed: they 'shared two metres of rice paddy' or were sent to 'make fertilizer'.[30]

But in Cambodia physical cruelty predominated over humiliation; it was mainly sympathy which was eroded or overridden. The psychology of the Khmer Rouge atrocities was one of willingness to kill and torture, partly created by stigmatizing and dehumanizing victims, as in the talk of 'microbes'. One Khmer Rouge document makes the sinister comment, 'Some of the filth of former classes remains; we will resolve this further.'[31]

Among those who had to carry out the brutal policies, sympathy was overcome by a training in cruelty. For this people were recruited as young as possible and separated from their families. François Bizot, a French ethnologist captured by the Khmer Rouge, saw the conditioning of very young children. He befriended a girl of about three whose father was marched away to probable death. He played with her and grew fond of her, but she was forced to attend indoctrination classes. Her smiling response to him was replaced by sullenness. One evening, looking him in the face, she tried to insert her finger between his ankle and the rope that bound him. Finding that she could, she called the guard to tighten the ropes. This became a regular spiteful routine, a demonstration of the vulnerability of children to conditioning in cruelty.[32]

Prince Sihanouk understood the value of this to the Khmer Rouge: 'Pol Pot and Ieng Sary quite rightly thought that if they trained their young recruits on cruel games, they would end up as soldiers with a love of killing and consequently war.' Sihanouk saw the process at close quarters. For three years he watched the Khmer Rouge who guarded him 'constantly take pleasure in tormenting animals . . . The Khmer Rouge loved to make their victims suffer as much as possible.' They would kill dogs or cats with clubs or bayonets, or would play a game of throwing animals into 'the fires of hell'. Dostoyevskian atrocities were carried out against pregnant Vietnamese women. Sihanouk thought the cause was that for years the young men had entertained themselves with cruelty: they were 'addicted to torture'.[33]

Tuol Sleng

The obsession with enemies grew. Documents produced by the leadership were full of exhortations like 'our side for its part must have mastery in continuously blocking and intercepting, seeking out and scattering the enemy's traitorous networks in the future'.[34] It was suggested that struggle against enemies was to be a permanent feature of life: 'We must nurture this standpoint; that there will still be enemies in ten years, twenty years, thirty years into the future.'[35]

'Enemies' were to be made to confess and then killed. For this purpose camps were set up, of which the most notorious was Tuol Sleng, a large camp set up round a former school in Phnom Penh. As the anxiety about enemies infiltrating the Party grew, those sent to Tuol Sleng were increasingly 'traitors' from within the Khmer Rouge.

Tuol Sleng was a place of appalling cruelty. Written confessions were demanded. The interrogation was backed by solitary confinement and torture. Prisoners were chained naked to beds in small cells. Sometimes they were suspended upside down from a gallows. They were whipped, or nearly drowned, or exposed to reptiles. After confessing they were killed. All this was carried out bureaucratically. Each prisoner was photographed on arrival and at death. Voluminous written records of torture and interrogations were kept. The instructions to the torturers noted that secrecy about the prisoners' fate helped the interrogation: 'we do whatever is necessary to make them uncertain about the question of life and death so that they will still hope that they may survive'.[36]

Foreign prisoners had to obey the 'Regulations of Security Agents', including:

Don't try to escape by making pretexts according to your hypocritical ideas. It is strictly forbidden to contest me.

During the bastinado or the electrization you must not cry loudly.

Do sit down quietly. Wait for the orders. If there are no orders, do nothing. If I ask you to do something, you must immediately do it without protesting.

If you disobey every point of my regulations you will get either ten strokes of whip or five shocks of electric discharge.[37]

Kang Kek Ieu ('Comrade Deuch') imposed the rules of interrogation. Deuch's mother later said that he himself had probably been tortured during his three years in jail under Sihanouk, and that before, 'He was a good, respectful boy who helped his parents . . . He was something of a loner. He read a lot and seldom played with the other children in the village.' By the time he reached Tuol Sleng, he had become the kind of person his 'regulations' suggest. Ing Pech, one of the few Tuol Sleng survivors, said of him, 'He had a kind and gentle manner, but everyone was terrified of him. His favourite expression was "This man is bad and needs to be re-educated." When you heard that you knew Deuch meant tortured and killed.'[38]

A Culmination of Stalinism

16,000 people passed through Tuol Sleng. Perhaps 2 million were killed by the Khmer Rouge, out of a population of fewer than 8 million. The regimes of Stalin and Mao each killed many more people, but to kill around a quarter of the population seems like the culmination of Stalinism. Although there were features which made Pol Pot's Cambodia special – the degree of paranoia about enemies; the obsession with purity; and the related belief in tipping out the fruit basket to start again – these were developments of trends already visible under Stalin and Mao. The shared central project of the three regimes was the total redesign of society, in ways unrestrained by human feelings or morality. Without these, people who did not fit the plan could be redesigned or eliminated.

Behind these three Stalinist projects was the theory that such huge social experiments held some hope for humanity. This theory has, tragically, been tested to destruction.

CHAPTER 32

Utopia and Belief

The thinkers of the Enlightenment planned the rebuilding of society on rational lines. Religion and tradition were seen to have no authority to dictate what the future world should be like. Where they conflicted with human interests they should give way.

Pol Pot had almost certainly never heard of the Enlightenment. But he was indirectly influenced by it, if only through his reading of the Communist newspaper *L'Humanité*, in his student days in Paris. The 'philosophers', Stalin and Mao, were also probably barely aware of the Enlightenment and would have had little patience with its thinkers. Kant was on the reading list of the philosophy course which provoked Stalin to ask, 'Who uses all this rubbish in practice?' But Stalin and his heirs were in thrall to the Enlightenment. They accepted the Marxist version: the revolution which would bring about the reconstruction of society along 'scientific' lines, which would in the end give people better lives. Yet these leaders did not reflect much on what would constitute better lives.

In one way we cannot escape the Enlightenment. The authority both of religion and of tradition has been challenged by questions that cannot be answered or easily suppressed. So the shape of society can only be justified in the spirit of the Enlightenment: in terms of effects on people's lives. And some social redesigning can make people's lives better. The replacement of market forces in medicine by a National Health Service is not part of the 'road to serfdom'. A world ruled by market forces, with no diversion of resources to the poor, is one of lives avoidably stunted and shortened. The aim of shaping society so that the greatest human needs are put first is not one we should give up.

Communism, the major sustained attempt to put an extreme version of the Enlightenment outlook into practice, was a human catastrophe. This was not because of some peculiarities of Stalin or of people in the USSR. The pattern of the disaster, under Stalin, Mao and Pol Pot, was too similar for that.

The Stalinist Pattern

Stalin's Soviet Union, Mao's China and Pol Pot's Cambodia had many differences, but in all three versions the shared enterprise (here for convenience to be called 'Stalinist') had the same central defects.

It was grandiose: given our intellectual and imaginative limitations, the total reconstruction of society is not a project on a human scale.

It was rigid. It was not an empirical, tentative enterprise. There was no provision for the project being changed in the light of feedback about what was not working. Those giving such feedback risked hard labour or death.

It was coercive: a society directed from the top, imposed on people rather than freely chosen.

It was inhuman. It was not restrained by sympathy or by respect for individual people. Those who did not fit were to be 're-educated'.

It was crude in its view of the good life. Mixed with other motives was a genuine desire to improve people's lives. 'Socialism' and 'the revolution' were seen as holding out hope for mankind, but the picture of the good life was too uniform and too materialistic. People need the food, housing, medical care and goods which poverty often denies them, but beyond these are many needs which the Stalinist project was oblivious to. I will mention just two: a need for self-respect, which is hard to satisfy if you have to lie to your children to keep them out of trouble; and a need for a degree of autonomy in choosing your own version of the good life, which is hardly possible where the public project is so invasive.

The pattern of Stalinist faults is utterly familiar, but worth repeating because it gives clues to the underlying psychology.

Stalinism dominated society partly by terror. Out of fear, nearly everyone went along with the regime at least a little. The minimum was passive acquiescence: no one caught Nadezhda Mandelstam's eye. Dictators have always inspired such fear – except in its degree, Stalinist terror was no novelty.

Dominating society through Belief was Stalinism's original contribution. What marked it off from predecessor authoritarian regimes was its large-scale utopianism. And the distinctive psychology of the utopian project is that of Belief.

Parts of the pattern of Stalinism came from the psychology of Belief in general. Other parts came from the crudely consequentialist content of Stalinist beliefs.

Grandiosity, Rigidity and Belief

The grandiose side of the Stalinist project was linked to over-confidence in the system of belief. The Marxist account of the processes of economic and social change appeared to have the objectivity and authority of science. This gave believing Marxists a misplaced confidence in their ability to succeed in vast social transformations, which were thought of on the analogy with applied science, as in the comparison with a hospital basing its practice on the established teachings of pathology.

The rigidity also came partly from this over-confidence in the belief system. No feedback or modifications were needed because the theory gave all the answers in advance. (In this respect the 'scientific' approach was strikingly unscientific.) The rigidity also came from religious commitment to the cause. The 'political somersaults' carried out by Maurice Cornforth and others resulted from the need to hold rigidly to belief in the rightness of Soviet policy: 'If one loses anything of that faith . . . one is done for as a Communist and Socialist.' Faith is holding beliefs rigidly. Corrective feedback is irrelevant.

According to Marxist theory, beliefs are of little intrinsic importance. They are the product of material and economic causes and are at best of instrumental importance in furthering the new society. The impression comes across that the Believers did not always act on this. No doubt propaganda was used partly to induce conformity of behaviour, but its effectiveness at getting inside people (making Jung Chang feel guilty about regretting the removal of the 'bourgeois' grass and flowers) suggests its aims may have gone beyond this.

The widespread use of 're-education' shows the importance attached to what people believed. When Chin Yueh-lin was forced to say that the new philosophy, being scientific, was the supreme truth, it is hard to see that this was only to make him behave as his re-educators required. There are simpler ways to do that. The suspicion is that those who thought the new philosophy was the supreme truth really cared that he should come to think so too. Belief creates an urge to make new Believers. Paradoxically, those who created Thought Reform did so partly because they shared this unreformed piece of human psychology.

The Stalinist Version of Consequentialism

Stalinist coercion came from the simple-minded version of consequentialism which dominated the belief system. Traditional moral restraints were supposedly discredited by the belief that Marxism had shown them to have class origins. The goal of socialism was taken to justify whatever means, however cruel, were necessary to reach it. To hope to make a revolution without executions was impermissible weakness, pacifist illusion, and so on: you can't make an omelette without breaking eggs; surgery cannot be performed without spilling blood.

The inhuman side of Stalinism came from the same beliefs, which discredited the human responses as whimpering or rotten liberalism. Respect for people was replaced by the manufacture of Communist man out of the human material of the capitalist age. Sympathy was discredited: mercy to the enemy was cruelty to the people.

'The imagination and the spiritual strength of Shakespeare's evildoers stopped short at a dozen corpses, because they had no idcology.' Belief is not the whole story. Unlike Macbeth, Stalin commanded the bureaucratic and technical resources of a modern state. But Solzhenitsyn was right about the role of ideology. The ideology which purported to justify the terror in large part made it possible for the leaders to live with themselves while doing what they did.

Their inhuman side was reinforced by the way the belief system undermined people's moral identity by discrediting their values. There was the process of 'turning into wood' which comes over those who lose their sense of values. One value put under particular pressure by the hard and crude consequentialism was truthfulness. Lying in turn created pressures to slide over into self-deception, so that people's beliefs sometimes became a partly delusional system. A residual awareness of this can lead to an uneasy relationship with one's own beliefs, with further corrosive effects on the sense of moral identity.

Even someone who was not at all inclined to 'turn into wood', like Bukharin, had to live with the tension between his human instincts and the hard beliefs he defended. This tension, and the sense of moral identity it shaped, probably contributed to his impressive but paradoxical perform-ance at his trial. Even then, the struggle between his human side and the official hard consequentialism continued, without clear victory for either side.

The crudity of Stalinism also had its origins in the beliefs. The version of consequentialism was not only ruthless but also shallow. Socialism was thought of as a means to greater and more widely distributed material abundance and it was assumed that this was what the good life was about. As in Marx's thought, there was a lack of reflection about ends. The picture was not informed by much sense of the contours of human psychology. There was an obliviousness to the importance of self-respect and of autonomy, and to the variety of different conceptions of the good life.

And, perhaps above all, there was no idea that ends can themselves be tentative. As people pursue their goals, their values may change, or, through experience, they may come to think they have been mistaken about what matters most to them. This open-endedness of human values makes a whole society dominated by a single big idea particularly Procrustean.

The obvious message from the history of Stalinism is the importance of avoiding grandiose utopian social projects. But another message is as important. It comes from the role of ideology in Stalinism. We have seen how, for instance, tribalism makes atrocities possible by overwhelming the moral resources. Among such psychological dispositions, Belief is at least as dangerous as tribalism.

PART SIX

THE WILL TO
CREATE MANKIND ANEW:
THE NAZI EXPERIMENT

Those who see in National Socialism nothing more than a political movement know scarcely anything of it. It is more even than a religion: it is the will to create mankind anew.

Adolf Hitler, *Hitler Speaks*

dein goldenes Haar Margarete
dein aschenes Haar Sulamith

Paul Celan, *Todesfuge*

CHAPTER 33

The Core of Nazism

The numbers of people murdered by Stalin's tyranny far surpass those killed in the Nazi camps. The numbers of Mao's victims are yet greater. Pol Pot killed a far higher proportion of the population than Hitler did. Yet, even after thinking about Stalin, Mao and Pol Pot, to turn towards Hitler still seems to be to look into the deepest darkness of all. If we hope for a humane world, Nazism is what Nietzsche might have called our antipodes.

The Nazi policy towards the Jews was implemented by degrees. They were excluded from professions. Their shops were boycotted and attacked. They were stigmatized by vicious propaganda and forced to wear a yellow star. They were segregated. They were rounded up and deported in conditions of extreme cruelty. They were held in camps of unimaginable horror. And, in their millions, in a mechanized industrial form of killing, they – men, women and children – were systematically murdered.

How did Nazism, which led to all this, win so much support? In a mixture of great psychological power, it combined tribalism and belief.

Nazism's emotional power came from tribalism: the 'bent twig' resentful nationalism created by the outcome of the First World War. The sense of national humiliation was fertile ground for Nazism. The Nazi project of national renewal gave many people beliefs and the hope of glory. Its belief system was a mixture of Social Darwinism and ideas from Nietzsche. Social Darwinism gave 'scientific' authority to tribalism and from Nietzsche came a belief in will, strength and power, together with a rejection of Judaeo-Christian morality.

Nationalism and the Jews as Scapegoats

Any successful movement needs a message people are willing to hear, but some movements more than others are the creation of a particular leader. Hitler's ideas *were* Nazism and at their core was nationalism. This was the deepest appeal of the movement. Many of Hitler's followers shared his sense of resentment at Germany's defeat in the First World War.

There is a photograph of the Odeonsplatz in Munich at the outbreak of the First World War. Visible among the cheering crowd is a jubilant young Adolf Hitler. Later he described his feelings: 'I fell down on my knees and thanked Heaven from an overflowing heart for granting me the good fortune of being permitted to live at this time.' He described the transfiguring power of the war: 'For me, as for every German, there now began the greatest and most unforgettable time of my earthly existence. Compared to the events of this gigantic struggle, everything past receded to shallow nothingness.'[1]

After this, defeat and the imposition of harsh peace terms were a terrible humiliation. The strength of the resulting resentful nationalism can be glimpsed in a moment when the defeat was avenged. In 1918, at Compiègne, the German representatives had signed the Armistice terms in Marshal Foch's private railway coach. After the fall of France in 1940, Hitler dictated his terms to the French representatives. The ceremony was again held at Compiègne, in the same coach at exactly the same spot, this time with Hitler in Foch's seat. The CBS correspondent William Shirer saw Hitler arrive: 'I observed his face. It was grave, solemn, yet brimming with revenge ... There was something else, difficult to describe, in his expression, a sort of scornful, inner joy at being present at this great reversal of fate – a reversal he himself had wrought.'

Hitler read the inscription on the French memorial to victory over Germany in 1918. Shirer again looked at his face:

> I have seen that face many times at the great moments of his life. But today! It is afire with scorn, anger, hate, revenge, triumph. He steps off the monument and contrives to make even this gesture a masterpiece of contempt. He glances back at it, contemptuous, angry – angry, you almost feel, because he cannot wipe out the awful, provoking lettering with one sweep of his high Prussian boot. He glances slowly round the clearing, and now, as his eyes meet ours, you grasp the depth of his hatred. But there is triumph there too – revengeful, triumphant hate ... He swiftly snaps his hands on his hips, arches his shoulders, plants his feet wide apart. It is a magnificent gesture of defiance, or burning contempt for this place now and all that it has stood for in the twenty-two years since it witnessed the humbling of the German Empire.[2]

The anger visible in this moment had been there since 1918.

A common response to the defeat was to look for scapegoats. Hitler blamed the Jews for causing the war: 'That race of criminals has on its conscience the two million dead of the First World War, and now already thousands more.'[3] Hitler claimed that Jews took safe jobs as clerks instead of fighting and that they ruined the German economy: 'The spider was slowly beginning to suck the blood out of the people's pores. Through the war corporations, they had found an instrument with which, little by little, to finish off the national free economy.'[4]

Hitler also blamed the defeat on a stab in the back, the betrayal of those at the front by Jewish agitators for revolution. Boiling anger dominates *Mein Kampf*: 'It would have been the duty of a serious government, now that the German worker had found his way back to his nation, to exterminate mercilessly the agitators who were misleading the nation. If the best men were dying at the front, the least we could do was to wipe out the vermin.'[5]

The nationalism was tribal, based not on a shared culture but on racial unity. This excluded fellow citizens who were members of the 'alien' groups blamed for the stab in the back. The unity transcended national boundaries to include Austrians and the Sudeten Germans in Czechoslovakia. Hitler's hatred of cosmopolitan variety comes out in his reaction to inter-war Vienna: 'I was repelled by the conglomeration of races which the capital showed me, repelled by this whole mixture of Czechs, Poles, Hungarians, Ruthenians, Serbs and Croats, and everywhere, the eternal mushroom of humanity, Jews and more Jews.'[6]

Opposed to this cosmopolitan mixture, and also opposed to the fragmentation of the race into bearers of German, Austrian, Czech or Polish nationality, was the idea of the tribal nation-state. This required a sense of tribal identity, with favourable emotionally charged characteristics authenticated by a tribal narrative, which went back to Roman times. Tacitus wrote *Germania* in AD 98. In contrast with the decadence of Rome, he praised the rough, brave warrior tribes who lived in the inhospitable German forests.

One strand in the German tribal story is place: the German woods and forests. Tacitus emphasized the numinous quality of the forest and its role in German life: 'Their holy places are the woods and groves, and they call by the name of god that hidden presence which is seen only by the eye of reverence.' It was in 'a wood hallowed by the auguries of their ancestors and the awe of ages' that the Semnones gathered to make ritual human sacrifice.[7]

Tacitus thought that, because it 'either bristles with woods or festers with swamps', and had so little coast, Germany had not been much visited. This gave Germans a rare racial unity:

The Germans themselves, I am inclined to think, are natives of the soil and extremely little affected by immigration or friendly intercourse with other nations ... For myself I accept the view that the peoples of Germany have never been tainted by intermarriage with other peoples, and stand out as a nation peculiar, pure and unique of its kind. Hence the physical type, if one may generalize at all about so vast a population, is everywhere the same – wild, blue eyes, reddish hair and huge frames that excel only in violent effort.[8]

For some Nazis *Germania* was a sacred document. Heinrich Himmler liked the ideas of primordial roots and racial unity so much that in 1943 an SS unit took time out from the war to ransack an Italian villa in an unsuccessful search for the original text of *Germania*.[9]

The idea that the German people had distinctively pure roots had been revived with nineteenth-century nationalism. In 1807, in French-occupied Berlin, Johann Gottlieb Fichte had given his 'Addresses to the German People'. Fichte thought the Germans had a living language because they were primordial in a way other peoples were not. They had kept 'the primordial language of the ancestral stock', while most other languages had become mixed. Only in people with a living primordial language did philosophy influence life, only German philosophy could create the national consciousness which the age required. The German identity had to be preserved: 'If you go under, all humanity goes under with you, without hope of any future restoration.'[10]

Later in the nineteenth century the nationalist idea of Germans as primordial was bound up again with forests and trees. Simon Schama quotes one sociologist of the period as saying the woods were 'what made Germany German'.[11] The simple life and moral community of the woodlanders was set against the foreign influences of technology and industrial capitalism. Urban life, in an anti-Jewish phrase which uses another contrast with trees, was seen as breeding 'rootless cosmopolitan-ism'.

For the Nazis, as for Fichte and his nineteenth-century successors, the preservation of German identity was crucial. They too had a great interest in forestry and conservation, but they also had more sinister concerns. For them, the recent chapter in the national narrative was the 'stab in the back' in 1918. Their version of national self-assertion and renewal was, to use Schiller's tree image, the bent twig springing back. It required the avenging of 1918 and the seizing of Lebensraum, living space for a united German nation. It also required the exclusion of the Jews, who were supposedly responsible for the stab in the back.

Hitler's own memories of the 'stab in the back' were linked to his experience of poison gas. In October 1918 he had endured a British gas attack.

As early as midnight, a number of us passed out, a few of our comrades forever. Towards morning I, too, was seized with pain which grew worse with every quarter hour, and at seven in the morning I stumbled and tottered back with burning eyes ... A few hours later, my eyes had turned into glowing coals; it had grown dark around me. Thus I came to the hospital at Pasewalk in Pomerania, and there I was fated to experience – the greatest villainy of the century.

This 'villainy' was the revolution in Germany, which declared a republic and accepted defeat in the war:

Was it for this that these boys of seventeen sank into the earth of Flanders? Was this the meaning of the sacrifice which the German mother made to the fatherland when with sore heart she let her best-loved boys march off, never to see them again? Did all this happen only so that a gang of wretched criminals could lay hands on the fatherland?[12]

The gas attack influenced the imagery of Hitler's political thinking. He said a Social Democratic political tactic would succeed 'unless the opposing side learns to combat poison gas with poison gas'. It also influenced the content of his thinking: 'If at the beginning of the war and during the war twelve or fifteen thousand of these Hebrew corrupters of the people had been held under poison gas, as happened to hundreds of thousands of our very best German workers in the field, the sacrifice of millions at the front would not have been in vain.'[13]

The treatment of Jews originated only partly in the hatred and resentment felt by Hitler and by those who followed him. Nazi tribalism differed from other versions in having the backing of a supposedly 'scientific' system of beliefs. This was crucial in turning resentment into genocide.

The Belief System: Social Darwinism and 'Racial Hygiene'

Social Darwinism had continued to flourish in Germany. Together with Mendelian genetics, it was widely thought to provide a scientific basis for the eugenic 'Racial Hygiene' movement. Racial hygiene was conceived of as improving and protecting the gene pool of the race. In 1933 a leading advocate of racial hygiene became Rector of the University of Berlin. In his rectoral address, Professor Eugen Fischer said that Germany's new leadership was forcefully intervening in the course of history and the life of the nation, with 'a biological population policy, biological in this context signifying the safeguarding by the state of our hereditary endowment and our race'.

The plan for improving the racial gene pool was to encourage those with 'good' genes to have children and to discourage or prevent those with hereditary defects from doing so. It was championed by Fritz Lenz, Professor of Racial Hygiene at Munich, who thought that 'as things are now, it is only a minority of our fellow citizens who are so endowed that their unrestricted procreation is good for the race'.[14]

In 1933 the Nazis introduced a sterilization law, with compulsory sterilization for 'congenital mental defect, schizophrenia, manic-depressive psychosis, hereditary epilepsy, hereditary chorea, hereditary blindness, hereditary deafness, severe physical deformity, and severe alcoholism'. Fischer and Lenz were both involved in examining possible candidates for sterilization. Lenz was confident of his own assessment of people's genetic potential. He thought he could tell musical from non-musical people instantly by their appearance. Size of head showed degree of intelligence and size of chest showed degree of vigour. Genius required a head circumference of at least 56 centimetres. Great men tended to have long noses.[15]

Racial hygiene was partly motivated by the worry that modern society had eliminated natural selective pressures. Welfare stopped the poor from dying of starvation and medicine stopped the weak dying from illness. As a result, the genes of losers in the Social Darwinist struggle were no longer eliminated, but were transmitted to future generations.

Hitler believed in the natural selective pressures. He said that 'Nature' allowed unlimited procreation but then weeded out the weak. He also said that man tried disastrously to improve on Nature's method of keeping population growth in check:

> He is not carved of the same wood, he is 'humane'. He knows better than the cruel queen of wisdom. He limits not the conservation of the individual, but procreation itself . . . man limits procreation, but is hysterically concerned that once a being is born it should be preserved at any price . . . the natural struggle for existence is obviously replaced by the desire to 'save' even the weakest and most sickly at any price . . . but sooner or later vengeance comes. A stronger race will drive out the weak, for the vital urge in its ultimate form will, time and again, burst all the absurd fetters of the so-called humanity of individuals, in order to replace it by the humanity of Nature which destroys the weak to give his place to the strong.[16]

Another motive was more theoretical. The biologists and anthropologists who led the racial hygiene movement knew the evidence against Lamarck's view that acquired characteristics could be passed on genetically to future generations. They drew the conclusion that environmental changes could influence only one generation and so were relatively unimportant. They thought that genetic policies were the only strategy for lasting improvement.

This reasoning rests on the assumption that the only transmission from one generation to other generations is genetic. It overlooks cultural transmission. The influence of scientific discoveries, Darwin's, for instance, lasts for centuries. This is not because the knowledge is genetically passed on, but because it is preserved and transmitted in the culture. Overlooking cultural transmission was a mistake shared by both Stalinists and Nazi racial theorists. Lysenko thought the defence of progress through social change required Lamarck's theory that environmentally triggered improvements are passed on through the genes. Stalinism imposed this view in characteristic fashion. Nazi biologists scorned Lysenko and other Soviet Lamarckians, but, equally mistakenly, they thought that the falsity of Lamarck's view left eugenics as the only strategy for progress. The Nazis then acted on this in characteristic fashion.

Their eugenic policy centred on the so-called 'euthanasia' programme. This bore little resemblance to euthanasia as debated and sometimes practised in non-Nazi societies. The Nazi policy was not based on respect for autonomy, on the idea that an individual person may choose to die. Nor was it based on compassion for someone facing a terrible illness and unable to express a choice. Respect and concern for individuals did not come into it. The Nazis' aim was to 'improve' the 'race', to tidy up the world by killing people who did not fit the biological blueprint.

The unimportance of the individual was stressed by the theorists of the euthanasia programme, Professors Karl Binding and Alfred Hoche in their book *Permission for the Destruction of Worthless Life: Its Extent and Form.* Binding wrote, 'The relatives would of course feel the loss badly. But mankind loses so many of its members through mistakes that one more or less hardly matters.'

Following up this line of thought, Hoche made use of a chilling comparison between a disabled person and a defective bodily part:

> Viewed from the standpoint of a higher state morality, it cannot be doubted that the endeavour to sustain worthless life at all costs has been taken to excess. We have got out of the habit of regarding the state organism as a whole, with its own laws and requirements like, for example, a self-contained human organism which, as we doctors know, abandons and rejects individual parts which have become worthless or damaging.[17]

Nazi eugenics also aimed to produce a higher proportion of the 'right' sort of children. Part of this was the compulsory sterilization of people whom the Nazis thought had 'life of lesser value'. These included Klara Nowak, who was sterilized in 1941. Her hope had been to marry a farmer and to have a big family. Half a century later, she still felt the loss:

I had always wished for a large family. I was always thinking what I would do better in the upbringing of my children, different from how my parents had done it. That was my big wish, to have a lovely, healthy family . . . When nowadays my neighbours, older ladies, tell me about their grandchildren and great grandchildren, this hurts bitterly, because I do not have any children or grandchildren, because I am on my own, and I have to cope without anyone's help.[18]

As well as the sterilization of the 'wrong' sort of people, there was Heinrich Himmler's Lebensborn programme, which aimed at more births of the 'right' sort of children. Members of the SS were exhorted to have more children, especially sons. Lebensborn homes provided support for the resulting large families, and also for racially preferred single mothers. Another bizarre aspect of the programme was mentioned by Himmler, speaking of the Poles: 'Obviously in such a mixture of peoples there will always be some racially good types. Therefore I think that it is our duty to take their children with us, to remove them from their environment, if necessary by robbing or stealing them.'[19] About 200,000 Polish children were stolen as part of the programme. Even on the Nazis' racist and Social Darwinist assumptions, it is hard to believe that this side of the project can have seemed to have a solid scientific basis.

After racial improvement, the second goal of racial hygiene was the protection of the gene pool. This was a matter of preserving racial purity: of avoiding 'contamination' by genes of other races.

Eugen Fischer's early work had been on children of mixed race in South Africa. Their parents were Boers and Hottentots. Fischer said these children were of 'lesser racial quality' and he thought they should only be allowed to live as long as they were doing useful work.[20]

In 1939 Fischer applied his thinking to Germany:

When a people wants, somehow or other, to preserve its own nature, it must reject alien racial elements, and when these have already insinuated themselves, it must suppress them and eliminate them. The Jew is such an alien and, therefore, when he wants to insinuate himself, he must be warded off. This is self-defence. In saying this, I do not characterize every Jew as inferior, as Negroes are, and I do not underestimate the greatest enemy with whom we have to fight. But I reject Jewry with every means in my power, and without reserve, in order to preserve the hereditary endowment of my people.'[21]

The desire to tidy up anomalous groups which did not fit into the Nazi picture of a pure German race led to the attack on the other victim groups. Even the Nazis did not blame homosexuals or the Sinti and Roma peoples for the loss of the First World War.

The two projects of racial hygiene sometimes came together; the imagery used in connection with racial improvement could carry over to racial purity. Like Alfred Hoche, Konrad Lorenz used the analogy of defective bodily parts. Both men advocated racial 'improvement' by means of 'eliminating' people. Lorenz wrote in 1940:

> There is a certain similarity between the measures which need to be taken when we draw a broad biological analogy between bodies and malignant tumours, on the one hand, and a nation and individuals within it who have become asocial because of their defective constitution, on the other hand . . . Any attempt at reconstruction using elements which have lost their proper nature and characteristics is doomed to failure. Fortunately, the elimination of such elements is easier for the public health physician and less dangerous for the supra-individual organism, than such an operation by a surgeon would be for the individual organism.[22]

Ideas have consequences. The 'euthanasia' programme proved Lorenz right about how easy 'the elimination of such elements' was. The idea carried over from racial improvement to the project of racial purity. One of those involved in the process was Dr Fritz Klein. After the war, he was asked how he could reconcile his oath as a doctor with his work in Auschwitz. His reply echoed the thoughts of Binding and Hoche, and of Lorenz: 'Of course I am a doctor and I want to preserve life. And out of respect for human life, I would remove a gangrenous appendix from a diseased body. The Jew is the gangrenous appendix in the body of mankind.'[23]

The Belief System: the Dark Side of Nietzsche

The darker side of Nietzsche's ideas was incorporated into the Nazi belief system. Part of the link was straightforward: some things Nietzsche said were pure Nazi doctrine. His comments that 'The extinction of many types of people is just as desirable as any form of reproduction' and that 'the tendency must be towards the rendering extinct of the wretched, the deformed, the degenerate' could come from any work on racial hygiene.[24]

Nietzsche's central contribution was not these explicitly Social Darwinist views, but his rejection of the Judaeo-Christian morality of compassion for the weak. Self-creation required hardness towards oneself: a strong will imposing coherence on conflicting impulses. It also required hardness towards others. Conflicts between the self-creative projects of different people made inevitable the attempt to dominate others. The whole of life was a struggle in which victory went to the brave and to the strong-willed.

Noble human qualities, linked with the will to power, were brought out in combat but atrophied in peace. Compassion was weakness, cowardice and self-deception. The Judaeo-Christian emphasis on it was poison. In drawing these consequences from his beliefs about the death of God and from Social Darwinism, Nietzsche provided the part of the Nazi belief system which 'justified' the cruel steps they took to implement their other beliefs.

The title of Leni Riefenstahl's film *Triumph of the Will* caught the side of Nazism which echoed Nietzschean self-creation. German renewal was the self-assertion of a national will and those who took part in it were seen as creating themselves anew, their own wills growing strong as they triumphed over the constraints of a discarded morality.

The choice of conflict and hardness over compassion was central to the Nazi outlook. Hitler rejected 'the loathsome humanitarian morality', which he followed Nietzsche in seeing as a mask for people's defects: 'In the end, only the urge for self-preservation can conquer. Beneath it so-called humanity, the expression of a mixture of stupidity, cowardice, and know-it-all conceit, will melt like snow in the March sun. Mankind has grown great in eternal struggle, and only in eternal peace does it perish.'[25]

Hitler also followed Nietzsche in seeing humanitarian morality in terms of poisoning. The military collapse of 1918 was the consequence of 'an ethical and moral poisoning, of a diminution in the instinct of self-preservation and its preconditions, which for many years had begun to undermine the foundations of the people and the Reich'. For Hitler, unlike Nietzsche, the Jews were the chief poisoners: 'The nationalization of our masses will succeed only when, aside from all the positive struggle for the soul of our people, their international poisoners are exterminated.'[26]

In the more repulsive passages of Nietzsche there is always an element of ambiguity. Because of his views on truth, and because of his ironical and aphoristic style, it is always possible to wonder how literally he means comments about 'rendering extinct' certain groups of people. Sometimes it seems that his desire to shock makes him say things which seem outrageous in the safe knowledge that they will not be acted on. If this was his tactic, it was a dangerous one. It may have contributed to a climate in which dilettante followers also seemed daring by repeating the same ambiguously meant thoughts. But with the arrival of Hitler, the talk of extermination turned serious. The Führer said:

Today the old wives of the literary world are everywhere croaking at me, charging me with 'betrayal of the spirit'! And they themselves have been betraying the spirit to this day in their fine phrases. So long as it was just a literary pastime, they prided themselves on it. Now that we are in earnest with it, they are opening wide their innocent eyes.[27]

The Assault on the Moral Resources

To carry out the policies required by their nationalism, their Social Darwinism and their belief in 'racial hygiene', the Nazis had to overcome both the human responses to their victims and ideas about moral identity which were not adjusted to participation in mass murder.

As in Stalin's Russia and Mao's China, the social pressures were thrown into reverse. The moral resources were overwhelmed by pressures to believe, to obey and to conform. In addition, the Nazi belief system was effective in making people internalize them. Not only were people afraid: many also thought disobedience would be wrong.

The Nazis systematically attacked the human responses. They set out to erode the moral status of Jews, homosexuals and others, denying them the protection of respect for their dignity. In the spirit of what they took from Nietzsche, they worked to replace sympathy with hardness.

In withholding respect and sympathy from their victims, the Nazis again resembled the regimes of Stalin and Mao. What, most of all, set Nazism apart was the degree and thoroughness of its assault on moral identity. People were to be transformed. There was to be a new Nazi identity, rooted in an outlook actively hostile to the responses which constitute our humanity. Stalinism and Maoism were twisted forms of consequentialism. In them, hardness and inhumanity were defended, implausibly, as the supposed means to a more humane world. Nazism was a more fundamental assault on moral values. It was a twisted deontology: hardness and inhumanity were seen as desirable in themselves, aspects of an identity that expressed 'the will to create mankind anew'.

In Stalin's Soviet Union inner moral resources were overwhelmed by Belief. After Yugoslavia they were overwhelmed by tribalism. In Nazi Germany they were overwhelmed by a lethal combination of both. Because of their system of belief, the central Nazi psychological projects were the substitution of hardness for sympathy and the reconstruction of moral identity.

CHAPTER 34

Obedience and Conformity

The National Socialism of all of us is anchored in uncritical loyalty, in the surrender to the Führer that does not ask for the why in individual cases, in the silent execution of his orders. We believe that the Führer is obeying a higher call to fashion German history. There can be no criticism of this belief.

> Rudolf Hess, in a speech, June 1934

> Accurate scholarship can
> Unearth the whole offence
> From Luther until now
> That has driven a culture mad,
> Find what occurred at Linz,
> What huge imago made
> A psychopathic god:
> I and the public know
> What all schoolchildren learn,
> Those to whom evil is done
> Do evil in return.
>
> W.H. Auden, 'September 1, 1939'

In the early stages of the mass murder of the Jews, the Nazis used vans, killing their victims with the exhaust fumes. Gustav Laabs was a driver and saw naked people being herded into his van before the door was locked after them. He obeyed orders:

Then [Hans] Bothmann . . . ordered me to start the engine and let it run for ten minutes. I carried out this order and after about a minute I heard terrible cries and groans from inside the van. I got scared and leapt from the cab. Now I understood that the exhaust fumes had been fed into the inside of the van to kill the people. Bothmann then snapped at me asking if I had gone mad. He ordered me to get behind the steering wheel again. I sat behind the wheel again and waited. I didn't dare do anything because I was afraid of Bothmann. After a few minutes the cries and groans of the people gradually died away.

He then drove away, under Bothmann's orders, to a mass grave, in which about fifty bodies were dumped from the back of the van. Then, 'after the van had been cleaned and the grids put back, the police official . . . ordered me to drive to the ramp again. The same process which I have just described in detail repeated itself.'[1]

Many people, like Gustav Laabs, obeyed out of fear. Sometimes it was hard to resist the pressure to participate in cruel Nazi policies. But this is not the whole story. The same pressures also existed in Stalin's Soviet Union, but it is hard to avoid the impression that the idea of a duty to obey and conform was more strongly internalized in Nazi Germany. If so, there are various possible explanations. Perhaps more Germans were receptive to Nazi ideology than Russians were to Communist ideology. Stalin's victims were chosen so capriciously that no one felt safe. Perhaps 'ordinary' Germans (those who were not Jews, Communists, socialists or homosexuals) felt safer, and so were more willing to identify with the regime. Perhaps Nazi propaganda was more effective. Perhaps Russian traditions were less accommodating to obedience and conformity.

The Leader and the Magic of Authority

In Nazi Germany obedience was linked to acceptance of the Führer's authority. Acceptance was linked to Hitler's deliberately cultivated religious-style charisma, which was apparent in his speeches:

> Once you heard the voice of a man, and it spoke to your hearts, it awakened you, and you followed that voice. Year in, year out, you followed it, without even having seen the speaker; you only heard a voice and followed it. Now that we meet here, we are all filled with the wonder of this gathering. Not every one of you can see me and I do not see each one of you. But I feel you, and you feel me! It is faith in our nation that has made us little people great, that has made us poor people rich, that has made us wavering, fearful, timid people brave and confident.

The religious appeal worked. Among comments made about his speeches at rallies were these: 'His never-to-be-forgotten words affected me as the words of a prophet.' 'The experience was a revelation to us, and we should have rushed blindly anywhere Hitler commanded us to go. The sun shone all the time he was there, in proverbial "Hitler weather". Before his arrival and after he left, it rained so hard we were drenched.'[2]

The legend was carefully cultivated. The Nazi success with Keynesian policies to deal with unemployment was ascribed by propaganda to Hitler personally. Typical was one newspaper, which had a picture of a German worker and an autobahn, together with the text: 'Germany is working again. Everywhere hands are active in the common work! One people, one will, one deed! The German people has the Führer to thank for all that!'[3] Joseph Wagner said he was the greatest artist of all times. Robert Ley said he was the only man in history who never erred. Rudolf Hess said he was 'pure reason in human form'. And Heinrich Himmler said that from its earliest beginnings Aryan humanity had not produced anything to compare with him.[4]

One absent cultural tradition may have played a part. Although there were political satirists in the Weimar Republic, there seems to have been no widespread irreverence towards political leaders. In some places everybody laughs when someone says the Leader is pure reason in human form.

Obedience and Upbringing

Theodor Adorno and his colleagues studied the psychology of 'potential fascists': people identified as such by their answers to questionnaires about Jews and other topics. The study suggested that such people often have an 'authoritarian personality', typified by rigidity of thought and behaviour, an emphasis on power and will rather than imagination and gentleness, superstitious thinking, rigid adherence to conventional values and aggression towards those who violate them. A central feature is a submissive, uncritical attitude towards authority. Those who scored highly on tests for the authoritarian personality tended to report having had a stricter upbringing than those who had a low score. The high scorers more often reported having dominant and disciplinarian fathers. Punishment for breaking rules played a big role. Neither emotional warmth nor reasoning about moral principles figured much in the accounts. Their descriptions of their parents were submissive and uncritical, but praise of them seemed conventional rather than showing real warmth.[5]

The study on which these claims were based was carried out in the United States towards the end of the Second World War. There are obvious questions about extrapolating across cultures. Americans who gave 'fascist' answers to questionnaires are likely to have differed in many ways from the Germans, Austrians and others who actually obeyed Nazi orders. But the rigidity, superstition, obedience, conformity, aggression and the emphasis on power and will are all striking features of many leading Nazis. And, as one of the authors of the study pointed out, the suggestion that father-dominated families breed authoritarian attitudes could make it 'more understandable why the German family, with its long history of authoritarian, threatening father figures, could become susceptible to a fascist ideology'.[6]

Many leading Nazis had an authoritarian upbringing. Heinrich Himmler, some of the concentration camp commanders, and some of the others most involved in mass murder, had all been very strictly conditioned to absolute obedience. Alice Miller makes the striking claim that among all the leading figures of the Third Reich, she cannot find a single one who did not have a strict and rigid upbringing.[7]

One example is Rudolf Höss, the Commandant of Auschwitz:

> It was constantly impressed upon me in forceful terms that I must obey promptly the wishes and commands of my parents, teachers and priests, and indeed of all grown-up people, and that nothing must distract me from this duty. Whatever they said was always right. These basic principles on which I was brought up became part of my flesh and blood . . . In my parents' house it was insisted that every task be exactly and conscientiously carried out. Each member of the family had his own special duties to perform. My father took particular care to see that I obeyed all his instructions and wishes with great meticulousness. I remember to this day how he hauled me out of bed one night, because I had left the saddle-cloth lying in the garden instead of hanging it in the barn to dry, as he had told me to do.[8]

Hitler's own upbringing fits this pattern. He described his battle with his father Alois over his career plans. His father wanted him to be a civil servant and utterly opposed the idea of his being an artist. Despite this conflict, Hitler's comments on his father were praising, though in a distant, conventional way: 'He bought a farm, which he worked himself, and thus, in the circuit of a long and industrious life, returned to the origins of his forefathers . . . In my thirteenth year I suddenly lost my father. A stroke of apoplexy felled the old gentleman who was otherwise so hale, thus painlessly ending his earthly pilgrimage, plunging us all into the depths of grief.'[9]

Others gave more details about the upbringing Alois Hitler gave Adolf. A woman who worked in the house as a cook said Alois was very strict and had a terrible temper. His colleagues at work noticed his unprovoked bad temper. They said he was a 'demon' about punctuality. In the family, he insisted on silence. The children never dared to speak in his presence unless told to. They were not allowed to call him 'du', but had to call him 'Herr Vater'. He did not use the name Adolf to call his son, but instead put two fingers in his mouth and gave the whistle he used to call his dog. A close friend, who became Adolf's guardian after the death of Alois, said that 'the boy stood in awe of him . . . he was strict with his family. No kid gloves as far as they were concerned; his wife had nothing to smile about.' Hitler's half-brother talked about Alois's 'very violent temper', and how he often beat the dog until it urinated on the floor, often beat the children, and would sometimes beat his wife.

It goes without saying that the central features of the authoritarian personality (will, power and aggression, rather than imagination and gentleness) fit Hitler perfectly. But the rigidity was also present, even about small things. He took his dog for exactly the same walk every day, throwing a stick for it at exactly the same place in the same direction. Any suggestion of varying the routine made him agitated and angry.[10]

The Human Disposition to Obey

There is a widespread human willingness to obey even terrible orders. The evidence for this comes partly from other 'crimes of obedience', from My Lai to Mao's China. It also comes from the well-known psychological studies carried out in New Haven, Connecticut, by Stanley Milgram.[11] Volunteers for a psychology experiment were told that they were taking part in a study of the effects of learning. When the 'learner' gave a wrong answer, each participant was ordered to press a switch, having been told that this would give the 'learner' an electric shock. The 'learner' was attached to an electrode and strapped to a chair in the next room. (In fact, there were no electric shocks and the 'learner' was only acting the part.) Participants were made to think that, by pressing different switches, they were giving increasingly severe shocks, and the 'learner' acted as if this were so.

There were thirty switches, ranging from 15 to 450 volts. At 75 volts the 'learner' grunted. At 120 volts he protested. At 150 he demanded to be released from the experiment. As the voltage increased, the protests rose, reaching an agonized scream at 285 volts. Participants who hesitated were ordered to continue. Those asking for guidance were advised to continue after a brief pause. After the 315-volt 'shock', the victim kicked on the wall again, but the participant was ordered to continue right up to the maximum of 450 volts. To reach this apparent voltage, it was necessary to pull the switch through positions marked 'slight shock/moderate shock/ strong shock/very strong shock/intense shock/extreme intensity shock/ danger: severe shock/XXX 450 volts'.

Of the 40 participants, 26 continued all the way to the last shock on the generator. A number showed obvious signs of stress, suggesting that they really did believe they were obeying orders to inflict severe pain.

Some of the response to Milgram's work has concentrated on the question of whether experiments involving both deception of the subjects and exposing them to severe stress were ethical. These are real issues, but there is a danger that they may obscure the importance of the studies.

In Nazi Germany, the charismatic appeal of Hitler may have acted on people often conditioned to obedience by an authoritarian upbringing. But Milgram's 'experimenter' had no special magic, and there is no reason to think that people in New Haven in the early 1960s had been brought up in a very authoritarian way. The disquieting results of Milgram's studies suggest a widespread human tendency to give uncritical obedience to authority, even when the orders are appalling.

David Rosenhan repeated the Milgram study at Princeton. Eighty per cent of his subjects were fully obedient. The widespread tendency to obey was confirmed, but it was not universal. The kind of person someone is can make a difference. There is something satisfying about the fact that Ronald Ridenhour, who later blew the whistle on the massacre at My Lai, refused to give even the first shock.[12]

Conformity

In Nazi Germany there were 'vertical' pressures from superiors to obey terrible orders. There were also 'horizontal' pressures to conform with members of the group.

In July 1940 a police battalion was given the job of clearing the village of Józefów of Jews. Old people, women and children were sent to the forest to be shot by members of the battalion. Each victim was paired off face to face with a policeman. The major in charge gave members of the battalion a chance to opt out of the task. Out of 500 men, only a dozen took this chance. Some of those who took part later admitted that they did so out of fear of losing face with the others. As one put it, 'If the question is posed to me why I shot with the others in the first place, I must answer that no one wants to be thought a coward.' Some who started shooting were revolted and dropped out. But 80 per cent carried on all day, until 1,500 people had been killed.[13]

Pressures to obey and to conform can reinforce each other. Where there is less pressure to conform, people may be more willing to disobey. In one version of Milgram's study, twenty-six out of forty obeyed the orders to 'give' the shocks. When the experiment was varied by letting it be known that two refused to obey, the figures were reversed and only four of the forty obeyed.[14]

In the shooting at Józefów, those who dropped out did not find so many followers. The orders, this time real, were far more terrible. The pressures on the members of the police battalion were quite different. There were the effects of their training, together with fears that dropping out would be held against them. There was also their reputation with other members of the battalion: 'no one wants to be thought a coward'.

Often conformity was reinforced by the emotional charge which existed among groups of believing Nazis. Sometimes, as at the Nuremberg rallies, this was a matter of crowd psychology. In response to the hypnotic voice of Hitler, many felt the intoxication of submerging their individuality in co-ordinated mass action.

Sometimes, especially among the SS, more lasting emotional bonds grew out of this. The widow of Karl Fritsch (one of the most sadistic camp officers) described it: 'Once or twice they ... travelled specially to Nuremberg to hear Adolf Hitler. At some point it caught him, it seems. He became very enthusiastic ... Looking back, it seems that he discovered a new kind of friendship; it was very powerful. That friendship eventually became everything to him.'[15]

The emotional bonds could create a sense of regaining youth and self-respect. Hans Hüttig, Commandant of the concentration camp at Natzweiler, joined the SS under the influence of younger friends: 'It was as if they returned my youth to me. Gave me another chance. I loved to be in the company of young warriors. I felt that I had something to offer them, and of course, the officer's rank they promised me tempted me ... I found comradeship in the SS, and a new faith in myself, and that was worth more than money.' The male bonding could be a kind of love. Joseph Kramer worked at Dachau and at Auschwitz. His widow said of his Nazi work that 'this joint effort, the new faith, brought them closer to each other. They had something to give each other. When I thought about that years later I said to myself that my Kramer felt more comfortable among men than among women.' Johannes Hassebroeck, Commandant of the camp at Gross Rosen, said:

> even the ties of love between a man and a woman are not stronger than that same friendship there was among us. This friendship was all. It both gave us strength and held us together, in a covenant of blood. It was worth living for; it was worth dying for. This was what gave us the physical strength and courage to do what others did not dare to do because they were too weak.[16]

Obedience as a Virtue and a Vice

The excuse of 'obedience to orders' has been discredited because of its use by Nazis, notably Adolf Eichmann. Pressure to conform is no more impressive as an excuse. But there are hard questions about when to stand out against obedience and conformity, and about how much we can reasonably expect of people.

Criticism of the those in the Milgram study who obeyed is too easy. Of course the results are disturbing. They seem to be a laboratory demonstration of the obedience that implemented the Nazi horrors. One response is that the disposition to obey is a disastrous aspect of human psychology, something as far as possible to be eradicated. This is partly right, but also too simple.

Autonomy is inevitably limited. We have not the time or ability to think out for ourselves every decision. We need to take short cuts, and these include trusting authorities. Many things depend on some uncritical obedience. Surgeons need assistants who will obey without a lot of debate. The efficiency of the fire service, the army, the ambulance service, the police, or even an airline, depends on people surrendering some autonomy and most of the time obeying instructions. They have to assume their superiors are not guilty of outrageous blunders or moral enormities. Without such trust, social life would be difficult.

Thinking about the Nazis and about the Milgram study may incline us to abandon these short cuts, but that is unrealistic. The best approach may be to carry on with them, but with much more alertness to the possibility that they may go wrong. We need to abandon them as soon as they look like doing so.

There is a parallel with issues about civil disobedience and the authority of law. The smooth functioning of society depends on a strong general presumption in favour of obeying the law. In a democratic society the case for this presumption is greatly increased. Everyone has at least an indirect say in what the law should be. And there is the chance of changing it by democratic means. But, even in a democracy, obedience to the law is a presumption, not an absolute. If some outrageously immoral law is enacted, the case for civil disobedience may outweigh the presumption in favour of obedience. Laws have instrumental value, and do not command obedience by some magic of their own.

The same applies to more informal rules. Of course, in the operating theatre the surgeon's instructions should normally be obeyed immediately, but in the one in a million case where the surgeon cracks up and orders the patient to be killed, the order should, of course, be disobeyed. In armies, at least officially, there is recognition of this. Obeying orders is normally essential, but, when a war crime is ordered, disobedience is a right and perhaps a duty. Those taught in general to obey should also be taught the sentence written on the flyleaf of Bertrand Russell's family bible: 'Thou shalt not follow a multitude to do evil.'

Internalization and the Role of Belief

Nazi obedience was reinforced by fear. It was also supported by the general human disposition to obey, and by the rigid cast of mind perhaps created by an authoritarian upbringing. There was also the emotional appeal: the magic of Hitler's authority and the felt emotional bonds with comrades.

Normally, such influences would meet resistance from the moral resources. But these were at least partly discredited by the Nazi belief system. Nazi obedience came from belief in the authority of orders and in the moral duty to obey.

In his interrogation Adolf Eichmann suggested that his promise to obey orders made obedience morally obligatory:

> When I received an order, I obeyed. An oath is an oath. In the observance of that oath I was uncompromising. Today I'd never take an oath. No one could make me, no judge for instance, could make me take a witness's oath. I refuse; I refuse on moral grounds. Because I've learned by experience that if you let yourself be bound by an oath, you'll have to take the consequences someday.

And, asked about whether there were ways of circumventing Hitler's orders, he said, 'I can only say that no man is justified in circumventing an order.'[17]

It is not necessary to believe in Eichmann's sincerity. The impression left by his interrogation is of someone straining to belittle his own role. Responsibility was sometimes shifted to his juniors: clerks who drafted letters which he merely signed. Most often, it was shifted to his seniors. Against much evidence, he presented himself as the functionary who had merely obeyed orders to arrange some transport.

Eichmann used obedience to orders in trying to escape responsibility, but, at the time of his participation in the Nazi crimes, he really did believe in obedience. When Germany was defeated, the collapse of the system of orders which had shaped his life left him disoriented: 'I sensed I would have to lead a leaderless and difficult individual life, I would receive no directives from anybody, no orders and commands would any longer be issued to me, no pertinent ordinances would be there to consult – in brief, a life never known before lay before me.'[18]

For many others, as for Eichmann, obedience was not just from fear or in response to pressure. The commitment to obey was deeply internalized, underpinned by Nazi beliefs. Those who obeyed in Milgram's study were in a highly artificial situation. They obeyed on a single day, in isolation from the restraining influence of their family, friends, neighbours, and the people they worked with. Their situation was like that of police in Pinochet's Chile or Galtieri's Argentina, who tortured their victims in remote, private places. Those who obeyed Milgram's 'experimenter' might not have done so routinely over years. Going back each evening to their families in New Haven, and describing their day giving people massive electric shocks, might have awakened them. The moral resources – their own human responses and sense of their moral identity, as well as the aghast reactions of those around them – could impose restraints. Nazi obedience can only be fully understood in the context of the Nazi beliefs which weakened or discredited those restraints.

CHAPTER 35

The Attack on Humanity

A revaluation of values under whose novel pressure and hammer a
conscience would be steeled, a heart transformed to brass, so that it might
endure the weight of such a responsibility . . .
>Friedrich Nietzsche, *Beyond Good and Evil*, section 203

My pedagogy is hard. What is weak must be hammered away. In my
fortresses of the Teutonic Order a young generation will grow up before
which the world will tremble. I want the young to be violent, domineering,
undismayed, cruel. The young must be all these things. They must be able
to bear pain. There must be nothing weak or gentle about them. The free,
splendid beast of prey must once again flash from their eyes.
>Adolf Hitler, quoted in Alice Miller, *For Your Own Good:*
>*the Roots of Violence in Child-rearing*

Human responses to other people, the responses of respect and sympathy,
are the heart of our humanity. Under Stalinism the human responses were
repressed on instrumental grounds. With extreme implausibility, this
repression of people's humanity was claimed to be the route to a more
humane world. In Nazi Germany the demand that the young should be
violent, domineering and cruel was not merely instrumental. The attack on
people's humanity was carried out partly for its own sake.

The Stripping of Dignity and of Human Status

The Nazis stripped their victims of protective dignity. They were
distanced and so pushed outside the boundaries of the moral community.
   People can be made psychologically distant by impersonal ways of
talking about them. The SS insisted that those in the camps had to be
called 'prisoners', rather than 'men' or 'women'. There is a bureaucratic
way of thinking and talking, which could be found in the Nazi 'euthanasia'

programme. In 1939 Victor Brack chaired a meeting which discussed who should be killed in the programme. The minutes report him as saying:

> The number is arrived at through a calculation on the basis of a ratio of 1,000:10:5:1. That means out of 1,000 people 10 require psychiatric treatment; of these 5 in residential form. And, of these, one patient will come under the program. If one applies this to the population of the Greater German Reich, then one must reckon with 65–75,000 cases. With this statement the question of 'who?' can be regarded as settled.[1]

Jews were marked off as different by being forced to wear the yellow star. This denied them normal human claims. In Vienna a Jew with an artificial leg (the result of a First World War disablement) fell over on an icy pavement. For three hours he asked passers-by to help him, but they all left him there. He broke his wrist when he finally managed to raise himself.

Hostile stereotypes were used, as in the cartoons in *Der Stürmer*. These cartoons are at the edge of one of the most extreme forms of distancing: the suggestion that some people are not even human.

Sometimes people are dehumanized by being thought of as animals. The milder, implicit version of this is to withdraw from them the normal distinguishing marks of respect for other humans. It strips away the protection of human status, but without suggesting any specific animal likeness. The stronger, explicit, version is positively to identify people with unattractive species of animals.

The implicit form of dehumanizing can be seen in the Nazi 'euthanasia' programme for mental patients. A nurse described one of the first transports, from the asylum at Jestetten:

> The senior sister introduced the patients by name. But the transport leader replied that they did not operate on the basis of names but numbers. And in fact the patients who were to be transported then had numbers written in ink on their wrists which had been previously dampened with a sponge. In other words, the people were transported not as human beings but as cattle, though without any maltreatment.[2]

The use of cattle trucks to transport victims came later. Within the camps, treatment as animals was common. Partly because of language difficulties, the guards often conveyed things to the prisoners, as with animals, by violence rather than words.[3] Victims of the appalling medical experiments were thought of as laboratory animals. The I.G. Farben Chemical Trust wrote to Auschwitz:

> In contemplation of experiments with a new soporific drug, we would

appreciate your procuring for us a number of women ... We received your answer but consider the price of 200 marks a woman excessive. We propose to pay not more than 170 marks a head. If agreeable, we will take possession of the women. We need approximately 150 ... Received the order of 150 women. Despite their emaciated condition, they were found satisfactory ... The tests were made. All subjects died. We shall contact you shortly on the subject of a new load.[4]

Explicit comparison with animals was used in the propaganda against Jews. One SS pamphlet drew on the creatures of nightmares:

From a biological point of view he seems completely normal. He has hands and feet and a sort of brain. He has eyes and a mouth. But, in fact, he is a completely different creature, a horror. He only looks human, with a human face, but his spirit is lower than that of an animal. A terrible chaos runs rampant in this creature, an awful urge for destruction, primitive desires, unparalleled evil, a monster, subhuman.[5]

Much Nazi propaganda likened opponents and victims to repulsive real forms of life. Nazi films intermingled shots of Jews with shots of rushing hordes of rats. Hans Frank, when Governor of Poland, called it a country 'which is so full of lice and Jews'. And Hitler wrote about Vienna after the First World War: 'Was there any form of filth or profligacy, particularly in cultural life, without at least one Jew involved in it? If you cut even cautiously into such an abscess, you found, like a maggot in a rotting body, often dazzled by the sudden light – a little Jew!'[6]

Lice and vermin also carry disease. It was a common Nazi device to liken Jews to dirt, to disease-bearing creatures, or to disease itself. When Jews were driven out of a place it was said to be 'Judenrein': clean of Jews. Hitler himself again provides an extreme case. In conversation over dinner one evening, he said, 'The discovery of the Jewish virus is one of the greatest revolutions that have taken place in the world. The battle in which we are engaged today is of the same sort as the battle waged, during the last century, by Pasteur and Koch. How many diseases have their origin in the Jewish virus! ... We shall regain our health only by eliminating the Jew.'[7] Those who took part in excluding and murdering Jews used these images as part of their self-justification. Friedrich Uebelhoer, ordering the setting up of a ghetto in Lodz, said that 'we must burn out this bubonic plague'.[8]

These stereotypes were images rather than literal beliefs. Hitler did not literally think Jews were viruses or maggots. (The question of whether he was mad would have been easier to answer if he had.) Such images and metaphors create a psychological aura or tone which once again may be at least as important as explicit beliefs which can be criticized as untrue.

Humiliation

These attempts to think them out of the human race meant Jews were humiliated in countless ways which reflected this loss of moral standing.

In a discussion in 1938 about trains, Goebbels and Goering expressed their desire to humiliate Jews. Goering proposed that the trains should have a segregated coach for Jews.

> GOEBBELS: Suppose, though, there aren't many Jews going on the express train to Munich, suppose there are two Jews on the train and the other compartments are overcrowded. These two Jews would then have a compartment all for themselves. Therefore, I say, Jews may claim a seat only after all Germans have secured a seat.
>
> GOERING: I'd give the Jews one coach or one compartment. And should a case like you mention arise and the train be overcrowded, believe me, we won't need a law. We'll kick him out and he'll have to sit all alone in the toilet all the way![9]

These cruel fantasies became reality. One American journalist described the scenes when the Nazis took over Vienna:

> On the streets today gangs of Jews, with jeering storm troopers standing over them and taunting crowds around them, on their hands and knees scrubbing the Schuschnigg signs [Schuschnigg was the former Chancellor of Austria] off the sidewalks. Many Jews killing themselves . . . Jewish men *and* women made to clean latrines . . . The wife of a diplomat, a Jewess, told me today she dared not leave her home for fear of being picked up and put to 'scrubbing things' . . . We had been told that the Jews had been made to scrub out the toilets with the sacred praying bands, the *Tefillin*.[10]

The humiliation was often a prelude to something even worse. When a police battalion entered Bialystok in June 1941, they drove Jews out of their quarter of the town, beating and shooting them. Some religious Jews had their beards set alight. When Jewish leaders went to beg a general for army protection, one member of the police battalion urinated on them. This stripping of protective dignity breached a moral barrier, making it easier to go the whole way in atrocity. All that day in Bialystok, Jews were shot. Over 700 were herded into the synagogue. Petrol and a grenade ensured that they were all burnt alive.[11]

The Cold Joke and Desecration

There is a distinctive Nazi laughter which echoes a remark of Nietzsche's: 'Laughter means: being *schadenfroh* but with a good conscience.'[12] Goebbels wrote of having 'enough courage to destroy, laughingly to shatter what we once held holy, such as tradition, upbringing, friendship and human love'.[13] Eichmann said that the feeling of having killed 5 million enemies of the state had given him so much satisfaction that he would jump laughingly into the grave.

The contemptuous laughter went with the cold joke. In the camp at Majdanek at the end of 1943 a huge increase in killings was described as a 'harvest festival'. In Treblinka the road to the gas chambers was known as the 'Himmelweg', or road to heaven. The cold joke is a display of power over its victims. It is also a way of easing the conscience, both by making light of what is being done and by a flaunting display of the joker's own hardness in the face of the claims of compassion.

The cold joke is not always verbal. And it can be deadly. In one company of a police battalion guarding the Warsaw Ghetto, shooting Jews was treated as a sport. In the bar a mark was made for each Jew killed, with celebrations when the numbers were large. The same grim playfulness appeared in the death camps, as one victim testified at Eichmann's trial: 'On Sundays there was no work, and we were placed in a row; each man had a bottle on his head, and they amused themselves by shooting at the bottles. When the bottle was hit, the man survived, but if the bullet landed below the target, he had had it.'[14]

The cold joke is related to desecration. When victims are seen as less than human, the murderers find it hard to treat their remains with respect. The cold joke was used to deny the dignity of the 'euthanasia' victims. When the thousandth corpse was cremated, one of the Nazi staff dressed as a clergyman and gave a parody of a funeral address. Any serious funeral would have been a reminder of the victims' humanity.

The Nazis carried dehumanizing to relentless extremes after death. Women's hair from Auschwitz was sold for making mattresses. Recognizable human ashes from the crematoria, often containing teeth or vertebrae, were used as thermal insulation between wooden walls, as fertilizer, and instead of gravel for the paths of the nearby SS village. It is hard to believe the main motive was economic. As Primo Levi put it, this treatment 'was intended to declare that these were not human remains, but indifferent brute matter, in the best of cases good for some industrial use'.[15]

In the death camps the Nazis turned the cold joke into an art form, with increasingly imaginative embellishments on the themes of cruelty and humiliation. At Auschwitz and also at a camp in Lvov Jewish prisoner musicians were put into an orchestra. Knowing that their own stay of execution was only temporary, they were forced to play cheerful music, particularly the tango, while graves were being dug or people were being shot. In 'Todesfuge', Paul Celan wrote of this:

he whistles his hounds to come close
he whistles his Jews into rows has them shovel a grave in the ground

he commands us play up for the dance . . .[16]

The ramifications of the cold joke were endless. Christian Wirth commanded the 'Clothing Works' at Lublin, where starving Jews were worked to death sorting the clothes of those already killed. Wirth's victims were allowed no hope for their own lives. They also knew there was no hope of their line being continued, as the children had been removed and killed. Wirth allowed one exception, as a cold joke of his own. One Jewish boy aged about ten was given sweets and dressed up as a little SS man. Wirth and he rode among the prisoners, Wirth on a white horse and the boy on a pony, both using machine-guns to kill prisoners (including the boy's mother) at close range.[17] To this ultimate expression of contempt and mockery, no reaction of disgust and anger is remotely adequate.

Circles of Confirmation

Seeing some people as less than human can create conditions which seem to confirm that view. In the Warsaw Ghetto the Nazis' linking of Jews with disease led them to post notices that it was an area threatened by typhus. The imposed conditions of starvation, overcrowding and filth soon created epidemics of typhus and other fevers.

People going to the camps were crushed together in freight cars without lavatories for a journey which could take days or weeks. Sometimes they would be let out for a short time to relieve themselves. Primo Levi describes the response when this happened during a stop at a station in Austria.

> The SS escort did not hide their amusement at the sight of men and women squatting wherever they could, on the platforms and in the middle of the tracks, and the German passengers openly expressed their disgust: people like this deserve their fate, just look how they behave. These are not *Menschen*, human beings, but animals, it's clear as the light of day.[18]

In the camps the inmates were partly stripped of their human appearance. This made things easier for those in charge, by confirming the belief that they were sub-human. Rudolf Höss, asked by his brother-in-law what the term *Untermensch* meant, replied, 'Look, you can see for yourself. They are not like you and me. They are different. They look different. They do not behave like human beings.' Ruth Kalder, the widow of another of the camp commanders, still thought in this way in 1975, saying in an interview, 'They were not human like us. They were so foul.'[19]

The policy of selecting prisoners to run the crematoria may also have served to confirm the Nazi view of the prisoners. As Levi again puts it: 'it must be shown that the Jews, the sub-race, the sub-men, bow to any and all humiliation, even to destroying themselves'. The message was 'we can destroy not only your bodies but also your souls'.[20]

In these ways the Nazis denied any moral standing to their victims. They convinced themselves that there was no dignity there to respect. The removal of this barrier helped to make the killings possible. Years later Franz Stangl, the Commandant of Treblinka, was asked, 'Why, if they were going to kill them anyway, what was the point of all the humiliation, why the cruelty?' His answer was, 'To condition those who actually had to carry out the policies. To make it possible for them to do what they did.'[21]

Hardness, not the 'Weakness' of Compassion

As well as undermining respect for the dignity of their victims, the Nazis attacked the other restraining human response: sympathy. Their propaganda extolled the replacement of compassion by hardness. The belief in hardness was rooted both in their Nietzschean outlook and in their Social Darwinism.

Like their obedience, the Nazis' hardness may have come from an authoritarian upbringing. Klaus Theweleit has given it a Freudian interpretation. Using documents from the Freikorps and from other precursors of Nazism, Theweleit gives many examples of the obsession with turning men into the hard, steel-like components of a disciplined collective machine. He quotes Ernst Jünger on the German soldiers of the First World War: 'This was a whole new race, energy incarnate, charged with supreme energy. Supple bodies, lean and sinewy, striking features, stone eyes petrified in a thousand terrors beneath their helmets. These were conquerors, men of steel tuned to the most grisly battle . . .'[22]

Those who think of themselves as men of steel have to subdue anything which threatens to return them to the old type of person with soft flesh and disorganized human feelings. Theweleit's Freudian account is that, as children, they never had the kind of relationships which would allow them to develop a sense of self from the inside. Instead, 'they must acquire an enveloping "ego" from the outside'. He says the punishments they receive 'remind them constantly of the existence of their periphery (showing them their boundaries) until they "grow" a functioning and controlling body armour, and a body capable of seamless fusion into larger formations with armourlike properties. If my assumptions are correct, the armour of these men may be seen as constituting their ego.'[23] (Like many Freudian interpretations, Theweleit's account is suggestive but hard to test.)

The hardness came partly from belief in Social Darwinism, with its suggestion that compassion is misplaced sentimentality. Nietzsche also believed in hardness as self-discipline. The man he admired had an abundance of desires and impulses, but self-creation meant having them under the control of a strong will. Nietzsche's advocacy of this Stoic hardness towards oneself sometimes included advocacy of hardness towards others. The Nazis made hardness towards others the test of a strong will.

Hardness was not a marginal value for the Nazis. Hitler said, 'I am the hardest man the German nation has had for many decades, perhaps centuries.'[24] He also admired the hardness of Stalin. He praised the Russians for disregarding 'the namby-pamby utterances about humanitarianism which they spread so assiduously in Germany', and said, 'Stalin, too, must command our unconditional respect. In his own way he is a hell of a fellow! He knows his models, Genghiz Khan and the others, very well.' He called Stalin 'half beast, half giant' and said, with apparent admiration, 'The people can rot for all he cares.'[25] Unsurprisingly, respect for Stalin's hardness did not lead Hitler to any softness in response. In the Commissar Decree he ordered the war in Russia to be waged with 'unprecedented, unmerciful and unrelenting hardness'.

Others echoing Hitler included Hans Frank, the Governor of Poland: 'Gentlemen, I must ask you to arm yourself against all feelings of sympathy. We have to annihilate the Jews wherever we find them and wherever it is at all possible.'[26] Reinhard Heydrich said, 'We must be as hard as granite, otherwise the work of our Führer will perish.'[27] At Eichmann's trial Pastor Grüber, who had often pleaded with him on behalf of Jews, said, 'the impression he made on me was that of a block of ice or marble, completely devoid of human feelings'.[28]

In those carrying out atrocities, hardness was a defence against the horror of what they were doing, like the hardness of soldiers in combat, but Nazi hardness was also something aspired to and deliberately cultivated. Instructions about the need for hardness were passed down the line to those engaged in killing. The guidelines given to the Order Police about partisan warfare were explicit: 'The enemy must be *totally destroyed*. The incessant decision over life and death posed by the partisans and suspects is difficult even for the toughest soldier. But it must be done. He behaves correctly who, by setting aside all possible impulses of personal feeling, proceeds ruthlessly and mercilessly.'[29]

Cultivation of the ability to overcome feelings of sympathy was central to SS training. Johannes Hassebroeck said that this marked off the requirements of the SS from the strength and courage required in other armies: 'The SS making you tough on yourself – demanded more. A man was ordered, for example, to shoot the dog he loved, or better – to kill him with a knife. Being tough on yourself means overcoming your weaknesses.'[30]

Rudolf Höss described a time when two small children were so absorbed in a game that they refused to let their mother tear them away from it to enter the gas chamber. 'The imploring look in the eyes of the mother, who certainly knew what was happening, was something I shall never forget.' Höss says, 'I might not show the slightest trace of emotion', and describes how he nodded to a junior non-commissioned officer, who carried the screaming, struggling children into the chamber, followed by their mother.[31] This is the reality behind the vague Nietzschean rhetoric about the triumph of the will over the emotions.

Breakthrough

Sometimes the crust of hardness cracks and ordinary human sympathy breaks through. The physical presence of victims makes breakthrough more likely. Being present as a spectator at the Nazi mass shootings could have an impact even on those most responsible for them. In 1941 Himmler watched a hundred people being shot at Minsk. He seemed nervous as the firing started, and during every volley he looked to the ground. When two women did not die, he yelled to the police sergeant not to torture them.

Being present as a participant certainly had a psychological impact on soldiers in the Einsatzgruppen, the units which carried out mass shootings. After Himmler saw the shooting at Minsk, Obergruppenführer von dem Bach-Zelewski said to him, 'Reichsführer, those were only a hundred . . . Look at the eyes of the men in this Kommando, how deeply shaken they are! These men are finished for the rest of their lives. What kind of followers are we training here? Either neurotics or savages!'[32]

There is some medical support for Bach-Zelewski's point about neurotics. A former Wehrmacht neuropsychiatrist, who had treated many such soldiers, estimated that 20 per cent of those doing the killing had psychological problems such as severe anxiety, nightmares, tremors and numerous bodily complaints. He said these were like the combat reactions of ordinary troops, except that they were more severe and lasted longer. Their greatest psychological problems were related to shooting women and children.[33] Bach-Zelewski himself became ill. The SS doctor who reported this to Himmler said that Bach-Zelewski experienced 'visions in connection with the shootings of Jews that he himself had led, and from other difficult experiences in the East'.[34]

These symptoms of inner conflict are an extreme case of what Socrates said about how the happiness of those who do immoral things is destroyed. But the fact that 80 per cent did *not* report these problems is grim testimony to the power of psychological mechanisms of adjustment.

Physical closeness does not always cause the breakthrough of human responses. The members of the police battalion who shot 1,500 Jews in the village of Józefów were paired off with their victims face to face, and yet most of them took part in the massacre all day. But more personal contact could still make a difference. One man took part in the first shooting, but was allotted a mother and her daughter as victims for the next shooting: 'I began a conversation with them and learned that they were Germans from Kassel, and I took the decision not to participate further in the executions. The entire business was now so repugnant to me that I returned to my platoon leader and told him that I was sick and asked for my release.' When those engaged in the massacre showed mercy it was usually the result of having to focus on the individual person. In Józefów, a girl of ten with a bleeding head was brought to Major Trapp, who was in charge of the evacuation and shooting. He took her in his arms and said, 'You shall remain alive.'[35]

Those who gassed the victims of the Nazis were physically very close to them. (By an evil twist, some of those involved were themselves prisoners and future victims acting under duress.) But, as with those participating in the mass shootings, if those operating the gassing were forced to focus on an individual this could bring about emotional breakthrough.

Miklos Nyiszli describes a case where a gas chamber was being cleared and a sixteen-year-old girl was found alive at the bottom of the pile of corpses. She was given a coat, while Nyiszli revived her with injections. Of those clearing the gas chamber, 'one ran to the kitchen to fetch some tea and warm broth. Everybody wanted to help, as if she were his own child.' Those now helping were themselves prisoners forced into the job they were doing. But some degree of breakthrough took place even in Oberscharführer Müssfeld, the Commandant of the crematorium, who often himself shot people in the back of the neck. Müssfeld came in and saw the girl. Nyisli tried to persuade him to spare her life. Müssfeld eventually decided that this would be too dangerous for himself, since she was only sixteen and might talk. He had her shot in the neck (by someone else). But before reaching this conclusion, he toyed with the idea of slipping her into a group of women who worked nearby and so saving her. Even an enthusiastic Nazi participant wobbled for a moment when faced with an individual girl.[36]

Emotions could be released by any weakening of distancing. Rudolf Höss said:

> when at night I stood beside the transports, or by the gas chambers or the fires, I was often compelled to think of my wife and children, without, however, allowing myself to connect them closely with all that was happening. It was the same with the married men who worked in the crematoria or at the fire pits. When they saw the women and children going into the gas chambers, their thoughts instinctively turned to their own families.[37]

These associations could cause strong emotional breakthrough. One person could not take part in shooting: 'Because there were children among the Jews we had brought and at the time I myself was a father with a family of three children, I told the lieutenant something to the effect that I was unable to shoot and asked if he couldn't assign me to something else.'[38]

Odilo Globocnik, the SS and Police Leader in Lublin, was thinking about the Polish children freezing to death while being transported from Lublin to Warsaw. He said to Sturmbannführer Höfle that he could not look at his three-year-old niece without thinking about the Polish children. Höfle 'looked at Globocnik like an idiot'. Later, Höfle's own baby twins died of diphtheria. At the cemetery Höfle shouted that it was heaven's punishment for his misdeeds.[39]

The Barriers Against Breakthrough

One of the features of Nazi ideology was the way it made people apologetic about any breakthrough of human responses. In 1940, during the 'euthanasia' programme, a Nazi doctor at the Eglfing-Haar asylum wrote a letter to the asylum's director, Dr Pfannmüller, explaining his reluctance to take part in the children's programme:

> The new measures are so convincing that I had hoped to be able to discard all personal considerations ... despite my intellectual understanding and good will, I cannot help stating that I am temperamentally not fitted for this. As eager as I often am to correct the natural course of events, it is just as repugnant to me to do so systematically, after cold-blooded consideration, according to the objective principles of science, without being affected by a doctor's feeling for his patient ... I feel emotionally tied to the children as their medical guardian, and I think that this emotional contact is not necessarily a weakness from the point of view of a National Socialist doctor ... I prefer to see clearly and to recognize that I am too gentle for this work than to disappoint you later.[40]

It is possible to catch a glimpse, in apologies of this kind, of the strength of the ideological barriers erected against emotional breakthrough, and of their similarity to Nietzsche's view of compassion as a weakness to be overcome.

Because the emotions held back by the barriers can be so powerful, it was easier to admit no exceptions at all. Primo Levi has pointed out that the Nazis included even women in their nineties in the transports to the death camps. It was not necessary for the Nazi policy to remove people well past bearing children and with little time left to live, but to have allowed exceptions might have opened the emotional floodgates. Rigid exclusion of consideration of the individual case made things easier for those carrying out the policy.

It is understandable that the Nazis saw emotional breakthrough as a threat, but breakthrough was not normally sufficient to make people refuse to participate. It was often treated as a psychological problem to be overcome, a response sometimes tinged with a grotesque note of self-pity. Rudolf Höss wrote, 'If I was deeply affected by some incident, I found it impossible to go back to my home and my family. I would mount my horse and ride, until I had chased the terrible picture away. Often, at night, I would walk through the stables and seek relief among my beloved animals.'[41]

Breakthrough has limitations. Only in a few cases was it followed by refusal. Himmler did not give up his job. Müssfeld had the girl shot. Globocnik and Höfle spared not a single life. And Höss stayed among his beloved animals to run Auschwitz.

CHAPTER 36

The Erosion of Moral Identity

For the things we have to learn before we can do them, we learn by doing them, e.g. men become builders by building and lyre-players by playing the lyre; so too we become just by just acts, temperate by doing temperate acts, brave by doing brave acts. This is confirmed by what happens in states; for legislators make the citizens good by forming habits in them . . . It makes no small difference, then, whether we form habits of one kind or of another from our very youth; it makes a very great difference, or rather *all* the difference.

Aristotle, *Nicomachean Ethics*

Once the killing began, however, the men became increasingly brutalized. As in combat, the horrors of the initial encounter eventually became routine, and the killing became progressively easier. In this sense, brutalization was not the cause but the effect of these men's behaviour.
Christopher R. Browning, *Ordinary Men: Reserve Police Battalion 101 and the Final Solution in Poland*

Some who carried out the Nazi policies were perhaps sadists or psychopaths. Rudolf Höss, the Commandant of Auschwitz, had participated in a particularly brutal political murder, in which the victim was beaten almost to death with clubs and branches, had his throat cut, and was then shot.[1] The participation in Nazi atrocities of someone like that is not much of a psychological puzzle. But many Nazis had no history of violence. A familiar Nazi figure is the quiet, boring, dutiful official. Even after giving due weight to obedience and conformity, the question arises how a 'normal' doctor or civil servant could help to murder huge numbers of men, women and children.

The quiet officials who took part must have been brought up to have a non-Nazi moral identity, which included the sense of not being a mass murderer. This was overcome: the old identity was eroded, and a new one created. Aristotle's view that virtues are cultivated by making a habit of virtuous actions was applied in reverse. The sense of not being the kind of person who would commit atrocities was gradually eroded by the habit of participation.

This suggests they started to participate while the old identity was in place. And this must have been psychologically painful. A crude method of deadening the pain was drink. One policeman commented that they 'drank so much solely because of the many shootings of Jews, for such a life was quite intolerable sober'.[2] There were less crude ways for people to evade recognition of their responsibility and role. And there were ways of denying either the reality or the terribleness of what they did.

Evasion: the Division of Labour and the Narrowing of Attention

Division of labour made evasion of personal responsibility easier. Those who rounded up Polish Jews from their homes, and were also made to shoot them, were acutely aware of participating in atrocity. But those who rounded people up had far less sense of this when the killing was done elsewhere by other people.

One strategy of evasion narrows the focus of attention to bureaucratic matters. Officials in the Reichsbahn sent carefully worked-out bills to the government department in charge of transporting Jews in freight cars to their death. The fare was third class for each person, except for half-price tickets for children under ten and free travel for those under four. It was business as usual on the Reichsbahn: a return fare for the guards and a one-way fare for the Jews.

Bureaucratic rivalries often occupied the foreground of attention. In 1942 a memorandum from the Office of Jewish Affairs in Paris described a call from Adolf Eichmann about the cancellation of a transport of Jews to Auschwitz:

> Obersturmbannführer Eichmann pointed out that this was a matter of prestige. To obtain the trains, long discussions with the Ministry of Transportation had been required, and now Paris was cancelling a train. Such a thing had never happened to him before. It was most embarrassing . . . He would have to consider dropping France altogether as a deportation country. I begged him not to do that, adding that it was not the fault of this office and that the other trains would leave on schedule.[3]

Sometimes the narrowing of focus was technical. In the camps SS doctors worked out numbers of people who should live, weighing the work they would do against the health problems created by keeping weak people alive.

Vans were developed in which people were killed by carbon monoxide from the exhaust. Willy Just proposed shortening the vans so that they could kill people more quickly. The manufacturers had said that shortening the vans would overload the front axle, but Willy Just worked out that this was not so: 'Actually a compensation in the weight distribution takes place automatically through the fact that the cargo in the struggle toward the back door during the operation always is preponderantly located there.' There was another problem. The pipe which fed in the exhaust fumes was being rusted away by urine, menstrual blood, excrement and vomit. Willy Just had a solution for that too. He suggested the floor should slope towards a hole in the middle: 'thin fluids' would exit during the operation, and 'thicker filth' could be hosed out later.[4]

Denial

Evasion blurs awareness of the agent's role. This can be contrasted with denial, which is a defence against recognizing the reality of what is happening. In atrocities denial tends to be centred on the victims rather than the agents. It minimizes or obscures the horror of what is being done.

Denial is not found only in atrocities. A doctor can tell someone they are going to die, only to find later that the news seems not to have been taken in. The person is still discussing long term plans. The imminence of death has been denied.

With atrocities, denial may occur in the potential victims. Some German Jews did not escape abroad because they could not bring themselves to see the danger facing them. In your own house, surrounded by your possessions and other familiar objects, and by people you have always known, it can be very hard to break through the illusory sense of security and see the need to abandon all this and start again in a foreign country.

For the perpetrators, denial works either by making the horrors seem unreal or by distancing the victims.

One way people deny the nature of what they are doing is by having a taboo on talking about it. Himmler referred to this in a speech in 1943:

> I want to mention here very candidly a particularly difficult chapter. Among us it should be mentioned once, quite openly, but in public we will never talk about it . . . It was with us, thank God, an inborn gift of tactfulness, that we have never conversed about this matter, never spoken about it. Every one of us was horrified, and yet every one of us knew that we would do it again if it were ordered and if it were necessary. I am referring to the evacuation of the Jews, to the extermination of the Jewish people.[5]

No doubt this 'tactfulness' made it easier not to be overcome by feelings of being 'horrified' while rounding up people and murdering them.

The taboo on discussion was accompanied by the use of orders which avoided the clear, plain statement. In the 'euthanasia' programme, senior doctors would often give the order to kill by innuendo. The soldiers and police who 'resettled' people who lived in Poland and Russia were often given their worst tasks by innuendo. One police battalion started by moving everyone living in a village:

> We endeavoured to fetch all people out of the houses, without regard for whether they were old, sick, or small children. The commission quickly found fault with our procedures. They objected that we struggled under the burden of the old and sick. To be precise, they did not initially give us the order to shoot them on the spot, rather they contented themselves with making it clear to us that nothing could be done with such people.

Soon members of the battalion were shooting the old people.[6]

Officially the policy had started off as one of deportation, with resettling Jews in Madagascar under consideration. Because the transition to extermination was blurred, conveyed by oral innuendo rather than by explicit written order, it was possible at any particular moment to avoid facing its meaning. Either it was too early to be sure that extermination was intended, or else it was too late because they had been involved for some time.

Denial of the terribleness of what is done can be helped by euphemisms. Jews deported to their death were 'evacuated', 'resettled', or 'sent to the East'. The death camps were 'work camps' or 'concentration camps'. Those selected for death were to be given 'special treatment'. In Auschwitz, the gas chambers and crematoria were called 'special installations' and 'bath houses'. And the whole policy was called the 'Final Solution'.

Sometimes denial exploits the 'unreality' of the context. 'A plain without a feature' makes killing in battle seem unreal. The Nazi killings were helped in the same way: in 1935 Hitler had said, 'if war came, he would take up and carry out this question of euthanasia, because it was easier to do so in wartime'.[7] And Eichmann spoke of the 'different personal attitude' to death when 'dead people were seen everywhere'.

The sense of unreality was most intense in the extermination camps. One of the prisoner doctors in Auschwitz, asked about the selections of prisoners to be killed, said, 'The whole thing was utterly unreal ... I'm sure that I'm not the only one who had the feeling that you were in a kind of ivory tower and it [was] not happening.' The SS doctors who carried out these selections were able to do so partly through a sense that Auschwitz was morally separate from the rest of the world, that it was 'extraterritorial' as one doctor put it.[8] Rudolf Höss, the Commandant of Auschwitz, was asked by Fritz Hensel, his brother-in-law, how he was able to function in such a place. Höss said that Hensel could not understand, as he belonged to a different world: 'Here you are on another planet. Don't forget that.'[9]

The role of a sense of unreality in helping those running Auschwitz to do their jobs (or in helping soldiers kill in war) brings out the way in which a psychological atmosphere can be as important as explicit beliefs. The SS doctors in Auschwitz did not literally believe that what they saw or took part in was not really happening. And Rudolf Höss was not psychotic: he did not literally believe that he was on another planet. The unreal atmosphere enabled people to do things they would otherwise have found unthinkable. But in those who got as far as running Auschwitz, repeated participation had thoroughly eroded the old moral identity.

The Residue of Moral Identity: Embarrassment

Even in the inner circle of Nazis, there was sometimes a minimal residue of an older moral identity. Some were capable of feeling embarrassment.

It was fear of embarrassment, together with fear of a public outcry, which led to policies of concealment. The euthanasia programme was concealed under the code name T4, after Tiergartenstrasse 4, the Berlin address of its headquarters. Front organizations were set up with such names as 'The Reich Association of Asylums' and 'The Community Foundation for the Encouragement of Asylums'. Victor Brack, who chaired the steering group running the programme, operated under the assumed name 'Jennerwein'.

The cover-up was incompetent. The death notice of one victim gave the cause of death as appendicitis, although the appendix had been removed years before. One man's death was said to have been caused by spinal disease, when his relations had seen him perfectly healthy a few days before. A death notice was sent out for a woman still alive and healthy. One family was mistakenly sent two urns of ashes. Despite the incompetence, an effort was made to cover tracks.

The extermination camps were concealed as far as possible. Secluded sites were chosen. Trees were planted round the Auschwitz crematoria. The International Red Cross was fobbed off with visits to the specially prepared model camp at Theresienstadt. At the extermination camps graves were opened, corpses burned, and the ashes disposed of as Himmler ordered: 'in such a way that it would be impossible at some future time to calculate the number of corpses burned'. As the sterilization expert of the Interior Ministry, Dr Linden, said: a future generation might not understand these matters.[10] As the German armies were driven back, camp survivors were transferred in huge numbers to places further from the Allied armies in an effort to keep their story from coming out. Efforts were also made to destroy the camps without trace. Pine trees were planted at Belzec and a farm was created on the site of Treblinka.

Some of the motives for concealment were linked to the furtherance of Nazi aims. They did not want to stir up opposition, nor did they want their extermination policies to be used in Allied propaganda. In the later stages of the war they were afraid of what would happen to them if they were caught. But they may also have needed to protect themselves from exposure to the reactions of others. It mattered that a future generation 'might not understand'. It probably mattered that some of their family and friends also might 'not understand'. The reactions of mothers or of old schoolfriends might reveal weakness in these toughened functionaries. Because the way people see themselves is moulded partly by others, there would be a risk to their self-respect, a risk of seeing themselves from the perspective of their older moral identity. They might feel ashamed, or at least embarrassed.

Some of the horror and revulsion which the Nazi policies in Poland created in those who saw them at first hand did filter back indirectly to Berlin. During the dissolution of the ghettos, one Polish policeman saw children being thrown on the floor and their heads trampled with boots. He also saw that many Jews had their bones broken with rifle butts and were then thrown into graves covered with calcium. When the calcium began to boil in the blood, their cries could still be heard. The policeman told a German woman that he had now become acquainted with German culture and asked whether she was not ashamed to be a German. She wrote about this anonymously to Berlin, and her letter reached the Reich Chancellor's office.[11]

Hitler and his circle did not like to be exposed to what their policies did to people. Even they could be embarrassed. Henriette, the wife of Gauleiter von Schirach, saw Jews being rounded up one night in Amsterdam. She was distressed by the terrible screams of the women. On the advice of her husband, she told Hitler about this. Hitler listened 'ungraciously', with interruptions rebuking her sentimentality. Everyone there found the episode 'very embarrassing'. The conversation stopped. The Schirachs left the room and went away without saying goodbye.[12]

Even the top Nazis could feel the pressure of social disapproval. Perhaps even the top Nazis sometimes felt awkwardness, linked to the residue of an older moral identity. They tried to conceal the murder of the Jews. And they could be embarrassed by comments such as those by Henriette von Schirach. But their response did not go beyond embarrassment. The policy continued. They had developed a new, Nazi, identity.

CHAPTER 37

The Nazi Moral Identity

To teach man the future of man as his will, as dependent on a human will, and to prepare for great enterprises and collective experiments in discipline and breeding . . . for that a new kind of philosopher and commander will sometime be needed, in face of whom whatever has existed on earth of hidden, dreadful and benevolent spirits may well look pale and dwarfed.

Friedrich Nietzsche, *Beyond Good and Evil*

The Nazi outlook was, in a selective way, Nietzschean, but the Nazis were not amoralists. They thought of themselves as living by a post-Christian morality, which gave them a strong sense of their own moral identity.

The Death of the Christian God and the Revaluation of Values

The Nazis disagreed with Nietzsche about the death of God. Hitler himself retained a belief in a supernatural power and at times he seemed to think that he himself had some supernaturally ordained destiny: 'If my presence on earth is providential, I owe it to a superior will.'[1] And in a speech in Linz in 1938 he said, 'I believe that it was the will of God to send a boy from here into the Reich, to make him great, to raise him up to be the Führer of the nation.'

But Hitler was passionately hostile to Christianity: 'I shall never come to terms with the Christian lie . . . Our epoch will certainly see the end of the disease of Christianity. It will last another hundred years, two hundred years perhaps. My regret will have been that I couldn't, like whoever the prophet was, behold the promised land from afar.' He accepted a broadly Nietzschean account of Christianity as a conspiracy of Jews for a slave revolt against their Roman conquerors: 'Christianity is a prototype of Bolshevism: the mobilisation by the Jew of the masses of slaves with the object of undermining society.'

Although he was passionately hostile to Christianity, Hitler said that he did not 'want to educate anyone in atheism'.[2] A Nazi was encouraged to be a *Gottgläubiger*, a believer in God, but the term carried no suggestion of Christianity. SS members were encouraged to leave the churches. Adolf Eichmann, taking the view that 'the God I believe in is greater than the Christian God',[3] left the Protestant Church and registered as a *Gottgläubiger*. In his case the Christian outlook was replaced by something more Nietzschean. In his final statement in court in Israel, Eichmann also spoke of the 'revaluation of values prescribed by the government'. And Joseph Goebbels used the same phrase: 'Children of revolt, we call ourselves with a poignant tremor. We have been through revolution, through revolt to the very end. We are out for the radical revaluation of all values.'[4] Hitler thought conscience was a Jewish invention. The effort to break free from the constraints of conscience was one of the central aspects of the Nazis' own revaluation of values. They believed in crossing the moral or emotional barriers against cruelty and atrocity.

The Nazis' Own Moral Boundaries

Nazism was conceived as a way of life, and its scope extended to the inner life. Harald Ofstad has reconstructed the total nature of its claims: 'To fulfil one's nazi duties and then relax is not enough. One must think, feel, fantasize – even relax like a nazi. The nazi faith must permeate one's entire being, penetrate the very core of one's soul.'[5]

One of the Nazis' most incongruous features is their capacity for moral disapproval, vehement even when disproportionate or inappropriate. When Eichmann was in Jerusalem, a police officer lent him a copy of *Lolita*. After two days he returned it, indignantly describing it as 'quite an unwholesome book'.[6]

Hitler, too, was strongly against prostitution and 'filth':

> No, anyone who wants to attack prostitution must first of all help to eliminate its spiritual basis. He must clear away the filth of the moral plague of big city 'civilisation' and he must do this ruthlessly and without wavering in the face of all the shouting and screaming that will necessarily be let loose ... Theatre, art, literature, cinema, press, posters and window displays must be cleansed of all manifestations of our rotting world and placed in the service of a moral, political and cultural idea.[7]

Superimposed on the racism and Social Darwinism was this additional morality, whose categories were 'filth' and 'cleansing'.

It is hard to see any coherent reasons for this moral mixture. The official moral theory was mainly a selective version of Nietzsche. There was also a highly distorted version of Kant. During his interrogation Eichmann claimed to believe in 'fulfilment of duty', saying, 'In fact it's my norm. I have taken Kant's categorical imperative as my norm, I did long ago. I have ordered my life by that imperative, and continued to do so in my sermons to my sons when I realized that they were letting themselves go.'[8] He made a similar remark at his trial, and when asked about this by Judge Raveh, he said that he had read the *Critique of Practical Reason*, and gave a decent account of the Categorical Imperative: 'I meant by my remark about Kant that the principle of my will must always be such that it can become the principle of general laws.'

Kant, who believed that people are to be treated as ends in themselves and not merely as means, would have been appalled by this particular Kantian. But there is a side of Kant to which the Nazis could claim a sort of adherence: the emphasis on obedience to rules for their own sake. Kantian rules are supposed to be generated purely rationally, in a way that is independent of their impact on people. And they should be obeyed out of pure duty, rather than out of any sympathy for people. For Kant, to act out of feelings of sympathy for others is to act on a mere inclination rather than out of duty, and so to do something without moral worth. The Nazis produced a grim variant of this austere, self-enclosed morality.

The sense of duty was important. As Martin Bormann put it, 'But you know, don't you, that in my dictionary DUTY is written in capitals.'[9] And Eduard Wirths, one of the leading Nazi doctors in Auschwitz, wrote to his wife in 1945, 'I can say that I have always done my duty and have never done anything contrary to what was expected of me.'[10]

Eichmann was also punctilious in carrying out small duties. At the end of the war, he sent his men home and gave the remaining money to his legal adviser, 'because, I said to myself, he is a man from the higher civil services, he will be correct in the management of funds, he will put down his expenses . . . for I still believed that accounts would be demanded some day'.[11] Sometimes at his trial he congratulated himself for his refusal to act for personal gain, as when he wanted to learn Hebrew: 'It would have been easy to say, let's grab a rabbi and lock him up and he'll have to teach me; but no, I paid three marks per hour, the usual price.' Martha Gellhorn described how he was bewildered by the reaction this provoked in the court: 'How could he know, this hollow man, that what seemed to him a natural phrase exposed wastelands of feeling to people who, under no circumstances on earth, would have imagined that you could "grab" an innocent scholar and jail him in order to get lessons for nothing.'[12]

Himmler too attached great importance to SS members not stealing anything from Jews for themselves, in contrast to the ease with which he felt he could justify their other actions:

We had the moral right vis-à-vis *our* people to annihilate *this* people which wanted to annihilate us. But we have no right to take a single fur, a single watch, a single mark, a single cigarette, or anything whatever. We don't want in the end, just because we have exterminated a germ, to be infected by that germ and die from it. I will not stand by while a slight infection forms. Whenever such an infected spot appears, we will burn it out. But on the whole we can say that we have fulfilled this heavy task with love for our people, and we have not been damaged in the innermost of our being, our soul, our character.[13]

The view that duties are quite independent of any concern for other people, and yet that they are binding, gave rise to a striking piece of moral indignation in Franz Stangl, the Commandant of Treblinka. When Gitta Sereny interviewed him after his trial, she asked him about his reputation for being superb at his job: 'Would it not have been possible for you, in order to register *some* protest, if only to yourself, to do your work a little less "superbly"?' She reports that this was one of the few questions that made him angry: 'Everything I did out of my own free will I had to do as well as I could. That is how I am.'[14]

The SS saw the very repulsiveness of what they did as evidence of a devotion to duty which made criticism particularly unfair. SS-Obersturm-bannführer Strauch arrested seventy Jews employed by a colleague, Kube, who criticized him for this. Strauch said:

I was again and again faced with the fact that my men and I were reproached for barbarism and sadism, whereas I did nothing but fulfil my duty. Even the fact that expert physicians had removed in a proper way the gold fillings from the teeth of Jews who had been designated for special treatment was made the topic of conversation. Kube asserted that this method of our procedure was unworthy of a German man and of the Germany of Kant and Goethe.

Strauch said it was regrettable that his men, 'in addition to having to perform this nasty job, were also made the targets of mudslinging'.[15]

The more horrible the acts the SS committed, the more they were able to think of themselves as showing heroism, remaining morally pure themselves at the same time as overcoming revulsion against atrocities in order to obey the commands of duty. Himmler, in 1943, congratulated his men on this:

Most of you know what it means when 100 corpses lie there, or 500 lie there, or 1,000 lie there. To have gone through this and – apart from the exceptions caused by human weakness – to have remained decent, that has hardened us. That is a page of glory in our history never written and never to be written.[16]

The SS, despite its central role in the brutality and killings, had a conception of itself as a moral elite. Its catechism said that 'the prisoner must know that the guard represents a philosophy superior to his, an unblemished political approach and a higher moral level, and the prisoner must take these as a personal example as part of his efforts to correct himself so that he may be once again a loyal citizen of his community'.[17] But their idea of a higher moral level is a dramatic illustration of the limitations of a morality detached from concern for others. It was based on taking very seriously duties which were trivial in human importance. Again the contrast is between this sense of duty and how they saw the human disaster they were creating. It is a contrast which displays an overwhelming distortion of perspective. One senior officer wrote: 'On that same pile of trash . . . were used articles of clothing and blankets. It was a terrifying sight. What horrible waste. A large portion of the uniforms thrown there were still usable. It is hard to believe that something like this could happen here.'[18] 'Here' was Auschwitz.

CHAPTER 38

The Willingness to Believe

The philosophy of the movement endowed my hitherto aimless life with a meaning and a purpose.
  In Nietzsche I discovered a bit of my primal self.
    Early supporters of the Nazi Party, quoted in J.P. Stern,
      Hitler: the Führer and the People

The belief system was central to Nazism. The pressures to obey were internalized because the beliefs were accepted. The beliefs motivated the repression of human responses and the erosion of people's previous moral identity. A new moral identity grew round acceptance of Nazi beliefs.

Hitler's hatred of Jews seems mainly to have come from his own psychology, shaped by a harsh childhood and by his experience of the First World War. But the psychopathology of Hitler and other leading Nazis does not account for the wider hostility to Jews. Among those attracted by the Nazi project of national renewal, there were people who were not anti-Semitic, but many Germans and Austrians were persuaded to become true believers.

Hitler laid out his views on propaganda in *Mein Kampf*:

Its effect for the most part must be aimed at the emotions and only to a very limited degree at the so-called intellect . . . The art of propaganda lies in understanding the emotional ideas of the great masses and finding, through a psychologically correct form, the way to the attention and thence to the heart of the broad masses.[1]

To resist propaganda, people need the ability to think critically. Some lacked this. Heinrich Himmler thought the SS should have leeks and mineral water for breakfast. He thought people could be made to confess by telepathy. Following King Arthur and the round table, he would have only twelve people to dinner. He believed that Aryans had not evolved from monkeys or apes like other races, but had come down to earth from the heavens, where they had been preserved in ice from the beginning of time. He established a meteorology division which was given the task of proving this cosmic ice theory. He also thought he was a reincarnation of Heinrich the First.[2] Himmler was an extreme case: the picture is perhaps one of someone quite mad. But one of his characteristics was much more widely shared – his mind had not been encouraged to grow. Filled with information and opinion, he had no critical powers.

To resist propaganda people have to want to think critically. Some Nazis, like Albert Speer, found it a relief not to think:

> My inclination to be relieved of having to think, particularly about unpleasant facts, helped to sway the balance. In this I did not differ from millions of others. Such mental slackness above all facilitated, established, and finally assured the success of the National Socialist system.[3]

The effectiveness of Nazi propaganda was only partly a matter of people lacking sceptical intelligence or the desire to use it. There were needs which Nazism met.

The Soul and the Hunger for Belief

In 1940 George Orwell wrote a review of *Mein Kampf*, in which he commented on the rigidity of Hitler's mind. In its unchanging monomaniac vision, the future was to be 'a horrible brainless Empire in which, essentially, nothing ever happens except the training of young men for war and the endless breeding of fresh cannon-fodder'.

How had people been persuaded to support this vision? Hitler's personality played a part, but Orwell thought Hitler's appeal also came from his seeing the falsity of the belief that people want only ease, security and no pain. Hitler knew that 'human beings *don't* only want comfort, safety, short working-hours, hygiene, birth-control and, in general, common sense; they also, at least intermittently, want struggle and self-sacrifice, not to mention drums, flags and loyalty-parades'.[4]

Hitler addressed psychological needs going beyond materialism and economics. People need a system of beliefs to make sense of the world and sometimes the most helpful system is a simple one. Johannes Hassebroeck, Commandant of the camp at Gross Rosen, valued this in what the SS taught him:

> I was full of gratitude to the SS for the intellectual guidance it gave me. We were all thankful. Many of us had been so bewildered before joining the organization. We did not understand what was happening around us,

everything was so mixed up. The SS offered us a series of simple ideas that we could understand, and we believed in them.[5]

People want their lives to add up to something, to contribute to something larger than themselves. Many Germans found Nazism gave their lives a meaning and a purpose. Glory came from participating in the project of national renewal, in helping to build the Thousand-Year Reich. The beliefs were held with great intensity and sustained some Nazis through running the death camps and the resulting trials. Before his execution, the Commandant of Auschwitz, Rudolf Höss, wrote to his wife that he still believed in everything he had done.

Part of the appeal of the SS to relatively unsuccessful people was that they were able to feel appreciated and important. Joseph Kramer, a camp Commandant, had been unemployed for nine years apart from brief periods as a door-to-door salesman. His widow said:

> The Party promised solutions to all his problems. From the day he understood this, he gave himself over to Nazism with all his heart. I think he remained ever grateful to his movement. Without the Party and the SS, he would have remained a failure for the rest of his life . . . The movement gave him great hope. He would say that, for him, Nazism was a deep emotional experience. The movement caught him. It allowed him to believe in himself once again.[6]

There is a need for transcendence: for something that reaches to the soul. Even the most cruel and brutal functionaries sometimes gave inarticulate expression to this side of Nazism's appeal. Interviewed many years after, Hans Hüttig, a camp Commandant, said, 'Today it seems so cruel, inhuman and immoral. It did not seem immoral to me then: I knew very well what I was going to do in the SS. We all knew. It was something in the soul, not in the mind.'[7]

Acceptance: the Case of Jim Keegstra

Accepting implausible beliefs does not always reflect deep emotional needs. Nor does it always require a whole society like Nazi Germany, with emotionally powerful propaganda and strong pressures to conform. People have a disposition to believe what they are told, especially when they are told it by someone in authority. There is also a disposition towards scepticism, but this depends on education or experiences which correct credulity.

The disposition to believe starts early. In a few years, children have to learn an enormous amount about the world. They are not born knowing how to test claims against evidence, and to test everything would take far too long. Adults give them more true information than false, so the disposition to accept most of what they are told is useful, but it does make children vulnerable to propaganda. The disposition and the associated vulnerability last beyond childhood.

A demonstration of the vulnerability of teenagers to Nazi propaganda comes, surprisingly, from Canada in the 1970s and 1980s. Jim Keegstra taught a class in the High School in Eckville, Alberta. He was a Bible-reader and a member of the Diamond Valley Full Gospel Church. He decided that Jews, by denying that Christ was God, were calling God a liar.[8]

Mr Keegstra's outlook influenced his teenage class. One young woman wrote in her essay: 'Hitler was one of the most successful people in the world ever to go against the Jews. If people would have been listening, he could have rid the world of Jews for ever. It's funny how people never want to hear the truth.' Mr Keegstra added the comment: 'But the Jews control the press, mass media and the propaganda.' One young man wrote a paper about the Jewish plots for world government, to abolish marriage and confiscate private property, and the Jewish assassination of Abraham Lincoln. Another student wrote that Jewish-controlled thugs rode around in packs, bashing in children's heads, raping and drowning women, and cutting open men's stomachs so they would bleed to death. The writer suggested, 'In my opinion, this must come to a dead halt . . . We must get rid of every Jew in existence so we may live in peace and freedom.'

Some parents complained and Keegstra's teaching was stopped. His replacement, Dick Hoeksema, found the students kept asserting Keegstra's point of view. Hoeksema raised this with other teachers and found that Keegstra had persuaded many of them. 'I would say World War Two started because Hitler invaded Poland and they'd say, "No, Hitler *liberated* Poland." I was starting to think that I was crazy. That I was the only person who thought that way.' The school library had many books supporting Keegstra's view. When Hoeksema took into class a book with pictures from the Nazi camps, they were dismissed as fakes. Evidence from other books was rejected because all textbooks were censored by Jews. Keegstra's removal was further evidence of the conspiracy. One member of Keegstra's class had his mind changed by a trip to Dachau paid for by a Calgary businessman, but for some this was more evidence that the Jews were determined to eradicate knowledge of their conspiracy.

The Keegstra case shows how, in a society utterly different from Nazi Germany, people can be persuaded to accept anti-Semitic beliefs verging on paranoia. There was the authority of the teacher, together with his apparent command of a large body of 'evidence'. There was the support of the books he had put in the library.

And there was the holistic character of a belief system. This parallels the way some members of the Central Committee of the British

Communist Party in 1939 had faith in the Soviet Union as the rigid point and preserved this by making whatever adjustments were necessary to other parts of their system. For his followers, belief in Keegstra's rightness about the Jewish conspiracy was the fixed point. To preserve this, they made adjustments to beliefs about the reliability of textbooks and so on to discredit countervailing evidence.

The Lack of a Climate of Criticism

The hunger for belief makes people receptive to propaganda which goes beyond materialism and, however spuriously, appeals to the soul. Those with this hunger want to believe more than they want to think critically.

But even people whose spiritual needs are not touched by the propaganda may find it hard to resist. If Keegstra could be so successful in Canada, it is less surprising that so many succumbed to the propaganda bombardment in Nazi Germany. There, too, the willingness of children to believe was exploited. One popular children's book was *The Poisoned Mushroom*, an illustrated account of the evil of Jews.[9] It included a way of discrediting anything Jews did that seemed good: the poisoned mushroom looks fine, but is actually deadly. The effect on a Jewish child's chances of making friends can be imagined.

The propaganda worked with adults as well as children. In Nazi Germany, as in Mao's China, it was hard to think critically when the pressures to conform and the testimony of those in authority all tended the same way. Rational people check their beliefs and ways of thinking against those of others. While some people have a marvellous scepticism and independence, most of us find our thoughts drawn by a kind of gravitational pull towards the larger mass of belief around us. This can be resisted, but the larger the mass the more strength resistance requires.

The most effective opposition to the pull of Belief comes from a tradition and culture of criticism. The public intellectual climate matters. Even before Nazism, Germany had a culture where respect for authority was stronger than criticism, scepticism or irreverence. In the dominance of German society by anti-Semitism, racial hygiene and Social Darwinism, a part was played by the lack of a climate of criticism.

CHAPTER 39

Philosophers

The pro-Nazi atmosphere was created partly by thinkers. Hitler knew that the intellectual mood mattered – he did not like thinkers, but understood their role. In a speech to the German press in 1938, he said of the 'intellectual classes' that 'Unfortunately we need them; otherwise we might one day, I don't know, exterminate them or something like that. But unfortunately we need them.'[1] The public role of philosophers exists because the intellectual climate matters. This role is to keep alive the critical examination of beliefs. For philosophers themselves to look critically at beliefs is only part of the job. There is also the encouragement of independence and rationality in others and the incitement not to defer to authority or to conventional views.

Where were the philosophers in Nazi Germany?

The Removal of the Philosophers

Many who might best have performed the public role were driven out because of their political opinions or because they were Jewish.

The 1920s and 1930s were a time of greatness in philosophy written in the German language. Ludwig Wittgenstein was developing ideas on language and mind which dominated much of philosophy for the rest of the century. Hans Reichenbach was showing how the theory of relativity overthrew Kantian assumptions about space and time. From the Vienna Circle (which, apart from Reichenbach, included Moritz Schlick, Rudolf Carnap, Otto Neurath, Carl Hempel and Ludwig Waismann) came a powerful challenge to the very idea of philosophy as an enquiry separate from science. In *Logik der Forschung*, Karl Popper set out ideas which were to be developed or opposed in much of what was worth reading in later twentieth-century philosophy of science. Karl Jaspers published what is still the greatest philosophical work on psychiatry. The Frankfurt School (which included Max Horkheimer, Herbert Marcuse, Theodor Adorno and Walter Benjamin) applied their own version of Marxism to politics, culture and psychology.

A number of these philosophers in different ways might have challenged the Nazi belief system. This was prevented: all these philosophers were political opponents of the Nazis, or were Jews, or were married to Jews. They were all removed from their posts, went into exile or were killed. Their ideas spread round the world, sometimes posthumously, sometimes through their writing and teaching in exile. But they were no longer there, in German and Austrian universities, to ask the necessary questions.

The Nazi Philosophers

The philosophers who remained were not of the same order. Many saw the relationship between philosophy and Nazism in very different terms.

Some thought, as Fichte had done, that philosophy was tied to a distinctively German cast of mind. The German Philosophical Society in 1934 accepted 'the duty to use the power of German philosophy for the construction of the German worldview'. They said, 'We must and will join in the work on the life of the German spirit as a whole in which the timeless content of our people's mission has gained temporal concrete shape and historical reality.'[2]

This national approach stressed characteristics appealing to the Nazis. Some supported 'the organic world-view', based on 'a real integration of Destiny, History, Blood.'[3] Others urged the superiority of will and action to reason and thought. Professor Lothar Tirala wrote that the absolute dominance of the world of action 'is a chief characteristic of the Aryan race, which didn't stem from clever intellectualizing. To a greater or lesser extent aware of this reality, all German philosophers have acknowledged the primacy of actions over pure thought: *action is all, thought nothing.*'[4]

The archetypal Nazi philosopher was Alfred Bäumler, who wrote on Nietzsche as a political thinker. He was less enthusiastic about reason than about darkness, heat and magic:

> It is not the logic of cautious calculation that is appropriate to our action, but powerful dark impulses, red-hot images, and ideas charged with magic. Reason gives us valuable service towards reaching part of our destination, but she can never tell us what we actually want. Our real will is a constant knocking on the door of a future in the shadows, a question to Destiny. And, in our act, our always renewed conversation with ourselves is temporarily concluded with the answer we get from Destiny.[5]

He saw something of this outlook in the 'heroic realism' of Nietzsche's views on the Will to Power.

Unsurprisingly, Bäumler saw Nazism as the expression of this version of Nietzsche:

> If today we see German youth on the march under the banner of the swastika, we are reminded of Nietzsche's 'untimely meditations' in which this youth was appealed to for the first time. It is our greatest hope that the state today is wide open to our youth. And if today we shout 'Heil Hitler!' to this youth, at the same time we are also hailing Nietzsche.[6]

In 1933 he joined the ideological office of the Nazi Party and was given the chair of Philosophy and Political Pedagogy at the Humboldt University in Berlin.

Bäumler's inaugural lecture was given in the presence of two SA men and a Nazi flag. He talked about replacing the neo-humanist view of man, and instead thinking of men in terms of their particular race. On the other side of the Unter den Linden from the Humboldt University was the Opernplatz. There, after the lecture finished, was to be a burning of books by Freud, Marx, Heine and by other Jews, liberals, socialists or pacifists. Bäumler spoke about this: 'You are leaving now to burn books in which an alien spirit uses the German word to fight us.' Then came a low point in the history of philosophy. Alfred Bäumler led his audience out of the building, and across the Unter den Linden, to join the Nazi book-burning.

The Case of Martin Heidegger

Martin Heidegger, who saw it as his mission to re-awaken people to an awareness of Being, was the most famous philosopher to support the Nazis. His enthusiasm went well beyond conformity; his lectures and classes included the Nazi salute. He was opposed to Jewish influence on German cultural life: in 1929 he wrote, 'either we will replenish our *German* spiritual life with genuine native forces and educators or we will once and for all surrender it to the growing Judaisation in a broader and narrower sense'.[7]

Heidegger's sense of his German identity was bound up with an intense interest in trees and forests. Photographs show him in a jacket with oak leaves embroidered on the lapels. His pupil Hans Jonas mentions his 'Blood and Soil' point of view, linked with the fact that 'he emphasized his Black Forest-ness a great deal'. He made a cult of his clothes, 'a kind of traditional costume that accentuated the landscape: knee breeches with long socks, a vest, I think it was an Alemannic one, a costume, which he also wore during lectures, that was half thought up by him and half copied from the Black Forest peasants'.[8]

Supporting national consciousness against a cosmopolitan outlook,

Heidegger thought in terms of trees and soil: 'Does not the flourishing of any genuine work depend upon its roots in a native soil?'[9] Writing about being revived by going to his cabin high in the woods at Todtnauberg, Heidegger used an image of himself as a tree: 'Up there the seeds germinate and grow, while down here the ripe fruits fall.'[10]

The rootedness which Heidegger contrasted with cosmopolitanism was something he felt in the Black Forest in the evenings:

> when I sit with the peasants by the fire or at the table in the Lord's corner, we mostly say nothing at all. We smoke our pipes in silence. Now and again someone might say that the woodcutting in the forest is finishing up . . . The inner relationship of my work to the Black Forest and its people comes from a centuries-long and irreplaceable rootedness in the Alemannian-Swabian soil.[11]

Sometimes students were invited to Todtnauberg. One party included Gunther Stern, who was a Jew, and of whom Heidegger had a low opinion. The philosopher admired the ability to stand on one's head for a long time. When Stern did this for five minutes, much longer than the other students, Heidegger was 'speechless' and 'seemed virtually insulted, because this was at odds with the negative picture he had of me'. But Heidegger's wife Elfride was impressed. Walking back to Freiburg next day, Stern and Elfride held hands. Unaware that he was a Jew, she suggested he should join the Nazi Party.

Heidegger's interest in the bodily side of Being went beyond standing on one's head. When Karl Jaspers asked, 'How can a man as coarse as Hitler govern Germany?', Heidegger replied, 'Culture is of no importance. Just look at his marvellous hands.'[12]

Heidegger joined the Nazi Party in a public ceremony on 1 May 1933. He wrote, 'My warmest thanks for your words of welcome upon my entry into the Party. We must now commit all our struggle to conquering the world of educated men and scholars for the new political spirit. It will be no easy passage of arms. Sieg Heil! Martin Heidegger.'[13]

The philosopher had his own private version of Nazism. He believed the usual version laid too much emphasis on biology. For him, the true goal of the movement was to replace the technological mode of thinking by a re-awakened awareness of Being. On this version of National Socialism, Heidegger himself was its great theorist. As he told Karl Jaspers, he wanted 'den Führer zu führen': to lead the Leader.[14] His attempt to have a meeting with Hitler, no doubt to put him right about Nazism, was unsuccessful. It is hard to imagine an encounter between two such disparate minds. Hitler, who once said of novels 'that kind of reading annoys me', had a mind which was rough, crude, impatient and consumed by resentment. Heidegger's mind was abstract, impenetrable, convoluted and consumed by vanity. To imagine the meeting between them, with

Heidegger glancing at Hitler's marvellous hands and talking about the unity of the outside-of-itself in the raptures of the future, is to be reminded how easily the Führer was moved to rage. That the two men did not meet is one of surrealism's great losses in the twentieth century.

Heidegger won the 1933 election for Rector of the University of Freiburg, the first in which Jews had no vote. He advised students, 'Let not propositions and "ideas" be the rules of your Being. The Führer alone *is* the present and future German reality and its law.' Academic freedom was rejected: 'The much-lauded "academic freedom" will be expelled from the German university; for this freedom was not genuine because it was only negative.' He also wanted a code of honour for lecturers to 'cleanse our ranks of inferior elememts and thwart the forces of degeneracy in the future'.[15] For the Rectoral Address, the hall was decorated with Nazi flags. Those present sang the Horst Wessel song, which the new Rector had helpfully had printed on the back of the programme.

Heidegger put Nazism before loyalty to his students and colleagues. In 1933 he damaged the academic career of his doctoral student Eduard Baumgarten by writing that he was

> anything but a National Socialist. In terms of family background and intellectual sympathies his roots lie in the Heidelberg circle of liberal-democratic intellectuals around Max Weber. Having failed to secure an appointment with me, he established close contact with the Jew Fraenkel, who used to teach in Göttingen and has now been dismissed from here.[16]

Nazism also came before loyalty to his own teacher, Edmund Husserl. *Being and Time* was 'Dedicated to Edmund Husserl, in respect and friendship. Todtnauberg, in the Black Forest, 8 April 1926.' In 1928 Husserl pushed through Heidegger's appointment to the Chair at Freiburg. Husserl was Jewish. In April 1933 he was notified of his compulsory 'leave of absence'. Partly because of this the Rector, von Möllendorf, resigned. On 28 April Martin and Elfride Heidegger sent Edmund and Malvine Husserl some flowers and an awkward note of sympathy. But Heidegger replaced von Möllendorf as Rector. And on 1 May, with public fanfare, he joined the Nazi Party.

In a letter, Husserl wrote of his disappointment with some colleagues:

> the most recent, and the most hurtful, being Heidegger; what hurt me most was the fact that I had put my trust, for reasons I no longer fully understand myself, not just in his talent, but also in his character . . . The perfect ending to this supposed bosom friendship between philosophers was his very public, and very theatrical, entry into the National Socialist Party on 1 May . . . Before this he broke off all relations with me (and very soon after his appointment) and in recent years he has allowed his anti-Semitism to come increasingly to

the fore, even in his dealings with his group of devoted Jewish students and his faculty colleagues.

Husserl also wrote about being devastated by his exclusion:

But the events of the last few weeks and months have struck at the deepest roots of my existence . . . The future alone will judge which was the true Germany in 1933, and who were the true Germans – those who subscribe to the . . . racial prejudices of the day, or those Germans pure in heart and mind, heirs to the great Germans of the past, whose traditions they revere and perpetuate.[17]

In 1934 Heidegger resigned as Rector, a move he was to cite after the war as showing disillusionment with Nazism. He was still a Nazi in 1936 when he met Karl Löwith in Rome. He was lecturing on 'Hölderlin and the essential nature of poetry' and wore his swastika badge. Löwith, in a card to Karl Jaspers, wondered 'what the essential nature of this poetry has to do with the swastika'.

Any change in Heidegger's outlook after resigning as Rector did not extend to defending his former teacher and mentor. In 1935 Husserl was banned from teaching. In 1936 his name was removed from the lecture list. In 1938 he died. Heidegger paid no tribute. He did not write to Malvine Husserl and did not go to the funeral. In the 1941 edition of *Being and Time*, the dedication to Husserl had been removed.

After the war, Heidegger was investigated by a de-Nazification commission, which included Karl Jaspers, who had been a friend of his and who had lost his university post in philosophy because of his marriage to a Jew. Jaspers wrote a fair-minded report. He mentioned Heidegger's impeccable behaviour towards his Jewish assistant in the Philosophy Department, but he also accepted that Heidegger had become anti-Semitic. He wrote of the shock he had felt on reading Heidegger's report on Baumgarten and his association with 'the Jew Fraenkel'. He thought Heidegger had been naïve about his relationship with Nazism and had not understood its main aims.

Jaspers thought that Heidegger's philosophy had insights and that he should not be stopped from writing, but he was uncommonly uncritical: 'He sometimes comes across as a blend of the earnest nihilist and the mystagogue-cum-sorcerer. In the full flow of his discourse he occasionally succeeds in hitting the nerve of the philosophical enterprise in a most mysterious and marvellous way.' Jaspers thought Heidegger should not be allowed to teach. Total academic freedom was the ultimate aim, but young people first had to be taught to think for themselves. The problem was not mainly Heidegger's opinions, but his mode of thinking, 'which seems to me to be fundamentally unfree, dictatorial and uncommunicative'. He should not teach until a 'genuine rebirth' could be seen in him.[18]

There was no rebirth. A philosopher might be expected to have had some reflections on how the movement he had supported had done some of the most evil things in history. Heidegger's response was silence. Or worse: silence punctuated by occasional bits of high-flown evasiveness which sought to minimize his own role, to imply that there was still something good at the core of Nazism, and to suggest that the Nazi atrocities were not anything very special. He said:

> To those and those alone who take pleasure in focusing on what they see as the shortcomings of my rectorship, let me say this: in themselves these things are of as little account as the fruitless rooting around in past efforts and actions, which are so utterly insignificant within the planetary will to power that they cannot even be termed minuscule.[19]

Edmund Husserl was not alive to hear this way of putting his problems in perspective.

In 1935 Heidegger had given the lectures later translated into English as *Introduction to Metaphysics*. In the lectures as delivered, one passage read: 'What is nowadays touted as the philosophy of National Socialism, but in fact has nothing whatsoever to do with the inward truth and greatness of National Socialism, is given to fishing around in these murky waters of "values" and "totalities".' When the lectures were published after the war, Heidegger could have deleted the phrase about the inward truth and greatness of National Socialism. Better would have been to leave it in, with a note apologizing for the huge political misjudgement.

What Heidegger chose to do was to publish a different version of the passage. 'The inward truth and greatness of National Socialism' was turned into 'the inward truth and greatness of the movement (namely with the encounter between technology on a planetary scale and modern man)'.[20] The swastika was no longer visible. Asked about this revision, Heidegger said the parenthesis was in his original manuscript and corresponded exactly to his conception of technology at the time: 'The reason I did not read that passage aloud was because I was convinced that my audience would understand me correctly.'[21] Even if we accept this account, presumably the 'movement' mentioned in the new version is still National Socialism. After the war Heidegger was prepared, obscurely but without apology, to suggest it had truth and greatness.

In 1946, one year after even the most sheltered person knew about Auschwitz, Heidegger wrote his *Letter on Humanism*. In it, he said, 'Perhaps the distinguishing feature of the present age lies in the fact that wholeness as a dimension of experience is closed to us. Perhaps this is the only evil.'[22]

The story is dismal. The anti-Semitism. The Nazism. The betrayal of Baumgarten and of Husserl. And then, afterwards, the mixture of silence and grandiose evasion. Despite all this, some who admired the philosophy still hoped for some redeeming words. The greatest poet of the time, Paul Celan, was one.

One night in June 1942 it was known there would be a round-up of Jews. Paul urged his parents to go with him into hiding, but they did not. When he went back next day, the house was sealed up and empty. His parents did not long survive the deportation. His father died of typhus later that year. His mother, either that year or in early 1942, was classified as unfit for work and shot. Paul himself was sent to a labour camp. He heard of his mother's death only 'in bits and pieces'.

Celan and Heidegger had read each other's work. Celan was influenced by Heidegger, but also knew of his Nazism. John Felstiner tells the story of their meeting.[23] In 1967 Celan gave a reading of his poems at the University of Freiburg, which Heidegger attended. At the reading, Heidegger gave Celan one of his books and invited him next day to Todtnauberg.

Heidegger still believed in the beneficial power of trees. He said, 'I know about his difficult crisis. It would be salutary to show P.C. the Black Forest.' They walked together in the forest, talking of plants, animals and philosophy. At Todtnauberg, Celan drank from Heidegger's well with its star on top. He had not forgotten Heidegger's silence about Nazism. In the visitors' book he wrote: 'Into the hut-book, looking at the well-star, with a hope for a coming word in the heart. On 25 July 1967 Paul Celan.' Poets have responded more impressively to the dark events of recent times than – with a few exceptions – have philosophers. The meeting between Celan and Heidegger is an extreme case, but still perhaps a symbolic one. A week later in his poem 'Todtnauberg', Celan expressed the same hope for a coming word. He sent the poem to Heidegger, but received only polite thanks.

Is it possible to put aside Heidegger the man and to consider only Heidegger the philosopher? What are the links between the two? There is probably no twentieth-century philosopher about whom opinion is more divided. Some have seen Heidegger as a major thinker. This view is more popular with others than with philosophers. But his admirers include Jean-Paul Sartre, Hannah Arendt, Richard Rorty and George Steiner.

Large claims have been made for him. Hannah Arendt wrote:

the storm that blows through Heidegger's thinking – like the one that still sweeps toward us from Plato's works after thousands of years – does not originate from the century he happened to live in. It comes from the primeval, and what it leaves behind is something perfect that, like all that is perfect, returns home to the primeval.[24]

(Minor consequences of studying the Nazis: a dwindling interest in trees and getting thoroughly sick of the primeval.)

Those who enthuse about the primeval wind blowing through Heidegger's philosophy usually do so at some distance from particular pages of his work. Sceptics point to the doubts an actual paragraph of Heidegger may raise.

His huge book, *Being and Time*, is written in a style of its own. Heidegger has the thought that some objects (like pens) have uses, which often require other useful objects (like paper). He calls these useful objects 'equipment'. He tries to get the point across to the reader:

> In our dealings we come across equipment for writing, sewing, working, transportation, measurement. The kind of Being which equipment possesses must be exhibited. The clue for doing this lies in our first defining what makes an item of equipment – namely its equipmentality. Taken strictly, there 'is' no such thing as *an* equipment. To the Being of any equipment there always belongs a totality of equipment, in which it can be this equipment that it is. Equipment is essentially 'something in order to . . .' A totality of equipment is constituted by various ways of the 'in-order-to', such as serviceability, conduciveness, usability, manipulability. In the 'in-order-to' as a structure there lies an *assignment* or *reference* of something to something. Only in the analyses which are to follow can the phenomenon which this term 'assignment' indicates be made visible in its ontological genesis. Provisionally, it is enough to take a look phenomenally at a manifold of such assignments. Equipment – in accordance with its equipmentality – always is *in terms of* its belonging to other equipment: ink-stand, pen, ink, paper, blotting pad, table, lamp, furniture, windows, doors, room.

Heidegger is then struck by a second thought: seeing a room someone lives in, we may notice several of these useful objects together. He has a go at saying this too:

> These 'Things' never show themselves proximally as they are for themselves, so as to add up to a sum of *realia* and fill up a room. What we encounter as closest to us (though not as something taken as a theme) is the room; and we encounter it not as something 'between four walls' in a geometrical spatial sense, but as equipment for residing. Out of this the 'arrangement' emerges, and it is in this way that any 'individual' item of equipment shows itself.[25]

The inarticulate complexity is Heidegger's trademark. Can someone whose thinking is so blurred be a serious philosopher? One difficulty is identifying what his books are about. A central theme is the 'question of Being'.

Heidegger introduces the question with an everyday example:

Over there, across the street, stands the high school building. A being. We can look over the building from all sides, we can go in and explore it from cellar to attic, and note everything we encounter in that building: corridors, staircases, schoolrooms, and their equipment. Everywhere we find beings and we find them in a very definite arrangement. Where is the Being of this high school? For after all it *is*. The building *is*. If anything belongs to this being, it is its Being; yet we do not find the Being inside it.

In this passage Heidegger appears to suggest that its Being is something additional the building possesses as well as its staircases, rooms, etc. And he thinks this extra feature is very important: the difference between Being and beings is 'the *one* basic differentiation whose intensity and fundamental cleavage sustains history'.[26]

All this results from thinking of existence as a property which objects possess. Looking round the school, we notice its corridors but not its existence. So its Being must be a different kind of possession: an unobservable, metaphysical one. But, as Paul Edwards points out, a cat's existence is not a metaphysical extra, behind its fur and claws: '"Cats exist" means "something is a cat".'[27] In logic the existential quantifier (introduced on the basis of the work of Gottlob Frege, half a century before Heidegger) captures the special function of a statement that something exists. The objection to treating 'Being' as a 'real predicate' had been made a century before Frege by Kant.[28]

For many philosophers, Heidegger's thoughts about Being are only comic or embarrassing. But some philosophers found themselves in circumstances from which Heidegger appeared in a harsher light.

Jean Améry, describing his life as a prisoner in Auschwitz, said thinking about metaphysics was impossible, because of 'the cruel sharpness of an intellect honed and hardened by camp reality'. But he sometimes remembered Heidegger, 'that disquieting magus from Alemannic regions . . . who said that beings appear to us only in the light of Being, but that man forgot Being by fixing on beings'. Améry's comment was:

> Well now, Being. But in the camp it was more convincingly apparent than on the outside that beings and the light of Being get you nowhere. You could *be* hungry, *be* tired, *be* sick. To say that one purely and simply *is* made no sense. And existence *as such*, to top it off, became definitively a totally abstract and thus empty concept. To reach out beyond concrete reality with words became before our very eyes a game that was not only worthless and an impermissible luxury but also mocking and evil.[29]

From the perspective of Auschwitz, the frivolity and emptiness of the philosophy might well seem mocking and evil. Some raise another question about a further kind of evil. Did Heidegger's Nazism grow out of the philosophy?

For Heidegger, the distinctively human mode of existence consists in questioning Being. Human beings alone have the possibility of choosing to live authentically. We find ourselves 'thrown' into particular historical circumstances, we live in a particular society at a particular time. Someone who lives inauthentically takes both for granted, playing conventional social roles and accepting without question the opinions of the time.

Authentic existence is to live a life in which you are most truly yourself. This partly comes from understanding your own past and your possibilities for the future. These possibilities always include death. Because life is finite, not everything can be done. Awareness of death prompts people to choose actions which add up to a life expressing who they are. People are autonomous. They cannot but choose the kind of life they lead, even if, inauthentically, they choose by default.

Authentic existence also comes from awareness of our partly social nature. Authentic awareness includes 'historicality' or 'historicity': awareness of the past and future potential of the community whose traditions have shaped us. This provides a perspective from which to stand back from conventional opinion. From this perspective the present can be seen in terms of what is at stake for the destiny of the community.

Heidegger himself saw commitment to Nazism as an expression of his authenticity: of his awareness of what he took to be the destiny of the German people. When Karl Löwith suggested to him that 'a partisanship for National Socialism lay in the essence of his philosophy', he 'agreed with me without reservation and elucidated that his concept of "historicity" was the basis of his political "engagement". He also left no doubt about his belief in Hitler.'[30]

There has been much debate about whether Heidegger's philosophy is discredited by his Nazism. Some argue that the philosophy contained the seeds of the politics. Others say that Heidegger's Nazism is only a contingent embarrassment. Perhaps someone with different politics might have interpreted standing back from conventional opinion in an anti-Nazi way. The philosophy is too nebulous and elusive for this debate to have a determinate conclusion.

The moral case against Heidegger the man is obvious. The central moral case against Heidegger the philosopher is easier to get wrong. It is not about a link between his theories and Nazism. It is about undermining philosophy's role in developing a climate of critical thought. His books are an embodiment of the idea that philosophy is an impenetrable fog, in which ideas not clearly understood have to be taken on trust. Karl Jaspers was right in seeing this 'incommunicative' mode of thought as linked to being dictatorial.

Deference is encouraged by having to take it on trust that the obscure means something important. And since things not understood cannot be argued about, the critical faculties atrophy. Philosophy could not have served the Nazis better than by encouraging deference and by this softening of the mind.

A Footnote on Gottlob Frege

The clearest way of indicating Heidegger's confusion about Being derives from Gottlob Frege. But Frege's contributions to philosophy and to logic go far beyond this. They transformed both subjects.

Frege's book *The Foundations of Arithmetic* was a revolution in the philosophy of mathematics. Some of his essays mark the start of modern philosophy of language. His *Begriffschrift*, published in 1879, laid the basis of modern formal logic. He influenced Russell, Wittgenstein and all subsequent logicians and philosophers of mathematics and of logic. In their history of logic, William and Martha Kneale say that his work 'contains all the essentials of modern logic, and it is not unfair either to his predecessors or to his successors to say that 1879 is the most important date in the history of the subject'.[31] Michael Dummett claims that questions about knowledge, which Descartes made people scc as the most fundamental in philosophy, have been displaced in that role by questions about logic and language. He credits Frege, together with Wittgenstein, with ending the Cartesian period in philosophy.[32]

Whatever the long-term estimate of Frege's work, he was serious in a way which contrasts with Heidegger. His style was austere but always in sharp focus. Rigour was all. There was no staginess, rhetoric, pretentiousness or waffle.

In 1924 Frege was in his mid-seventies. That year he kept a diary, which reveals him to have been an extreme nationalist. He thought Germany needed a strong leader to escape from French oppression. On 19 April he wrote of the disadvantage of joint-stock companies in that foreigners might acquire German shares. He was also anti-Semitic. On 22 April he wrote about his home town of Wismar. He looked back nostalgically to his boyhood days when a law banned Jews (except at the time of the fair) from staying in the town overnight. On 24 April he was regretting that the Reich had developed 'the cancer of Social Democracy'.

His anti-Semitism came out again on 30 April: 'One can remember that there are the most worthy Jews and still regard it as a misfortune that there are so many Jews in Germany and that in future they will have full political equality with German citizens.' He goes on to express sympathy with the wish that the Jews in Germany 'would get lost, or better would like to disappear from Germany'. He was also worried about another question: 'How can one reliably distinguish Jews from Non-Jews? Sixty years ago it would have been comparatively easy. Now it seems to me undoubtedly difficult.' (The Nazis' answer to this problem was the yellow star.) Frege suggested the thing to do was to concentrate on the kinds of jobs in which Jews did so much harm. Removing Jews' civil rights would exclude them.

After this, it is unsurprising to find that he was a reader of *Deutschlands Erneuerung* (Germany's Renewal), an extreme nationalist journal edited by Houston Stewart Chamberlain and others. On 5 May Frege comments on an article he found of interest: 'Adolf Hitler correctly writes in the April number of *Deutschlands Erneuerung* that, since Bismarck's guidance, Germany has not had a clear political goal. He thinks one must either go ahead with England against Russia or with Russia against England . . .'

Frege compartmentalized his mind. When thinking about philosophy and logic, he had no regard for conventional views. He undermined them by argument and worked out alternatives with a more rational basis. When thinking about politics and society, he accepted uncritically the worst conventional prejudices of his place and time.

There is the hope that the philosophical habit of exposing assumptions to clear and rational thought may make it harder for prejudices and unfounded beliefs to survive. For those of us who have that hope, the story of Frege is disheartening. It shows how even superb work in philosophy can leave the rest of a person's thinking unaffected. Uncritical acceptance of a set of political or religious beliefs is no bar to distinction in molecular biology or in chemistry. Done in the spirit of Frege, philosophy too becomes one technical subject among others.

Much Western philosophy in recent times has been divided into the 'analytical' tradition started by Frege and the 'continental' tradition coming partly from Heidegger. (The names, absurdly, contrast a method of thought with a geographical location.) The stories of Heidegger and Frege are a hostile caricature of the two traditions: one full of important-sounding rhetoric about the human condition, but without the intellectual equipment to ask critical questions about Nazism; the other full of logical analysis, which is kept quite sealed off from anything of human importance.

The defects of Heidegger have been often rehearsed. Because of Frege's merit as a philosopher, his failure in the face of Nazism is more troubling. No philosophers follow his political views. Some of his philosophical followers, such as the vigorously anti-racist Michael Dummett, have expressed loathing for his politics.[33] Yet, in current philosophy, there is some pressure to treat philosophy in the compartmentalized way Frege did.

It is not bad if some people do so. There are many ways of doing philosophy and not everyone can think about everything. There is room for philosophers who specialize in highly abstract questions and treat them as self-contained. But if this became the norm, there would be a loss. It would stop philosophy making difficulties for Belief. It would also stop philosophy making a difference to anyone's life. The voice of Socrates would trouble people no more.

CHAPTER 40

Bystanders

And there is another, vaster shame, the shame of the world. It was memorably pronounced by John Donne, and quoted innumerable times, pertinently or not, that 'no man is an island', and that every bell tolls for everyone. And yet there are those who faced by the crime of others or their own, turn their backs so as not to see it and not feel touched by it.

Primo Levi, *The Drowned and the Saved*

Societies are not made of sticks and stones, but of men whose individual characters, by turning the scale one way or another, determine the direction of the whole.

Socrates, in Plato, *The Republic*, Book Eight

It has sometimes been thought that most Germans and Austrians did not know what happened to the Jews and others who were taken away. The truth is more terrible. Many were willing to take part and many others knew well what was being done. There were administrators, typists, drivers, workmen and others, who did not kill people but provided necessary back-up. They usually knew what was going on, but kept their consciences quiet with the thought that their own role was harmless.

Near the death camps, people could not escape knowing. At Mauthausen there were thick plumes of smoke in the sky, day and night, and an appalling smell. Sister Felicitas, who lived nearby, said, 'The people suffered dreadfully from the stench. My own father collapsed unconscious several times, since in the night he had forgotten to seal up the windows completely tight.' She described stores of bones, often dumped in the river, and how tufts of hair blew onto the street out of the chimney.[1]

There was a degree of local revulsion, but people who expressed concern for the victims sometimes seemed more concerned for themselves. One woman near Mauthausen saw people who had been shot taking several hours to die. She wrote to protest: 'One is often an unwilling witness to such outrages. I am anyway sickly and such a sight makes such a demand on my nerves that in the long run I cannot bear this. I request that it be arranged that such inhuman deeds be discontinued, or else be done where one does not see it.'[2]

Others went beyond acquiescence. They were enthusiastic. In April 1945 Jews on forced labour were moved away from the advancing Soviet army and marched towards Mauthausen. At Eisenerz stones were thrown at some of them by townspeople coming out of the cinema. Others were ordered to run down a hill. A squad of local militia opened fire and killed 200 of them. One observer noted a festive mood among the militiamen before the massacre: 'it was for the men of the company seemingly a special joy to be able to seize the weapons'. The squad leader said, 'Today we are going to have some fun.'[3]

When prisoners in Mauthausen escaped, many local people enthusiastically joined the hunt. A priest in Allerheiligen described one man laughing as he shot a prisoner pleading for his life. The grocer in Schwertberg collected seven recaptured prisoners from the local cell and shot them one at a time in the courtyard of the town hall. In Tragwein, the butcher's daughter said, 'Drive them right inside onto the meat bench, we'll cut them right up like the calves.' Afterwards, the local people used to talk of the escape as the 'rabbit hunt'.[4]

Fear and Passivity

Many were afraid to help Jews or to speak out on their behalf. Years later, Karl Jaspers wrote:

> But each of us is guilty insofar as he remained inactive . . . But passivity knows itself morally guilty of every failure, every neglect to act whenever possible, to shield the imperilled, to relieve wrong, to countervail. Impotent submission always left a margin of activity which, though not without risk, could still be cautiously effective.[5]

Most people kept quiet. Inge Deutschkron was a Jewish girl who survived in hiding in Berlin. She later described Berliners' responses as their Jewish neighbours, paralysed with fear, were pushed into cars and taken away: 'People stopped in the street, whispered to each other, and then quickly went on their way, back to the safety of their homes, peering out from behind curtained windows to watch what was happening.'[6] After a few days all the Jews were gone.

Some Berliners were appalled, both at what was being done, and at the discovery of the limits of their own moral courage. One woman wrote about these feelings in her diary:

'They are forced to dig their own graves,' people whisper. 'Their clothing, shoes, shirts are taken from them. They are sent naked to their death.' The horror is so incredible that the imagination refuses to accept its reality. Something fails to click. Some conclusion is simply not drawn ... Such indifference alone makes continued existence possible. Realizations such as these are bitter, shameful and bitter.[7]

Coercive Moral Dilemmas

The Nazis coerced people with moral dilemmas. Critics had a terrible moral choice. They could acquiesce in genocide or they could speak out, but this might add their own family to the victims while saving no one else. The dilemmas for individuals were mirrored by those for groups. In occupied countries the Nazis pursued a deliberate policy of dividing potential opposition. Each fragment of opposition then had terrible choices to make.

In Holland the Nazis never made it clear that they intended to deport all Jews. By a complicated policy of distinctions and exceptions, they deflected some of the resistance into attempts to have particular groups reclassified. They presented Dutch civil servants with a dilemma about collaboration, by asking for a list of Jews who should be exempt because of distinction in science and the arts. They applied the same strategy to the churches. When the deportation of Jews was announced, the Catholic bishops and Protestant leaders joined in a letter of protest, to be read from all pulpits. The Protestant leaders were promised that, if they withdrew from this, Jews converted to Protestantism would be exempted. The Protestant leaders accepted this offer. The public reading of the letter in Catholic churches was followed by a large deportation of Catholic Jews to Auschwitz.[8]

Collaboration often brought relief in the short term. The Protestant Jews were spared from going in that transport. Those of us who have not been faced with these dilemmas should not be too quick to condemn the Protestant leaders. It is easy to understand how they must have seen things. Where lives are at stake, even temporary protection is something.

But, in the long run, such decisions may have helped the Nazis. There is truth in what Pastor Niemöller wrote:

> First they came for the Jews
> and I did not speak out –
> because I was not a Jew.
> Then they came for the communists
> and I did not speak out –
> because I was not a communist.

> Then they came for the trade unionists
> and I did not speak out –
> because I was not a trade unionist.
> Then they came for me –
> and there was no one left
> to speak out for me.

The Origins of Civil Courage

Some Germans and Austrians took risks. Sergeant Anton Schmidt, in charge of a German army patrol in Poland, gave forged papers and the use of military trucks to the Jewish underground until he was arrested and executed. His help was described at Eichmann's trial in Jerusalem. Hannah Arendt wrote of the silence that came over the courtroom, partly in honour of Anton Schmidt, and partly in response to the thought that such help had been so rare.[9]

Some thought opposition might succeed. In 1943 some Catholic anti-Nazi students were executed for distributing subversive pamphlets in Munich. On the morning of her execution, Sophie Scholl said, 'What does our death matter if thousands will be stirred and awakened by what we have done? The students are bound to revolt.' It was not so. There was a huge demonstration that evening in support of the executions, with hundreds of students shouting and stamping to applaud the university beadle, who had denounced Sophie Scholl and her brother.[10]

People were, to different degrees, moved by sympathy and by conceptions of their own moral identity. There is evidence that both of these had roots going back to childhood. Samuel and Pearl Oliner studied people who had helped to rescue Jews in Nazi-occupied Europe and compared them with similarly placed people who had not given such help. They found, unsurprisingly, that the rescuers cared more than the others about people outside their families.[11] Less obviously, the rescuers' upbringing had been different from that of the others. The parents of the rescuers had set high standards for their children, especially about caring for others, but had not been strict. The emphasis was on reasoning rather than discipline. It was virtually the exact opposite of the upbringing of the leading Nazis. Upbringing was mentioned by Emilie Guth, who hid Jews in Marseilles. Her mother, although not rich, had always given food and help to people in need: 'When children see people in the house helping others, it makes them want to help. The things you learn in your own house are the things you grow up to do.'[12]

The Human Responses

For some the first step was a small human gesture towards the victims. Even a friendly face made a difference. Prisoners in Mauthausen working away from the camp noticed people who looked at them sympathetically. Austrian workmen used their position on top of scaffolding to warn prisoners when they needed to work hard and when it was safe to let up. Some villagers put out glasses of water for the passing prisoners and threw them apples.[13]

Jews in Germany had minimal rations, but most Berlin Jews had friends who helped them. Inge Deutschkron describes how her family were given fruit and vegetables by the grocer Richard Junghans. Their old butcher, Mr Krachudel, sold them the same meat as before, without ration stamps. Mrs Krachudel would ask, as politely as ever: 'What will it be today? Stew meat, or maybe a roast?'[14] These small gestures called for courage. A story circulated in Berlin about a Jewish woman, with the Gestapo at her door, throwing lemons and apples out of the window to protect the shopkeeper who sold them to her.

Jean Améry remembered cigarettes. After he had been tortured in Breendonk, one soldier tossed him a lighted cigarette through the cell bars. Later, in Auschwitz-Monowitz, he shared the last cigarette of Herbert Karp, a disabled soldier from Danzig. Jean Améry remembered a few other people who made human gestures. They included Willy Schneider, a Catholic worker from Essen, 'who addressed me by my already forgotten first name and gave me bread'. There was the chemicals foreman, Matthäus, who on 6 June 1944 said, 'Finally, they have landed! But will the two of us hold out until they have won once for all?' But Jean Améry did not overlook how rare such gestures were: 'My good comrades are not to be blamed, nor am I, that their weight is too slight as soon as they stand before me no longer in their singularity but in the midst of their people . . . My Willy Schneider and Herbert Karp and Foreman Matthäus did not stand a chance of prevailing against the mass of the people.'[15]

Moral Identity

Civil courage could come from the sense of being a certain kind of person: of living by some standards rather than others. Sometimes the standards were professional. Some people in Germany refused to participate, even indirectly. Karl Wilhelm, a director of the Reichsbank, turned down a request to help distribute the property taken from murdered Jews, saying that 'the Reichsbank is not a dealer in secondhand goods'. Sometimes a lawyer would display commitment to traditional professional standards. One judge, Dr Lothar Kreyssig, made an accusation of murder against one of the euthanasia programme's leading directors. He refused to accept that Hitler's authorization made the murders legal.

Sometimes the integrity was an academic or scientific commitment to truth. An anthropologist at the University of Munich, Karl Saller, attacked the concept of a fixed Nordic race and said that modern Germans were racially mixed. Reinhard Heydrich banned him from teaching. Saller lost his chair at Munich. His fellow university teachers did not protest, instead they started to avoid him.

Sometimes patriotism played a part. One of the French nuns who hid and sheltered Jewish children, responding later to mention of her courage, said, 'Mais je suis Française, à la fin.'[16]

Religion often played a part. The response of the Christian churches to the Nazis was mixed. The Pope's muted public response to the Nazi murder of the Jews has rightly received much adverse comment. But often the values which led people to take risks to help came from religious commitment. All over Europe nuns gave shelter to Jewish children in their convents.

Sometimes people spoke out against the Nazis from their Christian beliefs. In Germany there were public protests against the euthanasia programme from certain Christian leaders. The Protestant Bishop of Württemberg wrote in protest to the Minister of the Interior. In Berlin the Catholic Bishop Preysing preached against it in St Hedwig's Cathedral. Pastor Braune, Vice-President of the Central Committee of the main Protestant welfare organization, wrote a long personal letter of protest to Hitler, which led to his arrest by the Gestapo.

A month after Braune's letter, the Catholic Bishop of Münster, Cardinal von Galen, preached against the euthanasia programme in forceful and highly specific terms. He spoke of reports that, on orders from Berlin, psychiatric patients were being killed. He had brought a charge of murder against those responsible, and had asked both the State Court and the Police President to protect the patients. In a sermon he said that, since he had received no reply, 'we must assume that the poor helpless patients will soon be killed'.

Bishop von Galen drew attention to the values behind what was being done:

> The argument goes: they can no longer produce commodities, they are like an old machine that no longer works ... What does one do with such an old machine? It is thrown on the scrap heap ... No, we are dealing with human beings, our fellow human beings, our brothers and sisters. With poor people, sick people, if you like unproductive people. But have they for that reason forfeited the right to life? ... even if initially it only affects the poor defenceless mentally ill, then as a *matter of principle* murder is permitted for all unproductive people ...[17]

Copies of the sermon were widely read. Nazi leaders suggested the Bishop should be hanged or sent to a concentration camp. To avoid conflict with the Catholic Church, Hitler did nothing, but said he would settle with the Bishop after the war.

On the murder of the Jews, the Church leaders were less impressive, but there were striking individual cases of Christian protest. Just before the round-up of Jews in Berlin, one Catholic priest, Bernard Lichtenberg, publicly prayed in St Hedwig's Cathedral for the Jews. He was imprisoned and died on his way to Dachau.

People could find themselves drawn into mild but increasing collaboration. They might gradually lose the self-respect which gave strength to their opposition. There is terrible danger in taking the first small step in collaboration and there is great value in early protest or refusal. Holland provides an instance. The Dutch people were not able to prevent transports of Jews to the death camps and many died. But large numbers of Dutch people gave help and support to Jews. Louis de Jong estimates that 25,000 Jews were hidden in Dutch homes, and that at least 2,000–3,000 resistance workers helped Jews with hiding places, papers, food coupons and money.

This record of opposition was present right at the beginning, before the corrupting effects of creeping collaboration could set in. In 1940 the German authorities started by saying that no more Jews should be admitted to the Dutch civil service. This was met by an immediate protest from all university student organizations and by a letter of protest signed by half of all the university teachers. The next step, the dismissal of all Jews from the civil service, was met by student strikes. The brutal rounding up for deportation of 400 Jews in Amsterdam was met with a virtually total strike in Amsterdam and nearby towns.[18] The self-respect maintained by these responses must have helped the many Dutch people who kept up resistance and gave shelter.

Le Chambon

Sometimes whole communities acted out of religious solidarity. In France the Protestant village of Le Chambon-sur-Lignon gave refuge to Jews. The pastor, André Trocmé, his wife Magda and the villagers had together created a community in which it would be unthinkable to turn away a refugee.

André Trocmé was a pacifist and a strong anti-Nazi. His sermons emphasized resisting evil. The resistance started when Marshal Pétain proposed schools should have a daily ceremony of saluting the flag. In Le Chambon there was none of the intended compulsion. Those who wished to salute the flag could do so. The numbers saluting dwindled. Then Trocmé and the school staff refused to sign an oath of unconditional loyalty to Pétain. The Mayor passed on to Trocmé an order from Pétain to ring his church bell as part of some Vichy celebration. Trocmé ignored the order. Amélie, the bell ringer, was part of an old dissenting Protestant tradition. When some visiting women tried to order her to ring the bell, she told them the bell belonged not to the Marshal but to God.

The village gave refuge to Jews. When the first, an old German Jewish woman, arrived on the doorstep, Magda Trocmé invited her in and gave the help she could. As she later put it, 'I do not hunt around to find people to help. But I never close my door, never refuse to help somebody who comes to me and asks for something. This I think is my kind of religion.'[19] Other refugees followed.

When Georges Lamirand, the Vichy Minister for Youth, visited the village, he was presented with a letter of protest about French police arresting Jews in Paris:

> We feel obliged to tell you that there are among us a certain number of Jews. But, we make no distinction between Jews and non-Jews. It is contrary to the Gospel teaching. If our comrades, whose only fault is to be born in another religion, received the order to let themselves be deported, or even examined, they would disobey the orders received, and we would try to hide them as best we could.

When the Prefect told Trocmé that he would have the Jews examined, Trocmé said, 'We do not know what a Jew is. We know only men.' When the authorities sent motor-cycle police and buses, the villagers warned the Jews to hide and Trocmé preached a sermon about the duty to protect the innocent. The search yielded one Jew. All the others were saved. Trocmé and two friends were arrested and spent about a month in an internment camp, before being released. At the time of the arrest the villagers brought gifts and sang hymns as the police and the arrested men were led away. The French policeman who arrested them was almost in tears.

During and after the internment, the policy of refuge went on. Documents were forged. The refugees were spread through the village and the houses of the surrounding country. Eventually 5,000 Jews, including many children, were in hiding in the village.

This stand must have had many sources. Among them were the Christian moral commitment to refuge, and the rapport between pastor and villagers. The warm responsiveness to people in need played a part. And the great rescue perhaps grew out of small things: the early refusals to salute the flag, to take the loyalty oath and to ring the bell for Pétain. These small things must have strengthened the sense of moral identity as surely as the opposite decisions would have weakened it. Emilie Guth worked in Marseilles, hiding Jews until they could be taken to Le Chambon. She found that an act of rescue would lead to further requests: 'Once you started to do one thing you couldn't stop because people came to you and begged for help. Even if you had just a little bit of feeling and were very afraid, you had to keep doing it.'[20]

There is another way in which the rescue may have grown out of small things. The people of Le Chambon did not think of themselves as heroes, but simply as doing the duty of any decent Christian. Laurence Thomas suggests that what they did fell into two stages, each of which seemed to them natural. Their Christianity made refusal of food and warmth to needy strangers impossible. And, having taken the needy strangers in, it became unthinkable to turn them out to their death.[21]

But, as Laurence Thomas also points out, it was important that the village was a community with a high moral base line. People who wanted to retain their self-respect could not depart far from the community's shared commitment to Christian charity. The capacity to resist is not only a matter of individual psychology, but also of a shared moral culture.

Denmark

In 1943, at the Jewish New Year, the Gestapo planned to round up all Jews in Denmark. An official at the German embassy leaked the plan to Danish politicians, who told the leading rabbi. He warned everyone to leave the synagogue and to tell all Jews to hide until transport to Sweden could be arranged. The Danish people gave massive support. Jews were stopped on the streets and given keys to people's homes. One ambulance driver went through the Copenhagen phone book and drove to the houses of people with Jewish names to take them into hiding. Doctors and nurses produced false medical records and hid Jews in hospitals. Taxis, ambulances, fire engines and other vehicles were used to take them to the coast. Of the 7,800 Jews in Denmark, 7,200 were hidden and helped to escape. Sweden made it clear that Jews would be welcomed and that boats in the rescue could fly the Swedish flag.

The rescue of the Danish Jews was helped by the fact that their numbers were relatively small, by the closeness and co-operation of Sweden, and by the warning. There is also reason to believe that the German authorities in occupied Denmark were not keen on the round-up and that a body of opinion in Berlin thought it would be unwise,[22] partly because of the likely Danish response. Immediately after the occupation, the German authorities sent a report to Berlin that steps against Jews would paralyse or seriously disturb economic life.[23]

Most countries are not monolithic and there were cases of betrayal of Jews by Danes. There was also a Danish Nazi Party of about 22,000 people. Despite these qualifications, the large number of Danes involved in the rescue suggests that much was owed to the climate of civil courage among the Danish people.

After the attempt to round up the Jews, the faculty and students at the University of Copenhagen agreed to suspend all classes 'in view of the disasters which have overtaken our fellow citizens'. The Danish Church was equally uncowed. The Bishop of Copenhagen issued a statement on behalf of all the bishops of Denmark, who had it read from the pulpit in the churches. Part of it read:

> Wherever Jews are persecuted because of their religion or race it is the duty of the Christian church to protest against such persecution, because it is in conflict with the sense of justice inherent in the Danish people and inseparable from our Danish Christian culture through centuries ... Our different religious views notwithstanding, we shall fight for the cause that our Jewish brothers and sisters may preserve the same freedom which we ourselves evaluate more highly than life itself. With the leaders of the Danish church there is a clear understanding of our duty to be law-abiding citizens who will not groundlessly rebel against the authorities, but at the same time our conscience bids us to assert the Law and protest against any violation of the Law. We shall therefore in any given event unequivocally adhere to the concept that we must obey God before we obey man.[24]

Perhaps the civil courage displayed in that public statement, and in the whole rescue operation, was not just a matter of individual psychology, but had its roots in Danish culture. Doubts have been expressed about thoughts of this kind. Steve Paulsson has said:

> The differences between nations are for the most part differences in their situations and not of intrinsic moral or other qualities; and one must not believe otherwise except on evidence much more rigorous than the historical discipline is capable of providing. Romanticism expressed along national lines is dangerous; to hold up whole nations to praise or blame is not only a questionable practice, it may even represent a subtle triumph of the Nazi ideal.[25]

To treat whole nations as collectively responsible for episodes is indeed objectionable. And to talk about 'intrinsic' moral qualities of nations is dubious, not least because the word 'intrinsic' is so vague. But the idea that people are to some extent shaped by the history and traditions of their culture need not be either romantic or subtly Nazi.

There seems no reason to disbelieve the account in the bishops' statement of some of the cultural roots of the rescue: a sense that Danish citizenship is bound up with ideas of freedom and of equal rights, and a Christian moral commitment which comes before obedience to men. The

Nazis were not up against a resistance movement pulled together out of nothing, but one which drew on character that had been growing a long time. The culture had shaped the characters of those who took part, but in turn what those people were like was part of what made the culture. The Danish rescue brings particularly strongly to mind what Socrates said about societies not being made of sticks and stones, but of people whose individual characters turn the scale.

Italy

The Nazis expected the Italians to co-operate in rounding up Jews for deportation. When Nazis demanded this from the Italian forces in Croatia, Mussolini wrote 'nulla osta' (no objection) across the paper about it; but other Italians often had different ideas.[26]

The Italian forces in Croatia interned the Jews for their own protection. General Roatta told the people interned at Kraljevice that, if he had submarines at his command, he would take them to Italy, where they would be safe.

When the Croatian Ustase were carrying out massacres, the Italian army sometimes saved the victims. Against orders, Lieutenant Salvatore Loi, with a corporal and two soldiers, saved 400 Serbs about to be killed, and protected a fleeing column of Serbs and Jews. Colonel Umberto Salvatores disobeyed orders by turning a blind eye. General Ambrosio invited refugees to return: 'The Italian armed forces are the guarantors of their safety, their liberty and their property.'

Baron Michele Scamacca, of the Italian Foreign Office, rejected a suggestion that Jewish refugees should be driven back to Croatia 'for obvious reasons of political prestige and humanity'. Jonathan Steinberg, who describes these events, comments on the way this 'obvious' reaction goes all the way up from Lieutenant Loi and his soldiers to the high officials of the Foreign Office, and rightly says that this chapter of glory in Italian history makes up for a good many defeats on the battlefield.

The Italians made masterly use of bureaucratic obstruction. The Office of Civilian Affairs of the Second Army had a document about how to seem to comply without actually doing so. And large complications were created about judging the 'pertinence' of Jews in occupied territory. One document said that the region would 'respond (without too much haste) to the Supreme Command'. There were endless delays while local commanders told the Germans that they had not yet had orders. When the Germans went higher up, the senior officials expressed surprise that their instructions had somehow not got through.

Italians occupying part of France blocked French efforts to implement the Nazis' Jewish policy. The Italian High Command, backed by the

Foreign Office, forbade the French to intern Jews or to impose the yellow star. And so it went on. To the constant exasperation of the Nazis, the Italians used every kind of obstruction and delay, combining deviousness with insistence on their rights as an occupying power.

The Jews in Italian-occupied Croatia had not been made to wear the yellow star. Mussolini was pressured to agree that they should be treated just as they would be in the German-occupied part of the country, but this was resisted right down the line. Count Luca Pietromarchi, the senior diplomat responsible for occupied territories, wrote in his diary that he had agreed with the liaison officer with the Second Army 'ways to avoid surrendering to the Germans those Jews who have placed themselves under the protection of our flag'. One colonel argued that 'our entire activity has been designed to let the Jews live in a human way', and that handing them over was impossible 'because we would not be true to the obligations we assumed'. The army's attitude was expressed in another document which said that 'the Italian army should not dirty its hands in this business'. The German authorities said they wanted the Jews in Mostar thrown out of their homes to provide houses for German mining engineers. The reply came that it was 'incompatible with the honour of the Italian army to take special measures against Jews'.

Jonathan Steinberg comments on how, in the Italian culture, the primary virtue of humanity so visible in these episodes is often surrounded by secondary vices found hardly at all in Germany: unpunctuality, bureaucratic inefficiency, evasiveness and corruption. He says that no sane person who has ridden a German bus or used a German post office would voluntarily use the Italian equivalents.[27] But at that time in Germany the secondary virtues of efficiency and incorruptibility were harnessed to inhuman ends. In Italy the secondary vices were in service to the primary virtue of humanity.

As with cultural comments about Denmark, there are reservations to make. Just as there were those in Germany who put humanity first, so there were Italians who did not. And atrocities were carried out by Italian forces in Abyssinia in the 1930s. But, taking account of exceptions and of the instability of national characteristics, the contrast with the Nazis does suggest something about the Italian culture of that time. The norm seems to have been for the human responses and the sense of moral identity to have been interwoven. For the Italian army to hand over Jews to their death would be to 'dirty its hands in this business'.

Free Bystanders and Moral Dilemmas

People living under Nazi rule often needed great courage to resist, sometimes risking themselves and their families. But this does not apply to 'free bystanders': those who lived outside Hitler's empire, and who had opportunities to help the victims of the Nazis.

Free bystanders were also sometimes presented by the Nazis with coercive moral dilemmas. This happened to the Red Cross. The World Jewish Congress asked the International Red Cross to say that Jews under Nazi rule in ghettos and concentration camps would be recognized as prisoners of war and so protected by the Geneva Convention. The request was refused because the Nazis had more than a million Allied prisoners of war, and they threatened to abandon the Geneva Convention if the Red Cross included the camps under it.

There were several occasions when British ministers and their officials had a chance of helping Hitler's Jewish victims. In judging the response, allowance has to be made for the fact that they were very occupied with the urgent need to defeat Hitler and help might have been given at the expense of the war effort. But, even allowing for this, the record is dismaying.

One conflict between the war effort and the chance of giving help was presented in May 1944 by Adolf Eichmann. He offered the Allies the lives of a million Jews in exchange for ten thousand trucks. Joel Brandt was allowed to take this offer to the British. He went to Aleppo, where the British authorities arrested him. Brandt said, 'Please believe me: they have killed six million Jews; there are only two million left alive.' British officials rejected the proposal. They said he could not return to Hungary. His reply was: 'Do you know what you are doing? This is simply murder! That is mass murder. If I don't return our best people will be slaughtered! My wife! My mother! My children will be first! You have to let me go! . . . I am here as the messenger of a million people condemned to death.'[28]

Even with hindsight, the decision was a difficult one. Suppose the trucks made it easier for Hitler to win the war? Suppose the blackmail was repeated and turned into a regular source of Nazi war supplies? Could Eichmann be relied on to keep his word?

Any adequate decision about the offer would have to be taken with the seriousness appropriate to what was at stake: the lives of a million men, women and children. It still might be right to turn down the deal, but with full emotional appreciation of what this meant such a decision would be agonizing.

'On Merely Humanitarian Grounds'

It is hard to see that the actual decision was made with this seriousness. In June 1944 representatives of the Jewish Agency met the British Foreign Secretary, Anthony Eden. They asked for some signal to be sent to Germany that the rescue of the Jews could be discussed. Eden said he could not act without the agreement of the American and Soviet governments. He said he 'doubted' that the deal was possible and expressed his 'profound sympathy'.[29] Someone imaginatively and emotionally engaged might not have offered this conventional condolence.

The impression that on this question Eden had a stunted moral imagination is reinforced by his earlier response to a plea to rescue the Jews of Bulgaria: he said, 'Turkey does not want any more of your people.' His imagination seems to have been stunted partly by anti-Semitism. His private secretary said that he loved Arabs and hated Jews. And Eden himself wrote in a private note that 'if we must have preferences let me murmur in your ear that I prefer Arabs to Jews'.[30]

And, where British ministers were responsive, they sometimes had to work against the anti-Semitism of their officials. The Colonial Secretary proposed to try to rescue Jewish children from Bulgaria. One of the Colonial Office's officials, J.S. Bennett, commented: 'It is difficult to prevent a convincing case on *security* grounds against letting in *children* as proposed here; particularly in view of our reception of Greek (non-Jewish) children . . . What is disturbing is the apparent readiness of the new Colonial Secretary to take Jewish Agency "sob stuff" at its face value.' Mr Bennett's response to eye-witness reports of what the Nazis were doing was to write: 'Familiar stuff. The Jews have spoilt their case by laying it on too thick for years past.'[31] One wonders what the Nazis would have had to do for Mr Bennett to find Jewish anguish justified.

Sometimes the political inadequacy seems to have come, not from anti-Semitism, but from the human responses being shrivelled by bureaucracy. A Foreign Office official, R.T.E. Latham explained the refusal to allow entry to some more Jewish refugees: 'I am afraid there is next to nothing we can do . . . in any case we simply cannot have any more people let into the UK on merely humanitarian grounds . . . Furthermore these refugees, pitiable as is their plight, are hardly war refugees . . . but simply racial refugees.'[32]

Bystanders and Ethics

Bystanders who looked away did so often because of the dangers of trying to help or protest. Rescuers often risked their lives. It is difficult for those of us who have not been in their position to be very condemnatory. We all hope we would be like the villagers of Le Chambon, while fearing we might be like the people Inge Deutschkron saw peering out from behind curtained windows.

The ethical position is fairly unproblematic if left vague. When people's lives are at risk from persecution, there is a strong moral obligation to do what is reasonably possible to help. It is not enough to seal up the windows against the smell. The world would be a terrible place if the whole truth about this aspect of us was what Norman Geras has called 'the contract of mutual indifference': we leave other people in peril unrescued and accept that others will do the same to us.[33] The problems start when we try to make the ethical position less vague. There is room for disagreement over what degree of risk it is reasonable to expect people to run for others. Particularly if rescuing a stranger means putting your family at risk, good people may divide about what morality requires.

Except in cases of coercive moral dilemmas, it is harder to find things to say for the free bystanders who refused to help. What comes over most strongly is the contribution made to their failure by distance and by lack of moral imagination. People immersed in bureaucratic rules easily forget what is at stake. A code of ethics for officials should include having the imagination to look through the rules to the human reality. This might undermine the thought that saving people's lives is 'merely' humanitarian.

Those bystanders under Nazi rule who protested or helped were people whose human responses and sense of moral identity had not been eroded or overwhelmed. Sometimes the sense of moral identity was bound up with the human responses. And a great difference could be made by the outlook prevalent in a community, whether a country or only a village.

Those who responded in more inspiring ways than sealing the windows sometimes did quite small things. They still made a difference. The small act of respect (Mrs Krachudel the butcher's wife still courteously asking what meat their Jewish customers wanted) mattered enough to be remembered. The same was true of the small gesture of sympathy: Herbert Karp sharing his last cigarette with Jean Améry. The small act of defiance (Amélie the bell ringer refusing to ring the bell because it belonged to God, not to Pétain) and the small act of generosity (Magda Trocmé telling the first Jewish refugee to come in and have a meal) can be enormously important. These small acts reinforce the ordinary, everyday human decencies, out of which the large heroic acts grow.

CHAPTER 41

Interpreting the Nazi Episode

The origins of Nazism were partly economic. In a few years people in Germany had experienced the hardships of the First World War, followed by runaway inflation and mass unemployment. Economic security had been destroyed. Unsurprisingly, promises of a new economic system were seized on. But economic hardship is only part of the story. That would equally have favoured Communism, which also offered the hope of building a new economic system through state action.

Before 1933 Nazism and Communism fought each other over how Germany should be re-created. The appeal of Nazism was deeper partly because it spoke to dimensions of the German crisis which were not economic. The defeat in the First World War, and the harsh and humiliating terms of the peace, strongly bent the twig of nationalist resentment. The Nazis and Communists both offered a planned economy to tackle poverty and unemployment, but the Nazis also promised to reverse the humiliation of Versailles. The phrase 'National Socialism' encapsulated the double promise and found an echo in people to whom Communist ideas of international working-class solidarity meant little. The extra emotional charge of Nazism was exploited powerfully by the songs, the uniforms and the mass rallies.

Nazi supporters felt their lives were given meaning by becoming part of a shared project, which in turn was justified by a system of beliefs which had deep emotional roots. As with Stalinism, the belief system played a central role by 'justifying' the Nazi atrocities. Stalinism, as a version of the Enlightenment idea of redesigning society on a rational basis, showed the catastrophic implications of carrying out such a project without moral or human restraints. Nazism was against the universalism of Kant and other Enlightenment thinkers. It was tribal: not the rights of man, but the German right to Lebensraum. If Stalinism shows what can go wrong when Enlightenment ideas are applied wrongly, Nazism shows what can happen when unenlightened ideas are applied rightly.

Intentionalism and Functionalism

To speak of Nazism in terms of ideas being applied may be to adopt an 'intentionalist' approach. This term was introduced in a classic paper by Tim Mason, in which he contrasts 'intentionalism' with 'functionalism'. The core of an intentionalist approach is to explain the genocide in terms of intentional actions chosen on the basis of beliefs. This approach entails trying to understand Nazism from the inside. (Mason mentions the German word 'verstehen'.) A functionalist approach does not give primacy to the beliefs and intentions of individuals. Instead it emphasizes that decisions are influenced by the way they are reached, especially by the interaction of different parts of the machinery of government.[1]

In his paper Tim Mason criticized intentionalism in particular. (Some of the criticisms assume the approach is only concerned with the intentions of Hitler. A version which ignores the intentions and outlook of those who supported or went along with Hitler is clearly too crude.) Mason's main criticism is that intentionalism has no explanatory power:

> to say, that is, that Hitler ordered the extermination of the Jews because he wanted to, is a form of intellectual surrender. Intention is an indispensable concept for historians, whether they are determinists or not, but we do not have to take people in the past at their own word concerning their intentions. The realm of their self-consciousness as presented in historical sources is not trivial, but it does not define the limits of our understanding. It is a starting point; it constitutes a problem, not an answer.[2]

A version of intentionalism which assumes that a speech by Hitler has to be taken at face value, with no scepticism about his sincerity or doubts about interpretation is again obviously too crude. That version would be intellectual surrender. And a version which left no room for questions about why Hitler wanted to kill the Jews, or why his orders were obeyed, can similarly be dismissed as a dogmatic dead end.

There is a range of middle positions between these naïve views and the functionalism which looks mainly to institutional factors to explain the genocide. The less crude intentionalist view is that the beliefs and outlook of the Nazis (not just of Hitler) were central. But, of course, economic and social factors contributed to the fact that those beliefs were held so widely. And the pattern of the genocide which sprang from the ideology was shaped by the government machine which implemented it.

If only the crude versions count as 'intentionalism', implausibility is built into the definition and the 'intentionalist-functionalist' contrast loses its interest. What matters is that the less crude way of giving weight to Nazi beliefs is able to be stated and defended. How much of value we learn from the genocide depends on how far we remember that it was not carried out impersonally, but was a series of things which people did.

The Distinctive Nazi Darkness

Another debate considers whether the Nazi genocide was unique. Some say that it takes its place with the other twentieth-century cases of political mass murder. Others argue that it possesses a moral enormity which makes it unique. The debate is blurred by the vagueness of the idea of an episode being unique. Every event is in some ways unique and in other ways not.

In some important aspects the Nazi genocide was not unique. In numbers killed, Hitler was surpassed by Stalin and by Mao. In proportion of the population killed, he was surpassed by Pol Pot. But, in other ways, there was a unique moral horror to what the Nazis did. There was an intensity of positive hatred in those who planned the genocide, which was not matched in the Stalinist exterminations. The uniqueness has been well put by Eberhard Jäckel, replying to some who would minimize it. He said:

> the National-Socialist murder of the Jews was unique because never before had a nation with the authority of its leader decided and announced that it would kill off as completely as possible a particular group of humans, including old people, women, children, and infants, and actually put this decision into practice, using all the means of governmental power at its disposal.[3]

I would not be discussing Nazism in the context of the other topics of this book unless I thought there were some common patterns to be found. But to say this is not to deny that the Nazi genocide has a terrible darkness all its own. A lot of the darkness came from Social Darwinism and from Nietzsche's version of amoralism. Nietzsche's belief in the struggle between the will to power in different individuals and groups was a psychological variant on Social Darwinism. It encouraged his view that a morality of compassion was discredited. The Nazis selectively took this part of his theory to justify their own dark views about cruelty and hardness, and the appalling new Nazi moral identity.

The Nazis showed how the technology of killing, combined with the robotic obedience of human functionaries, could be put to ends of unparalleled inhumanity. Some of the lessons are obvious: the dangers of Social Darwinism, the power and danger of tribalism, and the implications of unconditional obedience. But I believe that the central lesson Nazism holds for ethics is that a sense of moral identity is not enough. Moral identity needs to be rooted in the human responses, rather than, as with the Nazis, adversarial to them. It matters that people keep their humanity alive and retain their scepticism in the face of leaders or theories telling them otherwise.

PART SEVEN

ON THE RECENT MORAL
HISTORY OF HUMANITY

Trying to learn from the twentieth-century atrocities can seem absurd. Hiroshima, the Gulag, the cruelties of Mao or of Pol Pot: their enormity transcends our imagination. Any 'lessons' drawn are bound to seem puny beside the events themselves.

A few years ago a group of British philosophers was visiting Cracow. One day we were taken by bus to Auschwitz. On the way there was the buzz of philosophers' conversation: a mixture of gossip and 'People say such and such, but is it really rational?' Returning, we were silent. It was hard to take in emotionally what we had seen. The fine distinctions of ethical analysis would have been grotesque on the bus back to Cracow.

Inevitably, the discussion here is in the same way dwarfed by its subject. No ethical reflections, no thoughts, seem adequate.

All the same, we do need to learn from these events. One thought after a visit to Auschwitz is that 'never again' is the only morally serious response. The battlefields of the First World War provoke the same thought. I have not been to Hiroshima or Nagasaki, or to the sites of the Gulag, or to Cambodia, but the same thought must come there too. So this last section of the book contains comments on the threats from some parts of human nature and on our defences against them. Against the backdrop of the events of recent times, the fragility of these defences will be obvious.

CHAPTER 42

Some People and Not Others

If only it were all so simple! If only there were evil people somewhere insidiously committing evil deeds, and it were necessary only to separate them from the rest of us and destroy them. But the line dividing good and evil cuts through the heart of every human being . . . it is after all only because of the way things worked out that they were the executioners and we weren't.

Alexander Solzhenitsyn, *The Gulag Archipelago*

I do not know, and it does not much interest me to know, whether in my depths there lurks a murderer, but I do know that I was a guiltless victim and I was not a murderer. I know that the murderers existed . . . and that to confuse them with their victims is a moral disease or an aesthetic affectation or a sinister sign of complicity; above all, it is a precious service rendered (intentionally or not) to the negators of truth.

Primo Levi, *The Drowned and the Saved*

The causes of these catastrophes are partly political and social. Solutions to them cannot be purely in the realm of psychology or ethics: the political dimension has to be central. There is a need for proper policing of the world, with a legitimate and properly backed international authority to keep the peace and to protect human rights. There is a need for independent sources of information as alternatives to propaganda. There is a need to avoid large-scale utopian political projects.

But the solutions are also ethical and psychological. This is partly because the political solutions need a supportive public opinion. More generally, a climate of opinion can make a difference as to whether a disaster is avoided. The politics and the psychology are interwoven.

The psychology is partly about groups and partly about individual differences. One question about those who ran the Gulag or the Nazi genocide is about the rest of us too. Could *anyone* have done these things?

Primo Levi is right. It does no service to truth to blur the moral contrast between the victims and the murderers. Some people were willing to become murderers and some were not.

Alexander Solzhenitsyn exaggerates when he says that it was 'only because of the way things worked out' that some became murderers and some did not. That suggests the differences were only external, only of circumstances. Qualities of character made a difference too. In similar circumstances, different people made different decisions.

Yet Solzhenitsyn is partly right too. Character makes a difference, but character is itself shaped by genetic and environmental factors beyond our control. Self-creation is at best only partial. So, to some extent, character itself is a matter of 'the way things worked out'.

It is not necessary to create a false opposition between these two great chroniclers of the atrocities they lived through. The writings of each include recognition of the truths contained in both the passages quoted.

Solzhenitsyn knew from experience the difference character made: 'Those people became corrupted in camp who before camp had not been enriched by any morality at all or by any spiritual upbringing.'[1]

And Primo Levi knew how much there was in common between murderers and victims. He thought the word 'torturers' was inappropriate because it suggested twisted sadists, with some innate flaw: 'Instead, they were made of our same cloth, they were average human beings, averagely intelligent, averagely wicked: save for exceptions, they were not monsters, they had our faces, but they had been reared badly.'[2] Their bad upbringing had made them followers and functionaries, some of them Nazi believers, some careerists, some afraid, some too obedient.

There are two truths. One is that people with different characters respond very differently to moral crises. There is a difference between those who go along with murder and those who do not. The other truth is that differences of character are, for the most part, not just innate. (Though there may be an innate component. For instance, males participate more than females in war, violence and atrocities. Perhaps the Y chromosome and environmental differences both make some contribution to this. These things are still too poorly understood for confident answers.)

The sense of moral identity is one relevant aspect of character. Those who have a strong sense of who they are and of the kind of person they want to be have an extra defence against conditioning in cruelty, obedience or ideology.

Towards a Robust and Connected Moral Identity

However, the sense of moral identity does not always hold people back from doing terrible things. It may fail in several ways. Most crudely, it may be overridden. This may be by fear, either of the bullying sergeant or of a whole apparatus of state terror. Or it may be overridden by the pressures of obedience or conformity.

Sometimes people's actions seem to be disconnected from their sense of who they are. This may be because they slide into participation by imperceptible degrees, so that there is never the sense of a frontier being crossed. This gentle slide can be a feature of the training of torturers. It was what the Nazis aimed at in securing collaboration in occupied countries. With the atomic bomb, the slide was gradual from making it only as a deterrent against Hitler to making it for actual use against Japan. One version of the slide involves comparison with other people. This was a feature of the gradual abandonment of the prohibition on the intentional killing of civilians in war.

There is another form of disconnection between what people do and their sense of moral identity. The division of labour can make the contribution of any single person seem unimportant. The history of the atomic bomb was one case. Scientists saw themselves as making an atomic bomb which politicians decided to use. Politicians each thought the decision was not theirs. Individual scientists and politicians could avoid the thought that they had harmed anyone. Another case was the operation of the Nazi bureaucracy. Nazi officials were arranging trains which someone else had decided were needed for taking people to the death camps. Again, those involved could go on thinking of themselves as people who were not killers.

People clearly vary in the robustness with which their sense of moral identity resists being overwhelmed or being disconnected from action. This robustness may be partly luck, depending on things outside the person's own control. The patchy evidence suggests it may be influenced by upbringing and by the climate of a culture.

The evidence suggests that those who rescued victims of the Nazis had not been given a rigidly disciplined upbringing. When they were children, parents had shown them respect, giving them reasons rather than orders. Respect may create a climate where moral identity can grow. Evidence from Nazi-occupied countries suggests that cultures may have climates which vary in their support for the growth of moral identity.

Although most people can do little about their own upbringing or about the culture they live in, the robustness of the sense of moral identity is not entirely outside a person's own control. There is scope for partial self-creation. To see how actions can be severed from the sense of moral identity can be a warning to guard against such disconnection.

A Human Moral Identity

To hold people back from atrocities, it is not enough for the sense of moral identity to be robust and to be connected to actions.

Sometimes it is neither overwhelmed nor disconnected, but instead subverted. When terrible orders are given, some people resist because of their conception of who they are. But there may be no resistance when a person's self-conception has been built round obedience. In the same way, if someone's self-conception is built round a tribal identity or round some system of belief, resistance to tribal or ideological atrocities may have been subverted from within. A lot depends on how far the sense of moral identity has been narrowed to a merely tribal or ideological one. Again, seeing how this happens can prompt resistance.

Avoiding the kind of Belief that narrows the sense of identity means keeping scepticism alive. It means not distorting everything else to maintain a political or religious faith: not saving belief in Stalin by telling yourself Britain and France are the real aggressors against Hitler. It means, when under pressure to believe, staying alert to awkward evidence: noticing, like Jung Chang, that Mao's parents were heroes while other rich peasants were class enemies. It means not giving so much of yourself to Communism that you accept Palme Dutt's claim that a Communist has no private opinions apart from the collective thinking of the movement.

Another defence against the narrowing of moral identity is to keep tribal psychology under control. This means struggling, as Slavenka Drakulić did, to maintain an identity beyond being one of 4.5 million Croats. It means keeping alive the other commitments which enabled Dr Mujkanović to treat wounded Serbian soldiers in Srebrenica side by side with Bosnian ones.

To function as a restraint against atrocity, the sense of moral identity most of all needs to be rooted in the human responses. The chilling Nazi moral identity, built around hardness and the willingness to be cruel, is a clear warning. Franz Stangl, doing everything at Treblinka as well as he could, because 'that is how I am', did not lack a sense of moral identity, nor did Himmler, when he said that SS men should not steal a single fur or watch and that they had not been damaged in their soul, their character.

The two moral resources singled out here, the sense of moral identity and the human responses, are both needed as defences against atrocity, but the Nazi case brings out the primacy of the human responses. The humanity of the sense of moral identity is crucial. When severed from the human responses, or even hostile to them, it is useless or worse.

CHAPTER 43

Ethics Humanized

If you have no God then your moral code is that of society. If society is turned upside down, so is your moral code. The communists made a virtue of being beastly to each other.

> Jung Chang, *Independent on Sunday* (10 September 1995)

We have seen the triumph of evil after the values of humanism have been vilified and trampled on. The reason these values succumbed was probably that they were based on nothing except boundless confidence in the human intellect. I think we may now find a better foundation for them, if only because of the lessons we have drawn from our experience.

> Nadezhda Mandelstam, *Hope Against Hope*

One feature of our time is the fading of the moral law. The idea of a moral law external to us may never have had secure foundations, but, partly because of the decline of religion in the Western world, awareness of this is now widespread.

Those of us who do not believe in a religious moral law should still be troubled by its fading. The evils of religious intolerance, religious persecution and religious wars are well known, but it is striking how many protests against and acts of resistance to atrocity have also come from principled religious commitment. (A handful of names: Bishop George Bell, Elizabeth Anscombe, Bishop von Galen, Pastor Braune, Bernard Lichtenberg, André and Magda Trocmé and the villagers of Le Chambon, and the bishops of Denmark in 1943.) The decline of this moral commitment would be a huge loss. If the decline of religion means this, then Jung Chang's worrying thought, that if you have no God your moral code is that of society, might be true.

Reconstructing Ethics

Not all sceptics about a non-human moral law see much to admire in Nietzschean amoralism. The alternative is to keep ethics afloat without external support. If there is no external moral law, morality needs to be humanized: to be rooted in human needs and human values. (These may of course include caring about other species.)

Morality interpreted in this way becomes tentative, exploratory and partly empirical. It is exploratory on the model of Socrates. Our deepest values are not just obvious. They are not all on the surface. Questioning and argument are needed to discover some of them. But ethics is also exploratory in a different, more empirical, way. It includes seeing the consequences of living by a code or set of values. A human disaster shows the need to think again about the values.

With disasters on the scale of some in the twentieth century, any ethical theory which either justifies them or can give no help in avoiding them is inadequate. The thought at Auschwitz and at other places, 'never again', is more compelling than any abstract ethical principle. (There is a parallel with a thought sometimes expressed about another part of philosophy: belief in the existence of the physical world is more compelling than belief in any philosophical theory which purports to disprove it.) If persuaded that an otherwise convincing ethical theory could justify the Nazi genocide, I should without hesitation give up the theory. In reconstructing ethics, revulsion against these things which people have done has a central place.

It is necessary to see the size and urgency of the problem. For those of us whose everyday life is in relatively calm and sheltered places, the horrors of Rwanda or Bosnia or Kosovo seem unreal. The atrocities can be put out of mind. The television news reports torture or a massacre and we feel relief when it moves on to political scandals or sport. We bystanders look away. Repressing each atrocity maintains the illusion that the world is fundamentally a tolerable place. Yet it is almost certain that, as you read this sentence, in some places people are being killed and in others people are being tortured.

Bystanders know enough to see that knowing more will be uncomfortable. Looking away, there is little sense of an enormous evil it is urgent to stop. The first step is not to look away. As Norman Geras has written in his fine book on this topic, 'Under the sign of a different moral reality, the duty would be to take the pain of thinking about these things. It would be to take it enough to feel obliged to act against them.'[1]

The moral resources give some hope of opposing atrocities with a strategy which fits human psychology. The sense of moral identity and the human responses are parts of our psychology, independent of any external metaphysics. The sense of moral identity is important, but in the prevention of atrocities it is reliable only when it is rooted in the human responses. At the core of humanized ethics are the human responses.

But one obvious fact of recent history is that the human responses have often failed to prevent these catastrophes. First, a sketch of the pattern of failure.

How the Human Responses Fail

The propaganda of atrocity is often directed against the dignity of the victims. There are acts which humiliate the victims, often accompanied by the cold joke. Such acts remove one of the main inhibitions against further horrors. This was true both in Nazi Germany and in the Chinese Cultural Revolution. And those responsible for atrocities are often people whose own dignity has not been respected. The persistent humiliation of Lieutenant Calley in front of his men cannot have done much for his willingness to respect the dignity of the Vietnamese villagers. And how much the world owes to the childhood humiliation of Hitler by his father cannot be known for sure. It is not a universal truth that those to whom evil is done do evil in return, but it is true often enough, and Hitler is one instance. The spiral of vendetta in rival versions of 'bent twig' nationalism provides others.

Sympathy can also fail as a restraint. Sometimes people are trapped in ways which make it ineffective. The trap of Hobbesian fear can do this. So can military traps: the human responses of those trapped in the trenches did little to mitigate the horror. The same goes for the thought of the navigator after his first bombing raid on Hamburg: 'What about those poor sods under those fires?'

Sometimes sympathy is overwhelmed. This happens in combat with emotional explosion or release. It can also be overwhelmed by pressures to obey or conform, which is especially the effect of state terror. Under Stalin, Mao and Hitler, people were afraid to act on their generous protective impulses. And people were trapped in moral dilemmas created by threats to those they loved.

Sympathy can be defeated by Belief, of which the extreme case is the deliberately cultivated hardness of the Nazis.

Sympathy can be weakened or narrowed. It may be weakened by distance, either physical or psychological. When General Groves said that the atomic bomb 'went with a tremendous bang', he was thousands of miles away from its victims. For Nazis, Jews were psychologically distanced by being dehumanized. In the Cultural Revolution the victims were distanced by being seen as enemies of the people or as bourgeois. Tribalism and belief, by creating psychological distance, succeed in catastrophically narrowing the human responses, cutting them off to whole groups of people.

Sympathy can be eliminated through a sense of unreality. Combat on a plain without a feature, where the landscape could be that of the moon, where family, friends and neighbours seem to be a world away, creates this unreality. Auschwitz was another planet. Remoteness makes it natural to think all this is not really happening, I am not really doing this. People do not even have to go away. If war comes to you, this can sufficiently disrupt the everyday context in which horrors seem real. In the Terror during the French Revolution, 90 per cent of the executions took place in only twenty of the eighty-six departments of France. Apart from Paris, all those areas were war zones.[2]

There are common psychological patterns. The human responses are overwhelmed, weakened, narrowed or eliminated in ways which recur in Vietnam and Afghanistan; they recur in the use of the blockade, of area bombing and of the atomic bomb; they recur under Hitler, Stalin, Mao and Pol Pot. To see the unity in the underlying psychology is to make the development of 'a different moral reality' a more manageable task.

For many of us the catastrophes are remote from everyday life. It would be absurd for children's moral education to take as the main theme how not to become commander of a concentration camp. But, luckily, the ethics of preventing atrocities are an extension of the ethics of everyday life. At the supermarket people do not park in the disabled space partly because they do not want a disabled person to have the indignity and difficulty of struggling to carry groceries. They may also not want to be someone who is mean enough to cause this. The moral resources here are the same as those needed in the moral emergencies. It is a question of knowing and guarding against the ways in which they fail in those emergencies.

Breakthrough and the Moral Imagination

Most of all, the functioning of the human responses as a restraint requires the moral imagination. When Nixon and others planned the bombing of Cambodia, they sent death and suffering to people they hardly felt were real. In one way the psychology was like that of the people in Milgram's study who gave what they thought were electric shocks. They were more reluctant to give the shocks if the victims were visible. Without that, distance played its role. Neither Nixon nor those who gave the shocks to the unseen 'victims' had the moral imagination to overcome distance. This was also true of some of the hawks in the Cuba crisis. On the other hand, the imagination of Kennedy and the doves had been stimulated by being taught about the human effects of nuclear war. Emotional responses to the possible victims came alive.

Central to the moral imagination is seeing what is humanly important. When it is stimulated, there is a breakthrough of the human responses, otherwise deadened by such things as distance, tribalism or ideology. It checks conformity and obedience, bringing to the fore what matters humanly rather than the current norm or the official policy. It makes vivid the victims and the human reality of what will be done to them.

Sometimes the breakthrough is a simple emotional response, triggered by the visible reminder of someone's humanity: by the family letters and photographs of girlfriends found by soldiers in the pockets of those on the other side, or by seeing the fascist soldier holding up his trousers as he runs.

Sometimes the moral imagination involves both the emotions and the intellect. It can be stimulated by information, as in Kennedy's briefing about nuclear war. It can be stimulated by awareness of the effects of distance or of dehumanizing people, and a determination to resist those effects.

Questions and thinking are important for overcoming the effects of the social and technological division of labour. Take someone who works at a computer in a British company making aircraft. He may be relatively untroubled by knowing the aircraft are sold to Indonesia and then used for genocidal bombing. The victims are distant. The division of labour makes one person's contribution almost invisibly small.

The same British engineer at the computer might move to work in a country where punishments include being stoned to death. He would undoubtedly be horrified if asked to carry out a stoning. ('She committed adultery. All you have to do is pelt her with these heavy stones. Do not be put off by her screams, or by the blood, or by what the stones do to her face. Just keep going until she is dead.') The questions which need to be pressed are about the rationalizations which make the computer work seem so different. You would not do it alone, but would you take part in a collective stoning? Would you be the person who passes the stones to the killers? Would you help to make more punishments possible by inventing a remote-control technology for mass stoning?

Ethics Now

There are features of our time which make it particularly important to build up moral defences against barbarism. Most obviously, there is the way technology hugely increases the scale of atrocities. But there is the increasing awareness of the fading of the moral law. As authority-based morality retreats, it can be replaced by a morality which is deliberately created. The best hope of this is to work with the grain of human nature, making use of the resources of moral identity and the human responses. But changes and additions to common-sense attitudes will be needed. Many of these involve the social and personal cultivation of the moral imagination. To advocate this may sound like vague uplift with little content. The truth is the opposite. Real cultivation of the moral imagination is a threat to many comforting conventional attitudes. It is likely, for instance, to destroy the conventional explanations of why what the computer engineer does is so different from the stoning.

If a humanized version of ethics is developed, people later will see the end of belief in the moral law as just a stage in the evolution of morality. But, if we do not start on man-made moral traditions, there will be a gap. Particularly in relations between groups, amoralism may start to seem the natural state. And, once this happens, the idea of starting inter-group morality may come to seem utopian.

EPILOGUE

The Past Alive in the Present

So long as the past and the present are outside one another, knowledge of the past is not of much use in the present. But suppose the past lives on in the present; suppose, though encapsulated in it, and at first sight hidden beneath the present's contradictory and more prominent features, it is still alive and active; then the historian may very well be related to the non-historian as the trained woodsman is to the ignorant traveller.

R.G. Collingwood, *Autobiography*

This book would not have been written without the belief that the past is alive in the present. It started with another sentence from R.G. Collingwood: 'The chief business of twentieth-century philosophy is to reckon with twentieth-century history.' The aim has been to participate in a little of that true business, taking Collingwood's sentence in the obvious way. This is the moment to apologize for taking Collingwood's remark out of context: he was urging philosophers to reckon, not with the events of the century, but with the practice of twentieth-century historians. Despite this, I like to think he would also have sympathized with the other interpretation. At the end of the autobiography he published in 1939 he described how his opposition to fascist irrationalism had made him see links between philosophy and politics: 'I know that all my life I have been engaged unawares in a political struggle, fighting against these things in the dark. Henceforth I shall fight in the daylight.'[1]

One way in which the past is alive in the present is in the use of precedent as a justification. Sir Arthur Harris used the First World War blockade as a precedent for his bombing policy in the Second World War. He also took the mass slaughter in the trenches as a precedent to avoid. Harris's policy made easier the fire bombing of Japan, which itself paved the way to the use of the atomic bomb. The First World War was alive at Hiroshima.

The past can live on as resentment, in the support given to the spiral of tribal hatred by historical narratives and by personal memories. More generally, people are shaped by their experiences of public events. The influence of the First World War on Hitler's outlook is clear. There was his resentment that the war, whose outbreak made him ecstatic in the Odeonsplatz, ended in defeat and a humiliating peace. There was also his belief that the defeat came from betrayal, and the stimulus of his own experience of poison gas to suggest the form of revenge.

Keeping the past alive may help to prevent atrocities. There can be terrible significance in what some people expect others to forget. In a speech to SS men going to Poland, Hitler told them to kill men, women and children without pity. He suggested their acts would be forgotten: 'Who remembers now the massacres of the Armenians?' There is a chilling similarity between this and Stalin's comment while signing death warrants: 'Who's going to remember all this riff-raff in ten or twenty years' time? No one. Who remembers now the names of the boyars Ivan the Terrible got rid of? No one.'

At the other extreme, someone's conscience may be stimulated by awareness of a historical parallel. Hugh Thompson protected otherwise defenceless villagers at My Lai partly because he remembered the Nazis also shot people in ditches. Sometimes statesmen too want to avoid repeating the past. In the 1962 missile crisis, Khrushchev remembered the horrors of the Second World War and Kennedy wanted to avoid repeating 1914.

Most of all, there is the thought that patterns to be found in the past may tell us things helpful to know now. If so, Collingwood may have been right in his comparison between the historian and the trained woodsman.

Remember the absurdly simple view of the major political evils of the twentieth century which ascribed them all to the assassination of Archduke Ferdinand at Sarajevo. The reasoning was simple. No assassination, no First World War. If there had been no First World War, there would have been no Russian Revolution and so no Stalin. If there had been no German defeat in the war, there would have been no Hitler. Without Hitler, there would have been no Nazi genocide and no Second World War, no nuclear weapons and so no Hiroshima. Without Stalin or the Second World War, there would probably have been no Mao or Pol Pot.

This view is absurd, yet each part of the chain of reasoning is plausible. To rebut the view, we have to appeal to general tendencies. Without the assassination, the First World War as we know it would not have happened, but, with the arms race and the system of alliances as they were, there is a strong chance that a different First World War would have broken out later. (The military and political state of Europe in the early part of the century can be seen as a heap of combustible material. If one of the sparks flying around did not set it on fire, almost certainly another one would have done.) Without the First World War as we know it, there might have been no Revolution in October 1917, but the state Russia was in created a strong chance of some kind of revolution.

As we get further from history as it did turn out, thinking gets more speculative. Would a different Russian Revolution have avoided Stalinism? Would a different First World War a year or two later have led to a German victory? Might Hitler have been killed in it? We have no way of answering these questions.

But, if we move still further back from history as it did turn out, we get to a region where some plausible suggestions again can be made. Just as early twentieth-century Europe can be seen as combustible material, so the psychology of the human species can be seen as having a strong propensity both for getting trapped into conflict and also for cruelty and mass killing. Twentieth-century wars, massacres and genocides come from combining this psychology with modern technology. Without Sarajevo, without Stalin or Hitler, it seems likely that the destructive technology would still have been developed and used. (Here, perhaps a grim nod is appropriate to Heidegger's phrase about the planetary encounter with technology.)

The psychology so visible in the twentieth century is a recurring one. The French Revolution gives striking instances. Fabre d'Eglantine produced a poster urging townspeople to 'let the blood of traitors be the first holocaust'. An exhortation by Jacques Roux makes him seem a precursor of Pol Pot: 'It is time that the liberty of the people was consolidated by the shedding of impure blood.' Humiliation of victims before atrocities was common and often included the cold joke. Before the execution of Louis XVI, the guards scrawled graffiti for him to see: pictures of a crowned figure hanging from a gibbet captioned 'Louis Taking a Bath in the Air', or a fat figure having just been guillotined. Only by fainting did Marie Antoinette escape being made to look at the head of one of her ladies-in-waiting stuck on a pike. On the counter-revolutionary side in the Vendée, atrocities included forcing chains of prisoners to dig their own graves before being shot over them.[2]

This cruel psychology seized on the technology of mass killing even in its early and primitive forms. There was the guillotine, with some people enjoying watching its operation while others kept bureaucratic records of those killed. In Nantes Jean-Baptiste Carrier had holes made in barges which could then be filled with bound prisoners for mass drownings in the Loire. Over 2,000 people were killed in what the cold joke of the day called 'republican baptisms' or 'the national bath'. There was the search for a more efficient technology. One revolutionary leader asked a distinguished chemist to look into 'mines, gassings or other means to destroy, put to sleep or asphyxiate the enemy'.[3]

Inhumanity can be seen here stretching from our own time back to the eighteenth century. Of course it goes back further. It goes as far back as we know. The Tollund Man, whose peat-preserved body was found near

Aarhus, had been executed in prehistoric times. In Northern Ireland in the 1970s Seamus Heaney wrote that he would go to Aarhus:

> Out there in Jutland
> In the old man-killing parishes
> I will feel lost,
> Unhappy and at home.[4]

But the French Revolutionary guillotine and the republican baptisms – and the interest in the possibilities of gassing – all show how naturally inhumanity combines with technology. No doubt the facts of twentieth-century history would have been different if the assassination of the Archduke had not taken place, but inhumanity would still have been combined with modern technology. It is hard to see that there was much chance to escape some variant of the bloody twentieth century we know.

To avoid further disasters, we need political restraints on a world scale. But politics is not the whole story. We have experienced the results of technology in the service of the destructive side of human psychology. Something needs to be done about this fatal combination. The means for expressing cruelty and carrying out mass killing have been fully developed. It is too late to stop the technology. It is to the psychology that we should now turn.

References

Chapter 1   Never Such Innocence Again

1   Inaugural Lecture on the Study of History, Cambridge, 1895, reprinted in *Lectures on Modern History* (London, 1906).
2   *Independent* (6 February 1991).
3   *The Brothers Karamazov*, trans. Richard Pevear and Larissa Volokhonsky (London, 1990), Book 5, chs 3–4.
4   *The Letters of Charles Hamilton Sorley*, quoted in Jon Glover and Jon Silkin (ed.), *The Penguin Book of First World War Prose* (London, 1990).
5   Milan Kundera, *The Book of Laughter and Forgetting* (London, 1982), Part One, Section Five.
6   J. Glenn Gray, *The Warriors: Reflections on Men in Battle* (New York, 1959), p. 220.
7   Ed Vulliamy, *Seasons in Hell: Understanding Bosnia's War* (London, 1994), pp. ix–x.
8   Ibid., p. 201.
9   J.M. Keynes, 'My Early Beliefs', in *Two Memoirs* (London, 1949).

Chapter 2   Nietzsche's Challenge

1   *The Gay Science*, Section 125.
2   *On the Genealogy of Morals*, Essay One, Section 7.
3   Ibid., Section 9.
4   *Beyond Good and Evil*, Section 48.
5   *The Gay Science*, Section 344.
6   Ibid., Section 335.
7   *The Will to Power*, Section 864.
8   Ibid., Section 933.
9   *Twilight of the Idols*, Part Nine, Section 49.

10 *Beyond Good and Evil*, Section 265.
11 Ibid., Section 258.
12 *Nietzsche Werke: Kritische Gesamtausgabe*, Section 3, vol. 2, p. 261. Quoted in Bruce Detwiler, *Nietzsche and the Politics of Aristocratic Radicalism* (Chicago, 1990), p. 106.
13 *The Genealogy of Morals*, Essay One, Section 12.
14 *The Will to Power*, Section 872.
15 Ibid., Section 685.
16 *The Genealogy of Morals*, Essay One, Section 13.
17 *Thus Spake Zarathustra*, Part One, 'Of War and Warriors'.
18 *Beyond Good and Evil*, Section 62.
19 Ibid., Sections 212, 225.
20 Ibid., Section 210.
21 *Thus Spake Zarathustra*, Part Three, 'Of Old and New Law-Tables'.
22 *Beyond Good and Evil*, Section 293.
23 *The Genealogy of Morals*, Essay Two, Section 6.
24 *The Antichrist*, Section 2.

Chapter 3   Self-interest as a Restraint

1 Robert Axelrod, *The Evolution of Co-operation* (New York, 1984).
2 Matt Ridley, *The Origins of Virtue* (London, 1996), ch. 3.
3 Thomas Hobbes, *Leviathan* (London, 1651), ch. 13.
4 R.M. Hare, *Moral Thinking: Its Levels, Method and Point* (Oxford, 1981), ch. 11.

Chapter 4   The Moral Resources: Humanity

1 Immanuel Kant, *The Metaphysics of Morals*, trans. Mary Gregor (Cambridge, 1991), p. 255.
2 Alfred Draper, *The Amritsar Massacre: Twilight of the Raj* (London, 1985), chs 5 and 6.
3 Brian Keenan, *An Evil Cradling* (London, 1992), p. 46.

Chapter 5   The Moral Resources: Moral Identity

1 Brian Keenan, *An Evil Cradling* (London, 1992), p. 204.
2 Plato, *Gorgias*, 482.
3 Thucydides, *History of the Peloponnesian War*, Book Five.
4 Milovan Djilas, *Conversations with Stalin* (Harmondsworth, 1963), pp. 87–8, 90.
5 *The Will to Power*, Section 429.

Chapter 6   The Festival of Cruelty

1   Report by Matthew Engel, *Guardian* (2 March 1991).
2   Report by Tim Kelsey, *Independent on Sunday* (10 March 1991).
3   Report by Julie Flint, *Observer* (3 March 1991).
4   *Independent* (29 March 1991).
5   *Independent* (6 May 1991).
6   *Amnesty International Report* (London, 1991).
7   Jacobo Timerman, *Prisoner Without a Name, Cell Without a Number*, trans. Toby Talbot (New York, 1988), pp. 37–41.
8   Ronald Dworkin, 'Report from Hell', *New York Review of Books* (17 July 1986).
9   *Torture in Brazil: a Report by the Archdiocese of Sao Paulo*, trans. Jaime Wright, ed. Joan Dassin (New York, 1986), pp. 28–32.
10 Quoted in Simon Schama, *Citizens: a Chronicle of the French Revolution* (London, 1989), p. 670.
11 Brian Keenan, *An Evil Cradling* (London, 1992), pp. xii–xiii, 122.
12 Timerman, *Prisoner Without a Name*, pp. 82–3.
13 *Nunca Mas: a Report by Argentina's National Commission on Disappeared People*, English trans. (London, 1986), pp. 19, 25.
14 *Nunca Mas*, pp. 67–72.
15 Timerman, *Prisoner Without a Name*, pp. 60–1.
16 *Guardian* (2 March 1991).
17 Ibid. (30 March 1991).
18 Timerman, *Prisoner Without a Name*, p. 7.
19 Breyten Breytenbach, *The True Confessions of an Albino Terrorist* (London, 1985), p. 349.
20 *Observer* (13 January 1991).
21 Immanuel Kant, *The Metaphysics of Morals*, trans. Mary Gregor (Cambridge, 1991), p. 255.

Chapter 7   Answering Nietzsche

1   Jean Améry, *At the Mind's Limits: Contemplations by a Survivor on Auschwitz and Its Realities*, trans. Sidney and Stella Rosenfeld (New York, 1986), p. 68.
2   Ibid., pp. 11–12.

Chapter 8   Close Combat

1   William Eckhardt, in Ruth Leger Sivard, *World Military Expenditures* (1988 and 1989 edns).
2   Svetlana Alexievich, *Zinky Boys: Soviet Voices from a Forgotten War*, trans. Julia and Robin Whitby (London, 1992), pp. 35, 79.
3   Quoted in Robert Jay Lifton, *Home from the War: Vietnam Veterans: Neither Victims Nor Executioners* (New York, 1985).

4 Alexievich, *Zinky Boys*, pp. 116–17.
5 Tim O'Brien, *If I Die in a Combat Zone* (London, 1973), p. 105.
6 J. Glenn Gray, *The Warriors: Reflections on Men in Battle* (New York, 1959), p. 150.
7 John Keegan, *The Face of Battle: a Study of Agincourt, Waterloo and the Somme* (London, 1976), p. 18.
8 Lifton, *Home from the War*, p. 202.
9 *Independent* (6 February 1991).
10 Jeff Needle, *Please Read This*, quoted in Lifton, *Home from the War*, p. 109.
11 Gray, *The Warriors*, p. 163.
12 Ibid.
13 Lifton, *Home from the War*, p. 69.
14 Alexievich, *Zinky Boys*, p. 76.
15 Erich Maria Remarque, *All Quiet on the Western Front*, trans. A.H. Wheen (London, 1929), p. 21.
16 Alexievich, *Zinky Boys*, pp. 23, 45.
17 Peter G. Bourne, MD, 'From Boot Camp to My Lai', in Richard A. Falk, Gabriel Kolko and Robert Jay Lifton (ed.), *Crimes of War* (New York, 1971).
18 Tim Lynch, 'Taught to Kill, Not to Pity', *Independent On Sunday* (21 March 1993).
19 Lifton, *Home from the War*, pp. 41–3.
20 Alexievich, *Zinky Boys*, p. 110.
21 Ibid., p. 16.
22 Lifton, *Home from the War*, p. 114.
23 George Orwell, 'Looking Back on the Spanish War', in *The Collected Essays, Journalism and Letters of George Orwell*, vol. 2, *My Country Right or Left, 1940–3* (Harmondsworth, 1970), pp. 291–2.
24 Alexievich, *Zinky Boys*, pp. 171–2.
25 John Simpson, *From the House of War* (London, 1991), p. xiii.
26 Gordon S. Livingston, 'Letter from a Vietnam Veteran', in Falk, Kolko and Lifton (ed.), *Crimes of War*.
27 Bernard Edelman (ed.), *Dear America: Letters Home from Vietnam* (New York, 1985), pp. 184–5.
28 Alexievich, *Zinky Boys*, pp. 6, 16–17, 76.
29 Gray, *The Warriors*, pp. 44, 45.
30 Alexievich, *Zinky Boys*, p. 111.
31 *Guardian* (19 January 1991).
32 Gray, *The Warriors*, pp. 29, 36.
33 Alexievich, *Zinky Boys*, pp. 78–9.
34 Ibid., pp. 23–4.
35 Gray, *The Warriors*, p. 51.
36 William Broyles, 'Why Men Love War', *Esquire* (1984), and in Walter Capps (ed.), *The Vietnam Reader* (New York, 1991).

Chapter 9   The Case of My Lai

1   Michael Bilton and Kevin Sim, *Four Hours in My Lai* (New York, 1992), p. 80.
2   Ibid., pp. 53, 55.
3   Ibid., p. 20.
4   Ibid., pp. 18–19.
5   Robert Jay Lifton, *Home from the War: Vietnam Veterans: Neither Victims Nor Executioners* (New York, 1985), p. 50.
6   Bilton and Sim, *Four Hours in My Lai*, p. 21.
7   Ibid., p. 79.
8   Ibid., p. 78.
9   Ibid., pp. 94–5.
10   Ibid., p. 80.
11   Ibid., pp. 73–4.
12   Quoted in Lifton, *Home from the War*, p. 48.
13   Ibid., p. 52.
14   Ibid., p. 53.
15   Bilton and Sim, *Four Hours in My Lai*, p. 7.

Chapter 10   The Shift to Killing at a Distance

1   B.H. Liddell Hart, *The Real War, 1914–18* (London, 1930), pp. 89–94, 503.
2   Ibid., p. 503.
3   Recent views on the numbers are discussed in Alyson Jackson, 'Germany, The Home Front (2): Blockade, Government and Revolution', in Hugh Cecil and Peter H. Liddle (ed.), *Facing Armageddon: the First World War Experienced* (London, 1996).
4   Walter Duranty, *I Write as I Please* (London, 1935), p. 14.
5   Winston S. Churchill, *The World Crisis*, vol. 5, *Aftermath* (London, 1922), p. 66.
6   Ibid., p. 67.
7   Ulrich von Brockdorff-Rantzau, speech of the German delegation, Versailles, 7 May 1919, in Anton Kaes, Martin Jay and Edward Dimendberg (ed.), *The Weimar Republic Sourcebook* (Berkeley, Cal., 1994), p. 10.
8   John Maynard Keynes, *Dr Melchior: a Defeated Enemy*, in *Two Memoirs* (London, 1949).

Chapter 11   Bombing

1   Letter quoted in Max Hastings, *Bomber Command* (London, 1979), p. 62.
2   Sir Charles Webster and Noble Frankland, *The Strategic Air Offensive Against Germany, 1939–45*, vol. 1 (London, 1961), pp. 218–19.
3   Report of D.M. Butt to Bomber Command, 18 August 1941, Appendix 13 in Webster and Frankland, *Strategic Air Offensive*, vol. 4.
4   Winston S. Churchill, *The Second World War*, vol. 4, *The Hinge of Fate* (London, 1951), pp. 431, 437–8.

5   Albert Resis (ed.), *Molotov Remembers: Inside Kremlin Politics: Conversations with Felix Chuev* (Chicago, 1993), pp. 45–7.

6   Churchill, *The Hinge of Fate*, p. 432.

7   W. Averell Harriman and Elie Abel, *Special Envoy to Churchill and Stalin, 1941–6* (London, 1976), pp. 152–3.

8   Richard Overy, *Why the Allies Won* (London, 1995), p. 129.

9   Albert Speer's diary in Spandau prison, quoted in Hastings, *Bomber Command*, p. 287.

10   Albert Speer, *Inside the Third Reich*, trans. Richard and Clara Winston (London, 1971), p. 469.

11   Sir Arthur Harris, *Bomber Offensive* (London, 1947; reprinted 1990), p. 176.

12   Letter to Sir Norman Bottomley, quoted in Hastings, *Bomber Command*, p. 452.

13   Webster and Frankland, *Strategic Air Offensive*, vol. 4, Appendix 37, interrogation of Albert Speer.

14   Ibid., pp. 40–56.

15   Harris, *Bomber Offensive*, pp. 78–9.

16   Webster and Frankland, *Strategic Air Offensive*, vol. 1, p. 45.

17   Churchill's reply to Portal, September 1941. Quoted in Hastings, *Bomber Command*, p. 141.

18   Cherwell's letter to Tizard, quoted in Earl of Birkenhead, *The Prof in Two Worlds: the Official Life of Professor F.A. Lindemann, Viscount Cherwell* (London, 1961), pp. 251–3.

19   Webster and Frankland, *Strategic Air Offensive*, vol. 1, pp. 345–6.

20   Hastings, *Bomber Command*, p. 398.

21   Letter of 12 November, quoted in ibid., p. 399.

22   Ibid., pp. 400–1.

23   Speer, *Inside the Third Reich*, p. 392.

24   Noble Frankland, *The Bombing Offensive Against Germany: Outlines and Perspectives* (London, 1965), p. 92.

25   Quoted in Hastings, *Bomber Command*, p. 253.

26   Ibid., p. 197.

27   Martin Middlebrook, *The Battle of Hamburg: The Firestorm Raid* (London, 1980), p. 257.

28   Ibid., p. 276.

29   Hastings, *Bomber Command*, p. 388.

30   Erika Dienel, 'Half a day in hell', *Independent on Sunday* (3 May 1992).

31   Margaret Freyer, in Alexander McKee, *Dresden, 1945: The Devil's Tinderbox* (London, 1982), reprinted in John Carey (ed.), *Eyewitness to History* (New York, 1987), pp. 611–12.

32   Commander D.J. Childs, 'Saints, Bombs and Civilian Casualties', *Independent* (1 May 1993).

33   Letter from Douglas Smith, *Independent Magazine* (9 February 1991).

34   C.P. Snow, 'Science and Government', in C.P. Snow, *Public Affairs* (London, 1971), pp. 126–7.

35   Letter to Sir Norman Bottomley, in Hastings, *Bomber Command*, p. 452.

36   Harris, *Bomber Offensive*, pp. 176, 177.

37   Quoted in Middlebrook, *The Battle of Hamburg*, p. 368.

38 Smith, *Independent Magazine*.
39 Martin Gilbert, *The Second World War* (London, 1989), pp. 440–1.
40 Lord Cherwell, Cabinet Paper, quoted in Webster and Frankland, *Strategic Air Offensive*, vol. 1, pp. 331–2.
41 14 July 1941.
42 Air Marshal Sir Robert Saundby, Foreword to David Irving, *The Destruction of Dresden* (London, 1963).
43 Harris, *Bomber Offensive*, pp. 77–8.
44 Michael Walzer, *Just and Unjust Wars* (Harmondsworth, 1978).
45 John Collins, *Faith Under Fire* (London, 1966), p. 89.
46 Lord Woolton, quoted in Ronald C.D. Jasper, *George Bell, Bishop of Chichester* (London, 1967), p. 277.
47 Bishop George Bell, speech to House of Lords, 9 February 1944.
48 J.M. Spaight, *Bombing Vindicated* (London, 1944), pp. 119–20.
49 Harris, *Bomber Offensive*, p. 176.

Chapter 12   Hiroshima

1   *The Times* (12 September 1933), quoted in Richard Rhodes, *The Making of the Atomic Bomb* (Harmondsworth, 1988), p. 27.
2   Spencer R. Weart and Gertrud Weiss Szilard (ed.), *Leo Szilard: His Version of the Facts* (Cambridge, 1978), p. 53.
3   Otto Frisch, *What Little I Remember* (Cambridge, 1979), p. 126.
4   Frisch–Peierls Memorandum, in Ronald W. Clark, *Tizard* (London, 1965), pp. 215–17.
5   Heisenberg, quoted in Robert Jungk, *Brighter than a Thousand Suns* (Harmondsworth, 1964), p. 101.
6   Letter from Rudolf Ladenburg to Samuel Goudsmit, quoted in Mark Walker, *German National Socialism and the Quest for Nuclear Power, 1939–49* (Cambridge, 1989), p. 225.
7   Memorandum signed by Hahn, Heisenberg and others, 8 August 1945, *Operation Epsilon: the Farm Hall Transcripts* (Bristol, 1993), pp. 102–6.
8   Diebner, quoted in Rhodes, *The Making of the Atomic Bomb*, p. 517.
9   *Farm Hall Transcripts*, pp. 70, 80, 82.
10 Ibid., pp. 77, 78.
11 Walker, *German National Socialism*, p. 224.
12 *Farm Hall Transcripts*, pp. 77–8.
13 Eric Lomax, *The Railway Man* (London, 1995), chs 5–9.
14 John W. Dower, *War Without Mercy: Race and Power in the Pacific War* (New York, 1986), pp. 40–1.
15 Dwight D. Eisenhower, 'Ike on Ike', *Newsweek* (11 November 1963), quoted in Rhodes, *The Making of the Atomic Bomb*, p. 688.
16 A.H. Compton, *Atomic Quest* (Oxford, 1956), p. 242.
17 Gar Alperovitz, *The Decision to Use the Atomic Bomb* (London, 1995), pp. 163–4.

18 Henry L. Stimson, 'The Decision to Use the Atomic Bomb', reprinted in Amy Gutman and Dennis Thompson (ed.), *Ethics and Politics: Cases and Comments*, 2nd edn (Chicago 1990), pp. 5–15.

19 Jungk, *Brighter than a Thousand Suns*, pp. 163, 190.

20 Szilard, quoted in Alperovitz, *The Decision to Use the Atomic Bomb*, p. 147.

21 Cable from Shigenori Togo, quoted in Herbert Feis, *Japan Subdued: the Atomic Bomb and the End of the War in the Pacific* (Princeton, 1961), p. 65.

22 Winston S. Churchill, *The Second World War*, vol. 4, *The Hinge of Fate* (London, 1951), pp. 614–15.

23 Dr Koyama, quoted in Dr Michihiko Hachiya, *Hiroshima Diary*, trans. and ed. Warner Wells (London, 1955), p. 131.

24 Arata Osada, *Children of the A-bomb*, (Midwest Publishers International, 1982), p. 194; quoted in Rhodes, *The Making of the Atomic Bomb*, p. 716.

25 Hachiya, *Hiroshima Diary*, p. 108.

26 Mr Katsutani, quoted in ibid., p. 28.

27 Ibid., p. 117.

28 The Committee for the Compilation of Materials on Damage Caused by the Atomic Bombs in Hiroshima and Nagasaki, *Hiroshima and Nagasaki: the Physical, Medical, and Social Effects of the Atomic Bombings*, trans. Eisei Ishikawa and David L. Swain (London, 1981), ch. 8, and p. 115.

29 Ibid., ch. 9.

30 Osada, *Children of the A-Bomb*, pp. 77, 83, quoted in Rhodes, *The Making of the Atomic Bomb*, p. 723.

31 Osada *Children of the A-Bomb*, p. 264, quoted in Rhodes, *The Making of the Atomic Bomb*, p. 734.

32 Ernest Lawrence, quoted in Rhodes, *The Making of the Atomic Bomb*, p. 648.

33 Gunther Anders and Claude Eatherly, *Burning Conscience*, 2nd edn (New York, 1989), p. 82.

34 Ibid.

35 Frisch, *What Little I Remember*, p. 176.

36 Truman, quoted in Rhodes, *The Making of the Atomic Bomb*, pp. 690–1.

37 Henry Wallace's diary, quoted in ibid., p. 743.

38 Oppenheimer, quoted in Jungk, *Brighter than a Thousand Suns*, p. 266.

39 Ibid., p. 203.

40 *Memoirs of Harry S. Truman*, vol. 1, *Year of Decisions* (New York, 1955), p. 491.

41 Compton, *Atomic Quest*, pp. 238ff.

42 Interview with Oppenheimer, *Le Monde* (29 April 1958), quoted in Jungk, *Brighter than a Thousand Suns*, p. 291.

43 A.F.L. Beeston, letter in the *Oxford Magazine* (Michaelmas Term, 1995).

44 *Mr Truman's Degree* (Oxford, 1957), reprinted in G.E.M. Anscombe, *Ethics, Religion and Politics: Collected Philosophical Papers*, vol. 3 (Oxford, 1981).

45 Margaret Gowing, *Britain and Atomic Energy, 1939–45* (London, 1964), pp. 354, 355, 371.

46 Ibid., p. 355.

47 Ibid., Appendix 8, p. 447.

48 *Open Letter to the United Nations* (Copenhagen, 1950).

Chapter 14 Rwanda

1 African Rights, *Rwanda – Death, Despair, Defiance*, rev. edn (London, 1995), pp. 264–5.
2 Ibid., pp. 305–13.
3 Fergal Keane, *Season of Blood: a Rwandan Journey* (London, 1995), pp. 68–72, 75–81.
4 African Rights, *Rwanda*, pp. 42–3.
5 Ibid., pp. 76–7.
6 Alain Destexhe, *Rwanda and Genocide in the Twentieth Century*, trans. Alison Marschner (London, 1995), pp. 30–2.
7 African Rights, *Rwanda*, pp. 1117–18.

Chapter 15 The Tribal Trap

1 Laura Silber and Allan Little, *The Death of Yugoslavia* (London, 1995), p. 37.
2 Ibid., p. 77.
3 Ibid., pp. 91–2.
4 Mark Thompson, *A Paper House: the Ending of Yugoslavia* (London, 1992), p. 99.
5 Ed Vulliamy, *Seasons in Hell: Understanding Bosnia's War* (London, 1994), pp. 195–201.
6 Peter Maass, *Love Thy Neighbour: a Story of War* (New York, Toronto and London, 1996), pp. 38–9, 72–3, 78.
7 Rezak Hukanović, *The Tenth Circle of Hell: a Memoir of Life in the Death Camps of Bosnia*, trans. Colleen London and Midhat Ridjanović (London, 1996).
8 Maass, *Love Thy Neighbour*, pp. 45, 50, 75.
9 Vulliamy, *Seasons in Hell*, ch. 7.
10 Warren Zimmermann, 'The Last Ambassador: a Memoir of the Collapse of Yugoslavia', *Foreign Affairs* (1995).
11 Ibid., p. 8.
12 Article Nineteen, *Forging War: the Media in Serbia, Croatia and Bosnia-Hercegovina* (London, 1994), p. 34.
13 Ibid., p. 90.
14 Noel Malcolm, *Bosnia: a Short History* (London, 1994), p. 228.
15 Article Nineteen, *Forging War*, pp. 73, 185.
16 Slavenka Drakulić, *Balkan Express: Fragments from the Other Side of War* (London, 1993), p. 131.
17 Zimmermann, 'The Last Ambassador', p. 12.
18 Article Nineteen, *Forging War*, p. 83.
19 Survey by the Institute of Political Studies, quoted in ibid., p. 127.
20 Stojan Cerović, quoted in ibid., p. 129.
21 Thucydides, *History of the Peloponnesian War*, trans. Rex Warner (Harmondsworth, 1954), Book One, Introduction.

22 Thomas Hobbes, *Leviathan* (London, 1651), ch. 13.
23 Silber and Little, *The Death of Yugoslavia*, pp. 89, 143.
24 Drakulić, *Balkan Express*, p. 20.

Chapter 16   The Political Containment of Tribalism

1 Thomas Hobbes, *Leviathan* (London, 1651), ch. 17.
2 Martin Bell, *In Harm's Way: Reflections of a War Zone Thug* (London, 1995), pp. 136, 258.
3 Peter Maass, *Love Thy Neighbour: a Story of War* (New York, Toronto and London, 1996), p. 189.
4 Jan Willem Honig and Norbert Both, *Srebrenica: Record of a War Crime* (London, 1996).
5 Maass, *Love Thy Neighbour*, pp. 176–81.
6 Bell, *In Harm's Way*, pp. 261–2.
7 Maass, *Love Thy Neighbour*, pp. 267–70.
8 *Independent* (9 September 1993).
9 Maass, *Love Thy Neighbour*, p. 57.
10 Noel Malcolm, *Bosnia: a Short History* (London, 1994), p. 251.

Chapter 17   The Roots of Tribal Conflict

1 C. Haney, C. Banks and P. Zimbardo, 'Interpersonal Dynamics in a Simulated Prison', *International Journal of Criminology and Penology* (1973).
2 Konrad Lorenz, *On Aggression*, trans. Marjorie Latzke (London, 1966), p. 20.
3 W.D. Hamilton, 'The Evolution of Altruistic Behavior', *American Naturalist* (1963); W.D. Hamilton, 'The Genetical Evolution of Social Behavior', I and II, *Theoretical Biology* (1964).
4 R. Paul Shaw and Yuwa Wong, *Genetic Seeds of Warfare: Evolution, Nationalism and Patriotism* (Boston, 1989).
5 Giuseppe Mazzini, quoted in Eric Hobsbawm, *Nations and Nationalism since 1780: Programme, Myth, Reality* (Cambridge, 1990), p. 101.
6 Benedict Anderson, *Imagined Communities: Reflections on the Origin and Spread of Nationalism* (London, 1983); Ernest Gellner, *Nations and Nationalism* (Oxford, 1983).
7 Hobsbawm, *Nations and Nationalism since 1780*, p. 44.
8 Isaiah Berlin, 'The Bent Twig', in *The Crooked Timber of Humanity: Chapters in the History of Ideas* (London, 1990).
9 Mark Almond, *Europe's Backyard War: the War in the Balkans* (London, 1994), pp. 5–6.
10 Michael A. Sells, *The Bridge Betrayed: Religion and Genocide in Bosnia* (Berkeley, Cal., 1996), pp. 1–2.
11 Ed Vulliamy, *Seasons in Hell: Understanding Bosnia's War* (London, 1994), pp. 353–6.

12 Ibid., p. 205.
13 Slavenka Drakulić, *Balkan Express: Fragments from the Other Side of War* (London, 1993), p. 55.

Chapter 18 The Capacity to Unchain Ourselves

1 Archbishop Desmond Tutu, Obituary for Bishop Trevor Huddleston, *Guardian* (21 April 1998).
2 *Independent* (28 September 1996).
3 Seamus Heaney, *Crediting Poetry* (Nobel Lecture, 1995).
4 Slavenka Drakulić, *Balkan Express: Fragments from the Other Side of War* (London, 1993), p. 51.
5 Peter Maass, *Love Thy Neighbour: a Story of War* (New York, Toronto and London, 1996), p. 252.

Chapter 19 The Trap of the Trenches

1 Martın Middlebrook, *The First Day on the Somme, 1 July 1916* (London, 1971), p. 107.
2 Ibid., pp. 156-7.
3 John Keegan, *The Face of Battle: a Study of Agincourt, Waterloo and the Somme* (London, 1976), p. 260.
4 Lyn Macdonald, *Somme* (London, 1983), p. 83.
5 Lyn Macdonald, *1914–1918: Voices and Images of the Great War* (London, 1988), p. 160.
6 Erich Maria Remarque, *All Quiet on the Western Front*, trans. A.W. Wheen (London, 1929), p. 136.
7 Macdonald, *Somme*, p. 119.
8 Siegfried Sassoon, *Memoirs of an Infantry Officer* (London, 1930), pp. 82–3.
9 Captain A.F.P. Christison, MC, quoted in Macdonald, *1914–1918*, p. 230.
10 Captain Chudleigh, *Daily Telegraph* article, quoted in Denis Winter, *Death's Men: Soldiers of the Great War* (London, 1978), pp. 220–1.
11 Macdonald, *1914–1918*, pp. 46–8.
12 Ibid., p. 52.
13 Edmund Blunden, *Undertones of War* (1928, repr. Harmondsworth, 1937), p. 154.
14 Robert Graves, *Goodbye to All That*, rev. edn (London, 1960), p. 162.
15 Tony Ashworth, *Trench Warfare, 1914–18: the Live and Let Live System* (London, 1980), pp. 46–7.
16 J. Reith, *Wearing Spurs* (London, 1966), quoted in Winter, *Death's Men.*
17 Robert Axelrod, *The Evolution of Co-operation* (New York, 1984), ch. 4.
18 Lieutenant Cyril Drummond, in Macdonald, *1914–1918*, p. 52.
19 *Poil et Plume* (October 1917), quoted in Stéphane Audoin-Rouzeau, *Men at*

War, 1914–18: National Sentiment and Trench Journalism in France during the First World War, trans. Helen McPhail (Oxford, 1992).
20 Private Moodie, quoted in Winter, *Death's Men*, p. 216.
21 Macdonald, *1914–1918*, p. 52.
22 Ibid., pp. 116–17.
23 Blunden, *Undertones of War*, pp. 81–2.
24 Macdonald, *1914–1918*, p. 118.
25 Blunden, *Undertones of War*, pp. 44, 62.
26 Graves, *Goodbye to All That*, p. 198.
27 Remarque, *All Quiet on the Western Front*, pp. 110–12.
28 Graves, *Goodbye to All That*, p. 188.

Chapter 20   The Home Front

1   Immanuel Kant, *Perpetual Peace*, trans. M. Campbell Smith (London, 1903), pp. 120–8.
2   Letter from Professor Peter Goodhew, *Independent* (17 January 1991).
3   Letter of 28 July 1914, quoted in Michael and Eleanor Brock (ed.), *H.H. Asquith: Letters to Venetia Stanley* (Oxford, 1982), p. 130.
4   John W. Dower, *War Without Mercy: Race and Power in the Pacific War* (New York, 1986), pp. 59–60.
5   Robert S. McNamara, with Brian Vandemark, *In Retrospect: the Tragedy and Lessons of Vietnam* (New York, 1995).
6   *The Organization and Function of the Ministry of Information*, cd 9161, 1918, quoted in Cate Haste, *Keep the Home Fires Burning: Propaganda in the First World War* (London, 1977), p. 21.
7   Phillip Knightley, *The First Casualty* (London, 1975), p. 109.
8   Colonel Harry G. Summers Jr, quoted in Michael Bilton and Kevin Sim, *Four Hours in My Lai* (New York, 1992), p. 11.
9   Svetlana Alexievich, *Zinky Boys: Soviet Voices from a Forgotten War*, trans. Julie and Robin Whitby (London, 1992), p. 18.
10 Bilton and Sim, *Four Hours in My Lai*, pp. 20, 362, 375.
11 *Guardian* (7 February 1991).
12 Ibid. (18 January 1993).
13 Haste, *Keep the Home Fires Burning*, p. 68.
14 Knightley, *The First Casualty*, p. 416.
15 James Fenton, *All the Wrong Places: Adrift in the Politics of Asia* (London, 1988), p. 21.
16 Martin Bell, *In Harm's Way: Reflections of a War Zone Thug* (London, 1995), p. 214–15.
17 John Simpson, *From the House of War* (London, 1991), pp. 17–36, 89–94.
18 John R. Macarthur, *Second Front: Censorship and Propaganda in the Gulf War* (Berkeley and Los Angeles, 1993), ch. 2.
19 *New York Times* (May 1991), quoted in ibid., p. 7.
20 Middle East Watch, *Needless Deaths in the Gulf War: Civilian Casualties*

During the Air Campaign and Violations of the Laws of War (New York, 1991), pp. 113–17.

21 Alex Thomson, *Smokescreen: The Media, the Censors, the Gulf* (Tunbridge Wells, 1992), pp. 215–21.
22 Ibid., pp. 235–8.
23 Ibid., p. 260.
24 Simpson, *From the House of War*, p. 350.
25 Charles Glass, *Stains of War*, BBC 2, 6 November 1992.
26 Stephen Sackur, *On the Basra Road* (London, 1991), p. 18.
27 Thomson, *Smokescreen*, p. 25.
28 Macarthur, *Second Front*, p. 171.
29 Stanley Cloud, quoted in ibid., pp. 9, 155–6.
30 Sackur, *On the Basra Road*, p. 19.
31 Deborah Amos, quoted in Thomson, *Smokescreen*, pp. 51, 54.
32 Robert Fisk, 'Free to Report What We're Told', *Independent* (6 February 1991).
33 *The Times* (2 September 1914).
34 Haste, *Keep the Home Fires Burning*, p. 127.
35 Ibid., pp. 126–7.
36 Keith Butcher, 'The German War Memorial', *New College Record* (1995).
37 Dower, *War Without Mercy*, p. 217.
38 Ibid., pp. 242–9.
39 Ibid., pp. 53, 71, 78, 84, 85, 90–2, 162.
40 Ibid., pp. 66–7.
41 Ibid., pp. 53–5.

Chapter 21   The Stone Has Started to Roll: 1914

1 Z.A.B. Zeman, 'The Balkans and the Coming of War', in R.J.W. Evans and Hartmut Pogge von Strandmann (ed.), *The Coming of the First World War* (Oxford, 1988), pp. 22, 24.
2 *New York World* (29 June 1924), and in John Carey (ed.), *The Faber Book of Reportage* (London, 1987).
3 Telegram from Szápáry to Berchtold, 24 July 1914, and memorandum of the day of the Russian Ministry for Foreign Affairs, 24 July 1914, in Imanuel Geiss (ed.), *July 1914: the Outbreak of the First World War: Selected Documents* (London, 1967), pp. 174, 189.
4 Viscount Grey of Fallodon, *Twenty-five Years, 1892–1916*, vol. 1 (London, 1925), p. 310.
5 Protocol of the Council of Ministers for Common Affairs, 7 July 1914, in Geiss, *July 1914*, p. 86.
6 Telegram from Tschirschky to Jagow, 10 July 1914, in ibid., p. 107.
7 Letter from Berchtold to Tisza, 8 July 1914, in ibid., p. 102.
8 Letter from Schoen to Hertling, 18 July 1914, and telegram from Szögény to Berchtold, 25 July 1914, in ibid., pp. 128, 201.
9 Letter from William II to Jagow, 28 July 1914, in ibid., p. 256.

10 Telegram from Bethmann Hollweg to Tschirschky, 30 July 1914, in ibid., p. 293.

11 James Joll, *The Origins of the First World War*, 2nd edn (London, 1992), p. 21.

12 Ibid., p. 15.

13 Serge Sazonov, *Fateful Years, 1909–16* (London, 1928), p. 203.

14 Barbara Tuchman, *The Guns of August*, published in England as *August 1914* (London, 1962), p. 85.

15 Ibid., p. 62.

16 Ibid.

17 Sir Edward Grey, *Fly Fishing* (London, 1899).

18 Quoted in Tuchman, *August 1914*, p. 101.

19 Extract from the dispatch from His Majesty's Ambassador at Berlin respecting the rupture of diplomatic relations with the German government, in E. Barker, H.W.C. Davis, C.R.L. Fletcher, Arthur Hassall, L.G. Wickham Legg and F. Morgan, *Why We Are at War: Great Britain's Case*, by members of the Oxford Faculty of Modern History (Oxford, 1914), p. 200.

20 Prince von Bülow, *Memoirs, 1909–19* (London, 1932), p. 145.

21 Michael and Eleanor Brock (ed.), *H.H. Asquith: Letters to Venetia Stanley* (Oxford, 1982), p. 146.

22 Sazonov, *Fateful Years*, pp. 212–13.

23 Letter from Lichnowsky to Bethmann Hollweg, 9 July 1914, in Geiss, *July 1914*, p. 104.

24 Fritz Fischer, *Germany's Aims in the First World War* (London, 1967), pp. 32–3.

25 Ibid., p. 72.

26 The Saxon Military Attaché, quoted in V.R. Berghahn, *Germany and the Approach of War in 1914* (London, 1973), p. 203.

27 Konrad H. Jarausch, *The Enigmatic Chancellor: Bethmann Hollweg and the Hubris of Imperial Germany* (New Haven, 1973), p. 180.

28 Wilhelm II, in Geiss, *July 1914*, pp. 171, 182, 256, 290.

29 Berghahn, *Germany and the Approach of War in 1914*, p. 86.

30 Max Warburg to Gustav Krupp, quoted in ibid., p. 193.

31 Telegram from Szögény to Berchtold, 27 July 1914, in Geiss, *July 1914*, p. 236.

32 Fischer, *Germany's Aims*, pp. 70–1.

33 Quoted in Joll, *Origins of the First World War*, p. 92.

34 Herbert Samuel, quoted in ibid., p. 22.

35 Letter from Moltke to Bethmann Hollweg, 29 July 1914, in Geiss, *July 1914*, p. 283.

36 Telegram from Bethmann Hollweg to Pourtalès, 29 July 1914, in ibid., p. 285.

37 Memorandum of the day of the Russian Ministry of Foreign Affairs, 30 July 1914, in ibid., pp. 310–12.

38 A.J.P. Taylor, *The First World War: an Illustrated History* (Harmondsworth, 1966), pp. 17–20.

39 James Joll, 'Politicians and the Freedom to Choose', in Alan Ryan (ed.), *The Idea of Freedom: Essays in Honour of Isaiah Berlin* (Oxford, 1979), p. 110.
40 Joll, *Origins of the First World War*, pp. 20–1.
41 Grey, *Twenty-five Years*, vol. 2, p. 52.
42 Michael Howard, *The Lessons of History* (Oxford, 1993), p. 11; Paul Kennedy, 'Arms Races and the Causes of War, 1850–1945', in *Strategy and Diplomacy*, 1780–1945 (London, 1983).
43 Berghahn, *Germany and the Approach of War in 1914*, pp. 29 31.
44 Tirpitz, quoted in Paul Kennedy, 'Strategic Aspects of the Anglo-German Naval Race', in *Strategy and Diplomacy*, p. 131.
45 Tirpitz, quoted in ibid., p. 138.
46 Quoted in Berghahn, *Germany and the Approach of War in 1914*, p. 45.
47 Quoted in Winston Churchill, *The World Crisis*, abridged edn (New York, 1931), p. 46.
48 Michael Howard, 'The Edwardian Arms Race', in *The Lessons of History*.
49 Grey, *Twenty-five Years*, vol. 2, p. 273.
50 Quoted in Howard, 'The Edwardian Arms Race'.
51 Quoted in Fischer, *Germany's Aims*, p. 59.
52 Jarausch, *The Enigmatic Chancellor*, p. 149.
53 Berghahn, *Germany and the Approach of War in 1914*, p. 181.
54 Ibid., p. 172.
55 Geiss, *July 1914*, p. 295.
56 Statement of Imperial Chancellor Bethmann Hollweg, in *Official German Documents Relating to the World War* (New York, 1923), p. 21.
57 Berghahn, *Germany and the Approach of War in 1914*, p. 186.
58 Kurt Reizler, quoted in H.W. Koch (ed.), *The Origins of the First World War: Great Power Rivalry and German War Aims*, 2nd edn (London, 1984), p. 16
59 Telegram to Lichnowsky, 3 August 1914, in Geiss, *July 1914*, p. 355.
60 Memorandum by Sir E. Crowe, in letter from Crowe to Grey, 31 July 1914, in ibid., p. 330.
61 Jarausch, *The Enigmatic Chancellor*, p. 174.
62 Ibid., pp. 124, 145.
63 Brock, *Asquith*, p. 148.
64 Bertrand Russell, *Autobiography*, vol. 2, *1914–44* (London, 1968), p. 16.
65 Paul Crook, *Darwinism, War and History: the Debate Over the Biology of War from the 'Origin of Species' to the First World War* (Cambridge, 1994).
66 Quoted in Joll, *Origins of the First World War*, p. 179.
67 Zara Steiner, *Britain and the Origins of the First World War* (London, 1977), p. 16.
68 *Aus Meiner Dienstzeit* (Vienna, 1923), quoted in James Joll, *The Unspoken Assumptions* (London, 1968), pp. 13–14.
69 Fritz Fischer, *War of Illusions*, trans. Marion Jackson (London, 1975), p. 30.
70 Berghahn, *Germany and the Approach of War in 1914*, p. 35.
71 Kennedy, 'Arms Races', pp. 124–5, 157–8.
72 Quoted in Howard, 'The Edwardian Arms Race', p. 95.
73 Quoted in Berghahn, *Germany and the Approach of War in 1914*, p. 185.
74 Fischer, *War of Illusions*, pp. 193–4.

75 Count Hoyos, quoted in letter from Stolberg to Jagow, 18 July 1914, in Geiss, *July 1914*, p. 126.
76 Sazonov, *Fateful Years*, p. 203.
77 Letter from Moltke to Bethmann Hollweg, 29 July 1914, in Geiss, *July 1914*, p. 284.
78 Jarausch, *The Enigmatic Chancellor*, p. 149.
79 Grey, *Twenty-five Years*, vol. 1, pp. 327–8.
80 Telegram from Grey to Goschen, 30 July 1914, in Geiss, *July 1914*, p. 315.
81 Crowe's Memorandum, ibid., p. 331.
82 Joll, 'Politicians and the Freedom to Choose', p. 103.
83 Grey, *Twenty-five Years*, vol. 2, p. 15.
84 Asquith, quoted in Michael Brock, 'Britain Enters the War', in Evans and von Strandmann (ed.), *The Coming of the First World War*, p. 177.
85 Howard, 'Europe on the Eve of the First World War', ibid., p. 9.
86 Steiner, *Britain and the Origins of the First World War*, p. 229.
87 Joll, *Origins of the First World War*, p. 16.
88 Ibid., p. 23.

Chapter 22 Sliding Out of the Trap: 1962

1 Stevenson's letter to the President, 17 October, in Laurence Chang and Peter Kornbluh (ed.), *The Cuban Missile Crisis, 1962: a National Security Archive Documents Reader* (New York, 1992), p. 119.
2 Ernest R. May and Philip D. Zelikow (ed.), *The Kennedy Tapes: Inside the White House During the Cuban Missile Crisis* (Cambridge, Mass., 1997), p. 264.
3 Ibid., p. 358.
4 Quoted in Chang and Kornbluh, *The Cuban Missile Crisis*, p. 189.
5 Quoted in ibid., pp. 185–8.
6 Quoted in Bruce J. Allyn, James G. Blight and David A. Welch, *Back to the Brink: Proceedings of the Moscow Conference on the Cuban Missile Crisis, 1989* (Cambridge, Mass., 1992), p. 77.
7 Robert Kennedy, *Thirteen Days: a Memoir of the Cuban Missile Crisis* (New York, 1969), p. 109.
8 James G. Blight and David A. Welch, *On the Brink: Americans and Soviets Re-examine the Cuban Missile Crisis* (New York, 1989; 2nd edn, 1990), p. 254.
9 11 November 1962, in Chang and Kornbluh, *The Cuban Missile Crisis*, p. 272.
10 Nikita S. Khrushchev, *Khrushchev Remembers* (New York, 1970), p. 494.
11 Aleksandr Fursenko and Timothy Naftali, *'One Hell of a Gamble': the Secret History of the Cuban Missile Crisis* (London, 1997), p. 169.
12 Burlatsky in Allyn, Blight and Welch, *Back to the Brink*, p. 46.
13 May and Zelikow, *The Kennedy Tapes*, p. 176.
14 Ibid., p. 114.
15 Blight and Welch, *On the Brink*, p. 188.

16 May and Zelikow, *The Kennedy Tapes*, p. 498.
17 Blight and Welch, *On the Brink*, p. 246.
18 In Allyn, Blight and Welch, *Back to the Brink*, pp. 86, 88.
19 May and Zelikow, *The Kennedy Tapes*, p. 136.
20 Chang and Kornbluh, *The Cuban Missile Crisis*, pp. 354, 356.
21 In Allyn, Blight and Welch, *Back to the Brink*, pp. 7, 9.
22 Blight and Welch, *On the Brink*, pp. 336, 339.
23 Raymond Garthoff, in ibid., p. 75.
24 May and Zelikow, *The Kennedy Tapes*, p. 188.
25 Ibid., p. 194.
26 Ibid., pp. 519, 635.
27 Robert McNamara, *In Retrospect: the Tragedy and Lessons of Vietnam* (New York, 1995), pp. 339–42.
28 In Allyn, Blight and Welch, *Back to the Brink*, p. 45.
29 Lord Kennet, letter to the *Independent* (10 October 1992).
30 Khrushchev, *Khrushchev Remembers*, pp. 493–4.
31 May and Zelikov, *The Kennedy Tapes*, p. 681.
32 Emilio Aragones, in Allyn, Blight and Welch, *Back to the Brink*, p. 52.
33 Khrushchev, *Khrushchev Remembers*, p. 493.
34 Dillon's memorandum of 17 October 1962, in Chang and Kornbluh, *The Cuban Missile Crisis*, p. 116.
35 Khrushchev, *Khrushchev Remembers*, p. 497.
36 May and Zelikow, *The Kennedy Tapes*, p. 133.
37 Ibid., pp. 259, 263–4
38 *I.F. Stone's Weekly* (8 October 1962), quoted in Bertrand Russell, *Unarmed Victory* (London, 1963).
39 Blight and Welch, *On the Brink*, pp. 244–5.
40 Arthur M. Schlesinger Jr, *A Thousand Days: Kennedy in the White House* (Boston, 1965), pp. 835–8.
41 May and Zelikow, *The Kennedy Tapes*, p. 92.
42 Blight and Welch, *On the Brink*, p 43.
43 May and Zelikow, *The Kennedy Tapes*, p. 342.
44 Ibid., pp. 128–9.
45 Kennedy, *Thirteen Days*, pp. 62, 127.
46 Minutes of 19 October meeting of Ex-Comm, in Chang and Kornbluh, *The Cuban Missile Crisis*, pp. 124, 126.
47 May and Zelikow, *The Kennedy Tapes*, p. 71.
48 Ibid., p. 258.
49 Kennedy, *Thirteen Days*, pp. 76–7.
50 Ibid., p. 98.
51 In Allyn, Blight and Welch, *Back to the Brink*, p. 32.
52 In ibid., pp. 38, 89.
53 In Blight and Welch, *On the Brink*, pp. 63–4.
54 *Saturday Review* (10 October 1977), cited in ibid., p. 347.
55 Ibid., p. 51.
56 Fursenko and Naftali, '*One Hell of a Gamble*', p. 274
57 Oleg Troyanovsky, 'The Caribbean Crisis: a View from the Kremlin',

International Affairs (Moscow, April–May 1992), p. 152, quoted in May and Zelikow, *The Kennedy Tapes*, p. 683.

58 Blight and Welch, *On the Brink*, p. 208.
59 May and Zelikow, *The Kennedy Tapes*, pp. 329–30, 336–7, 357.
60 Ibid., p. 142.
61 Blight and Welch, *On the Brink*, p. 78.
62 Ibid., p. 80.
63 Ibid., p. 105.
64 Ibid., p. 170.
65 Ibid., p. 147.
66 Ibid., pp. 169–70.
67 Ibid., p. 183.
68 Ibid., pp. 192, 188–9.
69 Ibid., p. 278.
70 Kennedy, *Thirteen Days*, pp. 31, 34.
71 Ibid., pp. 69–72.
72 In Allyn, Blight and Welch, *Back to the Brink*, p. 76.
73 Blight and Welch, *On the Brink*, p. 183.
74 May and Zelikow, *The Kennedy Tapes*, p. 198.
75 Blight and Welch, *On the Brink*, p. 182.
76 May and Zelikow, *The Kennedy Tapes*, pp. 143, 149.
77 Kennedy, *Thirteen Days*, p. 39.
78 Blight and Welch, *On the Brink*, pp. 142–3.
79 Ibid., p. 255.
80 Kennedy, *Thirteen Days*, pp. 108–9.
81 Fursenko and Naftali, *'One Hell of a Gamble'*, p. 284.
82 Dobrynin's version of letter of 30 October, in Allyn, Blight and Welch, *Back to the Brink*, p. 84.

Chapter 23   Ways Out

1 Martin Shubik, 'The Dollar Auction Game: a Paradox in Non-cooperative Behavior and Escalation', *Journal of Conflict Resolution* (1971).
2 Immanuel Kant, 'Perpetual Peace', in *Political Writings*, trans. H.B. Nisbet, ed. Hans Reiss, 2nd edn (Cambridge, 1991), pp. 103–4.
3 Ibid., p. 103.

Chapter 24   In Those Years

1 R.J. Rummel, *Lethal Politics: Soviet Genocide and Mass Murder since 1917* (New Brunswick, N.J., 1990).
2 Robert Conquest, *The Great Terror*, 2nd edn (London, 1990), pp. 484–7.
3 Sergo Mikoyan, quoted in ibid.
4 V. Tsaplin, discussed by Alec Nove, 'Victims of Stalinism: How Many?', in

J. Arch Getty and Roberta T. Manning (ed.), *Stalinist Terror: New Perspectives* (Cambridge, 1993).

5   Alexander Solzhenitsyn, *The Gulag Archipelago, 1918–56*, trans. Thomas P. Whitney and Harry Willetts, abridged Edward E. Ericson Jr (London, 1988), pp. 425–32.

6   Robert Conquest, *Harvest of Sorrow* (London, 1986).

7   Ibid., ch. 16, and Stephen G. Wheatcroft, 'More Light on the Scale of Repression and Excess Mortality in the Soviet Union in the 1930s', in Getty and Manning, *Stalinist Terror*.

8   D.P. Vitovsky, quoted in Solzhenitsyn, *The Gulag Archipelago*, p. 205.

9   Conquest, *The Great Terror*, p. 287.

10 Solzhenitsyn, *The Gulag Archipelago*, p. 60.

11 Conquest, *The Great Terror*, pp. 122–3.

12 Nadezhda Mandelstam, *Hope Against Hope*, trans. Max Hayward (Harmondsworth, 1975), p. 80.

13 Caroline Moorhead, 'Out of Darkness', *Independent Magazine* (26 January 1991).

14 Solzhenitsyn, *The Gulag Archipelago*, pp. 185–6.

15 Mandelstam, *Hope Against Hope*, pp. 251–?

Chapter 25   *The Trap of Terror*

1   Dmitri Volkogonov, *Lenin: Life and Legacy*, trans. and ed. Harold Shukman (London, 1994), pp. 69–70. Italics in original.

2   Nadezhda Mandelstam, *Hope Against Hope*, trans. Max Hayward (Harmondsworth, 1975), p 383.

3   Alexander Solzhenitsyn, *The Gulag Archipelago, 1918–56*, trans. Thomas P. Whitney and Harry Willetts, abridged Edward E. Ericson Jr (London, 1988), pp. 27–8.

4   Lars T. Lih, Oleg V. Naumov and Oleg V. Khlevniuk (ed.), *Stalin's Letters to Molotov* (New Haven, Conn., 1995), p. 210.

5   Robert Conquest, *The Great Terror*, 2nd edn (London, 1990), pp. 163–4.

6   Arkady Vaksberg, *Prosecutor and Prey: Vyshinsky and the 1930s Moscow Show Trials*, trans. Jan Butler (London, 1990), pp. 110–11.

7   Fitzroy MacLean, *Eastern Approaches* (London, 1949; Harmondsworth, 1991), pp. 85–8.

8   Ibid., pp. 109–13.

9   Ibid., p. 109.

10 Ibid., pp. 119–20.

11 Nikita S. Khrushchev, *Khrushchev Remembers*, (New York, 1970) p. 301.

12 Roy Medvedev, *All Stalin's Men*, trans. Harold Shukman (Oxford, 1983), p. 20.

13 Robert Conquest, *Stalin: Breaker of Nations* (London, 1993), pp. 208–9.

14 Stuart Kahan, *The Wolf of the Kremlin* (London, 1987), pp. 160–1.

15 Ibid., pp. 222–30.

16 *Molotov Remembers: Inside Kremlin Politics, Conversations with Felix Chuev*, ed. Albert Resis (Chicago, 1993), p. 323.
17 Ibid., p. 323.
18 S. Mikunis, quoted in Medvedev, *All Stalin's Men*, p. 99.
19 Svetlana Alliluyeva, *Twenty Letters to a Friend*, trans. Priscilla Johnson McMillan (New York, 1967), pp. 7–8.
20 Khrushchev, *Khrushchev Remembers*, p. 318.
21 Secret speech, quoted in Conquest, *The Great Terror*, p. 56.
22 Khrushchev, *Khrushchev Remembers*, p. 299.
23 Milovan Djilas, *Conversations with Stalin* (Harmondsworth, 1963), p. 103.
24 Plato, *The Republic*, trans. Robin Waterfield (Oxford, 1993), pp. 565–76.

Chapter 26   Belief: Ends and Means

1 *Victory*, organ of the Soviet writers of Lithuania (1950), quoted in Czeslaw Milosz, *The Captive Mind* (London, 1980), p. 231.
2 Milovan Djilas, *Conversations with Stalin* (Harmondsworth, 1963), p. 15.
3 Dmitri Volkogonov, *Lenin: Life and Legacy*, trans. and ed. Harold Shukman (London, 1994), p. 241.
4 Khrushchev's secret speech, quoted in Robert Conquest, *The Great Terror*, 2nd edn (London, 1990), p. 60.
5 D.A. Lazurkina, quoted in Volkogonov, *Lenin*, p. 309.
6 Roy Medvedev, *Nikolai Bukharin: the Last Years*, trans. A.D.P. Briggs (New York, 1980), p. 52.
7 *Critique of the Gotha Programme* (1875), English trans. (Moscow, 1966), p. 17.
8 V.I. Lenin, *Lessons of the Commune*, quoted in Richard Pipes, *The Russian Revolution* (New York, 1991), p. 790.
9 Leon Trotsky, *On Lenin*, quoted in ibid., p. 791.
10 S.J. Taylor, *Stalin's Apologist: Walter Duranty, the New York Times's Man in Moscow* (Oxford, 1990), pp. 185, 207.
11 I.D. Perfilyev, quoted in Volkogonov, *Lenin*, p. 310.
12 Stuart Kahan, *The Wolf of the Kremlin* (London, 1987), p. 309.

Chapter 27   Stalinism and the Moral Resources

1 *Independent* (5 March 1993).
2 Stalin, *Works*, vol. 12, quoted in Jonathan Lewis and Phillip Whitehead, *Stalin: a Time for Judgement* (London, 1991), p. 57.
3 Dmitri Volkogonov, *Lenin: Life and Legacy*: (London, 1994), p. 571.
4 Ibid., pp. 196–7, 245.
5 Alexander Solzhenitsyn, *The Gulag Archipelago, 1918–56*, trans. Thomas P. Whitney and Harry Willetts, abridged Edward E. Ericson Jr (London, 1988), p. 323.
6 Ibid., p. 326.

7 Nadezhda Mandelstam, *Hope Against Hope*, trans. Max Hayward (Harmondsworth, 1975), pp. 43–4, 63–4, 159, 414.

8 Lev Kopelev, *The Education of a True Believer* (New York, 1977), quoted in Robert Conquest, *Harvest of Sorrow* (London, 1986), p. 233.

9 Hatayevich, Central Committee Member, quoted in R.J. Rummel, *Lethal Politics: Soviet Genocide and Mass Murder since 1917* (New Brunswick, N.J., 1990), p. 81.

10 Andrei Sakharov, *Memoirs*, trans. Richard Lourie (New York, 1992), p. 21.

11 Mandelstam, *Hope Against Hope*, p. 281.

12 Robert C. Tucker, *Stalin as Revolutionary, 1879–1929* (London, 1974), pp. 102, 113.

13 Volkogonov, *Lenin*, pp. 293, 338–9.

14 Solzhenitsyn, *The Gulag Archipelago*, p. 74.

15 Mandelstam, *Hope Against Hope*, pp. 198, 212.

16 Roy Medvedev, *Nikolai Bukharin: the Last Years*, trans. A.D.P. Briggs (New York, 1980), p. 52.

17 *Economic Theory of the Leisure Class*, and speeches, quoted in Stephen F. Cohen, *Bukharin and the Bolshevik Revolution: a Political Biography 1888–1938* (London, 1974), pp. 167–8.

18 *Pravda* (16 March 1925), and other sources, quoted in Cohen, *Bukharin and the Bolshevik Revolution*, p. 169.

19 Stalin, quoted in Medvedev, *Nikolai Bukharin*, p. 25.

20 Volkogonov, *Lenin*, pp. 285–6.

21 Ibid., pp. 295–8.

22 Medvedev, *Nikolai Bukharin*, p. 144.

23 Ibid., p. 67.

24 Ibid., p. 160.

25 'To a Future Generation of Party Leaders', in Anna Larina Bukharina, *This I Cannot Forget*, trans. G.K. (London, 1993), pp. 343–5.

Chapter 28 The Working of the Belief System

1 Frank Ramsey, 'General Propositions and Causality', in *The Foundations of Mathematics and Other Essays* (London, 1931), p. 238.

2 Francis King and George Matthews (ed.), *About Turn: the British Communist Party and the Second World War: the Verbatim Record of the Central Committee Meetings of 25 September and 2–3 October 1939* (London, 1990).

3 Account by Kirill Shirinya of Dmitrov's diary, quoted in ibid., p. 20.

4 Ibid., pp. 60–1.

5 Ibid., p. 220.

6 Ibid., p. 30.

7 Ibid., pp. 251–4.

8 Ibid., pp. 263–4.

9 Ibid., pp. 130–1.

10 Ibid., p. 275.

11 Ibid., pp. 24–5.

12 Ibid., pp. 240–1.
13 Ibid., pp. 284–5, 293.
14 Ibid., p. 72.
15 Ibid., p. 59.
16 Ibid., p. 247.
17 Ibid., p. 128.
18 Ibid., p. 72.
19 Ibid., p. 141.
20 Ibid., p. 146.
21 Ibid., p. 246.
22 Ibid., p. 76.
23 Ibid., pp. 85–6.
24 Ibid., pp. 200, 202–3.
25 Ibid., p. 40.
26 Ibid., pp. 296–9.
27 Ibid., p. 56.
28 Ibid., pp. 72, 82.
29 Ibid., p. 278.
30 Ibid., p. 236.

Chapter 29   Stalinism, Truth and Moral Identity

1   Alexander Solzhenitsyn, *The Gulag Archipelago, 1918–56*, trans. Thomas P. Whitney and Harry Willetts, abridged Edward E. Ericson Jr (London, 1988), pp. 325–6.
2   Ibid., pp. 198–201.
3   Ibid., pp. 190–2.
4   George Orwell, 'Looking Back on the Spanish War', in Sonia Orwell and Ian Angus (ed.), *The Collected Essays, Journalism and Letters of George Orwell*, vol. 2, *My Country Right or Left, 1940–3* (Harmondsworth, 1970), pp. 295–7.
5   Karl Marx, 'Concerning Feuerbach', in *Early Writings*, trans. Rodney Livingstone and Gregor Benton (Harmondsworth, 1975), p. 422.
6   *Agrobiologiya*, quoted in Jasper Becker, *Hungry Ghosts: China's Secret Famine* (London, 1996), p. 65.
7   Quoted in Arkady Vaksberg, *Prosecutor and Prey: Vyshinsky and the 1930s Moscow Show Trials*, trans. Jan Butler (London, 1990), p. 161.
8   Quoted in Solzhenitsyn, *The Gulag Archipelago*, p. 43.
9   Dmitri Volkogonov, *Lenin: Life and Legacy*, trans. and ed. Harold Shukman (London, 1994), p. 361.
10 Leon Trotsky, 'The Party in the Fields of Art and Philosophy', in *Problems of Everyday Life* (New York, 1973), p. 321.
11 Nadezhda Mandelstam, *Hope Against Hope*, trans. Max Hayward (Harmondsworth, 1975), p. 463.
12 Dmitry Volkogonov, *Stalin: Triumph and Tragedy*, trans. Harold Shukman (Rocklin, Cal., 1991), pp. 230–2.

13 Obituary of Milovan Djilas, *Independent* (21 April 1995).

Chapter 30   Mao's Utopian Project

1 Zhisui Li, *The Private Life of Chairman Mao: the Memoirs of Mao's Personal Physician*, trans. Tai Hung-Chao (London, 1994), pp. 272–3, 277.
2 Roderick MacFarquhar, Timothy Cheek and Eugene Wu (ed.), *The Secret Speeches of Chairman Mao, from the Hundred Flowers to the Great Leap Forward* (Cambridge, Mass., 1987), quoted in Jasper Becker, *Hungry Ghosts: China's Secret Famine* (London, 1996), p. 68.
3 Becker, *Hungry Ghosts*, pp. 144–5.
4 Li, *The Private Life of Chairman Mao*, pp. 277–8.
5 Ibid., p. 165.
6 Ibid., p. 463.
7 Speaking at a meeting at Chengdu in 1958, quoted in ibid., pp. 234–5.
8 Elizabeth J. Perry and Li Xun, *Proletarian Power: Shanghai in the Cultural Revolution* (Boulder, Colorado, 1997), pp. 12–14.
9 Zhai Zhenhua, *Red Flower of China: an Autobiography* (New York, 1992), pp. 97–100.
10 Letter to the Red Guards, 1 August, 1966, in Jerome Ch'en (ed.), *Mao Papers: Anthology and Bibliography* (London, 1970), p. 115.
11 Li, *The Private Life of Chairman Mao*, pp. 489–90.
12 Ibid., p. 429.
13 Anchee Min, *Red Azalea* (New York, 1994), pp. 30–42.
14 Feng Jicai, *Ten Years of Madness: Oral Histories of China's Cultural Revolution* (San Francisco, 1996), p. 11.
15 Li, *The Private Life of Chairman Mao*, p. 140.
16 Ibid., p. 121.
17 Jung Chang, *Wild Swans: Three Daughters of China* (London, 1991), pp. 379, 407–8.
18 John Byron and Robert Pack, *The Claws of the Dragon* (New York, 1992), quoted in Becker, *Hungry Ghosts*, p. 33.
19 Zhai Zhenhua, *Red Flower of China*, p. 95.
20 Jung Chang, *Wild Swans*, pp. 436–8.
21 Chihua Wen, *The Red Mirror: Children of China's Cultural Revolution* (Boulder, Colorado, 1995), p. 38.
22 Jung Chang, *Wild Swans*, p. 359.
23 Michael Oakeshott, 'Political Education', inaugural lecture at the London School of Economics, 1951, reprinted in *Rationalism in Politics* (London, 1962).
24 Robert Jay Lifton, *Thought Reform and the Psychology of Totalism: a Study of 'Brainwashing' in China* (Harmondsworth, 1967), pp. 36–45.
25 Chin Yueh-li, 'Criticizing My Idealistic Bourgeois Pedagogical Ideology', *Kuang Ming Jih Pao* (Beijing, 17 April 1952), reprinted in ibid., pp. 537–49.
26 S.E. Asch, 'Effects of Group Pressure upon the Modification and Distortion

of Judgement', in H. Guetzkow (ed.), *Groups, Leadership and Men* (Pittsburgh, 1951).

27 Michael Cherniak, *Minimal Rationality* (Cambridge, Mass., 1986).
28 Jicai, *Ten Years of Madness*, p. 21.
29 William James, *The Principles of Psychology*, vol. 1 (New York, 1950), p. 293.
30 Jung Chang, *Wild Swans*, pp. 438–9.
31 *China Youth Journal* (27 September 1958), quoted in Becker, *Hungry Ghosts*, p. 106.
32 Jung Chang, *Wild Swans*, p. 659.
33 Li, *The Private Life of Chairman Mao*, p. 122.
34 Ibid., pp. 125, 217.
35 Mao Zedong, *Sixty Points on Working Methods* (Internal Party Document, circulated in Beijing, 1958), quoted in Jonathan D. Spence, *The Search for Modern China* (New York, 1990), pp. 577–8.
36 *China Youth Journal* (27 September 1958), quoted in Becker, *Hungry Ghosts*, p. 106.
37 Jung Chang, *Wild Swans*, pp. 658–9.

Chapter 31 Overturning the Basket: Cambodia

1 François Ponchaud, *Cambodia, Year Zero*, trans. Nancy Amphoux (Harmondsworth, 1978), p. 22.
2 Chhin Phoeun, quoted in Ben Kiernan, *The Pol Pot Regime – Race, Power, and Genocide in Cambodia under the Khmer Rouge, 1975–9* (New Haven, Conn., 1996), p. 43.
3 Jon Swain, *River of Time* (London, 1996), p. 147.
4 Sam Suon, quoted in Ponchaud, *Cambodia, Year Zero*, p. 42.
5 Ibid., pp. 62–3, 82.
6 Radio Phnom Penh, 11 March 1976, quoted in ibid., p. 116.
7 Suon Phal, quoted in ibid., p. 75.
8 *Kampuchea, Decade of the Genocide: Report of a Finnish Inquiry Commission*, ed. Kimmo Kiljunen (London, 1984), p. 5.
9 Ben Kiernan, obituary of Pol Pot, *Independent* (17 April 1998).
10 Peter W. Rodman, 'Sideswipe: Kissinger, Shawcross and the Responsibility for Cambodia', reprinted in William Shawcross, *Sideshow: Kissinger, Nixon and the Destruction of Cambodia* (London, 1986), p. 426.
11 Roger Morris, *Uncertain Greatness: Henry Kissinger and American Foreign Policy* (London, 1977), quoted in John Pilger, *Heroes* (London, 1986), p. 387.
12 Charles Meyer, quoted in Kiernan, *The Pol Pot Regime*, p. 20.
13 Chhit Do, interview with Bruce Pauling, quoted in ibid., p. 23.
14 Ibid., pp. 80, 95–7.
15 Ponchaud, *Cambodia, Year Zero*, pp. 37–8.
16 *The Party's Four-Year Plan to Build Socialism in All Fields*, in David P. Chandler, Ben Kiernan and Chanthou Boua, *Pol Pot Plans the Future:*

Confidential Leadership Documents from Democratic Kampuchea, 1976–7 (New Haven, 1988), p. 113.

17 'Examine the Control', Khmer Rouge document, 1975, quoted in Kiernan, *The Pol Pot Regime*, pp. 98–9.

18 Ponchaud, *Cambodia, Year Zero*, pp. 85–9.

19 Khuon Thlai Chamnan, quoted in Kiernan, *The Pol Pot Regime*, p. 154.

20 Pol Pot, quoted in Kenneth M. Quinn, 'Explaining the Terror', in Karl D. Jackson (ed.), *Cambodia, 1975–8: Rendezvous with Death* (Princeton, 1989), pp. 219–21.

21 *The Party's Four-Year Plan to Build Socialism in All Fields*, and *Preliminary Explanation Before Reading the Plan, by the Party Secretary*, in Chandler, Kiernan and Boua, *Pol Pot Plans the Future*, pp. 48, 160.

22 Michael Vickery, *Cambodia, 1975–82* (Boston, 1984), p. 81.

23 Ponchaud, *Cambodia, Year Zero*, p. 201.

24 *Preliminary Explanation Before Reading the Plan, by the Party Secretary*, in Chandler, Kiernan and Boua, *Pol Pot Plans the Future*, p. 158.

25 *Report of Activities of the Party Center According to the General Political Tasks of 1976*, in ibid., p. 183.

26 *Examine the Control*, quoted in Kiernan, *The Pol Pot Regime*, p. 98.

27 Ponchaud, *Cambodia, Year Zero*, pp. 86, 92.

28 Ibid., p. 25.

29 *Regrets for the Khmer Soul* (1977), quoted in Quinn, 'Explaining the Terror', p. 234.

30 Ponchaud, *Cambodia, Year Zero*, p. 89.

31 Party Center, *Abbreviated Lesson on the History of the Kampuchean Revolutionary Movement Led by the Communist Party of Kampuchea*, in Chandler, Kiernan and Boua, *Pol Pot Plans the Future*, p. 222.

32 Swain, *River of Time*, pp. 44–5.

33 N. Sihanouk, *War and Hope: the Case for Cambodia* (New York, 1980), quoted in Quinn, 'Explaining the Terror', pp. 237–8.

34 *Summary of the Results of the 1976 Study Session*, in Chandler, Kiernan and Boua, *Pol Pot Plans the Future*, p. 173.

35 *Excerpted Report on the Leading Views of the Comrade Representing the Party Organization at a Zone Assembly*, in ibid., p. 15.

36 Elizabeth Becker, *When the War Was Over: Cambodia's Revolution and the Voices of Its People* (New York, 1986), p. 296.

37 Swain, *River of Time*, pp. 257–8.

38 Ibid., pp. 258, 260.

Chapter 33 The Core of Nazism

1 Adolf Hitler, *Mein Kampf*, trans. Ralph Manheim (London, 1969), pp. 148, 150, 155.

2 William L. Shirer, *Berlin Diary, 1934–41* (London, 1941), pp. 328–32.

3 *Hitler's Table Talk, 1941–4*, introduced by Hugh Trevor-Roper (Oxford, 1988), p. 87.

4 Hitler, *Mein Kampf*, p. 175.

5 Ibid., p. 155.

6 Ibid., p. 113.

7 Tacitus, *Germania*, in *Tacitus on Britain and Germany*, trans. H. Mattingly (West Drayton, 1948), pp. 108–32.

8 Ibid., pp. 101–4.

9 Simon Schama, *Landscape and Memory* (London, 1996), pp. 75–134.

10 Johann Gottlieb Fichte, quoted in Hans Sluga, *Heidegger's Crisis: Philosophy and Politics in Nazi Germany* (Cambridge, Mass., 1993), pp. 34–41.

11 Schama, *Landscape and Memory*, pp. 100–20.

12 Hitler, *Mein Kampf*, pp. 183–5.

13 Ibid., pp. 41, 620.

14 Robert N. Proctor, *Racial Hygiene: Medicine Under the Nazis* (Cambridge, Mass., 1988), ch. 2; Benno Müller-Hill, *Murderous Science: Elimination by Scientific Selection of Jews, Gypsies and Others, Germany, 1933–45*, trans. George R. Fraser (Oxford, 1988), pp. 10, 112.

15 Proctor, *Racial Hygiene*, pp. 51–2.

16 Hitler, *Mein Kampf*, pp. 121–2.

17 J. Noakes and G. Pridham (ed.), *Nazism, 1919–45, a Documentary Reader*, vol. 3, *Foreign Policy, War and Racial Extermination* (Exeter, 1988), pp. 999–1000.

18 Klara Nowak, interviewed by Michael Burleigh (Hadamar, 1991), quoted in Michael Burleigh, *Death and Deliverance: 'Euthanasia' in Germany, 1900–45* (Cambridge, 1994), p. 58.

19 Catrine Clay and Michael Leapman, *Master Race: the Lebensborn Experiment in Nazi Germany* (London, 1995), p. 91.

20 Michael Burleigh and Wolfgang Wippermann, *The Racial State: Germany, 1933–45* (Cambridge, 1991), p. 38; Müller-Hill, *Murderous Science*, p. 113.

21 Müller-Hill, *Murderous Science*, p. 12.

22 Ibid., p. 14.

23 Robert Jay Lifton, *The Nazi Doctors: a Study in the Psychology of Evil* (London, 1987), p. 16.

24 Friedrich Nietzsche, *Nachgelassene Fragmente, Anfang 1880 bis Sommer 1882*, pp. 189, 250, quoted in Burleigh and Wippermann, *The Racial State*, p. 34.

25 Hitler, *Mein Kampf*, pp. 39, 124.

26 Ibid., pp. 210, 307.

27 Quoted in Joachim Fest, *The Face of the Third Reich*, trans. Michael Bullock (London, 1972), p. 394.

Chapter 34   Obedience and Conformity

1 J. Noakes and G. Pridham (ed.), *Nazism, 1919–45, a Documentary Reader*, vol. 3, *Foreign Policy, War and Extermination* (Exeter, 1988) p. 1141.

2 Quoted in J.P. Stern, *Hitler: the Führer and the People*, rev. edn (London, 1984), pp. 74, 171.

3   *Münchner Neueste Nachrichten*, (29 March 1936), quoted in Ian Kershaw, *The Hitler Myth: Image and Reality in the Third Reich* (Oxford, 1987), p. 78.
4   Quoted in Stern, *Hitler*, p. 99.
5   T.W. Adorno, Else Frenkel-Brunswik, Daniel J. Levinson and R. Nevitt Sanford, *The Authoritarian Personality* (New York, 1950).
6   Else Frenkel-Brunswik, in ibid., p. 370.
7   Alice Miller, *For Your Own Good: the Roots of Violence in Child-rearing*, trans. Hildegarde and Hunter Hannum (London, 1987), p. 65.
8   Rudolf Höss, *Commandant of Auschwitz*, trans. Constantine Fitzgibbon (London, 1961), p. 28.
9   Adolf Hitler, *Mein Kampf*, trans. Ralph Manheim (London, 1969), pp. 5, 16.
10 Robert G.L. Waite, *The Psychopathic God: Adolf Hitler* (New York, 1993), pp. 15, 131–8.
11 Stanley Milgram, *Obedience to Authority: an Experimental View* (London, 1974).
12 Gordon Bear, Internet communication, 1998.
13 Christopher R. Browning, *Ordinary Men: Reserve Police Battalion 101 and the Final Solution in Poland* (New York, 1992), pp. 71–7.
14 Milgram, *Obedience to Authority*, pp. 116–21.
15 Tom Segev, *Soldiers of Evil: the Commandants of the Nazi Concentration Camps* (New York, 1987), p. 139.
16 Ibid., pp. 49, 89–90, 190–1.
17 Jochen von Lang and Claus Sibyll, *Eichmann Interrogated: Transcripts from the Archives of the Israeli Police*, trans. Ralph Manheim (New York, 1983), pp. 198–9.
18 Eichmann, quoted in Hannah Arendt, *Eichmann in Jerusalem: a Report on the Banality of Evil* (Harmondsworth, 1977), p. 32.

Chapter 35   The Attack on Humanity

1   J. Noakes and G. Pridham (ed.), *Nazism, 1919–45: a Documentary Reader*, vol. 3, *Foreign Policy, War and Racial Extermination* (Exeter, 1988), p. 1010.
2   Ibid., pp. 1023–4.
3   Primo Levi, *The Drowned and the Saved*, trans. Raymond Rosenthal (London, 1988), pp. 70–1.
4   Bruno Bettelheim, *The Informed Heart: the Human Condition in Mass Society* (London, 1970), pp. 224–5.
5   Tom Segev, *Soldiers of Evil: the Commandants of the Nazi Concentration Camps* (New York, 1987), p. 80.
6   Adolf Hitler, *Mein Kampf*, trans. Ralph Manheim (London, 1969), p. 53. (I have altered the translation of 'Judlein'.)
7   *Hitler's Table Talk, 1941–4*, introduced by Hugh Trevor-Roper (Oxford, 1988), p. 332.
8   Raul Hilberg, *The Destruction of the European Jews*, student edn (New York, 1985), p. 80.
9   Ibid., p. 49.

10   William L. Shirer, *Berlin Diary, 1934–41* (London, 1941), p. 92.
11   Christopher R. Browning; *Ordinary Men: Reserve Police Battalion 101 and the Final Solution in Poland* (New York, 1982), pp. 11–12.
12   *The Gay Science*, Section 200.
13   Joachim Fest, *The Face of the Third Reich*, trans. Michael Bullock (London, 1972), pp. 495–6.
14   Martha Gellhorn, 'Eichmann and the Private Conscience', in *The View from the Ground* (London, 1990).
15   Levi, *The Drowned and the Saved*, p. 99.
16   Paul Celan, 'Todesfuge', trans. John Felstiner, in John Felstiner, *Paul Celan: Poet, Survivor, Jew* (New Haven, 1995), p. 31.
17   Daniel Jonah Goldhagen, *Hitler's Willing Executioners: Ordinary Germans and the Holocaust* (London, 1997), pp. 308–9.
18   Levi, *The Drowned and the Saved*, pp. 88–9.
19   Segev, *Soldiers of Evil*, pp. 201, 211.
20   Levi, *The Drowned and the Saved*, p. 37.
21   Gitta Sereny, *Into That Darkness: an Examination of Conscience* (London, 1977), p. 101.
22   Ernst Jünger, *Battle as Inner Experience*, quoted in Klaus Theweleit, *Male Fantasies*, trans. Chris Turner and Erica Carter, vol. 2 (Minneapolis, 1989), p. 159.
23   Ibid., p. 164.
24   8 November 1940, quoted in J.P. Stern, *Hitler: the Führer and the People*, rev. edn (London, 1984), p. 62.
25   *Hitler's Table Talk*, pp. 586–7, 624.
26   Hilberg, *The Destruction of the European Jews*, pp. 187–8.
27   Fest, *The Face of the Third Reich*, p. 169.
28   Gellhorn, 'Eichmann and the Private Conscience'.
29   Browning, *Ordinary Men*, p. 183.
30   Quoted in Segev, *Soldiers of Evil*, p. 86.
31   Rudolf Höss, *Commandant of Auschwitz*, trans. Constantine Fitzgibbon (London, 1961), pp. 172–4.
32   Hilberg, *The Destruction of the European Jews*, pp. 136–7.
33   Robert Jay Lifton, *The Nazi Doctors: a Study in the Psychology of Evil* (London, 1987), p. 15.
34   Browning, *Ordinary Men*, p. 25.
35   Ibid., pp. 67, 69.
36   Miklos Nyiszli, *Auschwitz: a Doctor's Eye-witness Account*, trans. Tibere Kremer and Richard Seaver (London, 1962), pp. 89–93.
37   Höss, *Commandant of Auschwitz*, p. 175.
38   Browning, *Ordinary Men*, p. 113.
39   Hilberg, *The Destruction of the European Jews*, p. 217.
40   Noakes and Pridham, *Nazism, 1919–45*, pp. 1014–15.
41   Höss, *Commandant of Auschwitz*, p. 174.

Chapter 36   The Erosion of Moral Identity

1   Rudolf Höss, *Commandant of Auschwitz*, trans. Constantine Fitzgibbon (London, 1961), p. 44.
2   Christopher R. Browning, *Ordinary Men: Reserve Police Battalion 101 and the Final Solution in Poland* (New York, 1992), p. 82.
3   Jochen von Lang and Claus Sibyll (ed.), *Eichmann Interrogated: Transcripts from the Archives of the Israeli Police*, trans. Ralph Manheim (New York, 1983), pp. 132–3.
4   Christopher R. Browning, 'The Development and Production of the Nazi Gas Van', in *Fateful Months: Essays on the Emergence of the Final Solution* (New York, 1985), pp. 64–5.
5   Raul Hilberg, *The Destruction of the European Jews*, student edn (New York, 1985), p. 281.
6   Browning, *Ordinary Men*, p. 40.
7   Hannah Arendt, *Eichmann in Jerusalem: a Report on the Banality of Evil* (Harmondsworth, 1977), p. 108.
8   Robert Jay Lifton, *The Nazi Doctors: a Study in the Psychology of Evil* (London, 1987), pp. 200, 228.
9   Tom Segev, *Soldiers of Evil: the Commandants of the Nazi Concentration Camps* (New York, 1987), pp. 3–4, 211.
10   Lifton, *The Nazi Doctors*, pp. 160, 249.
11   Hilberg, *The Destruction of the European Jews*, pp. 198–9.
12   Ibid., p. 281.

Chapter 37   The Nazi Moral Identity

1   *Hitler's Table Talk, 1941–4*, introduced by Hugh Trevor-Roper (Oxford, 1988), p. 343.
2   Ibid., p. 6.
3   Jochen von Lang and Claus Sibyll, *Eichmann Interrogated: Transcripts from the Archives of the Israeli Police*, trans. Ralph Manheim (New York, 1983), p. 39.
4   *Die Zweite Revolution*, quoted in Joachim Fest, *The Face of the Third Reich*, trans. Michael Bullock (London, 1972), pp. 138–9.
5   Harald Ofstad, *Our Contempt for Weakness: Nazi Norms and Values – and Our Own* (Stockholm, 1989), pp. 117–18.
6   Hannah Arendt, *Eichmann in Jerusalem: a Report on the Banality of Evil* (Harmondsworth, 1977), p. 49.
7   Adolf Hitler, *Mein Kampf*, trans. Ralph Manheim (London, 1969), pp. 231–2.
8   Von Lang and Sibyll, *Eichmann Interrogated*, p. 288.
9   Fest, *The Face of the Third Reich*, p. 191.
10   Robert Jay Lifton, *The Nazi Doctors: a Study in the Psychology of Evil* (London, 1987), p. 404.
11   Arendt, *Eichmann in Jerusalem*, p. 235.

12   Martha Gellhorn, 'Eichmann and the Private Conscience', in *The View from the Ground* (London, 1990), pp. 259–60.
13   Raul Hilberg, *The Destruction of the European Jews*, student edn (New York, 1985), p. 275.
14   Gitta Sereny, *Into That Darkness: an Examination of Conscience* (London, 1977), p. 229.
15   Hilberg, *The Destruction of the European Jews*, pp. 150–1.
16   Ibid., p. 227.
17   Tom Segev, *Soldiers of Evil: the Commandants of the Nazi Concentration Camps* (New York, 1987), p. 36.
18   Ibid., p. 47.

Chapter 38   The Willingness to Believe

1   Adolf Hitler, *Mein Kampf*, trans. Ralph Manheim (London, 1969), pp. 164–5.
2   Joachim Fest, *The Face of the Third Reich*, trans. Michael Bullock (London, 1972), p. 173; Robert Jay Lifton, *The Nazi Doctors: a Study in the Psychology of Evil* (London, 1987), p. 279.
3   Albert Speer, *Inside the Third Reich*, trans. Richard and Clara Winston (London, 1971), p. 51.
4   Sonia Orwell and Ian Angus (ed.), *The Collected Essays, Journalism and Letters of George Orwell*, vol. 2, *My Country Right or Left, 1940–3* (Harmondsworth, 1970), pp. 27–9.
5   Tom Segev, *Soldiers of Evil: the Commandants of the Nazi Concentration Camps* (New York, 1987), p. 74.
6   Ibid., p. 49.
7   Ibid., p. 9.
8   Robert Mason Lee, 'Keegstra's Children', *Saturday Night* (May 1985).
9   Daniel Jonah Goldhagen, *Hitler's Willing Executioners: Ordinary Germans and the Holocaust* (London, 1996), p. 394.

Chapter 39   Philosophers

1   Hitler, quoted in Joachim Fest, *The Face of the Third Reich*, trans. Michael Bullock (London, 1972), p. 391.
2   *Blätter fur Deutsche Philosophie*, quoted in Hans Sluga, *Heidegger's Crisis: Philosophy and Politics in Nazi Germany* (Cambridge, Mass., 1993), p. 86.
3   *Meyers Lexikon* (Leipzig, 1938), quoted in Monika Leske, *Philosophen im Dritten Reich: Studie zu Hochschul – und Philosophiebetrieb im faschistischen Deutschland* (Berlin, 1990).
4   'Rasse und Weltanschauung' in *Nationalsozialistische Monatshefte* (1934), quoted in ibid., p. 120.
5   Alfred Bäumler, 'Jugenddienstpflicht, Hitler-Jugend und Schule', in *Weltanschauung und Schule* (1938), quoted in ibid., p. 121.
6   Alfred Bäumler, *Studien zur Deutschen Geistesgeschichte* (Berlin, 1937), in George L. Mosse, *Nazi Culture: a Documentary History* (New York, 1981), pp. 100–1.

7   Elzbieta Ettinger, *Hannah Arendt, Martin Heidegger* (New Haven, Conn., 1995), pp. 36–7, 48.
8   Hans Jonas, 'Heidegger's Resoluteness and Resolve', in Gunther Neske and Emil Kettering, *Martin Heidegger and National Socialism: Questions and Answers*, trans. Lisa Harries (New York, 1990).
9   Martin Heidegger, *Discourse on Thinking*, quoted in Richard Wolin, *The Heidegger Controversy: a Critical Reader* (Cambridge, Mass., 1993), p. 9.
10 Hugo Ott, *Martin Heidegger: a Political Life*, trans. Allan Blunden (London, 1993), p. 379.
11 Martin Heidegger, *Creative Landscape: Why Do We Stay in the Provinces?*, in Anton Kaes, Martin Jay and Edward Dimendberg (ed.), *The Weimar Republic Sourcebook* (Berkeley, Cal., 1994), p. 427.
12 Ettinger, *Hannah Arendt*, p. 48.
13 Ott, *Martin Heidegger*, p. 169.
14 Sluga, *Heidegger's Crisis*, p. 172.
15 Martin Heidegger, 'The Self-assertion of the German University', in Neske and Kettering, *Martin Heidegger and National Socialism*, pp. 5–13.
16 Ott, *Martin Heidegger*, p. 190.
17 Husserl quoted in ibid., pp. 177, 184–5,
18 Jaspers, letter to Oehlkers, quoted in ibid., pp. 336–40.
19 Martin Heidegger, *Facts and Thoughts*, quoted in ibid., p. 139.
20 Ibid., p. 294.
21 Martin Heidegger, interview with *Der Spiegel* (1966), trans. Lisa Harries, in Neske and Kettering, *Martin Heidegger and National Socialism*, p. 54.
22 Martin Heidegger, *Letter on Humanism*, in David Farrell Krell (ed.), *Martin Heidegger: Basic Writings* (London, 1993), p. 254. I have used the translation of this sentence in Ott, *Martin Heidegger*, p. 167.
23 John Felstiner, *Paul Celan: Poet, Survivor, Jew* (New Haven, 1995), pp. 242–7.
24 Hannah Arendt, 'For Martin Heidegger's Eightieth Birthday', in Neske and Kettering, *Martin Heidegger and National Socialism*.
25 Martin Heidegger, *Being and Time*, trans John Macquarrie and Edward Robinson (Oxford, 1962), pp. 97–8.
26 Martin Heidegger, *An Introduction to Metaphysics*, trans. Ralph Manheim (New York, 1961).
27 Paul Edwards, 'Heidegger's Quest for Being', *Philosophy* (1989).
28 Immanuel, Kant, *Critique of Pure Reason*, trans. Norman Kemp Smith, 'Transcendental Dialectic', Book 2, ch. 3.
29 Jean Améry, *At the Mind's Limits: Contemplations by a Survivor on Auschwitz and Its Realities*, trans. Sidney and Stella Rosenfeld (New York, 1986), pp. 18–19.
30 Karl Löwith, 'Last Meeting with Heidegger', in Neske and Kettering, *Martin Heidegger and National Socialism*, p. 158.
31 William and Martha Kneale, *The Development of Logic* (Oxford, 1962), p. 511.
32 Michael Dummett, *Frege: the Philosophy of Language* (London, 1973).
33 Ibid., Preface.

Chapter 40   Bystanders

1   Gordon J. Horwitz, *In the Shadow of Death: Living Outside the Gates of Mauthausen* (London, 1991), pp. 60–1.
2   Ibid., p. 35.
3   Raul Hilberg, *The Destruction of the European Jews*, student edn (New York, 1985), p. 255; Horwitz, *In the Shadow of Death*, pp. 158–9.
4   Horwitz, *In the Shadow of Death*, pp. 132–4.
5   Karl Jaspers, *The Question of German Guilt*, trans. E.B. Ashton (New York, 1947), pp. 69–70.
6   Inge Deutschkron, *Outcast: a Jewish Girl in Wartime Berlin*, trans. Jean Steinberg (New York, 1989), pp. 151–2.
7   Horwitz, *In the Shadow of Death*, p. 5.
8   Louis de Jong, *The Netherlands and Nazi Germany* (Harvard, 1990), pp. 10–11.
9   Hannah Arendt, *Eichmann in Jerusalem: a Report on the Banality of Evil* (Harmondsworth, 1977), pp. 230–1.
10   J.P. Stern, *Hitler: the Führer and the People*, rev. edn (London, 1984), pp. 28–9.
11   Samuel P. Oliner and Pearl M. Oliner, *The Altruistic Personality: Rescuers of Jews in Nazi Europe* (New York, 1988).
12   Gay Block and Malka Drucker, *Rescuers: Portraits of Moral Courage in the Holocaust* (New York, 1992), p. 118.
13   Horwitz, *In the Shadow of Death*, pp. 121, 153.
14   Deutschkron, *Outcast*, p. 66.
15   Jean Améry, *At the Mind's Limits: Contemplations by a Survivor on Auschwitz and Its Realities*, trans. Sidney and Stella Rosenfeld (New York, 1986), pp. 73–4.
16   Gitta Sereny, *Into That Darkness: an Examination of Conscience* (London, 1977), pp. 284–5.
17   J. Noakes and G. Pridham, *Nazism, 1919–45, a Documentary Reader*, vol. 3, *Foreign Policy, War and Extermination* (Exeter, 1988), pp. 1036–8.
18   De Jong, *The Netherlands and Nazi Germany*, pp. 8, 20–1.
19   Philip Hallie, *Lest Innocent Blood Be Shed: the Story of Le Chambon and How Goodness Happened There* (New York, 1979), pp. 152–3.
20   Block and Drucker, *Rescuers*, p. 119.
21   Laurence Thomas, *Vessels of Evil: American Slavery and the Holocaust* (Philadelphia, 1993), pp. 65–72.
22   S. Paulsson, 'The "Bridge over the Oeresund": the Historiography on the Evacuation of the Jews of Nazi-occupied Denmark', *Journal of Contemporary History* (1995).
23   Leni Yahil, *The Rescue of Danish Jewry: Test of a Democracy*, trans. Morris Gradel (Philadelphia, 1969), p. 42.
24   Quoted in Samuel Abrahamsen, 'The Rescue of Denmark's Jews', in Leo Goldberger (ed.), *The Rescue of the Danish Jews: Moral Courage under Stress* (New York, 1987).
25   Paulsson, 'The "Bridge over the Oeresund" '.

26 Jonathan Steinberg, *All or Nothing: the Axis and the Holocaust, 1941–3* (London, 1990).
27 Ibid., pp. 170–1.
28 Hilberg, *The Destruction of the European Jews*, p. 329.
29 Ibid., pp. 329–30.
30 Bernard Wasserstein, *Britain and the Jews of Europe* (Oxford, 1988), p. 34.
31 Martin Gilbert, *Auschwitz and the Allies* (London, 1991), p. 99.
32 Wasserstein, *Britain and the Jews of Europe*, p. 109.
33 Norman Geras, *The Contract of Mutual Indifference* (London, 1998).

Chapter 41   Interpreting the Nazi Episode

1 'Intention and Explanation: a Current Controversy about the Interpretation of National Socialism', in Tim Mason, *Nazism, Fascism and the Working Class*, ed. Jane Caplan (Cambridge, 1995).
2 Ibid., p. 222.
3 Eberhard Jäckel, 'The Impoverished Practice of Insinuation: the Singular Aspect of National-Socialist Crimes Cannot Be Denied', in *Forever in the Shadow of Hitler? Original Documents of the Historikerstreit, the Controversy Concerning the Singularity of the Holocaust*, trans. James Knowlton and Truett Cates (New Jersey, 1993), p. 76.

Chapter 42   Some People and Not Others

1 Alexander Solzhenitsyn, *The Gulag Archipelago, 1918–56*, trans. Thomas P. Whitney and Harry Willetts, abridged Edward E. Ericson Jr (London, 1988), p. 319.
2 Primo Levi, *The Drowned and the Saved*, trans. Raymond Rosenthal (London, 1988), pp. 169–70.

Chapter 43   Ethics Humanized

1 Norman Geras, *The Contract of Mutual Indifference* (London, 1998), p. 47.
2 Donald Greer, *The Incidence of the Terror During the French Revolution: a Statistical Interpretation* (Cambridge, Mass., 1935), cited in Simon Schama, *Citizens: a Chronicle of the French Revolution* (New York, 1989), p. 785.

Epilogue   The Past Alive in the Present

1 R.G. Collingwood, *An Autobiography* (Harmondsworth, 1939), p. 112.
2 Simon Schama, *Citizens: a Chronicle of the French Revolution* (London, 1989), pp. 630, 635, 652–4, 693.
3 Ibid., pp. 789–90.
4 Seamus Heaney, 'The Tollund Man', in *Wintering Out* (London, 1972).

Sources and Acknowledgements

AFRICAN RIGHTS: from *Rwanda: Death, Despair and Defiance* (1995); ANNA AKHMATOVA: from 'Requiem' in *Selected Poems*, translated by D.M. Thomas (Penguin Books, 1992), reprinted by permission of Random House UK Ltd; SVETLANA ALEXIEVICH: from *Zinky Boys: Soviet Voices from a Forgotten War*, translated by Julia and Robin Whitby (Chatto & Windus, 1992); JEAN AMERY: from *At the Mind's Limits: Contemplations by a Survivor on Auschwitz and Its Realities* (Schocken Books, 1986); ANTON ANTONOV-OVSEYENKO: from *The Time of Stalin: Portrait of a Tyranny* (HarperCollins, 1981); W.H. AUDEN: from 'September 1, 1939' in *The English Auden: Poems, Essays & Dramatic Writings, 1927-1939* (Faber & Faber, 1986); from 'The Shield of Achilles' in *Collected Shorter Poems 1927-1957* (Faber & Faber, 1966); JAMES G. BLIGHT and DAVID A. WELCH: from *On the Brink: Americans and Soviets Re-examine the Cuban Missile Crisis* (Farrar, Straus & Giroux, 1989); CHRISTOPHER BROWNING: from *Ordinary Men: Reserve Police Battalion 101 and the Final Solution in Poland* (HarperCollins, 1992); WILLIAM BROYLES: from 'Why Men Love War' (*Esquire Magazine*, 1984); JUNG CHANG: from *The Independent on Sunday* (10 September 1995); from *Wild Swans: Three Daughters of China, from Warlords to Mao* (HarperCollins, 1992); JIWEI CI: from *Dialectic of the Chinese Revolution: From Utopianism to Hedonism* (Stanford University Press, 1994), reprinted by permission of the publisher; R.G. COLLINGWOOD: from *An Autobiography* (Oxford University Press, 1982); ROBERT CONQUEST: from *The Great Terror* (Pimlico, 1992); RENE DESCARTES: from *The Philosophical Writings of Descartes: Volume 1*, translated by John Cottingham (Cambridge University Press, 1985), reprinted by permission of the publisher; JOHN W. DOWER: from *War Without Mercy: Race and Power in the Pacific War* (Pantheon Books, 1986), reprinted by permission of the publisher; SLAVENKA DRAKULIC: from *Balkan Express: Fragments from the Other Side* (Hutchinson, 1992); JOHN FELSTINER: 'Todesfuge' by Paul Celan from *Paul Celan: Poet, Survivor, Jew* (Yale University Press, 1995), reprinted by permission of the publisher; GERALD FLEMING: from *Hitler and the Final Solution* (University of California Press, 1984), © 1984 The Regents of the University of California, reprinted by permission of the publisher; CHARLES FRANK (editor): from *Operation Epsilon: The Farm Hall Transcripts* (Institute of Physics Publishing, 1993); SIGMUND FREUD: from *The Future of an Illusion* (The Standard Edition), edited by James Strachey (Norton, 1990); MARTHA GELLHORN: from *The Face of War* (Granta, 1998), reprinted by kind permission of the publisher and the Martha Gellhorn estate; LEO GOLDBERGER (editor): from *The Rescue of the Danish Jews: Moral Courage Under Duress* (New York University Press, 1987), reprinted by permission of the publisher; ROBERT GRAVES:

from *Goodbye to All That* (Penguin Twentieth Century Classics, 1990), reprinted by permission of Carcanet Press Ltd; J. GLENN GRAY: from *The Warriors: Reflections on Men in Battle* (Harcourt Brace Jovanovich, 1959); EDWARD GREY: from *Twenty-Five Years: Volume 1: 1892-1916* (Hodder & Stoughton, 1925); MICHIHIKO HACHIYA: from *Hiroshima Diary: The Journal of a Japanese Physician, August 6 - September 30, 1945*, translated by Warner Wells, MD (University of North Carolina Press, 1955), © 1955 by the University of North Carolina Press, reprinted by permission of the publisher; INDIRA HADZIOMEROVIC: 'Mourning in Sarajevo' from 'Quote Unquote' in *The Independent* (8 August 1992), reprinted by permission of the publisher; MAX HASTINGS: from *Bomber Command*, (Michael Joseph, 1979); SEAMUS HEANEY: from 'The Tollund Man' in *Wintering Out* (Faber & Faber, 1972); MARTIN HEIDEGGER: from *Introduction to Metaphysics*, translated by Ralph Manheim (Yale University Press, 1974), reprinted by permission of the publisher; from *Being and Time*, translated by John Macquarrie and Edward Robinson (Blackwell, 1978), reprinted by permission of the publisher; RAUL HILBERG: from *The Destruction of the European Jews* (Holmes & Meier, 1985); ADOLF HITLER: from *Mein Kampf*, translated by Ralph Manheim (Hutchinson, 1969), reprinted by permission of Random House UK Ltd; GORDON J. HORWITZ: from *In the Shadow of Death: Living Outside the Gates of Mauthausen* (I.B. Tauris, 1991), reprinted by permission of the publisher; RUDOLF HÖSS: from *Commandant of Auschwitz*, translated by Constantine Fitzgibbon (Weidenfeld & Nicolson, 1959), reprinted by permission of The Orion Publishing Group; KONRAD H. JARAUSCH: from *The Enigmatic Chancellor: Bethmann Holweg and the Hubris of Imperial Germany* (Yale University Press, 1973), reprinted by permission of the publisher; ROBERT JUNGK: from *Brighter than a Thousand Suns*, translated by J. Cleugh (Victor Gollancz; Rupert Hart-Davis, 1958), reprinted by permission of The Orion Publishing Group; FERGAL KEANE, from *Season of Blood: A Rwandan Journey* (Penguin Books, 1996); BRIAN KEENAN: from *An Evil Cradling* (Hutchinson, 1992), reprinted by permission of Random House UK Ltd; ROBERT F. KENNEDY: from *Thirteen Days: A Memoir of the Cuban Missile Crisis* (Norton, 1971), © 1968 by McCall Corporation, reprinted by permission of W.W. Norton & Company Inc; FRANCIS KING and GEORGE MATTHEWS (editors): from *About Turn: Communist Party and the Outbreak of the Second World War – The Verbatim Record of the Central Committee Meetings, 1939* (Lawrence & Wishart, 1990), reprinted by permission of the publisher; PHILIP LARKIN: from 'MCMXIV' in *Collected Poems* (Faber & Faber, 1988); PRIMO LEVI: from *The Drowned and the Saved*, translated by Raymond Rosenthal (Michael Joseph, 1988); ZHISUI LI: from *Private Life of Chairman Mao: The Memoirs of Mao's Personal Physician* (Arrow Books, 1996); ROBERT JAY LIFTON: from *Home from the War: Vietnam Veterans – Neither Victims nor Executioners* (Beacon Press, 1985); PETER MAASS: from *Love Thy Neighbor: A Story of War* (Papermac, 1996); LYN MACDON-ALD: from *1914–1918: Voices and Images of the Great War* (Penguin, 1991); FITZROY MACLEAN: from *Eastern Approaches* (Penguin Books, 1991); ERNEST R. MAY and PHILIP D. ZELIKOW (editors): from *The Kennedy Tapes: Inside the White House During the Cuban Missile Crisis* (Harvard University Press, 1997); NADEZHDA MANDEL-STAM: from *Hope Against Hope: A Memoir*, translated by Max Hayward, first published by The Harvill Press in 1971, © Atheneum Publishers, 1970, translation © Atheneum Publishers, New York, and Harvill, London, reprinted by permission of The Harvill Press; MARTIN MIDDLEBROOK: from *The Battle of Hamburg: The Firestorm Raid* (Penguin Books, 1994); BENNO MULLER-HILL: from *Murderous Science: Elimination by Scientific Selection of Jews, Gypsies, and Others – Germany, 1933–45*, translated by G.R. Fraser (Oxford University Press, 1988), reprinted by permission of Tanja Howarth Literary Agency; FRIEDRICH NIETZSCHE: from *On the Genealogy of Morals*, translated by Walter

Kaufmann and R.J. Hollingdale (Random House, 1969); from *Beyond Good and Evil*, translated by R.J. Hollingdale (Penguin Classics, 1973); from *Thus Spake Zarathustra*, translated by R.J. Hollingdale (Penguin Classics, 1969); from *The Will to Power*, translated by R. J. Hollingdale and Walter Kaufmann (Weidenfeld & Nicolson, 1968), reprinted by permission of Random House Inc; JEREMY NOAKES and GEOFFREY PRIDHAM: from *Nazism 1919–45: Volume 3* (University of Exeter Press, 1988); GEORGE ORWELL: from 'Looking Back on the Spanish Civil War', © George Orwell 1942, and from 'The Lion and the Unicorn: Socialism and the English Genius', © George Orwell 1941, in *The Complete Works of George Orwell* (Secker & Warburg, 1998), reprinted by permission of A.M. Heath & Co Ltd on behalf of Mark Hamilton as the Literary Executor of the Estate of the Late Sonia Brownell Orwell, and Martin Secker & Warburg Ltd; HUGO OTT: from *Martin Heidegger: A Political Life*, translated by Allan Blunden (HarperCollins, 1993); PLATO: from *The Republic*, translated by H.D.P. Lee (Penguin Classics, 1970); from *The Republic*, translated by Robin Waterfield (Oxford University Press, 1994); FRANCOIS PONCHAUD: from *Cambodia, Year Zero*, translated by Nancy Amphoux (Penguin Books, 1978); J. REITH: from *Wearing Spurs* (Hutchinson, 1978); ALBERT RESIS (editor): from *Molotov Remembers: Inside Kremlin Politics, Conversations with Felix Chuev* (I.R. Dee, 1993); RICHARD RHODES: from *The Making of the Atom Bomb* (Penguin Books, 1988); SIEGFRIED SASSOON: from *Memoirs of an Infantry Officer* (Faber & Faber, 1965), copyright Siegfried Sassoon, reprinted by kind permission of George Sassoon; SERGE SAZONOV: from *Fateful Years, 1909–1916: Reminiscences* (Jonathan Cape, 1928); TOM SEGEV: from *Soldiers of Evil: The Commandants of the Nazi Concentration Camps* (McGraw-Hill, 1987); WILLIAM SHIRER: from *Berlin Diary, 1934–1941* (Hamish Hamilton, 1941), reprinted by permission of Noel Rae, Trustee of the William Shirer Literary Trust; KEVIN SIM and MICHAEL BILTON: from *Four Hours in My Lai: A War Crime and Its Aftermath* (Penguin Books, 1994); DOUGLAS SMITH: from 'Letter: A bomber pilot remembers' from *The Independent Magazine* (9 February 1991); ALEXANDER SOLZHENITSYN: from *The Gulag Archipelago, 1918–1956*, translated by Thomas P. Whitney and Harry Willetts (The Harvill Press, 1988); ALBERT SPEER: from *Inside the Third Reich*, translated by Richard and Clara Winston (Weidenfeld & Nicolson, 1971), reprinted by permission of The Orion Publishing Group; J.P. STERN: from *Hitler, The Führer and the People* (University of California Press, 1992); JON SWAIN: from *River of Time* (Heinemann, 1995); TACITUS: from 'Germania' in *Tacitus on Britain and Germany*, translated by H. Mattingly (Penguin Books, 1948); JACOBO TIMERMAN: from *Prisoner Without a Name, Cell Without a Number*, translated by Tony Talbot (Vintage Books, 1988), reprinted by permission of Alfred A. Knopf Inc.; DMITRI VOLKOGONOV: from *Lenin: Life and Legacy* (HarperCollins, 1995), reprinted by permission of the publisher; JOCHEN VON LANG and CLAUS SIBYLL: from *Eichmann Interrogated: Transcripts from the Archives of the Israeli Police*, translated by Ralph Manheim (Farrar, Straus & Giroux, 1983); ED VULLIAMY: from *Seasons in Hell: Understanding Bosnia's War* (Simon & Schuster, 1994); REBECCA WEST: from *Black Lamb and Grey Falcon* (Canongate Classics, 1993), reprinted by permission of the Peters Fraser & Dunlop Group Ltd; W. B. YEATS: marginal note, reprinted in his copy of *The Genealogy of Morals* by Friedrich Nietzsche (1897); from 'The Stare's Nest by My Window' (1928) from 'Meditations in Time of Civil War' in *Collected Poems* (Picador, 1990), reprinted by permission of A. P. Watt Ltd on behalf of Michael B. Yeats.

Every effort has been made to trace or contact all copyright holders. The publishers would be pleased to rectify any omissions or errors brought to their notice at the earliest opportunity.

Index